Lecture Notes in Computer Science   8809

Commenced Publication in 1973
Founding and Former Series Editors:
Gerhard Goos, Juris Hartmanis, and Jan van Leeuwen

More information about this series at http://www.springer.com/series/7410

 MyCopy

Dear MyCopy Customer,

This printed, personal Springer eBook is a unique service that is available at a low cost, only on link.springer.com because your library purchased at least one Springer eBook subject collection. This book is an exact, monochrome copy of the eBook on SpringerLink.

MyCopy books are strictly for individual use only, and not available for resale. You can cite this book by referencing the bibliographic data and/or the DOI (Digital Object Identifier) found in the front matter.

MyCopy is the ideal format for anyone who wants a physical copy for page-by-page study.

My Book, MyCopy.
Enjoy reading.

Springer Science+Business Media, LLC

Bruce Christianson · James Malcolm
Vashek Matyáš · Petr Švenda
Frank Stajano · Jonathan Anderson (Eds.)

Security Protocols XXII

22nd International Workshop
Cambridge, UK, March 19–21, 2014
Revised Selected Papers

 Springer

Editors

Bruce Christianson
James Malcolm
University of Hertfordshire
Hertfordshire
UK

Vashek Matyáš
Petr Švenda
Faculty of Informatics
Masaryk University
Brno
Czech Republic

Frank Stajano
University of Cambridge
Cambridge
UK

Jonathan Anderson
Memorial University of Newfoundland
St. John's, NL
Canada

ISSN 0302-9743   ISSN 1611-3349 (electronic)
DOI 10.1007/978-3-319-12400-1

LNCS Sublibrary: SL4 – Security and Cryptology

Springer Cham Heidelberg New York Dordrecht London

Printed on acid-free paper

Springer is part of Springer Science+Business Media (www.springer.com/mycopy)

Preface

This volume collects the revised proceedings of the 22nd International Security Protocols Workshop, held at Sidney Sussex College, Cambridge, England, from March 19 to 21, 2014.

The theme of this workshop was "Collaborating with the Enemy." There is an ambiguity about collaboration, as the dictionary definition[1] reveals:

col-lab-o-rate:
1. To work together, especially in a joint intellectual effort.
2. To cooperate treasonably, as with an enemy occupation force in one's country.

It has always been tricky to understand who is the enemy of Alice, under what circumstances that animosity might change, or what happens when Bob declares his stance (either toward Alice or her enemy). But we have certainly seen all our paranoid dreams of the last 20 years come true. And so the question becomes – what shall we wish for next?

"Attackers" now control so much of our infrastructure that we cannot achieve any serious distributed service without their cooperation. Interestingly, this remains true even if we interchange our view about whom we regard as the service provider, and whom as the protocol hacker subverting the (supposed) legitimate service. Spies have no privacy now either. Is this a zero-sum game, resulting in a straightforward shoving match, or are there security innovations that both parties have a positive incentive to support?

As with previous workshops in this series, each paper was revised by the authors to incorporate ideas that emerged during the workshop. These revised papers are followed by a revised transcript of the presentation and ensuing discussion.

Our thanks to Lori Klimaszewska for the initial transcription of the recorded workshop discussions, and to all but two of the authors for their kind and timely collaboration with revising these transcripts and their position paper. Particular thanks to Simon Foley and Virgil Gligor for joining us on the Program Committee. Last but not least, we thank GCHQ for providing us, perhaps appropriately, with financial support.

We hope that reading these proceedings will encourage you to join in the debate yourselves, and perhaps even to send us a position paper for the next workshop.

September 2014

Bruce Christianson
James Malcolm
Vashek Matyáš
Petr Švenda
Frank Stajano
Jonathan Anderson

---

[1] http://www.thefreedictionary.com/collaborate, accessed September 2, 2014

Previous Proceedings in this Series

The proceedings of previous International Security Protocols Workshops are also published by Springer Verlag as Lecture Notes in Computer Science, and are occasionally referred to in the text:

21st Workshop (2013)	LNCS 8263	ISBN 978-3-642-41716-0
20th Workshop (2012)	LNCS 7622	ISBN 978-3-642-35693-3
19th Workshop (2011)	LNCS 7114	ISBN 978-3-642-25866-4
18th Workshop (2010)	LNCS 7061	In preparation
17th Workshop (2009)	LNCS 7028	ISBN 978-3-642-36212-5
16th Workshop (2008)	LNCS 6615	ISBN 978-3-642-22136-1
15th Workshop (2007)	LNCS 5964	ISBN 978-3-642-17772-9
14th Workshop (2006)	LNCS 5087	ISBN 978-3-642-04903-3
13th Workshop (2005)	LNCS 4631	ISBN 3-540-77155-7
12th Workshop (2004)	LNCS 3957	ISBN 3-540-40925-4
11th Workshop (2003)	LNCS 3364	ISBN 3-540-28389-7
10th Workshop (2002)	LNCS 2845	ISBN 3-540-20830-5
9th Workshop (2001)	LNCS 2467	ISBN 3-540-44263-4
8th Workshop (2000)	LNCS 2133	ISBN 3-540-42566-7
7th Workshop (1999)	LNCS 1796	ISBN 3-540-67381-4
6th Workshop (1998)	LNCS 1550	ISBN 3-540-65663-4
5th Workshop (1997)	LNCS 1361	ISBN 3-540-64040-1
4th Workshop (1996)	LNCS 1189	ISBN 3-540-63494-5

No published proceedings exist for the first three workshops.

Previous Proceedings in this Series

The proceedings of previous International Security Protocols Workshops are also published by Springer Verlag as Lecture Notes in Computer Science, and are occasionally referred to in the text:

No published proceedings exist for the first three workshops.

Preface

This volume collects the revised proceedings of the 22nd International Security Protocols Workshop, held at Sidney Sussex College, Cambridge, England, from March 19 to 21, 2014.

The theme of this workshop was "Collaborating with the Enemy." There is an ambiguity about collaboration, as the dictionary definition[1] reveals:

col-lab-o-rate:
1. To work together, especially in a joint intellectual effort.
2. To cooperate treasonably, as with an enemy occupation force in one's country.

It has always been tricky to understand who is the enemy of Alice, under what circumstances that animosity might change, or what happens when Bob declares his stance (either toward Alice or her enemy). But we have certainly seen all our paranoid dreams of the last 20 years come true. And so the question becomes – what shall we wish for next?

"Attackers" now control so much of our infrastructure that we cannot achieve any serious distributed service without their cooperation. Interestingly, this remains true even if we interchange our view about whom we regard as the service provider, and whom as the protocol hacker subverting the (supposed) legitimate service. Spies have no privacy now either. Is this a zero-sum game, resulting in a straightforward shoving match, or are there security innovations that both parties have a positive incentive to support?

As with previous workshops in this series, each paper was revised by the authors to incorporate ideas that emerged during the workshop. These revised papers are followed by a revised transcript of the presentation and ensuing discussion.

Our thanks to Lori Klimaszewska for the initial transcription of the recorded workshop discussions, and to all but two of the authors for their kind and timely collaboration with revising these transcripts and their position paper. Particular thanks to Simon Foley and Virgil Gligor for joining us on the Program Committee. Last but not least, we thank GCHQ for providing us, perhaps appropriately, with financial support.

We hope that reading these proceedings will encourage you to join in the debate yourselves, and perhaps even to send us a position paper for the next workshop.

September 2014

Bruce Christianson
James Malcolm
Vashek Matyáš
Petr Švenda
Frank Stajano
Jonathan Anderson

---

[1] http://www.thefreedictionary.com/collaborate, accessed September 2, 2014

Introduction: Collaborating with the Enemy (Transcript of Discussion)

Bruce Christianson

University of Hertfordshire

Hello everybody, and welcome to the 22nd Security Protocols Workshop. Every year we have a theme, and it has become customary to announce this prior to the start of the workshop. This year's theme is Collaborating with the Enemy, which immediately gives rise to a number of questions: why do we want to collaborate? who is the enemy? might they be us? and would it matter if they were?

As academics we collaborate all the time, we tend not to be fussy who we're collaborating with, and we think collaboration is a good thing. Unless it turns out that the people with whom we're collaborating go on to lose the war, in which case we rapidly discover that history is written by the winners. There's a fine line between being a freedom fighter and being a terrorist, I guess George Washington being a case in point, but when the BBC aren't sure which side is going to win they usually refer to them as guerillas. So maybe we're all still guerillas.

I had a look at the MI6 handbook section covering collaboration on my way here, and it said the four motives for collaboration are greed, fear, ideology and egotism, and I guess most of the work to this point on . . .

Joan Feigenbaum: Isn't love supposed to be in there?

Reply: Well maybe it's in the CIA handbook, it's not in the MI6 handbook. I think it's buried under ego in the MI6 handbook.

But the work we've done so far on security protocols for collaboration is mainly I guess in the ideology chapter, except we tend to refer to it as security policy, rather than as ideology. The idea is that there's this security policy, which we all agree that we're going to act as if we believed. But it's clear that when you're collaborating with an enemy, which is almost by definition somebody who isn't on the same page of the security policy as you are, then a lot of what I'd loosely describe as the trust-management type approaches to collaboration need a radical reinterpretation, at the very least.

On the other hand, even in the familiar Alice and Bob scenario, it's never clear that Alice and Bob actually have the same agenda, and we seem to be able to work around that OK. It's quite unusual for security objectives to be diametrically opposed, so can we not somehow use the triangle of forces to allow greed, fear, egotism, and love[1], to do the heavy lifting for us? Maybe if we just thought more carefully about how we design our security infrastructure we'd be more easily able to tack against the wind.

---

[1] Thank-you, Joan.

There's a nice mix here of people who have been before, and people who haven't, so I'll just go quickly through the rules of engagement. This is supposed to be a workshop and not a conference, so if everybody listens politely until you've got to the end of your presentation, then you've failed. The idea is to get as rapidly as possible from presenting your position paper to leading a discussion about it, and the only rule about interrupting is please try and make sure that what you're about to say, if you interrupt, is at least as interesting as what the person you're interrupting would have said if you hadn't interrupted them. That's true regardless of whether you're the speaker or not.

The discussions are being recorded, and we will publish both the position papers and a transcript of the discussion that follows them. Don't panic, this isn't Hansard, both are very heavily edited before they see the light of day. This is a safe environment in which to speculate and try out new ideas, because we will not let you say anything egregiously stupid on the record. So if you feel the urge to have a punt and see where a line of argument goes, feel free, and if it turns out it didn't go anywhere good we'll just take it out. The other rule is, if you break somebody's protocol during their talk then it's expected that you will help them fix it at the tea break afterwards. We've had several rather good publications come out of that over the years.

If at any point you feel the urge just to tell somebody how wonderful the workshop is, and how well everything is going, then feel free to interrupt me regardless of what I'm doing. Conversely, if you have a problem, however large, James is just over there, and we do collaborate. In the spirit of the workshop, the organising committee has approached GCHQ who have agreed to pay for some, but not all, of your dinners, and we will be revealing more about that as the workshop proceeds[2].

Ockham's Razor says that we should start with the model that has the smallest number of moving parts, and only when we can prove that that doesn't work are we justified in using a more complicated model. The simplest model of security is not to have any, and so to put us in the correct boot state, Dieter Gollmann has kindly agreed to be the first speaker and talk about, why bother securing DNS?

---

[2] Philippe Golle and Ari Juels, Dining Cryptographers Revisited, EUROCRYPT 2004, LNCS 3027, pp. 456–473.

Contents

Why Bother Securing DNS?

Dieter Gollmann$^{(\boxtimes)}$

Security in Distributed Applications,
Hamburg University of Technology, Hamburg, Germany
diego@tuhh.de

Abstract. The current state of DNS security is characterized by two opposing developments. DNSSEC introduces a PKI to support message authentication in the DNS protocol; DANE proposes to use this PKI also for provisioning TLS certificates. At the same time, PKIs are perceived as a major point of weakness; mechanisms like certificate pinning attempt to reduce the trust one needs to place in a PKI. We note that DNS provides rendezvous, identification, and introduction services and argue that this differentiation can reduce the impact of compromised trusted third parties.

Keywords: Domain Name System · TLS · DANE · Identification · Rendezvous services · Critical infrastructures

If it is trusted it can hurt you. [Robert Morris Sr.]

1 Introduction

It has become commonplace to note that critical infrastructures are increasingly relying on the internet, and that the internet has become a critical infrastructure itself. Complaints about the insecurity of the internet and demands for securing this critical infrastructure then quickly follow from such observations. With apparent inevitability, endeavours for securing the internet – a communications infrastructure after all – are drawn towards cryptography. We will follow this path in the case of the Domain Name System (DNS), a critical component within the internet. We will briefly reflect on current DNS security incidents, argue why reliance on "security solutions" that involve trusted third parties is bad for security, and put forward the case that security is not improved by deploying stronger security mechanisms but by reducing reliance on the infrastructure. Specifically, we observe that DNS serves more than one purpose. It provides a *rendezvous service* and an *introduction service. Identification services* are in the process of being added. Addressing these three aspects separately may be a way towards improving the security of applications using the internet. Separation of concerns is, of course, a well established security strategy.

© Springer International Publishing Switzerland 2014
B. Christianson et al. (Eds.): Security Protocols 2014, LNCS 8809, pp. 1–8, 2014.
DOI: 10.1007/978-3-319-12400-1_1

2   Domain Name System

The Domain Name System plays a crucial rôle in the internet, mapping host names to IP addresses. *Authoritative name servers* manage zones and make statements about the bindings between host names and IP addresses for hosts in their zone. All other participants trust their statements. Resolvers use a hierarchy of root servers and global top level domain servers to find authoritative name servers. This is the *rendezvous service* service provided: given a host name, *name resolution* returns its current IP address. Security is based on trust in the name servers and in a simple authentication of server responses.

The authentication mechanism originally specified for DNS uses a challenge-response pattern (*return routability*): queries for a host name contain a 16-bit query id; a resolver accepts the first response that contains this host name and the query id sent (and arriving at the expected port) as authoritative. This message authentication mechanism does not rely on any trusted third parties or shared secrets.

2.1   DNS Cache Poisoning Attacks

This authentication mechanism is relatively weak, leaving recursive name servers open to *cache poisoning attacks* [6]. Recursive name servers keep a cache of the bindings they have received. Queries for host names with cached bindings are served directly, without involving the authoritative name server. Cache entries expire based on a time-to-live set by the authoritative name server.

A cache poisoning attack triggers name resolution for a target host at the resolver and then floods the resolver with spoofed answers with guessed query ids and an IP address of the attacker's choice. The attack succeeds if a spoofed answer with correctly guessed query id arrives before the genuine answer.

The attacker's chances improve considerably if a resolver will run several name resolutions for a given host name in parallel. The attacker triggers several name resolutions and floods the resolver with spoofed answers. Now, one of the attacker's guesses has to match one of the resolver's query ids; the probability for the attack to succeed is related to the birthday paradox. Such a vulnerability had been reported for BIND 4 and BIND 8 in a security advisory[1] in 2002.

A DNS cache poisoning attack launched against the DNS server operated by the Chaos Computer Club (CCC), dnscache.berlin.ccc.de (213.73.91.35), followed the same pattern[2]. The CCC had been running *djbdns*, highly praised for its randomization algorithms, as its name resolution software. A birthday paradox vulnerability in *djbdns* had been known since 2009 [2], a patch for *djbdns* had been provided, but the CCC was still running an unpatched version. We are faced with a known instance of a known problem with a known remedy. In this respect, securing the infrastructure is a practical software security issue.

---

[1] http://www.rnp.br/cais/alertas/2002/cais-ALR-19112002a.html

[2] https://www.fehcom.net/diary/2014/20140212.html,
     http://www.heise.de/newsticker/meldung/DNS-Server-des-CCC-Anfaellig-wegen-veralteter-Software-2112171.html

However, powerful attacks are possible even when query ids are chosen at random and when the search space is enlarged with further randomizations, e.g. the choice of port number and mixing upper and lower case characters in the spelling of the host name. Dan Kaminsky had shown an attack that exploits *additional resource records*, another performance optimization. A DNS response may contain an *additional section* where the authoritative name server includes bindings for hosts that resolver had not asked for but might want to resolve in the near future. For example, the response for a query for www.example.com might also include a record for mail.example.com. Resolvers do not blindly trust authoritative name servers on additional resource records but perform *bailiwick checking*. Only records for hosts in the same domain ("in the bailiwick") of the host the query has been issued for are cached.

The attack asks to resolve a random host name in the bailiwick of the target. This random host name has most likely no entry in the resolver cache, so name resolution is triggered, and most likely the host does not exist, so the authoritative name server would send a NXDOMAIN response. The attacker's spoofed responses contain a binding for the target in their additional section. If the attacker's response wins the race the cache entry for the target entry gets poisoned; if the attacker loses the race a new race for another random host name is started immediately. This attack convinced the DNS community that it was high time to move to cryptographic message authentication in the DNS protocol.

2.2   DNS Rebinding Attacks

Cryptographic message authentication strengthens defences against "outsiders" impersonating authoritative name servers. It does not stop authoritative name servers from exploiting the trust placed in them. In *DNS rebinding attacks* [3–5], an unsporting authoritative name server maps a host in the attacker's zone to an IP address of a host that is not. In this way, the attacker may, e.g., circumvent the *same origin policy* enforced by browsers and use a client as a proxy to access hosts outside the attacker's zone (but believed by the client to be in the zone).

Same origin policies regulate, e.g., where a script executed in the browser may connect to. To enforce this policy, the browser has to know the *origin* of the script (authentication of origin is not our concern here) and the IP addresses corresponding to that origin. The bindings issued by authoritative name servers can thus be viewed as policy rules in an access control system, which are evaluated in the browser. In the language of access control, authoritative name servers act as *Policy Information Points*.

Authoritative name servers are, by design, authoritative for binding hosts in their own zone to IP addresses. They thereby become authoritative for binding IP addresses to hosts in their zone, but without any restrictions on the IP addresses they may issue bindings for. They can thus hijack arbitrary IP addresses for their zone. This is a serious construction flaw in an access control system. The defence suggests itself: send a query to the IP address to check whether it "speaks for" the given host name. There are strong parallels to the defences against bombing attacks in networks with node mobility as discussed in [1].

3 DNS and Public Key Cryptography

Deploying cryptographic authentication in the internet is at its heart a key management challenge. Parties need to be provided with correctly attributed public verification keys. Certificates create cryptographically protected bindings between hosts and their public keys. The issuers of those certificates (a.k.a. certification authorities) become trusted third parties. We will look at the way this key management challenge has been addressed and, in particular, at the trust placed into certificate issuers.

3.1 DNSSEC

The attacks on DNS had re-ignited interest in cryptographic authentication based on digital signatures (DNSSEC, RFC 4033) as a replacement for the weak authentication mechanism mentioned above. This kind of authentication relies on a Public Key Infrastructure. The PKI for DNSSEC, by and large, mirrors the hierarchical structure of the DNS and is gradually becoming operational. The signed root zone, implemented by ICANN and Verisign with input from the U.S. Department of Commerce, exists since July 2010[3]. At the time of writing (2014-05-29), 403 of the 589 top level domains are signed, 395 have trust anchors published in the root zone[4]. Top level domains and the root zone are "roots of trust" in this PKI, but they are roots of trust in DNS anyway as far as name resolution is concerned.

A PKI needs a secure way of distributing public verification keys to the relevant parties. Accepted methods for public key delivery are listed in the *DNSSEC Practice Statement for the Root Zone KSK Operator*[5]. The internet draft on *DNSSEC Trust Anchor Publication for the Root Zone*[6] covers the same topic.

3.2 TLS

There exists a second – already widely used – PKI for the internet, created for facilitating access to secure web sites via *https*. This PKI puts certification authorities (CAs) in a very powerful position. They can issue certificates for any host in the web. Once a CA is included in the list of trusted roots on a client it becomes authoritative for the entire web (for that client).

An attacker who has compromised a certification authority can thus issue bogus but nevertheless valid certificates for arbitrary hosts. A well reported case is that of the Dutch CA DigiNotar. Google had noted in 2011 a DigiNotar issued certificate for google.com not contained in Google's own list of certificates for

---

[3] http://www.root-dnssec.org/
[4] http://stats.research.icann.org/dns/tld_report/
[5] https://www.iana.org/dnssec/icann-dps.txt
[6] http://tools.ietf.org/html/draft-jabley-dnssec-trust-anchor-07

google.com. The incident had serious impacts on IT services offered by the Dutch government[7] and on DigiNotar, which filed for bankruptcy.

Is the list of trusted certificates (public keys) at the client a solution to this problem? Clients could for important hosts define a set of authorized CAs (introduced as *certificate pinning* in Chrome, although CA pinning would be more accurate), thus moving those hosts out of the reach of all other CAs. Certificate pinning is also used to describe solutions where the certificate is hard coded in a client application and the certificate received in a TLS handshake is compared against this "pinned" certificate. In this case, the CA authorized for the application is fixed.

Is the list of trusted certificates (public keys) at the client a part of the problem? Consider Mikko Hyppönen's post[8] from April 2013 on finding that the US DoD certification authority is pre-installed on various Apple devices:

– *My phone carries a root certificate for a military.*
– *From one country.*
– *And it's not my country.*
– *And I can't remove it.*
– Issuer: C=US, O=U.S. Government, OU=DoD, OU=PKI, CN=DoD CLASS 3 Root CA

The average user is hardly in a position to judge the trustworthiness of a trusted CA, e.g., its proximity to the government of the country it is operating in.

3.3 DANE

The wish to restrict the impact of corrupted CAs in TLS takes us back to DNS. The idea of certificate (CA) pinning could be extended. CAs could be authorized to issue certificates only for a limited scope of hosts. We would then have to define a policy that states which CA is authoritative for which set of hosts.

In DNS, authoritative name servers are already trusted on mapping host names to IP addresses. With the introduction of DNSSEC, they are also trusted to sign resource records, to confirm the public keys of sub-authorities, and to protect their own private keys. It is then a plausible next step to build a PKI for *https* on the basis of DNS and let authoritative name servers (or registrars) issue certificates for hosts in their domain, but only for hosts in their domain. Such a PKI has been specified as *DNS-Based Authentication of Named Entities* (DANE, RFC 6698). Corrupted CAs can only affect their own zone.

On the other hand, compromise of an authoritative name server now lets the attacker not only provide a wrong IP address for a host (attack at the network layer) but also a wrong public encryption key (attack at the application layer). Have we improved security or made matters worse? This brings us to the main question of this discussion paper:

---

[7] http://www.onderzoeksraad.nl/uploads/items-docs/1833/Rapport_Diginotar_EN_summary.pdf

[8] https://twitter.com/mikko/status/327170802673917952

Have we been walking in the wrong direction by putting too many require-
ments on the Domain Name System, which made us rely more heavily
on DNS, forcing us in turn to look for stronger security mechanisms?

4   Splitting Services

Alternatively, we might treat DNS just as a *rendezvous service* providing the
current IP address of a host without any pretence of delivering authentication.

– Addresses can change in space and time.
– It matters when no rendezvous service is available.
– It does not matter when wrong information is provided as long as alternative
  services can be consulted.

Cryptographic protection may have a rôle at the network layer but not in the
rendezvous service itself. We do not want to trust rendezvous services in the
first place. DNS would just make a best effort to provide an IP address for a
host. Failure to provide a correct IP address is then an availability issue, not an
authentication issue, to be addressed with methods for improving availability.

A further service needs to confirm that the host a client is looking for is resid-
ing at the address obtained. We need such a service anyway because authoritative
name serves may lie. The fact that, with DNSSEC, their answers are signed does
not imply that they are true. The service used in the case where a host is already
known to the client can be different from the service used when there has been
no previous interaction.

In the first case, the client would not ask the host "who are you" but "are
you the one I want to connect to". The client could remember from a previous
visit how to recognize this host, and the host could answer this question by
providing evidence that it is the same as at the client's last visit. We call this
an *identification service*. Such a service confirms that a host is the same as
last time and not someone else pretending to be that host. This follows Pekka
Nikander's argument[9] that etymologically identity, stemming from Latin *idem
et idem*, means "the same as before". We are well aware that identification has
also other meanings in the field of IT security.

For identification a pinned public key of the host or a shared secret would do.
Current developments towards certificate pinning have been noted in Sect. 3.2.
In (our usage of) identification the client needs a local name for the host to
connect to. Identification does not need trusted third parties.

For hosts not known to the client, a service is needed that equips the client
with the means to authenticate the host. We call this an *introduction service*. The
TLS PKI is such a service. Host names have to be globally unique. The introducer
acts as a trusted third party. Asking several independent parties reduces the
impact of a compromised introducer.

---

[9] http://tools.ietf.org/html/draft-nikander-ram-ilse-00

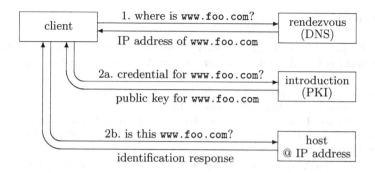

Fig. 1. Interplay of rendezvous, introduction, and identification services when connecting to a host.

Figure 1 describes how a client connects to www.foo.com. Step 1 retrieves an untrusted IP address for the host. An optional step 2a gets a credential from an introductions service; in the case of a PKI the credential is a public key. Step 2b is a run of an identification protocol run between the client and the host at the IP address obtained in step 1. The response is verified using either the credential from step 2 or a credential pre-installed at the client.

5   Conclusion

Infrastructures are critical because of critical applications using the infrastructure. In the first instance, it is not the critical infrastructure that needs to be secured but the applications that had turned the infrastructure critical. This in turn may point to security services the infrastructure should provide. The fewer parties these services have to trust the better.

We may be taking a wrong turn when we ask DNS to provide additional services and rely on cryptography for securing DNS. Authentication does not protect against lying insiders, i.e., against the very entities providing these services. Relying on DNS introduces an awful lot of trusted third parties, albeit with certain limits to the damage they can cause. Arguably, this does not secure the infrastructure but increases the attack surface.

DNS can be viewed as a rendezvous service returning the current IP address of a host; it needs an infrastructure of name servers such as the one we have got today, but it should not be necessary to trust this infrastructure. Certificate pinning is adding an identification service to TLS. Identification needs no trusted third party at all. Introduction services are, by definition, trusted third parties. The principle of *divide et impera* suggests that there may be benefits in splitting rendezvous from introduction services.

Acknowledgements. The author thanks Daniel Thomas for a constructive criticism of this paper.

References

1. Aura, T., Roe, M., Arkko, J.: Security of internet location management. In: Proceedings of the 18th Annual Computer Security Applications Conference, pp. 78–87, December 2002
2. Day, K.: Rapid DNS poisoning in djbdns, February 2009. http://www.your.org/dnscache/djbdns.pdf. Accessed 5 June 2014
3. Dean, D., Felten, E.W., Wallach, D.S.: Java security: from HotJava to Netscape and beyond. In: Proceedings of the 1996 IEEE Symposium on Security and Privacy, pp. 190–200 (1996)
4. Jackson, C., Barth, A., Bortz, A., Shao, W., Boneh, D.: Protecting browsers from DNS rebinding attacks. In: Proceedings of the 14th ACM Conference on Computer and Communications Security, pp. 421–431 (2007)
5. Johns, M.: (Somewhat) breaking the same-origin policy by undermining DNS pinning. Posting to the Bug Traq mailing list, August 2006. http://www.securityfocus.com/archive/107/443429/30/180/threaded. Accessed 5 June 2014
6. Schuba, C.: Addressing weaknesses in the domain name system protocol. Ph.D. thesis, Purdue University (1993)

Why Bother Securing DNS?
(Transcript of Discussion)

Dieter Gollmann[✉]

Hamburg University of Technology, Hamburg, Germany
`diego@tu-harburg.de`

As Bruce so kindly said, I was volunteered to give the first talk after he had successfully extracted more than two lines of a position paper from me. I will talk about what I see currently happening in and around the domain name system. I will start with a story, some of you might have heard about it, although I don't know how far it reached beyond Germany.

In Germany you have the Chaos Computer Club, which they quite proudly will tell you, has more or less the status of an NGO in Germany, they're not the evil hackers, they are the good guys. And because they're the good guys, and you can't trust the enemy running the entire infrastructure, they run their own DNS resolver, so you can have a proper trusted resolver. The software version they're running, Dan Bernstein's DJBDNS, which is Open Source, and therefore good.

Back in 2009 someone had a look at DJBDNS and found that there were some features in it that made it particularly susceptible to cache poisoning attacks. They contacted the author who was no longer interested in maintaining DJBDNS, they published their own patch, but the Chaos Computer Club is above installing patches, so they were hacked. That as a starting point, and here you can read on, and I guess it also has an English version where if you don't trust the automatic translation tools from German will tell you what had happened.

So I'm talking about DNS, a distributed directory system, mapping host names to IP addresses, authoritative name servers in charge of making statements about their domain, resolvers, caching whatever the authoritative name servers have told them. Authenticating the authoritative name server in a non-cryptographic fashion. Sending a query ID, maybe at a random port number, anything that comes back on that port contains the query ID, contains the host name, is the authoritative answer. To seasoned cryptographers this is of course ridiculous, and we are not surprised that there is a long history of cache poisoning attacks working on the simple principle of guessing this 16-bit number. Guessing is easy if the 16-bit number is generated by a counter.

It is moderately easy if the resolver runs several queries for the same host and at the same time, then you can use the Birthday Paradox to go down from a search space of 2 to the 16 roughly to a search space of square root of 2 to the 16, that was published by Vagner Sacramento in 2002 on BIND 4 and BIND 8. Strange enough it took another seven years to figure out that DJBDNS had the same problem, and even more strangely if you look at the world, it took another

© Springer International Publishing Switzerland 2014
B. Christianson et al. (Eds.): Security Protocols 2014, LNCS 8809, pp. 9–17, 2014.
DOI: 10.1007/978-3-319-12400-1_2

five years before someone really exploited this known vulnerability. 2008 Dan Kaminsky's famous paper explaining that if your cache poisoning attack failed you could immediately restart it, you did not have to wait for cache entries to expire, by querying for a random host name in the bailiwick of your target host, and eventually you would win the game using additional resource records. At that time some faces in the community, running the global Domain Name System, went very pale. This was Armageddon. They finally realised this type of non-cryptographic authentication doesn't work. We have been talking about DNSSEC since the late 1990s, and now we have to get serious about it.

So, a habit in our community, we see a problem, we run for cryptography. We have an authentication problem, we run for digital signatures. If we do that we need verification keys, we need a public key infrastructure for verification keys, and the public key infrastructure for verification keys that is emerging, as far as I can see, more or less mirrors the hierarchical structure of the Domain Name System, and the top level domains, generic top level domains, country code top level domains, take on the role of routes of trust, which is OK, which is perfectly OK because there are anyway roots of trust. They will say where to find the next authoritative server in the DNS hierarchy. If they want to cheat they could cheat before DNSSEC.

What have we achieved? We have protection against outsiders, proper cryptographic protection against outsiders. We do not have protection against insiders, insiders meaning authoritative name servers making false statements. They're allowed to make statements about hosts in their domain, and then they can claim that an IP address that does not belong to a host in their domain belongs to them. There is a range of papers on this topic starting from the mid 1990s. I think Drew Dean and his Princeton colleagues were one were one of the first to discover such a DNS rebinding attack.

One of the defences, potential defences, would be to write to the IP address and ask, I think you are in this domain, is this true? In past papers I have suggested, so instead of using authentication, we might treat this as authorization to connect. We ask the host at that address, are you happy to accept traffic for this domain?

Frank Stajano: In the case of this possible defence you talk about, if the malicious DNS server is saying, this is the guy you wanted, presumably it's for some attack, at which the thing that responds is colluding with the wrong DNS, so if you ask them, are you the host of this domain, they would say yes wouldn't they?

Reply: It's a different type of attack, it's an attack in the world of same origin policies, where the attacker's script according to the same origin policy would only be allowed to connect back to the domain it came from. But now the bad guy tells it, this IP address is in my domain, and then the browser gets an IP address to connect to, yes, permitted according to my policy, it's in the same domain, and defeats the same origin policy. So that is the background of the DNS rebinding attacks currently. Mike.

Michael Roe: So there's something similar in mobile IPv6 per return routability, where they are not talking about binding domain names by IP addresses, but the long lived IP address for the host relative to its mobile location, there you have precisely this check asking the mobile, sending a message to where the mobile node currently is saying, technically, are you at this house, which is the way against various binding attacks. There are similar sorts of things in DNS where you're careful about doing the reverse lookup.

Reply: Yes, indeed, a general principle, and yes, I could also have talked about return routability in this context. Now, tweet by Mikko Hyppönen, I have found this root certificate, country US, organisation US government, organisational unit DoD, on my iPhone. I can't even get rid of it, what does it do, what is the purpose? I mentioned this story at a workshop and there was a Taiwanese post-doc, and she said very cheerfully, yes, my government also has one of those certificates. And I remember an email from Ross saying, I have been to this conference mentioning one of the Turkish CAs is run by the Turkish secret services, and someone from Turkey violently opposed this view, working with the enemy, yes please.

Micah Sherr: Quick comment. OK, at least it's labelled, I mean, at least it's labelled as the US government.

Reply: Yes, there can be perfectly innocent reasons.

Bruce Christianson: Well it's labelled as the US government.

Michael Roe: So this is potentially an attack because the X.509 certification authority, certification hierarchy doesn't work quite the same way as the hierarchy does in DNS. So I think DNS say the authority for .mil has a key that says they can sign stuff for .mil, you don't care about that because you're not in .mil, they're not going to forge DNS entries for you. But a certificate that might have been intended just for signing certificates for .mil entries, because of the way X.509 does not bind the hierarchies together, that certificate could be used to sign anything, so you might be worried they might sign things outside their domain.

Reply: That is indeed my next point. All these root certificates, and I have produced stories like DigiNotar, who were compromised. Once a trusted CA is trusted it can issue certificates for anyone. I've called it a global point of failure, not a single point of failure, because there are two or three dozen of those points of failure on my machine. In the spirit of this Cambridge Protocols Workshop we had Robert Morris Senior around and hed said, trusted, remember, it meant it can hurt you. So all these trusted route certificates can hurt us. And there are incidents, I've mentioned DigiNotar, where it happened.

Natural response, can we restrict impact, can we make those trusted CAs less trusted? I'm walking back to the Domain Name System where the authoritative name servers can make statements about their domain only. Idea, can't we use this same infrastructure also for TLS certificates? So it would be some point in the domain name hierarchy that issues also certificates, not only for IP addresses, or signatures for IP addresses, but also certificates for public keys, this is known as DANE, DNS based authentication of named identities, RFC6698. I had a student in Hamburg doing his Master thesis whilst working for DFNCert, and the task was to establish, is this more or less secure than the traditional approach. My comment, this is something I see quite often. We have an infrastructure, we have a service, we ask it to do something else on top. DNS was here to resolve domain names to IP addresses, or host names to IP addresses. Now we also want DNS to tell us the public key of the host.

What have we achieved? We have restricted impact, as we wanted. We have achieved that the same entity can lie about your IP address and your public key. Separation of duties, I haven't done my homework, Saltzer and Schroeder, roughly from that time, 1970s, classic, ancient principle in security. And we have thrown it out of the window. Are we asking too much?

So coming to my proposal's questions. What do we need? We need a rendezvous service. Addresses change. With mobility, nodes move round in the network. In time a host might change its IP address. Does it matter when such a service is not available? Yes, because I can't look up your current address. Does it matter when I'm given wrong information? Not yet. I might do the checking independently of the rendezvous service. Cryptography might have a role at the network level below. I don't see it having a role in the construction of the rendezvous service itself, I do not want to trust, as the people who know me know very well.

Interlude. Pekka Nikander in his PhD thesis and in many other places, I have taken this from a draft IETF document as identity. Where does it come from? It comes from Latin identitas, which stems from early Latin, idem et idem, same and same, again, again, identidem, repeatedly. And he goes on in this draft to say that this implies in our understanding, unique ability, to uniquely identify, blah, blah, blah. I have not given you the entire blurb because it then goes on saying, aahh, I think we're moving in the wrong direction, it means something else. So what could one mean with identification?

In our traditional explanation computer security, you login, enter a user name, a password, user name, is identification, you tell who you are, authentication then checks it's really you. If you go to biometrics, they tell you, we have identification, we have verification. Identification means we have a database of fingerprints, and then we check, is this fingerprint from the crime site in our database. Given that we have already overloaded the term, I keep at it, and give it yet another meaning. It tells that it's the same as last time. That is the Pekka Nikander interpretation of identity, identification.

Now fortunately I'm not the only one to be old enough to say, remember around early 1990 s this very agitated discussion about X.509, about, does it make any sense to have globally unique names for access control. Isn't there a fundamental misunderstanding of the concept of names, aren't names meant to identify entities you already know? Is it the case that you only need local names for access control? And all of this comes back here again as far as I can see. So to continue my requirement analysis, I might need an identification service in this last sense, telling, I'm going to the host and check, are you who I believe you are, are you the one I wanted to contact? So the difference to authentication, authentication somebody else tells me who he or she is, and then I check. Now I tell you who you are and you have to confirm it by knowing some secret, for example. So bottom line here, it's easy if I already knew you, it's easy if we have common context, it's easy if we have common context we do not share with anybody else, like a secret key. It's tricky if we've never met before, we need someone to introduce us. So maybe we need in our world introduction services. And same as with the rendezvous services, maybe we have more than one introduction service. If you have independent introduction services, again, we reduce trust on a single service.

Conclusions. When one looks at DNSSEC, when one looks at DANE, are we taking the wrong turn. Are we expecting too much? In particular on DANE, digital signatures protect against outsiders, not against insiders. What are we doing? We've turned the entire DNS hierarchy into insiders we now have to trust. Madness really if you think in security terms, but that is what's going on, and as I've said before, trust is bad for security, we would like to reduce it. Last slide. I'm hearing a lot about critical infrastructures, but I don't think they need security. You should ask, why is the infrastructure critical, because of the services running on the infrastructure, and the services are critical. Secure the services, divide and conquer. And as a final word, I was at the talk by Scott Charney, Vice-President Microsoft, at the Führungsakademie der Bundeswehr in Hamburg, so the Academy of the Officers of the Germany army, and some German army major said, I've just been to the department of defence and the minister said the internet is a critical infrastructure, can we secure the internet? And Scott Charney said, you cannot boil the ocean. The internet was designed to be highly available in the case of a nuclear strike, and we have done quite well maintaining availability, and that is what I'd expect in the main from a critical infrastructure.

So with that I will shut up, up to you to throw your views at me.

Yvo Desmedt: So in your previous slide you mentioned, so the obligation does not protect against live insiders. In 1996 there were two schools that were actually looking at that problem, and so there was a paper by Mike Burmester, and myself, and Kabatianskii, at a workshop organised by Rebecca Wright and Peter Newman, where we exactly said that, but then in the context of certifying authorities. And then Reiter and Stubblebine also wanting to deal with untrusted CA. And later in 2004 Mike and myself published a paper in the Communications of the ACM, Is hierarchical public-key certification the next target for hackers? Obviously what can be said for CAs can also be said for DNS.

Reply: Absolutely.

Tim Goh: The thing is, the authentication things you propose seem to already exist at say various levels, you have TLS if you want to do it above, you've got IPSEC if you want to do it below. The key exchange mechanism already exists, ISAKMP will do web trust file, key exchange if you want it to, RFC recommends such a thing, it's not too far-fetched to implement such a thing. Good luck at getting users to actually establish a web of trust. But there is one major concern that I have that might not be mentioned, embedded systems. Do you have, embedded systems made with DNS, is it reasonable to ask another system to compete key exchange in any useful fashion because considering the systems may be on a 8 meg, 8-bit processor with less than 256 bytes of RAM.

Reply: I wasn't proposing any key exchange.

Tim Goh: Say for example, if you're doing, such an authentication mechanism.

Reply: I'm against using authentication mechanisms, I don't want to use them in the first place, they're useless. That's a very over the top remark. Yes, you're perfectly right. All these authentication mechanisms exist. We have them at the IP layer, we have them at the TCP layer, we have them at the application layer, we have them at the application layer above the application layer. They do not solve the problem. If an insider provides authenticated wrong information, then that is the challenge. Like when DigiNotar was hacked, somebody, the attacker, somebody issued certificates for Google Mail, and via real systems, did all the cryptographic properly, and concluded we are talking to Google Mail, only they weren't.

Tim Goh: But then I am separating the authentication from the trust issue here. Authentication is, I see it as something that needs to happen, but your trust issue is separate.

Simon Foley: Yes, so would you see this as something similar to the Perspectives project at CMU? They developed a browser-plugin that consults a network of notary servers to confirm that others have seen the same SSL certificate that is being presented to you when you visit a website.

Reply: It's more in this direction, yes. And it's also, I think in the context of TLS cache pinning, sorry, certificate pinning. I have been using this certificate with that server in the past, now for some reason I'm getting a different certificate, suspicious. It's no longer the same.

Hannan Xiao: I just wondered, in your introduction service, in your approach, for the first time we still have to rely on the introduction service.

Reply: Of course.

Hannan Xiao: But do you use trust in your introduction service? And somebody introduces someone, so do you use trust.

Reply: So the idea has been around again for ages. When did Phil Zimmermann introduce PGP, early 1990s, earlier, it had this idea. And it works in some communities. DFNCert, the Computer Emergency Response Team for the German research network has an annual conference, and part of their annual conference is a PGP signing meeting, where all the system administrators from German research institutions come and if they have not already shared their keys they can do it at that point, and then they can go back to their institution and introduce maybe certificates or keys to others in the organisation. That's where I see this idea being used, and this idea being used reasonably well. I have my doubts to which extent it can be automated and formalised. And again, if you go back to the research literature there are lots of trust evaluation algorithms. If I give you weight point 35, and you give me a certificate, which you have given a different weight, which weight will I now attribute to the certificate. And then if I have a particular transaction how good must the certificate be. There is a lot on paper, I see little in reality that works.

Virgil Gligor: By definition a trusted third party is trusted by both parties, that's why it's a third party that is trusted. An introduction service need not be trusted by both parties, it needs to be trusted by at most one. So there's a difference of trust there, there is a very clear difference, and you can even formalise that, but I know you don't like formalisation.

Reply: Oh no, I'm a mathematician, I like formalisation, but I like genuine formalisation, not bogus formalisation.

Virgil Gligor: You need not notation only.

Reply: Yes. I keep saying, you don't impress me by using the language of set theory, this was first year stuff in a mathematics course.

Virgil Gligor: So there is a difference.

Reply: Yes.

Bruce Christianson: Virgil's point is a very important one because in order for me to introduce Virgil to somebody I don't have to have any control over Virgil at all.

Virgil Gligor: Correct.

Frank Stajano: One of the things you said in one of the last few slides, I can't remember which one, about the point that establishing that you are talking with the same person you have talked with before, reminded me of the Guy Fawkes protocol, where you can have a strong chain, yes, that's the person who sent me the previous messages, I don't know where it starts from, and there was a big discussion at the time with Roger and Ross about whether you ever know the beginning of it. You can say, well how do you know your mother is your mother, you just know it's the one, for years you've called your mother, but how do you know, at the beginning you didn't have a commission. So that just, this continuity seems to be the authentication rather than the real origin. And something similar to that is in this things like in Android you get some signed installation that, you install a program and you have no clue what it is, it's malware, whatever, but you install it and the next time when it updates at least it's signed with the same key they used on the first time. So it may be completely bullshit, but at least it's the same one as before.

Reply: Yes, I think these are not novel ideas, these are ideas that have been around, but I think the wrong ideas, and simple crypto ideas like digital signatures, attract too much attention, and are not solving the problem we are really facing, in particular, if we are collaborating with the enemy, because the enemy is part of the network, or part of the system.

Tim Goh: Is it worth actually considering say RFC 2408, ISAKMP's original separation of the notion of authentication here, which seems to be conflated here with the notion of initial trust establishment. So before we actually suggest authentication between the host, both hosts, but before that, it's got a complete separate phas that you seem to be calling authentication here, but it's really trust establishment, and establishing some sort of may be signature, maybe, any mechanism somehow to verify as a person, instead of actually having a separate mechanism, and actually defined in those terms. ISAKMP is a horribly painful protocol, but it seems to be exactly what is being asked for here. There is a separate phase that is not, that your talk is not quite interested in, which is somehow given a signature, these two hosts are the thing that we established in the previous phase, but the thing they seem to be interested in is the previous phase where you actually somehow establish trust. So they do briefly talk about mechanisms like that, for at least the IPSEC layer, but ISAKMP can be used for other things.

Reply: I think we have to take that offline, because I didn't talk about authentication.

Yvo Desmedt: The solution has been discovered a long time ago in the reliability community, you just vote, they used it in the station poll, every time that you fly an aeroplane it's used there, and the answer is the same in this circumstance, just vote, don't trust a single party.

Reply: Yes.

Yvo Desmedt: I mean your computer votes. Then it talks to many DNS servers, and then basically your computer votes. That is the vote, and then it decides that the majority can be trusted.

Bruce Christianson: But how do you resist a Sybil attack, it seems very hard to prove that two voters are actually different. How do you prove that two computers are not actually the same computer?

Reply: Yes, that is the core word in my argument, it's the argument that what do we do for availability, we replicate, but we need to be guaranteed independence, how do we know that.

Bruce Christianson: Establishing identity is straightforward along the lines you're proposing. Establishing non-identity seems to be an almost intractable problem.

Virgil Gligor: Maybe a crowd source.

Reply: I think again you will find papers that suggest this as a solution to our present dilemma. Don't use a single server that tells you this is the public key of entity X, ask around, and if you have enough agreement then you take that, but then again, there is Bruce's point, if there are not many people interested in you, and we all collaborate, or we multiply ourselves, we can defeat this mechanism.

Yvo Desmedt: So as a solution in our 2004 paper we suggested that we actually cover all the CAs in that case, depending on the platform that they ran, so if they, for example, were Microsoft or they were Unix, all the Microsoft ones are the same colour, all the Unix ones are the same colour, because if you do a replicated attack, and whether you can attack one or all, is the same, so when you basically, and then you do the same in DNS, so if you say, OK all the CISCO ones, we need them the same colour, so that means that it is easy to hack one of those, and the outsider becomes an insider in that case, and that's how we should just deal with it.

Reply: That defends against the outsider becoming an insider, but it doesn't defend against the insider who is sitting there in the first place.

Yvo Desmedt: But if everybody is against you then you will lose, we know that. There's no solution. If the majority is corrupt then there is no solution.

Reply: Yes.

Alastair Beresford: So just coming back to Bruce's point earlier, so one of the things that bitcoin does is use, compute power for, it's sort of, for who gets to vote mechanism. I'm not sure I like that here, but it's something that does exist, at least as a market solution.

Collaborating as Normal: Detecting Systemic Anomalies in Your Partner

Olgierd Pieczul[1,2]([envelope]) and Simon N. Foley[2]([envelope])

[1] Ireland Lab, IBM Software Group, Dublin, Ireland
[2] Department of Computer Science, University College Cork, Cork, Ireland
olgierd@pieczul.net, s.foley@cs.ucc.ie

Abstract. It is considered whether anomaly detection techniques might be used to determine potentially malicious behavior by service providers. Data mining techniques can be used to derive patterns of repeating behavior from logs of past interactions between service consumers and providers. Consumers may use these patterns to detect anomalous provider behavior, while providers may seek to adapt their behavior in ways that cannot be detected by the consumer. A challenge is deriving a behavioral model that is a sufficiently precise representation of the consumer-provider interactions. *Behavioral norms*, which model these patterns of behavior, are used to explore these issues in a on-line photograph sharing style service.

1 Introduction

In today's digital world, individuals and organizations perform much of their computing and communications using third party services. These service *consumers* and *providers* interoperate according to their own, possibly conflicting, requirements. For example, an individual consumer uses a social media service provider to communicate with friends: the service is free, however, the consumer may wish to minimize advertisments/loss of privacy, while the provider may wish to maximize advertising revenue by weakening consumer privacy. Similarly, the provider of a public cloud infrastructure may be willing to risk degraded consumer service for the sake of additional consumer revenue, while consumers seek certain service agreements. Consumers and producers rely on each other to behave accordingly, however each have to recognize that it may be in the interest of the other to cut across their requirements.

In this paper we explore how consumers might detect malicious provider behavior that is at variance with consumer requirements, and how malicious providers, might in turn, adapt their behavior in ways that cannot be detected by the consumer. This malicious provider behavior is not a conventional Dolev-Yao style external attacker [5,13] since the consumer relies on the provider's 'normal' behavior. Nor is the behavior that of a insider-attacker [4,6] that is to be mitigated by security controls within the provider. We characterize this behavior as that of a *systemic* attacker: it is the provider itself that is the attacker. A systemic attack may result from the deliberate intentions of a provider or arise from an incompetent provider that itself has been compromised in some way.

© Springer International Publishing Switzerland 2014
B. Christianson et al. (Eds.): Security Protocols 2014, LNCS 8809, pp. 18–27, 2014.
DOI: 10.1007/978-3-319-12400-1_3

In principle, a consumer could use a reference monitor to check provider interaction against policies of acceptable behaviors. In practice, however, the scale and complexity of the systems involved mean that it is not reasonable to expect a complete and coherent specification of such behaviors, regardless of the consumer's understanding of the requirements. A proactive consumer might use browser-based security controls [11] in an attempt to prevent Cross Site Scripting attacks coming via an incompetent provider, write some network-packet controls in effort to block unwanted content, rely on protocols such as OAuth [9] to control access, or even use task-based polices [15] to control provider interaction sequences. Such consumer-side controls on provider interaction will likely be ad-hoc and incomplete, focusing on behavior perceived to be critical, with an assumption that other activities, known or unknown, are not significant. However, it is often the side-activities that can lead to security concerns.

We argue that log data of past interactions between consumer and provider(s) can be used to derive policies of acceptable behavior and that the consumer can use anomaly detection techniques to monitor provider compliance. When a consumer is unable to (fully) articulate their expectation of a provider, then the consumer should be interested in knowing when provider behavior deviates from what are considered 'normal' interactions of the past. This deviation may be an indication of a security concern. Such system log mining techniques have been used elsewhere to infer acceptable behavior/policies for anomaly detection [7,12] process mining [1–3] and security policy mining [8,10]. In this paper we consider how the system log mining techniques described in [12] might be used by a service consumer to discover models for these 'normal' interactions and which can be used to monitor for potential systemic attacks by service providers.

The paper is organized as follows. Section 2 sketches the operation of a simple online photograph sharing service. Section 3 outlines how a behavioral norm model might be generated from a consumer's log of their interaction with this service. Sections 4 and 5 explore how this behavioral norm model might be used to detect anomalies in single and collaborating provider services. While this paper is exploratory, Sect. 6 outlines how behavioral norms have been evaluated in practice. Section 7 concludes the paper.

2   An Online Photograph Sharing Service

Consider an on-line photograph hosting and sharing service. The service allows users to upload and store their photographs, establish a network of friends with whom to share photographs, comment on photographs, and so forth. The service also provides activity tracking of the users and their friends. Users can view the actions they have performed (for example, the photographs they uploaded and when), and limited tracking of the actions of other users (for example, accesses and comments on the photographs they share). For example, Fig. 1 provides a fragment of a log of such actions that are visible to the user Frank.

This activity data need not necessarily come from a conventional text log. Actions/events may be presented to the consumer by the provider using a web

```
time                     user   context  action         id      extra
--------------------------------------------------------------------------
2013-11-04 16:53:05      Frank  self     login          -       -
2013-11-04 16:55:21      Frank  self     upload_photo   img23   Holidays 2013
2013-11-04 16:57:55      Frank  self     upload_photo   img24   New bike
2013-11-04 17:01:03      Frank  self     share          img23   Lucy
2013-11-04 17:04:29      Lucy   friend   view_photo     img23   -
2013-11-04 17:05:18      Frank  self     share          img24   Bob
2013-11-04 17:05:19      Lucy   friend   comment        img23   I wish, I was there
2013-11-04 17:21:34      Bob    friend   view_photo     img24   -
2013-11-04 17:22:01      Bob    friend   comment        img24   Nice!
...
```

Fig. 1. Partial log from the photo hosting service

interface or as a feed in some common format such as RSS or ATOM and we assume that a consumer is be able to view the events relevant to its interaction with the provider. Events are comprised of attributes; the events in Fig. 1 have attributes that provide `time` of event, `user` name, `action` carried out, and whether the action is carried out by the user viewing the log (the `context` value `self`) a `friend` or `other` user, the image `id`, and any `extra` data.

Studying Fig. 1, we see that `Frank` logs-in, uploads two photographs, shares photographs with users `Lucy` and `Bob` who in turn view and comment.

Our goal is to discover a model that represents (provider) behavior from the event log that includes the fragment in Fig. 1. Analyzing the log events contiguously/in the order in which they appear in Fig. 1 does not provide much insight into the behavioral patterns of the provider. For example, representing the behavior in terms of short-range correlations between events, such as n-grams [7], does not reveal any interesting patterns of behavior.

However, a closer inspection of the log in Fig. 1 reveals what appears to be two, interleaving, transaction-like patterns of behavior. In the first, `Frank` uploads a photo `img23`, shares it with `Lucy` who then views and comments. In the second, the same sequence of actions occur in relation to `Frank` sharing `img24` with user `Bob`. This analysis identifies a simple transaction-style behavior in the log fragment:

<upload_photo, share_photo, view_photo, comment_photo>

In identifying these transaction style patterns it is important to distinguish the roles that are played by the different event attributes. Intuitively, the attribute value `action` represents the operation being carried out by the event and this operation is effectively parameterized by the image identifier (target attribute `id`). For the purposes of this paper we choose to ignore the `time` attribute as not playing a role in the behavior of the provider (other than providing event temporal ordering). Further study of the log is required to decide whether the `user`, `context` and `extra` attribute values should play a role in this transaction.

3   Behavioral Norms

Behaviorial norms [12] represent repeating patterns of behavior at different levels of abstraction that can be discovered from event traces/logs. A search process has been developed [12] can be used to determine the event attributes that represent the operations and parameters for potential norms discovered in the event log. These norms may be represented in various forms, such as a database of n-grams.

Considering the log fragment in Fig. 1, the search process discovers a behavioral norm depicted as:

```
<self.upload_photo, self.share_photo, friend.view_photo, friend.comment_photo>
```

This is a transaction-style sequence of actions. The search identifies attributes context and action values as representing the event operation on common target attribute id values while attributes time and extra are considered to have no discernible effect on behavior. Thus, the log sub-sequence

```
2013-11-04 16:55:21   Frank   self     upload_photo   img23   Holidays 2013
2013-11-04 17:01:03   Frank   self     share          img23   Lucy
2013-11-04 17:04:29   Lucy    friend   view_photo     img23   -
2013-11-04 17:05:19   Lucy    friend   comment        img23   I wish, I was there
```

is a valid instantiation of the above norm, while the sub-sequence

```
...
2013-11-04 16:55:21   Frank   self     upload_photo   img23   Holidays 2013
2013-11-04 17:01:03   Frank   self     share          img23   Lucy
2013-11-04 17:04:29   Lucy    friend   view_photo     img23   -
2013-11-04 17:05:19   Lucy    friend   comment        img24   I wish, I was there
...
```

is not a valid instantiation of the norm as it does not involve a common photograph id.

Figure 2 depicts likely behavioral norms that might be discovered if given a complete provider log for Frank. The first norm describes the behavior that can be observed from Fig. 1. The other norms represent additional kinds of typical 'normal' behavior, such as Frank viewing photos shared by other users, or connecting with friends.

```
1   <self.upload_photo, self.share_photo, friend.view_photo, friend.comment_photo>
2   <friend.upload_photo, friend.share_photo, self.view_photo, self.comment_photo>
3   <friend.upload_photo, self.view_photo, self.comment_photo>
4   <other.connect_request, self.accept_connect_request>
5   <self.connect_request, other.accept_connect_request>
```

Fig. 2. Norms for user's collaboration with photo hosting service provider

The norms in Fig. 2 represent provider (online service) behavior that could be discovered by a consumer (Frank) analyzing his event logs. These 'discovered' norms provide insight into the behavior of the provider. Frank and his community usage patterns and configuration, such as privacy settings, are reflected in these norms. For example, Frank uses the service's default privacy policy that considers newly upload photos as private. This requires him to explicitly share every photo before it is viewed by other users. Some of **Frank**'s friends have a similar configuration, and this is reflected in the second norm. Other friends configured their account differently to make all of their uploaded photos visible to their friends or public, by default. This behavior is captured in the third norm, which lacks an explicit sharing operation.

4   Provider Anomalies

Assume that **Frank**'s photo hosting service wishes to attract additional traffic and increase the amount of content that is available to their users. To do this, they decide to change their default application behavior. The change is to make all new content visible to the user's friends by default. Users can still configure the policy explicitly in order to override default behavior. Unaware of the new default setting, Frank continues to use the service and uploads new images. Frank's friends may now see the image instantly, without Frank's explicit action to share. This change is made to only the default behavior of the application. It does not modify application's terms of use nor the privacy policy. Frank still has the right to restrict his content, configure his policy differently, or remove any of his content. While this provider change may be done entirely legally it has a negative effect on Frank's use of the application.

Frank's set of norms may be used to detect this application change. His service provider, after the change, will start generating the logs that cannot be matched to the norms in Fig. 2. This unrecognized activity may be considered an anomaly and alert Frank to investigate the change. Performing norm discovery on the new log can reveal that a new norm has emerged:

<self.upload_photo, friend.view_photo, friend.comment_photo>

This anomaly is specific to Frank's interaction with the service. For other users, such as those whose photos are shared with others by default, the change has no impact. For such users, the above norm would already be considered an acceptable norm (based on the analysis of their logs).

5   Anomalies Across Multiple Collaborating Providers

Continuing the example, Frank uses an additional service provider: an on-line photograph printing service. Using this service he can order prints for his photographs on-line and have them delivered to the friends and family. The service is integrated with Frank's photograph hosting provider. This is convenient for Frank as he can give the printing site permission to access his photographs and order prints without the need to re-upload. The access delegation can be done using a standard protocol such as OAuth [9]. In a typical scenario, Frank accesses the printing service, and selects his hosting service as the location of images. The printing service accesses Frank's account and downloads photograph miniatures. Frank selects the photographs that he wants printed and for each of them the printing service, with its delegated authority from the photograph sharing service, downloads the full size image files.

The logs (visible to Frank) from both providers for such a scenario are presented at Listing 3. Log events now originate from two different service providers and this is distinguished by a new event attribute **provider** in the logs. In addition, events for actions performed on behalf of Frank by the printing service provider have a **context** attribute value **prtsvc** in the hosting provider log (Fig. 3).

```
PRINT SERVICE (provider=print)          HOSTING SERVICE (provider=host)
time     user  context action     id    time     user  context action        id
-------------------------------------   -------------------------------------------
19:31:05 Frank self    new_order
                                        19:31:19 Frank prtsvc  list_photos
                                        19:31:20 Frank prtsvc  get_thumbnail img01
                                        19:31:20 Frank prtsvc  get_thumbnail img02
                                        ...
                                        19:31:21 Frank prtsvc  get_thumbnail img08
19:33:41 Frank self    select     img03
19:33:52 Frank self    select     img07
                                        19:34:06 Frank prtsvc  get_fullsize  img03
                                        19:34:08 Frank prtsvc  get_fullsize  img07
19:36:02 Frank self    submit_order
```

Fig. 3. Two producers collaboration

Frank has given the printing service a permission to access his photos. While short-lived permission delegations are possible in schemes such as OAuth, many providers offer long-lived *offline* permissions, which are often requested by the third-party providers [14], irrespective of the dangers. The expected behavior is that the service will only access the photos when Frank places a print order. Technically however, there is no such restriction and the print service may access the photos at any time. Frank can only trust that this service provider will behave properly.

Analyzing the hosting service log in isolation the following norm may be discovered:

<prtsvc.list_photos, prtsvc.get_thumbnail, prtsvc.get_fullsize>

This norm represents the typical way in which a print service accesses user photographs when interacting with the hosting service. With its delegated permission from Frank, the printing service could decide to download all of Frank's photos in the background without interaction with Frank. This activity will generate a log in the hosting service. Based on the behavioral norm above, however, this activity can be regarded as 'normal'.

Building the behavioral norms from the individual printer service log is insufficient to fully capture the interaction between consumer and the two providers. The norms should be discovered from a single log that aggregates the events from both service providers. In this case, log operations are characterized in terms of three attributes: **provider.context.action** with a sample norm

<print.self.new_order, host.prtsvc.list_photos, host.prtsvc.get_thumbnail,
print.self.select, host.prtsvc.get_fullsize, print.self.complete_order>

This norm captures aggregated behavior of all of the parties collaborating together. Any activity of printing service unrelated to Frank's print ordering will be considered abnormal, as it will not match the norm.

6   Norms in Action

This paper explores the use of behavioral norms to help interpret anomalies in the interactions between a consumer with its providers. Previous research [12] evaluated the effectiveness of using behavioral norms to represent emergent behavior from system logs. The evaluation demonstrated that behavioral norms can be discovered in logs from a simulated system and in logs from a real-world enterprise on-line collaboration application. The logs contained relatively low-level system attributes and the norm discovery process identified attributes for event actions and targets for the norm transactions.

In practice, the sequence of operations may not be identical even if two parts of log represent the same behavior. For that reason, norms are represented as patterns that match sequences to certain degree of similarity. This similarity level, if set high, it produces large number of very precise norms. If it is low, model contains fewer, more general norms. During the norm search the suitable similarity level is identified.

In a further experiment, we considered how adverse changes in a system configuration might be detected in terms of changes in norms. The simulated application system in [12] was augmented to include a simple access-control mechanism that governed the operations carried out by users. The resulting behavioral norms for the application system reflected the constraints by the underlying access control system. The simulation was modified to reflect a security flaw whereby the access control policy was disabled and this resulted, as anticipated, in the identification of new application behavioral norms. These norms described new behaviors

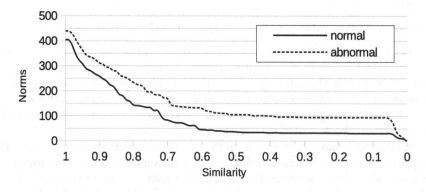

Fig. 4. Number of norms before and after configuration change [12]

corresponding to system activity with different then previously recorded access rights. Figure 4 depicts comparison between number of norms (for different levels of similarity) for system before and after the change. These experiments confirmed that behavioral model can be successfully built, and reasoned about, from arbitrary system logs with unknown structure of events. In this paper we used the behavior norms model to help interpret anomalies in service consumer-provider scenario. We are currently exploring how this might be evaluated in practice.

7   Discussion

Consumer security is impacted by the provider services with which it directly or indirectly interacts. Individually, providers may have different motivations in providing service and the security mechanisms available to the consumer to control interaction tend to be weak. For example, service providers often provide only coarse grained access controls to their consumers. When multiple applications need to collaborate, they may be given more access than is actually required.

We argue that anomaly detection style techniques can be used by a consumer to monitor interactions with providers. The challenge is to formulate a sufficiently precise model of 'normal' interaction and we propose that consumers mine their provider logs to build models of past, presumably acceptable, behavior. We propose using behavioral norms [12] to model multiple patterns of behavior in a system log.

Conventional anomaly detection is routinely used to help protect a provider from malicious consumers; we have considered using anomaly detection to protect a consumer from multiple, possibly collaborating, providers. A single consumer transaction may span multiple providers interacting with each other and the consumer. Prescribing rules for each of the providers separately is not sufficient. As seen in Sect. 5, an anomaly may not manifest itself when only single provider-centric rules are considered. The anomaly may be an acceptable activity from the individual provider, but be unacceptable when considered part of a value chain.

Another difficulty in determining normal interaction is distinguishing acceptable and unacceptable provider intertaction. Simply comparing provider behavior against known and precise access control rules is not sufficient. Section 4 illustrated how provider misbehavior can be subtle and within the boundaries of the contract, but is a deviation from normal/past interactions.

If consumers can use behavioral norms to detect malicious provider behavior then a malicious provider might attempt to use the same norms to guide behavior adaptation in ways that cannot be detected by the consumer. This corresponds to a *mimicry* style attack [16], used to bypass anomaly detection systems. For example, in an n-gram based model [7], the attacker crafts an attack sequence that contains malicious code but is built entirely of acceptable (n-gram) sequences.

Investigating whether a malicious provider constrained by behavioral norms would find it difficult to mount a successful mimicry attack is a topic for future research. Behavioral norms provide a model of discovered behavior that is considerably more precise than n-grams. To mimic a behavior, one must consider not only the operation itself, but the other attributes (`user` and `provider` in our example) that together represent the actions engaged for a common target attribute value (image `id` in our example) for a given behavioral norm. We conjecture that this provides less flexibility in designing malicious sequences that fit a behavioral norm. Furthermore, as shown in Sect. 5, the model may include aggregated behavior of multiple providers with the consumer. In this case, the malicious provider not only must adjust its own sequences, but must also be able to influence the sequences of the other providers.

Acknowledgments. This research has been partly supported by Science Foundation Ireland grant 08/SRC/11403.

References

1. van der Aalst, W.M., Weijters, T., Maruster, L.: Workflow mining: discovering process models from event logs. IEEE Trans. Knowl. Data Eng. **16**(9), 1128–1142 (2004)
2. Accorsi, R., Stocker, T.: Automated privacy audits based on pruning of log data. In: EDOCW 12th Enterprise Distributed Object Computing Conference Workshops, pp. 175–182 (2008)
3. Agrawal, R., Gunopulos, D., Leymann, F.: Mining process models from workflow logs. In: Schek, H.-J., Saltor, F., Ramos, I., Alonso, G. (eds.) EDBT 1998. LNCS, vol. 1377, pp. 469–483. Springer, Heidelberg (1998)
4. Bellovin, S.M.: The insider attack problem nature and scope. In: Stolfo, S.J., Bellovin, S.M., Keromytis, A.D., Hershkop, S., Smith, S.W., Sinclair, S. (eds.) Insider Attack and Cyber Security. Advances in Information Security, vol. 39, pp. 1–4. Springer, Heidelberg (2008)
5. Dolev, D., Yao, A.: On the security of public key protocols. IEEE Trans. Inf. Theory **29**(2), 198–208 (1983)
6. Foley, S.: A non-functional approach to system integrity. IEEE J. Sel. Areas Commun. **21**(1), 36–43 (2003)
7. Forrest, S., Hofmeyr, S.A., Somayaji, A., Longstaff, T.A.: A sense of self for unix processes. In: IEEE Symposium on Security and Privacy, pp. 120–128 (1996)
8. Frank, M., Buhmann, J., Basin, D.: On the definition of role mining. In: Joshi, J.B.D., Carminati, B. (eds.) ACM Symposium on Access Control Models and Technologies (SACMAT), pp. 35–44. ACM (2010)
9. Hardt, D.: The OAuth 2.0 Authorization Framework. RFC 6749 (Proposed Standard) October 2012. http://www.ietf.org/rfc/rfc6749.txt
10. Kuhlmann, M., Shohat, D., Schimpf, G.: Role mining - revealing business roles for security administration using data mining technology. In: Proceedings of the Eighth ACM Symposium on Access Control Models and Technologies, SACMAT '03, pp. 179–186. ACM, New York (2003)
11. Louw, M.T., Venkatakrishnan, V.N.: Blueprint: robust prevention of cross-site scripting attacks for existing browsers. In: Proceedings of the 2009 30th IEEE Symposium on Security and Privacy, pp. 331–346. IEEE Computer Society (2009)

12. Pieczul, O., Foley, S.: Discovering emergent norms in security logs. In: 2013 IEEE Conference on Communications and Network Security (CNS - SafeConfig), pp. 438–445 (2013)
13. Ryan, P.Y.A.: Mathematical models of computer security. In: Focardi, R., Gorrieri, R. (eds.) FOSAD 2000. LNCS, vol. 2171, pp. 1–62. Springer, Heidelberg (2001)
14. Sun, S.T., Beznosov, K.: The devil is in the (implementation) details: an empirical analysis of OAuth SSO systems. In: Proceedings of the 2012 ACM Conference on Computer and Communications Security, CCS '12, pp. 378–390. ACM, New York (2012)
15. Thomas, R., Sandhu, R.: Task-based authorization controls (TBAC): a family of models for active and enterprise-oriented autorization management. In: Proceedings of the IFIP TC11 WG11.3 Eleventh International Conference on Database Securty XI: Status and Prospects (1998)
16. Wagner, D., Soto, P.: Mimicry attacks on host-based intrusion detection systems. In: Proceedings of the 9th ACM Conference on Computer and Communications Security, CCS '02, pp. 255–264. ACM, New York (2002)

Collaborating as Normal: Detecting Systemic Anomalies in Your Partner (Transcript of Discussion)

Simon N. Foley[✉]

University College Cork, Cork, Ireland
s.foley@cs.ucc.ie

I'd like start with an analogy of the problem that we've been thinking about recently. Consider a bank ATM. The provider is the bank who provides this service. Within the bank they use various security controls; the simplest control is your ATM card and your PIN, and maybe there's a chip there as well. The bank also has terms and conditions about how you're allowed to use the ATM to withdraw cash. To go with this is a security infrastructure that the bank has put in place in an effort to ensure your ATM transaction is secure. Our view is that for such a complex system, one will never be able to articulate, or describe, all of the necessary security controls, or security mechanisms, that make the system secure. Therefore, in practice there's a lot of other things that the users of the system are doing that contribute to the overall security of the system.

Consider how the bank ATM is used in this picture[1]. You can see that there's a social norm, which is that when someone is standing at the ATM machine, other people stand back at a distance, and this gives some sense of safety, or security, to the person using the machine. You might say, that's just security theatre, but if that's the case then, would you use this ATM[2]? Consider this second picture; there's no queue, its seems to be a free for all. We have here what we think of as an anomalous norm. The social norm of orderly queuing is broken and as a consequence we're somewhat concerned about using this particular system; it does not feel secure.

Frank Stajano: But usually, when you look at the first picture, you would imagine that the person being one metre back is so that they cannot see your PIN. Now in the case of your second picture it's like they are they going to snatch the money when it comes out of the machine.

Reply: Yes, while the bank will install some security mechanisms, there's additional things that people do that help to make the overall system secure. You can think of the bank's security controls as being the regulation, those known things that we're trying to defend against, but then there's all of these social norms, which are all these other things that are, if you like, unspoken, or unspecified, that people do to make the system secure.

---

[1] Points to a picture of an orderly queue of people at an ATM.

[2] A disorderly ATM queue http://commons.wikimedia.org/wiki/File:ATM_Masalli.jpg.

© Springer International Publishing Switzerland 2014
B. Christianson et al. (Eds.): Security Protocols 2014, LNCS 8809, pp. 28–37, 2014.
DOI: 10.1007/978-3-319-12400-1_4

Jeunese Payne: Is it not the case that people just don't like to sit next to each other, or stand next to each other, like on the bus everybody will sit in a seat. I'm aware that I'm doing it right now, but is it not just the case that they don't care about the security, they just don't want to be seen as imposing on somebody else's personal space?

Reply: So would you be happy to withdraw money from this second ATM machine?

Jeunese Payne: No, I certainly wouldn't; not necessarily because of the money thing, but because everybody is around me: I'd think, oh what are they doing, this is my personal space. So do you think maybe it would be, is it really to do with, how do you know that it's to do with idea of security.

Frank Stajano: But then how would it apply to the other people in the queue who are just next to each other before the last one.

Peter Ryan: If you go to the first picture then the spacing between people, there's a very poignant space between them.

Jeunese Payne: Yes, there is a poignant space that's a good point.

Reply: It's a fair point, but if you're in a movie theatre on your own and somebody comes in and sits two spaces from you, then that's strange.

Jeunese Payne: It's a bit creepy.

Reply: Our position is that security is provided by both the bank's security mechanisms and the social norms. In this case, because of the breakdown in the social norms and even though they're not violating the bank's security policies or mechanisms, we'd still be somewhat concerned about using this ATM.

Peter Ryan: It looks like that one's spewing out money, doesn't it.

Reply: Yes, thanks Peter. Here's another picture of an ATM machine where somebody had accidentally put in, I think, £20 notes into the £10 note slot, and everybody was getting twice the amount that they withdrew. In this case, its not that there was a breakdown in the social norm, the breakdown was in the actual security mechanism itself. And of course what's interesting here as an aside is that, in some senses, because the mechanism has failed there's quite a different social norm going on here, there's people looking over their shoulder saying, you know, how much are you getting, and people seemed quite relaxed with that.

Our paper is about a systems equivalent to social norms. The outline of the talk is as follows. Our view is that when you consider security then there are the security controls that are prescribed and put in place to defend against those known threats, but then there are also these other patterns of normal behaviour—in society we think of them as social norms—which are a sort of a compliment to regulations and laws. In computer-based systems we call them behavioural norms, and I'll show you some examples of those later. What we're interested in, is when a consumer is using a service, the consumer is interested in detecting anomalies. Not just the anomalies from failures in the known controls that are put in place by the provider, or even by the consumer. For example, if I'm browsing the web and visiting websites, then I'm going to install various security mechanisms into my browser to help stop, for example, cross site scripting attacks. Thus there's a number of things that I should try to do myself as a consumer, but then again, I don't know about everything that might happen. What I'd like to do is to make sure that when I am using a service that there's a norm in the way I'm I'm using it. The way that I'm using it is similar to how I've used it in the past.

We're going to look at a very simple example about photograph hosting and printing services, and how people might use them. The main idea is that we've got security mechanisms, but the security of the system is more than just these controls, it's a combination of controls plus these patterns of normal behaviour.

The setup is as follows. We have a consumer who is interacting with various provider services. The consumer has access to a service log from the provider, which is a log of the actions, or API calls, a record of what has happened on the provider on the consumer's behalf. What the consumer wants to try to do is to build a collection of what we call behavioural norms that describe their patterns of normal behaviour with the provider. From the provider's point of view we know that they have some security controls in place, but they are possibly incomplete, perhaps because they've misunderstood them. Also perhaps, there's an internal attacker within the provider, or the provider itself could be the attacker. This is not just a simple internal attacker, it's what we call a systemic attacker. The provider might also get the consumer to sign up to a service agreement to avoid problems. From the consumers point of view they judge security as being normal based on their past interaction.

Consider the photograph hosting service. Frank, the consumer, is interacting with a photograph hosting service, that allows him to upload, share, comment, and view, on photographs. Its a very, very simple system. The photographs can be either public or private, so that when I upload a public photograph it means everybody can look at it, or if I upload a private photograph then it means that I have to explicitly share it with other people. And then there's the service default setting, which is private sharing. We'll assume that the hosting service has the usual terms and conditions that it won't misuse your photograph, and so on. Frank likes free services, he wants to share photographs with his friends, but he also likes his privacy, and he's going to rely on the default privacy setting. A very, very simple scenario.

Here's an example[3] of the log that might be available to Frank. What he'd like to do is to ask, what's my normal interaction with this particular service, or, what is this (what we call this behavioural norm) repeating pattern of behaviour? Frank might look at just the actions in the log and ask if there is any particular repeating pattern of behaviour here. Maybe he'll do something like an n-gram analysis and try to build a model from that. However, there's nothing terribly interesting going on when we consider n-grams built from just the action name.

---

[3] Points to the log in Fig. 1 of the paper.

If we also consider the context of the action, what we have in this line of the log is that Frank, as himself, uploads photograph 23, and then as himself he shares that photograph 23 with Lucy, and then Lucy, who's a friend, views that photograph, and then Lucy, who's a friend, comments on that photograph. You can see that this is the pattern of behaviour for image 23, and is also the same pattern for image 24. Olgierd's been working on a scheme whereby you data-mine your logs to extract these behavioural norms, these transaction-like behaviours, these patterns of behaviours in the logs. In this slide we've identified one example of a behavioural norm in the log. And of course we might identify other behavioural norms if we had a sufficiently large log. For example, here in the log a friend has a similar norm, which is: he uploads photos, he shares them, and then people can view them, or he can view it. Or here's another friend who uploads photographs and in this case Frank can directly view the photograph and comment on it, so it doesn't require an explicit share. In this case, this friend of Frank must have the public setting for his photograph sharing options.

Suppose that the previous log represented past normal behavior for Frank. The log in this next slide reflects a slightly different arrangement. The service provider decides to change the upload default setting from private to public. Perhaps their motivation is that if they can get more visitors looking at photographs on their website, then they get more advertising revenue. If everybody is sharing photographs privately then that's not enough public photographs, and not enough visits to the website. The service provider decides that they're going to change the upload default setting, and of course they send out an email to all their subscribers, and, of course, nobody reads these new terms and conditions. As a result the service log for Frank changes, you can see that: he uploads image 24, and then immediately Bob, a friend, can view it. Frank doesn't have to explicitly share. As a result we have a pattern of behaviour that's not in Frank's norms. Frank could use an anomaly detection system to alert him to these different behaviors. For Frank the social norm has changed.

Frank Stajano: Isn't this rather similar to what you were saying in the context of Dieter's talk that at the beginning you don't know what's normal, and then you sort of rely on something becoming normal, and it's a bit like the identity, you don't really know where to anchor that.

Reply: Right, absolutely. Maybe I've never used this photograph service before and I'm somewhat concerned about using it, and about using it properly. However, I see myself as being someone like you and therefore feel it would be safe if I adopted your norms as my norms. I'm happy enough following your normal patterns of behavior. But of course, the question is how do we bootstrap this.

Michael Roe: Isn't this what the intrusion detection plan is usually talking about, where they're mining logs of accesses that are permitted by policy to ensure that something that is happening is normal.

Reply: Yes, I think there are two differences. One is that intrusion detection is usually about intrusions or extrusions, where you're looking for anomalies in your system, or anomalies that your system is causing to its external environment. One slight difference in our case is that it's a consumer who's using a service who's looking for anomalies in the way that the consumer is using that particular service. That's not a big difference. The other difference is more technical. Consider anomaly detection schemes that are based on checking normal behavior, such as the original work by Stephanie Forrest on models of self. Built using n-grams, these Markov style models are less expressive as they were not used to distinguish transactional behavior in the system. Our position is that it's not just a case of discovering simple correlations between sequences of events in the log. There are separate sequences, which in our model correspond to the transaction like behavioural norms.

In addition to this, many of the existing anomaly detection systems require an a priori identification of the attributes in the log that are considered relevant, prior to mining the log. For example, in building a model of normal behavior, one might decide to mine Frank's log based on just the action attribute while not realizing that it is only by also considering the photo-id attribute that transactional like behavior is discovered. Olgierd has been investigating how, by analyzing the log, one can also discover what combination of log attributes generate the most precise behavioral norms that describe the system.

Olgierd Pieczul: One point is that some of the log attributes may not be obvious to an administrator or to someone configuring the anomaly detection system. Certain attributes may, in some unexpected way, contribute to the system's normal behaviour. Also one should bear in mind that these behavioral norms may identify completely unexpected behavior patterns in the system that works according to particular parties. Thus its valuable to consider all of the attributes and look for those that can result in repeating patters of behavior.

Alastair Beresford: What's the incentive for the provider of this free service to provide the log, why would do that?

Reply: That's a fair question. A malicious provider could decide to provide an incomplete log and while Frank can collect some of the information based on his interaction, there are other interactions he cannot easily discover for him self. For example, he does rely on the provider telling him in the log that Lucy looked at his photo.

Frank Stajano: Insofar as it's an adversarial game between the provider wanting to open up the settings, regardless of what the users want, then it does make sense to ask Alistair's question.

Reply: Absolutely, yes.

Olgierd Pieczul: The idea here was to have it like a wall with some information that the provider would show to the consumer, and in this host model it could be something like a basic blog, so its in the provider's interest to release the information. Also, there might be regulations requiring the provide to show that information.

Alastair Beresford: And there might be other, as you say, Facebook's motivation, might be to get more users as well as to see more sharing and more ads going out because they're all interlinked because in that case the log, they have some interest in doing the log.

Rebecca Wright: Certainly I think there are privacy and policy implications on the log itself. And you had the one where, I think you had Frank inferring that Bob made his photos public by default, and that may or may not be something that you would want shared, and that policy itself of sharing that in the log could change.

Reply: Yes.

Alastair Beresford: Photo's gone private here.

Reply: Yes. There's another example related to Alistair's question. It's an example that Roger Needham gave, which was that if a bank wants to improve its internal security then it should include details of who looked at your account on your account statement. In our case have to trust that the provider is going to provide all this information.

Frank Stajano: And also you're putting a non-trivial burden on Frank to check the log in a meaningful way because, you know, the way you look at bank statements, OK, another one, that's fine, you don't even read in there unless you are worried about stuff that might happen. And so here there has to be quite a bit of analysis from Frank in order to detect those things.

Reply: Yes, and there's two related observations. The first is that one would hope that maybe there's some automated support that will do this for Frank. The second, which I think the more interesting part of your question, is, how does Frank recognise that this is an issue? Perhaps the system has identified 200 different norms based on Franks past behavior. How does Frank decide how to interpret a previously unknown behavior that doesn't match these previous norms? Should Frank be concerned? You can imagine that the more norms we have then the harder it will be for a user to determine whether or not he has a problem.

Alastair Beresford: Another thing that's just popped into my head, they did some trials I think in the US where they put fake entries into the records, of people who were in hospital that had famous names, and went to see who looked at them. I don't know quite what the analogy would be here, but whether you could inject fake items into the log, or would be a useful thing.

Bruce Christianson: Following up on Frank's point, a lot of fraud detection mechanisms are simply trying to detect a typical transaction, or transactions where it is worth bothering the user by popping up a box, not endless boxes saying, allow or deny, but boxes saying, how do you feel about this transaction. And I guess you almost want, three answers, definitely yes, definitely no, or, yes I feel ambivalent about this one, because that says you're drawing the line in the right place.

Reply: If we know what valid transactions should look like beforehand then its relatively easy to look at the log and flag potentially anomalous behavior. However, what about the situation where you start to see repeating patterns of behaviour in your logs that you never expected and you don't necessarily know what they mean, mostly they are OK, except that there's this peculiar transactional like behaviour to the others. Maybe your looking at a cloud provider and when you start going down at the lower, layers, you start seeing some very strange behaviour down at the file system level due to caching, and it's this repeating pattern, and you've never put a name onto it, but perhaps it's important for the security.

Bruce Christianson: But I guess what you wanted to flag there is, when it changes.

Reply: Yes, that's it, so you know something has gone wrong. So it's like the social norm, and like the case of the social norm, it requires a analogous study to identify and recognise true norms.

Frank Stajano: There's still a shift of the burden towards the user who might not understand and says, you know, the system is very good at flagging anomalies and it says, well I'm just a system flagging anomalies, I don't understand what is security relevant really, I just see that it's different, so you user, what do you think about this, do you feel ambivalent, do you feel it is dangerous. And the user says, I don't understand this stuff you said, file system, caching, and I don't have a computer science degree, I just want to share my photos, and I will just go to another service that doesn't ask me these difficult questions because it's just too scary for me, you're putting all the responsibility on me to ask, and, you know, decide which one I should do of things I don't understand. So I think we should protect the user from having to take the decision themselves on the ultimate top-level part, which one is dangerous and which one isn't. How are they supposed to know.

Reply: Yes, Olgierd discussed a related issue this morning. Ignorance is bliss when it comes to security, and in some sense it's perhaps a case of you're better off not knowing that your norms are changing because if we start trying to tell you about all your norms then it's an overload, and you can't cope.

Nikita Borisov: But I was trying to understand, norms have two different meanings. Here you seem to talk about usual behaviours, what you usually do, but when I think of norms I often think about what is the expected behaviour, so to see the difference, for example, I always cross my hands like this, this is my usual behaviour, but nobody expects me, nobody would say, oh you're doing something wrong, if I did it like this, right. So are we really talking about social norms in terms of the expected behaviour from a social perspective, or are we talking about things that just have some behaviour.

Reply: These were social norms. For example, safety in society is made up of not just laws, but also the social norms that people follow. We can't rely just on regulation for people to feel safe in society, there's all those other things that people do which contribute to somebody feeling safe in society.

Nikita Borisov: So then I think that there's actually maybe a distinction between what typically we think about anomaly detection and these norms. For example, if I normally log into my work account at 9 am and I started doing it at 8.30 the next week, that's nothing to do with social norms, but might show up as a big anomaly.

Reply: Yes, the social norm is the analogy. We think of society, which is made safe by a combination of regulations and social norm, and then for a computer system or enterprise, we think of the security of it as being a combination of security mechanism, which is regulations, things we know about, plus these other behavioural norms, these repeated actions that perhaps don't apparently have any bearing on security, but have this repeated transactional like behaviours which are occurring in the system.

James Malcolm: I think when somebody breaks their norms you don't just have to say, stop. Uca Moriyama, a couple of years ago, suggested that all you need to do is change the screen colour a little bit to say, you may be in a slightly dangerous area here, you're doing something unusual, just be careful.

Reply: Yes.

Olgierd Pieczul: So like with the ATM example, if you really need to get money from the ATM then you would maybe still use it if there is a guy behind you.

James Malcolm: Exactly yes.

Dongting Yu: So earlier Alistair mentioned why the provider might have to provide logs. Suppose there is such a social log and the provider is forced to provide the logs, then what's preventing the provider from basically decreasing the signal to noise ratio in the log? One of the techniques might be just to insert records that you can't trace.

Reply: Agreed. In the next example Frank uses a hardcopy print service to get physical copies of the photographs, and this print service interacts with the hosting service to get access to the photographs. You can imagine the scenario as an OAuth style protocol whereby the *intention* is that Frank gives the print service temporary access to the hosting service so that it can access Frank's photographs. Frank gets to select those photographs and then prints them out. Again, we've got service logs that are being collected from both of these services.

Kosta Beznosov did a study on how OAuth was being used in practice and he found that it was not unusual for services to issue much longer delegation credentials than were required. In our example, its the print service getting a credential that it can use over to assess Frank's photos over and over again even when Frank hasn't necessarily initiated the request.

We have two simple logs[4] where Frank visits the print service and initiates a new printing order. Following OAuth, the print service then logs in as Frank to

---

[4] In Fig. 3 of the paper.

the hosting service and gets a list of the photographs. Frank selects the images that he wants to print, and then at the print service, the print service then, at the hosting service as Frank, gets the full sized images, prints them out, Frank submits the order.

If we were to look at the log of just the hosting service, you can see that there's a norm like behaviour where the print service, as Frank, lists the photos, and then gets thumbnail and full-size of an image. There's a very simple kind of norm pattern of behaviour here. If the print service was to subsequently, at a later date, access the hosting service without being initiated by Frank, then this would still be a valid norm. There's nothing here that involves Frank's participation when the print service accesses the hosting service as Frank. But if we considered the two logs together, and build a norm out of the two, you can see here that we have a norm, whereby Frank looks for a new order, lists photos, gets thumbnails, selects the photo, gets full-size and submits. And then, if the print service was to try to login as Frank at a later date with an offline permission, which it had gotten from a previous print transaction, then you can see that it would break the norm.

These are two very simple examples. When we think of the security of a consumer using a provider then it's a combination of whatever security controls might be in place, plus these behavioural norms. The view from a consumer's perspective is that if there's a change in norms then that perhaps points to some kind of anomaly. This is neither intrusion detection nor extrusion detection from the consumers point of view. We are also considering is mimicry attacks whereby an attacker attempts to generate a behavior that fits within the known norms, yet at the same time does something malicious.

Dongting Yu: How do you propose to differentiate between evolving norms and broken norms?

Reply: At the moment we haven't considered that. We've focussed on how to data-mine norms from system logs. You could look at a log, and if there's a small change in norms over time then perhaps that's acceptable. However, you wouldn't be entirely sure since some of the norms could be critical, and other ones less so. That's future work.

Shishir Nagaraja: I can emulate good behaviour and then I can be malicious. How do you address that?

Reply: I think that's the ideal scenario. If the provider is a well-behaved provider and does everything exactly as one would expect then from that I can build up the set of norms that represent good behaviour. If the provider then begins to be malicious, as in the example of the photograph scenario where the provider changes the default settings, then that's something that I flag because it's different from the previous behaviour.

Partha Das Chowdhury: I presume you can also spot other users being malicious, so if you had a system where you could share pictures and your friends had never done it before, and suddenly they start sharing on your pictures then that might be something.

Reply: Yes, if it's in the logs. However, I don't think Facebook will tell me whether my photograph is being used by somebody else.

Bruce Christianson: So that's part of their privacy policy.

Reply: Yes.

Henry Tan: I'm still curious why you don't look at it from the other point of view where the provider is looking at his access logs since he has all of them, and making sure that all of his users are using it innocently.

Reply: Yes, that's a good point, we could also do that. We just focused on the consumer who is interacting with a provider, and is not entirely sure whether he can trust the interaction with that provider. Of course the flipside is a provider who wants to check whether his consumers are behaving properly.

Henry Tan: Yes, and then they don't have to provide logs or anything because they have the logs.

Reply: Yes, they have all the logs. Olgierd has been looking at discovering norms from very large logs of transactions from a large-scale enterprise systems. What he found is that one discovers the patterns of behaviour from the high-level application level calls, as expected. However, as you increase the granularity of the event log and consider the lower level/system calls, you start seeing new and interesting behaviours that suggest other patterns that were not a priori anticipated. One might ask, if there was a change in these low-level patterns then does that mean that there's something wrong with the system? We're looking into this.

Remark!: A Secure Protocol for Remote Exams

Rosario Giustolisi, Gabriele Lenzini, and Peter Y.A. Ryan(✉)

Interdisciplinary Centre for Reliability, Security and Trust (SnT),
University of Luxembourg, Luxembourg, Luxembourg
{rosario.giustolisi,gabriele.lenzini,peter.ryan}@uni.lu

Abstract. This manuscript presents *Remark!*, an electronic exam protocol which achieves several authentication, (conditional) anonymity, privacy, and verifiability properties without trusted third parties. *Remark!* is primarily designed for invigilated Internet-based exams but it also fits computer-based exams with candidates taking their exam in classrooms.

Keywords: Electronic exams · Security analysis · Security protocol design · Authentication · Anonymity · Privacy · Verifiability

1 Introduction

There is a growing demand for tools able to evaluate remotely the skills and knowledge of people. Remote assessment promises in fact to be cheaper than traditional examination, which usually requires a considerable organizational effort. In its resorting to information and communication technology, computer-based assessment is also able to reach easily a worldwide audience of candidates. However, the use of computers exposes remote examinations to new threats, while it may require to change seasoned procedures successfully used against known threats. Hence, there is an interest in understanding how to design secure remote electronic exams (in short *e-exams*). To date, there has been very little investigation into the design and analysis of e-exams. In this paper we fill this gap: we discuss a number of security properties appropriate to e-exams, and we present and comment a novel scheme designed to achieve them.

1.1 Anatomy of an Exam

Traditional exams consist at least of four phases: *registration*, *testing*, *marking*, and *notification*. During the registration phase, an exam is arranged, usually by a manager, and candidates enrol for it. During the testing phase, the candidates receive and take a test and submit their answers. During the marking phase, examiners assess the answers and assign a mark. Finally, during the notification phase, candidates learn their marks.

E-exams are organized similarly and with the same principals involved in traditional exams: candidates, one or more examiners, and a manager. The roles of

© Springer International Publishing Switzerland 2014
B. Christianson et al. (Eds.): Security Protocols 2014, LNCS 8809, pp. 38–48, 2014.
DOI: 10.1007/978-3-319-12400-1_5

candidate and examiner are straightforward. Essentially, the candidate is responsible to provide answers to the test question, while the examiner is in charge of evaluating the provided answers. The role of the manager includes all remaining tasks necessary to fulfil the examination. Such tasks include: to register eligible candidates and examiners for an examination, to assign the test question to the candidates, to distribute the answered test to examiners, to gather the marks and notify them to the corresponding candidates. According to the specific implementation, the manager's tasks can be increased or split among other principals, such as question committee, invigilator, collector, and notifier.

1.2 Related Work

To our knowledge only a few works propose exam protocols with security in mind. Bella *et al.* propose WATA IV [GRG14], the latest version of computer-assisted exam systems that are paper-based, hence without support for remote examination. Castella-Roca *et al.* [JJA06] propose a computer-based e-exam system with a fully trusted manager. Huszti & Petho [AA10] advance a remote e-exam scheme with fewer trust requirements on principals, but their scheme turns out to have several problem of security. We have identified a number of security flaws but, at time of writing, the work that analyses this protocol and discusses its security is under review [DGK+14].

Contribution and Outline. This paper first identifies threats and requirements for e-exams, in particular the ones that *Remark!* has been designed to counter (Sect. 2). Then, it proposes the details of *Remark!*, an e-exam protocol primarily designed for invigilated internet-based exams (Sect. 3). As we shall see, the protocol also suits computer-based testing where candidates take the exam at examination venue, such as a classroom or a test centre. According to the security analysis provided, *Remark!* achieves authentication, verifiability, and conditional anonymity with minimal reliance on trusted parties (Sect. 4). The paper concludes discussing some future work (Sect. 5).

2 Threats, Security Requirements, and Assumptions

2.1 Threats

E-exams are threatened by outsiders as well as by insiders: each role has in fact incentives to misbehave. In traditional exams, most common threats are due to candidates, who may try to cheat in different ways during the testing phase [che]. In remote exams, candidates may also attempt to exploit the security flaws of the underlying e-exam protocol to abuse any exam phase. For instance, a dishonest candidate may want to tamper with her and other's marks, or find the identity of the examiner who evaluates her test in order to bribe him.

On the other hand, even exam authorities may misbehave as exposed in recent exam scandals [L.13,R.14]. Both managers and examiners might be strongly motivated to tamper with candidates' marks, especially when they collude with some candidates. This can lead to embarrassing situations as recently occurred in the U.S. Navy nuclear exam cheating scandal [usn].

As we shall see, *Remark!* cannot withstand all possible threats. It is a cryptographic protocol and for this reason designed to withstand network security threats. Plagiarism can still happen: to avoid it there is need of appropriate invigilation. Principals can still collude and communicate via subliminal channels, as it happens when a candidate reveals her identity to the examiner by using steganography. Although it is hard to rule out completely such a threat, steganalysis techniques can be of some help here. Other counter-measures may be needed against collusion attacks that exploit covert channels.

In particular, *Remark!* is designed to resist the following threats:

1. An intruder impersonating a candidate during the testing.
2. An intruder tampering with a candidate's test answer or mark.
3. A candidate seeking to get an higher mark than she deserved (overmarked).
4. A candidate seeking to coerce the examiner who evaluates her test.
5. The manager tampering with the marks.
6. An examiner seeking to assign a biased mark to a specific candidate's test.

2.2 Security Requirements

We have identified several fundamental security requirements that a secure e-exam should fulfil. The list outlined above takes inspiration and extends the requirements described in our previous work [GRG13]:

p1: *Test Answer Authentication:* the manager only accepts test answers submitted by registered candidates. This means that a candidate, the test assigned to her, and their association should be authenticated and preserved, for instance against collusion among candidates.

p2: *Examiner Authentication:* the manager only accepts evaluations provided by a registered examiner. This rather obvious requirement means that the mark assigned to a test answer is authentic.

p3: *Anonymous Marking:* no one learns the author of a test answer before the test is marked. This requirement states that only the candidate who wrote the answers knows the association between her identity and the test. Notably, this should be resistant to collusion between examiner and manager.

p4: *Anonymous Examiner:* no candidate learns the identity of the examiner who evaluates their test answers. This requirement ensures that no candidate can coerce an examiner before and even after he evaluates her test answer.

p5: *Question Secrecy:* no candidate learns the test question before the testing phase begins. This ensures a desirable degree of fairness among candidates as no one knows the questions in advance, provided that no one is illegitimately allowed to know the answers beforehand.

p6: *Question Privacy:* the manager does not learn which test question is assigned to a specific candidate. This requirement ensures that the manager cannot identify a candidate by looking at the test question once it has been submitted for evaluation. In contexts where all students for a given exam receive the same questions this requirement becomes superfluous.

p7: *Mark Privacy:* the candidate learns only her mark and not those of other candidates. This rather natural requirement, not always applied, means that the mark of a test is known only by the author of test, and possibly by the manager, who may need it for registering the mark.

p8: *Test Verifiability:* the candidate can verify that her test is considered for evaluation. This requirement states that the candidate has a way to check whether her submitted test has been accepted by the manager.

p9: *Mark Verifiability:* the candidate can verify that the manager registers the mark she was assigned to by the examiner. This ensures that the candidate can notice when the mark assigned to her test differs from the one registered by the manager.

2.3   Assumptions

Our design and analysis rely on the following assumptions:

1. Each principal holds a long-term public/private pair of keys.
2. The candidate holds a smart card. This carries the candidate's identity visibly engraved and stores her private key securely (*i.e.*, it cannot be extracted).
3. Candidates are invigilated during the testing. Invigilation mitigates cheating, and it can be done remotely by using software such as ProctorU [Pro].
4. The model answers are kept secret from the candidates until after the exam has completed. The examiners may be provided with the model answers after testing has finished.
5. An authenticated append-only bulletin board is available. Everyone is guaranteed to see the same data, though write access might be restricted to appropriate entities (*e.g.*, see [JPV13]). An implementation of a bulletin board together with a detailed description of its security requirements is given in Culnane *et al.* [CS14].
6. Channels ensuring integrity and confidentiality, *e.g.*, SSL/TLS, are available.
7. At least one mixnet server (see next) is honest.

3   *Remark!*: Protocol Description

Remark! relies on several servers that implement an *exponentiation mixnet* [RO11]. The peculiarity of this kind of mixnet is that each mix server re-encrypts the terms by a common exponent value in contrast to a conventional re-encryption mixnet in which each term is independently re-encrypted. As usual, we assume that at least one server among the ones in a mixnet behaves honestly.

Thus, if the mixnet is made of m servers and r_i is the exponent value chosen by the ith server, then the mixnet given the input X, outputs $X^{\bar{r}_m}$, where $\bar{r}_m = \prod_{i=1}^{m} r_i$.

Remark! makes use of exponentiation mixnets at registration, to create the pseudonyms for the candidates and examiners. The mixnet servers may also required at notification to revoke the candidates pseudonyms and retrieve the candidates' identities by revealing $\bar{r}_m$. In particular, the generation of pseudonyms for candidates is separated from that for examiners because, at notification, only the identities of candidates should be revealed.

A bulletin board is used to publish the pseudonyms, the questions, the tests, and the marks. As we shall see, the bulletin board is also used by the mixnet's servers to publish their intermediate shuffling. In so doing anyone can check the authenticity of each mix step.

The following paragraphs detail how to use exponentiation mixnets to generate pseudonyms, and describe all the phases of *Remark!*. The protocol's steps are also illustrated in Appendix in form of a message sequence chart. In the reminder, $\langle X_i \rangle$ is a shorthand for the list $\langle X_1, \ldots X_n \rangle$, and $\bar{r}_k$ is a shorthand for $\prod_{i=1}^{k} r_i$ (so, $\bar{r}_1 = r_1$, and $\bar{r}_2 = r_1 r_2$, *etc.*) and $\bar{\pi}_k$ for $\pi_k \circ \cdots \circ \pi_1$, (so, $\bar{\pi}_1 = \pi_1$, and $\bar{\pi}_2 = \pi_2 \circ \pi_1$, *etc.*).

Registration. The registration uses an exponentiation mixnet to generate pseudonyms for the candidates and examiners, in two independent runs.

In particular, let us assume n eligible candidates with identities $C_1, \ldots, C_n$. Let g denote a generator of a multiplicative subgroup $\mathbb{G}$ of order q. Each C_i has a pair of public/private keys (PK_i, SK_i), each $PK_i = g^{SK_i}$. The identities of the candidates as well as their public keys are public.

The first mix server mix_1 takes $\langle PK_i \rangle$ —the list of the public keys of the candidates— generates a fresh random $r_1 \in \{1, q-1\}$, and computes $\langle PK_i^{r_1} \rangle$ —the list of the public keys to the r_1. Then mix_1 signs and sends this list in a secret shuffled order (*i.e.*, it posts $\langle PK_{\pi_1(i)}^{r_1} \rangle$, where π_1 is the permutation of indexes applied by mix_1) to the bulletin board. It also sends g^{r_1} to the next mix server over a secure channel. Further mix servers repeat these steps as required. Each mix server signs and publishes the shuffled list on the bulletin board, as shown in Fig. 1. The last mixserver, mix_m, publishes also $g^{\bar{r}_m}$. We assume that the bulletin board has appropriate write access control mechanisms, (*i.e.*, only authorities can publish data therein). If the access control can be relied on, the signatures might not be necessary.

While the intermediate steps should be posted to a bulletin board, we do not post intermediate $g^{\bar{r}_1}, \ldots, g^{\bar{r}_{m-1}}$ terms. This is to avoid each candidate tracking their intermediate pseudonyms through the mixnet: although such eventuality is not an attack, it is an undesired feature. The last mix server mix_m publishes the final $h_C := g^{\bar{r}_m}$, and the list of pseudonyms $\langle \overline{PK}_i \rangle = \langle PK_{\bar{\pi}_m(i)}^{\bar{r}_m} \rangle$. Note that zero-knowledge proofs could be used to demonstrate that the mix servers behave correctly. Once the shuffled pseudonyms and the corresponding signatures have been posted along with h_C, each candidate, say C_k, can recognize her pseudonym

		mix_1	mix_2		mix_m	
C_1	PK_1	$PK_{\overline{\pi}_1(1)}^{\overline{r}_1}$	$PK_{\overline{\pi}_2(1)}^{\overline{r}_2}$	$\cdots$	$PK_{\overline{\overline{\pi}}_m(1)}^{\overline{r}_m}$	$= \overline{PK}_1$
C_2	PK_1	$PK_{\overline{\pi}_1(2)}^{\overline{r}_1}$	$PK_{\overline{\pi}_2(2)}^{\overline{r}_2}$	$\cdots$	$PK_{\overline{\overline{\pi}}_m(2)}^{\overline{r}_m}$	$= \overline{PK}_2$
$\vdots$	$\vdots$	$\vdots$	$\vdots$		$\vdots$	
C_n	PK_n	$PK_{\overline{\pi}_1(n)}^{\overline{r}_1}$	$PK_{\overline{\pi}_2(n)}^{\overline{r}_2}$	$\cdots$	$PK_{\overline{\pi}_m(n)}^{\overline{r}}$	$= \overline{PK}_n$
	g	$g^{\overline{r}_1}$	$g^{\overline{r}_2}$	$\cdots$	$g^{\overline{r}_m}$	$= h_C$

Fig. 1. Using exponentiation mixnet to generate pseudonyms. All the terms within the box are published on the bulletin board.

among those in the shuffled list $\langle \overline{PK}_i \rangle$ by computing $h_C^{SK_k}$ and finding the match. The pseudonym from now on serves as the pseudo identity for C_k.

After the pseudonyms of candidates have been published, the mixnet generates the pseudonyms for examiners in a similar way. Since a different random value is used by the mix servers to generate the examiner pseudonyms, a different h_E is published at the end of the mix.

Testing. Before starting the testing phase, the manager generates the test questions, signs them with its private key SK_M, and encrypts each test question under a candidate pseudonym. We do not specify how the manager generates the test questions in order to include different forms of assessment (e.g., multiple choice, open-ended, etc.) and assignments (e.g., single question, different questions for candidate, random question permutations, etc.). In general, we observe that a test question denotes a list of questions.

As soon as the testing starts, the manager authenticates the candidate via remote invigilation software. In particular, the manager checks whether the candidate details printed on the top of the smart card matches the candidate identity. When all candidates have been authenticated, the manager publishes the encrypted test questions in the bulletin board. Once all the candidates have received their test questions, they are allowed to work on their test answers.

When the candidate concludes to answer the test, she can submit the test as follows: the candidate appends her pseudonym and the test answer to the test question, so the filled test is $T_C = \langle ques, ans, \overline{PK} \rangle$. Then, she signs T_C with her private key SK_C using the generator h_C instead of g. Thus, the signature can be verified using the candidate's pseudonym $\overline{PK}_C$ with respect to h_C. The candidate then encrypts the signed test with the public key of the manager PK_M, and submits it to the manager. The manager collects and decrypts the test, and then signs a hash of T_C using his private key SK_M. The manager then encrypts the signed hash(T_C) under the corresponding candidate's pseudonym, and publishes the encryption as receipt.

Marking. The manager encrypts the signed test under an eligible examiner pseudonym $\overline{PK}_E$ previously published on the bulletin board by the mixnet.

The designated examiner marks the test. The mark is appended to the signed test, thus generating the evaluation $M_C = \langle Sig\{T_C\}_{SK_M}, mark \rangle$. The examiner then signs M_C with his private key SK_E and the generator h_E. Finally, the examiner encrypts M_C with PK_M and submits his evaluation to the manager.

Note that it is possible to introduce a universally verifiable deterministic assignment of answers to examiners. Thus, for example, the encrypted answers and the examiners pseudonyms could be posted in two lexically ordered lists and the assignment performed cyclically. Such an assignment algorithm should remove any suspicion that the authority might try to perform the assignment in some unfavourable way to the candidates.

Notification. The manager receives the encrypted evaluation from the examiner, which are decrypted and re-encrypted under the corresponding candidate pseudonym $\overline{PK}_C$. The manager publishes all the test evaluations together. Then, the manager asks the mixnet to reveal the random values r used to generate the candidates pseudonyms. In so doing, the candidate anonymity is revoked, and the mark can finally be registered. Note that each candidate (and only him) can see his mark before $\overline{r}_m$ is revealed.

Notification (alternative). Some universities allow candidates decide whether to know the mark or to withdraw their test entirely without knowing he mark. In this case, the mark is forgotten and it is not notified nor registered. This particular way to run a final exam is adopted, for instance, by those universities where candidates are conceded with a limited amount of failures during the exam season, mainly to discourage them from taking the exam without adequate preparation. Other universities, again to discourage candidates to sit at the exam just 'to try it out to get marked', have a rule saying that if a candidate chooses to know her mark and this turns out to be a fail, then she has to skip the next exam session. By giving a candidate the possibility to withdraw a test without knowing the mark, those universities soften the severity of such rules. A candidate can spare wasting one of her attempt token when she realizes, on her own, to have performed insufficiently.

Remark! can include such requirement via an alternative notification phase. In this case, the manager publishes a public commit of the mark instead of the mark. Then, if a candidate wants to know her mark, she proves the knowledge of her private key. If so, the manager reveals the commitment parameter to the candidate, and the candidate can check the commitment. Notably, the notification does not involve the mixnet.

4   Security Analysis

We discuss informally the security of *Remark!* and give arguments supporting the claim that it achieves our security requirements. We organize our argumentation in four sections. The first section discusses authenticity properties, the second anonymity properties, the third privacy properties, and the last verifiability properties.

4.1 Authentication

Test Answer Authentication (p1) is achieved because the manager accepts only the test whose signature can be verified with a pseudonym published by the mixnet. No one but the candidate who holds the corresponding private key can generate a correct signature. Colluding candidates who switch their smart cards are detected by invigilation.

Examiner Authentication (p2) holds because the manager encrypts the test with the examiner's pseudonym. Only the examiner who holds the corresponding private key obtains the test. The manager accepts the evaluation only if it can check the signature using the corresponding examiner's pseudonym.

4.2 Anonymity

The pseudonym guarantees the anonymity of the test submitted by the candidate. The mix servers cannot associate a pseudonym to a candidate's identity, unless all of them collude. Even if a malicious examiner colludes with the manager, Anonymous Marking (p3) holds unless all the mix servers reveal their secret exponents.

Remark! ensures Anonymous Examiner (p4) because the manager encrypts the test with the examiner's pseudonym. The examiner can fairly evaluate the anonymous test answers without fear of being coerced by any candidate, because the pseudonyms of the examiners are not revoked by the mixnet. Even in case of collusion between a candidate and an examiner, if the examination board consists of different examiners, the candidate has no guarantee that the colluding examiner will be assigned to evaluate her test answers.

4.3 Privacy

Question Secrecy (p5) is achieved because the manager publishes the test question once the candidate is under invigilation. The manager cannot learn which test question is assigned to a specific candidate because the test question are encrypted with the anonymous candidate's pseudonym. Thus, *Remark!* ensures Question Privacy (p6).

The protocol also ensures Mark Privacy (p7) because the mark is encrypted with the candidate's pseudonym and then published on the bulletin board. Thus, each candidate only learns her corresponding mark. Only the manager learns the mark after the mixnet reveals the secret exponents.

4.4 Verifiability

Each mix server publishes its generated list of signed pseudonyms (the intermediated and the last), and a zero-knowledge proof of correctness (*e.g.*, all pseudonyms are generated by using the same exponential value). This allows any observer to verify the authenticity and the correctness of the pseudonyms. Once the final pseudonyms are published on the bulletin board, each eligible candidate and examiner can only find their corresponding pseudonym.

Test Verifiability (p8) is guaranteed because the manager publishes the receipt after it receives a valid signature (i.e. the manager can verify a signature using a pseudonym as verification key). Thus the candidate can verify that her test is considered for evaluation. Moreover, she can also prove that her test has been accepted because the manager signs the receipt.

Remark! ensures Mark Verifiability (p9). In fact, the marks are published before the mixnet reveals their secret exponents. Thus, the candidate can verify that the manager registers the correct mark once the mixnet revokes her anonymity. Note that both the manager and the examiner sign the test to which the mark is assigned. Since the mark is signed by the examiner, if the manager registers an incorrect mark, the candidate can prove to an authority the correct mark the examiner assigned to her test.

Note that the manager may post the candidate pseudonyms alongside the marks, which allows everyone to verify the set of posted marks is correctly derived. In this way each candidate can still identify her own mark, while everyone can check, still anonymously, that the marks are distributed among all the candidates. However, such a modification is incompatible with assuring strong mark privacy (p7).

5   Conclusion

This paper proposes *Remark!*, an e-exam protocol that achieves heterogeneous security properties (authentication, privacy, anonymity, and verifiability) in a realistic threat model with minimal trust assumptions. Notably, it requires no trusted parties but that only one mix server behave honestly. *Remark!* can resist collusion of candidates, examiner and manager, or examiner and candidate. Although the paper presents an informal analysis of the protocol, a preliminary formal analysis of *Remark!* in the symbolic model confirms that it ensures all the nine security requirements. As future work, we plan to build a prototype of *Remark!*, and to engineer it as an extension of Moodle. Other future work includes extending our protocol with techniques to detect plagiarism and candidate cheating during the testing phase. We envisage that misbehaviour detection strategies such as data mining used to derive patterns described by Pieczul *et al.* in [OS14] can be useful for our purposes. Another interesting research direction includes the support for collaborative marking, in which the questions are categorised by subject, and examiners evaluate the test answers pertaining to their subject area. Finally, we observe the need of an efficient way to resolve disputes perhaps following the principles outlined in [SR14].

Acknowledgement. We thank Jannik Dreier, Ali Kassem and Pascal Lafourcade for helpful discussions on the security of our protocol.

A   *Remark!*: Message Sequence Chart

Notation. A test question is denoted by *quest*, and a test answer by *ans*. SK_X and PK_X denotes the ElGamal private and public keys of the principal X. We assume a common public generator g for the keys of all principals. $\overline{PK}_X$ denotes the pseudonym of the principal X, and r_{X_i} is the secret value used by the mix server i when processing the batch of the role X. The terms *Enc* and *Sig* denote respectively the encryption and signature functions of a message. In particular, the notation $Sig\{msg\}_{\overline{SK}_X, h_X}$ denotes the message *msg* and its signature using the private key SK_X and the parameter h_X rather than g.

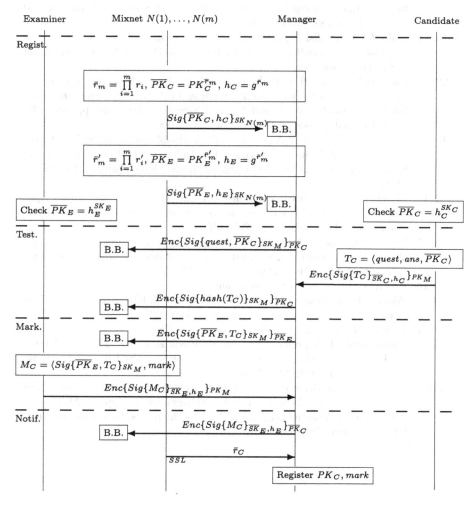

References

[AA10] Huszti, A., Pethõ, A.: A secure electronic exam system. Publicationes Mathematicae Debrecen **77**, 299–312 (2010)

[che]   How to Cheat on Test Using School Supplies. http://www.wikihow.com/Cheat-on-a-Test-Using-School-Supplies

[CS14] Culnane, C., Schneider, S.: A peered bulletin board for robust use in verifiable voting systems. CoRR, abs/1401.4151 (2014)

[DGK+14] Dreier, J., Giustolisi, R., Kassem, A., Lafourcade, P., Lenzini, G., Ryan, P.Y.A.: Formal analysis of electronic exams (work under review) (2014)

[GRG13] Bella, G., Giustolisi, R., Lenzini, G.: What security for electronic exams? In: 2013 International Conference on Risks and Security of Internet and Systems (CRiSIS), pp. 1–5 (2013)

[GRG14] Bella, G., Giustolisi R., Lenzini, G.: Secure exams despite malicious management. In: Proceedings of 12th Conference on Privacy, Security and Trust (PST) (to appear, 2014)

[JJA06] Castella-Roca, J., Herrera-Joancomarti, J., Dorca-Josa, A.: A secure e-exam management system. In: Proceedings of the First International Conference on Availability, Reliability and Security, ARES '06, pp. 864–871. IEEE Computer Society, Washington, DC (2006)

[JPV13] Benaloh, J., Ryan, P.Y.A., Teague, V.: Verifiable postal voting. In: Christianson, B., Malcolm, J., Stajano, F., Anderson, J., Bonneau, J. (eds.) Security Protocols 2013. LNCS, vol. 8263, pp. 54–65. Springer, Heidelberg (2013)

[L.13] Copeland, L.: School cheating scandal shakes up atlanta, April 2013.   http://www.usatoday.com/story/news/nation/2013/04/13/atlanta-school-cheatring-race/2079327/

[OS14] Pieczul, O., Foley, S.N.: Collaborating as normal: detecting systemic anomalies in your partner. In: Proceedings of 22nd International Security Protocols Workshop, Cambridge (to appear, 2014)

[Pro]   ProctorU. http://www.proctoru.com/

[R.14] Watson, R.: Student visa system fraud exposed in BBC investigation, February 2014. http://www.bbc.com/news/uk-26024375

[RO11] Haenni, R., Spycher, O.: Secure internet voting on limited devices with anonymized DSA public keys. In: Proceedings of the 2011 Conference on Electronic Voting Technology/Workshop on Trustworthy Elections, EVT/WOTE'11. USENIX Association (2011)

[SR14] Murdoch, S., Anderson, R.: Security protocols and evidence: where many payment systems fail. In: Financial Cryptography (to appear, 2014)

[usn]   U.S. Navy discloses nuclear exam cheating. http://edition.cnn.com/2014/02/04/us/navy-cheating-investigation/

Remark!: A Secure Protocol for Remote Exams (Transcript of Discussion)

Rosario Giustolisi[(✉)]

University of Luxembourg, Luxembourg, Luxembourg
rosario.giustolisi@uni.lu

[Omitted explanation of the paper.]

We categorize the security requirements for e-exam in authentication, anonymity and privacy requirements. For instance, we want that only the test answers submitted by registered candidates to be accepted. Similarly, we want that only registered examiners can evaluate the answers submitted by candidates. As an example of an anonymity property, we define anonymous marking, which means that no one can learn the link between a candidate and the answer she submitted. For instance, it is interesting to find out how to guarantee anonymity and authentication properties.

Frank Stajano: It seems to me this set of constraints will severely limit the type of exams you can deliver, because if you have some kind of free-form essay it would be easy to agree on some steganographic hint that, you know, if I am colluding with the examiner then I would say, it's me, if I say the following things.

Reply: Yes, that's true. I think that in remote exams you can communicate to an examiner in the way you said.[1]

Frank Stajano: Right, if I'm going to give you £300,000 if you give me this mark, and then I can always agree, and I send the signal that it was me, if I had a free form. So where does this apply, is this just multiple choice exams?

Reply: The exam setting aims to be as general as possible. You can do a stenographic attack, but it will work if the examiner who marks your test is the one colluding with you. In our protocol, the candidate doesn't know who is going to mark her test. So, the attack can work although the candidate is not 100 % surely it will work.

Alastair Beresford: Presumably if you want the same feature as an old traditional exam, and that you could have collusion, but you want to offer the student the opportunity that they can be anonymous if they want to be. So I could write my own exam, which is made in handwriting, my name is Alastair, please give me 100 % if I wanted to, if I had colluded with Frank for a good mark.

---

[1] In the post-proceeding version of the paper we clarified that some steganalysis techniques may help here although threats via subliminal channels are hard to rule out.

© Springer International Publishing Switzerland 2014
B. Christianson et al. (Eds.): Security Protocols 2014, LNCS 8809, pp. 49–54, 2014.
DOI: 10.1007/978-3-319-12400-1_6

Frank Stajano: Yes, you can do it more subtly, so that an auditor won't see that you did.

Alastair Beresford: Sure, and you can do that on physical paper at the moment. So one of the properties I presume you're trying to preserve is the add of a candidate number where the student if they want to be an anonymous candidate.

Frank Stajano: Yes, but what I'm saying is some of these properties are stronger than what we have in a normal exam. So, no one learns the author of a test answer before the mark has been committed. In the current exams thing that we run every year, this can be easily violated. Now, if you are serious about maintaining this then you are really constraining very narrowly the type of exams you can deliver with this.

Joseph Bonneau: It also seems like if it's that constraining then you don't need examiners at all, right, I think there are algorithms could work.

Reply: Yes, if there's an automatic algorithm. Actually, even if it is with open-ended questions I know there is also some algorithm[2], but it depends on the kind of the questions.

Dieter Gollmann: Anonymous examiners, in our examination systems you have the right to come back to me and ask me, why did you mark this question like that? So they have to know who the examiner is. And, if it was somebody else in the university, they would say: it wasn't me so I don't know who marked this.

Peter Ryan: Well, you can then revoke their anonymity.

Reply: Yes, that is also for an anti-revenge aspect.

Dieter Gollmann: In a typical examination situation, students would take a course in software security, and would then know who taught that course in software security, and would know who will have set the examinations on software security, and would know who examined the course for software security. So why try to hide something that is basically obvious?

Reply: It depends. If you think, for instance, a conference, you have anonymous reviewers.

Saar Drimer: But the scenario that you described at the beginning, right, there were brand names of remote exams online based, it doesn't apply to exams in Cambridge, I think, that's my understanding.

James Malcolm: The evaluation can be delegated to some PhD student.

Dieter Gollmann: Well that is different. What in fact is the security requirement?

---

[2] Two approaches for automatically grading open-ended questions have been proposed in http://aow2012.yolasite.com/resources/aow20120_submission_10.pdf and http://linc.mit.edu/linc2013/proceedings/Session3/Session3Mit-Par.pdf.

Peter Ryan: It may be one way of thinking that is a defence, who's worried about attacking whom, and what things a candidate may be worried about for example, the examiner affecting the results, and this mechanism does at least help that.

Reply: Considering anonymous marking, we want a way to revoke the candidate anonymity because we want to register the mark to someone. We don't want to revoke the anonymity of the examiner to avoid some future possible revenge. If you think about academic conferences you don't know who reviewed your paper.

So, this different anonymity requirements clashes with authentication requirements. There are also secrecy requirements, like question secrecy, to guarantee fairness among the candidates, such as the questions are not revealed before the testing phase. Verifiability properties are also interesting, because the candidate may not need to know who actually marked her test, but know if she got the correct mark for her answer. So, the candidate wants to verify that the examiner will be marking her submitted test, and she also wants to check if she got the mark she deserved.

[Omitted explanation of protocol description.]

Frank Stajano: Is there a different question for every candidate?

Reply: It depends on the exam. If all candidates receive the same question, we lose question privacy, but if they have different questions, or different order of questions, the manager doesn't know to whom each question is given because it's encrypted with the candidate pseudonym.

[Omitted explanation of paper conclusions.]

Yvo Desmedt: Have you taken into account that there are already many, many software systems that actually do these online exams, so for example, at UCL they were using Moodle, which is a system that allows you to basically do these online exams. So when assigning project for students in the classroom of computer security too, I actually did sniff around and found out that this whole communication was basically done in the open, so http was used, not https. So, then two students actually showed to the administration that using an Ipod they could actually change their grade, and only then did the University actually decide to use https instead of http. So there's interest to propose new systems, but what about the security, and the deployment of systems that are already in use.

Reply: So, would you like to use Moodle to run a public competition, or give a job to someone because he passes an exam in Moodle? Or for instance at entrance University exam, in which there is high competition, and you want to allow people from different places to compete...

Yvo Desmedt: I understood the problem, the question is, by proposing something new, there is already a lot of things that have been used, and they may not be good. It's just common.

Peter Ryan: It would be interesting to look at it, yes, we weren't aware of it, so thanks for the tip, and we'll take a look at it. If there are any other systems that people know of we'd be interested to hear about it. I mean this is not something you could easily stumbled on by Google or whatever.

Yvo Desmedt: No, you look at many universities and see what they actually use. So what seems to me, every different university uses some unique systems, but this is not true, because otherwise there would be as many as there are universities, which is false. But it seems there are many around of these systems. And I don't think many people are looking at how good they are.

Simon Foley: Moodle would be worth looking at. It's entirely Open Source, and it uses a plug-in software architecture for extensions so it might be possible to even implement these algorithms.

Yvo Desmedt: But the thing there was, at UCL, the university decided not to switch the https, they just used open, completely open, so that was an option in Moodle.

Simon Foley: Could these also be seen as examples of potential security vulnerabilities within in Moodle itself? Problems like cross site scripting, and a bunch of other implementation vulnerabilities. While the problem that you're looking at may be different, those types of problems are equally relevant when it comes to implementation.

Peter Ryan: And the other point, so I want to just carry on, what we're trying to stress here is a kind of analogy to what people have to tried to do in e-voting systems trying to minimise the trust, which you have to do, and I think most of these systems would have significant trust in what is the managing system, and we're trying to come up with something which tries to minimise that.

Vashek Matyas: The Blackboard company is developing lot of systems for North American colleges, so you just might, I don't really know whether they denote something like this, but I know that they do have a big coverage of systems there all related, and it's a big company for the area.

Saar Drimer: It seems to me that the main issue here is almost the exam administrators that in academic institutions are interested in this threats that's cheating and what you call plagiarism. Two examples I've seen in the news recently in exams such as TOEFL, and the one equivalent here in the UK. People who were taking the exam would come in, door closes, and then answers being read out. Another example, the people who were taking the exams come in, then the people who were going to take the exam, instead of them coming in and sitting next to them, take the exam, and then go away, that's, they're sitting next to each other for about three hours just reading the books. But that, I can see bits of this system dealing with some of the issues, and make it a bit harder, like randomisation of the questions and answers, and so on, but it doesn't seem to me like it's solving the real issue. Now, the other thing is that there are two different scenarios. There's the university exam taking scenario where there is some form of weak authentication when you go away and they recognise your face. In Cambridge I know that that's kind of system is a weak authentication mechanism.

Joseph Bonneau: But some schools, they are the same in US now.

Saar Drimer: Yes, that's a problem, and then there is the remote, pretty much anonymous, exam taking for getting into university, or getting into a language school, and so on, that here is trumped up in the news quite a bit. So I wonder what bits of this work alleviate some of these concerns.

Reply: Plagiarism, I think, is hard to combat cryptographically in the sense of designing a cryptographic protocol that counters plagiarism problem.

Saar Drimer: Yes, I understand, it's a hard problem.

Reply: So there are some tools like ProctorU and Remote Proctor Now that are designed for invigilation purposes. The UK scandal happened because the invigilator was colluding with all the candidates there, and he read the correct answers aloud.

Joseph Bonneau: So, to extend on Saar's point a little bit, I guess what are the target applications here where people care enough about privacy and having strong security properties is they would do this complex crypto protocol, but they don't have such security concerns that they require candidates to take tests in a secure facility without knowing quite where, etc. I mean, in the US at least it's pretty police state now for the important exams, for admissions, and for like things like I took an IT exam in the fall, and they did like metal detectors to see if I had any devices on me, and then sat down and hardware control, etc. There is like a professional company in the US that does this for multiple different professional exams and things. So there's kind of like that level for tests that people really have jobs riding on. And then it seems like for the Coursera right now that sort of people are mostly taking the courses just for fun really.

Reply: Yes, I think that MOOC plan is to give certification, and you can expect to get credit from the university. So, I think, if we don't propose secure exams with some secure properties, probably they won't use remote exam system to improve their examination system.

Simon Foley: To follow up on that, it might be an interesting to use ceremonies to help model both the physical infrastructure and the system itself.

Peter Ryan: Yes, absolutely. I mean, at the moment these issues are certainly important, but they're just brushed into the assumptions, but I think we will come back to them, and yes, ceremonies why not, maybe the right way to do that.

Joseph Bonneau: Another question. How would this effect the marking process, because, I mean, for smaller scale exams usually it's pretty iterative, where people sit down in a room and they compare answers, and they're sort of developing the criteria while they're looking at the answers, at least in my experience, grading university finals and things like that. I mean, would that violate the examiner anonymity properties here?

Reply: It depends. This is a general approach so if we consider a deterministic marking algorithm, so that the examiner is just a computer process which actually runs the algorithm, we don't have to bother about the examiner identity, because it's a marking algorithm. It is different when the examiner is a human, for instance with open-ended questions.

Joseph Bonneau: There's a couple of models, like in Cambridge, the one lecturer has to grade everything, right, with no help, right Frank?

Frank Stajano: Yes, well more or less, there may be exceptions, but that's the general model, yes.

Joseph Bonneau: Whereas like in, at least in the US usually like the professor doesn't do the grading, and they make like four TAs sit down in a room and churn through it all, but usually it's pretty collaborative grading as opposed to like one individual person grading each thing.

Daniel Thomas: Well the same thing happens in A-level and GCSE exams in school. The mark scheme that's produced isn't necessarily the mark scheme that's actually used. The examiners read some scripts, look at some answers, then they sit down together and then work out what the actual mark scheme to use is, and then they write that down handwritten on top of the actual mark scheme, and then use that. So again, there the examiners all sit down in a room together and chat before they decide how to mark the questions.

Reply: OK, that's not remote.

Daniel Thomas: That's not remote.

Reply: OK if you focus to this kind of applications, that is, educational. Probably, this is not for public competitions, or job hiring, in which you have not this kind of collaboration. The roles are different, so a candidate cannot participate on mark assignment. Did I understand you correctly?

Daniel Thomas: The examiners sit down together, not the candidates.

Reply: OK. In our protocol we have a pseudonym that belongs to each examiner. So, it would be interesting to see how to face that.

Red Queen's Race: APT Win-Win Game

Vit Bukac[1]([✉]), Vaclav Lorenc[2], and Vashek Matyáš[3]

[1] Faculty of Informatics, Masaryk University, Brno, Czech Republic
bukac@mail.muni.cz
[2] Institute of Computer Science, Masaryk University, Brno, Czech Republic
valor@mail.muni.cz
[3] Faculty of Informatics, Masaryk University, Brno, Czech Republic
matyas@fi.muni.cz

Abstract. Advanced persistent threats (APTs) are not only a very prominent buzzword, but often come with a costly impact. A popular approach how to deal with APTs is the kill chain concept. We propose an extension to the kill chain, where the attacker is allowed to continue his attack even after being discovered by defenders. Meanwhile, observing defenders collect valuable intelligence which is to be used to counter future attacks. Benefits and negatives of postponed remediation are presented and related issues are discussed.

Keywords: Advanced persistant threats · APT · Kill chain · Honeypot

1 Background

In the entire human history, economic or military contestants have used subtle techniques to achieve information dominance. They have used anything from bribery to gun threats to modification of satellite communications. Widespread and dependence on computer networks then provided abundant new attack vectors. Advanced persistent threat (APT) is a term coined for an advanced long term stealthy intrusion into a computer system, with the aim to steal an intellectual property of the owner [Man10]. APTs are quickly becoming a nightmare for security officers. APT groups are usually well-funded and possess extensive knowledge. They employ effective intrusion methods such as zero-day attacks or stealth techniques and often have vast infrastructure of compromised servers for support. Their attacks come in campaigns and are often aimed at only a single target globally, being tailored specifically to target with reliance on prior reconnaissance. Traditional security measures such as antivirus software, signature based IDSs and systems hardening are largely inefficient against APTs.

To combat the rapidly growing threat of APTs, security experts from Lockheed Martin recommended adopting the concept of *kill chain* [HCJA11]. The idea behind the kill chain is to create a knowledge base of indicators from all observed phases of an APT in order to continuously improve defenses. The struggle between APT actors and defenders leads to a game where APT actors are

© Springer International Publishing Switzerland 2014
B. Christianson et al. (Eds.): Security Protocols 2014, LNCS 8809, pp. 55–61, 2014.
DOI: 10.1007/978-3-319-12400-1_7

adapting their techniques to penetrate encountered defense measures and defenders are developing new signatures and indicators to have the upper hand in campaigns in the future. The kill chain concept is quickly becoming the weapon of choice against APTs, being fostered by renown companies such as RSA [RSA12], Dell SecureWorks [Sec13], Hewlett-Packard [HP13] or NSS Labs [FA12]. Relevant academic research focuses primarily on efficient data aggregation and analysis [BY13, ILCP13].

Cyber kill chain concept is not limited to APTs. Harris, Konikoff and Petersen investigated the application of kill chain on distributed denial of service (DDoS) attacks. While performing DDoS attacks can always be considered an intended Action on Objective, authors also look for DDoS-related events at other phases [HKP13].

2   Kill Chain

APTs can be split into several consecutive phases (Fig. 1). Failure to overcome the defense measures at any phase results in the interruption of entire process. Oppositely, intrusion detection during a certain phase implies that all previous phases executed successfully. Phases are as follows [HCJA11]:

1. Reconnaissance. The attacker learns about the target organization and its members from mailing lists search, social networks crawling and web page crawling.
2. Weaponization. Remote access Trojan is coupled with an exploit to create a deliverable payload. Payload is tested and modified as long as it can be detected by security systems that are known to be used by the organization.
3. Delivery. Payload is delivered to the target, usually in the form of an email, a clickable link or on an USB media.
4. Exploitation. Payload is applied to a vulnerable system, executing malicious code.
5. Installation. Tools of attacker's choice are deployed in the system. Persistence is achieved.
6. Command and Control (C2). Infected host informs the APT actor that the compromise was successful. APT actor may begin pursuing his goals.
7. Actions on Objectives. APT actor moves laterally in the environment, using legitimate methods after he gained access to user accounts. He exports intellectual property from the organization in obfuscated or encrypted containers. He cleans most observable traces from the systems that he no longer needs.

A piece of information that objectively describes an intrusion is called an indicator. APT actor's actions during each phase of the kill chain leave a trail of indicators that can be later examined and used to adjust appropriate countermeasures. Indicators are subsequently used to build an attacker model tailored to each separate APT actor. In turn, the attacker model enables allocation of resources towards most relevant security measures.

Fig. 1. Kill chain [HCJA11].

Indicator usage example: System is infected by a malware that was encapsulated in a PDF attachment of a spear phishing email. The infection was discovered during a failed attempt to export data to an IP address which is known to belong to APT group. After a forensic analysis of the system, numerous improvements are implemented. A list of all users who received and opened this mail is created and basic security training is scheduled for them. Company antivirus vendor is supplied with binaries of the malware that was installed, along with the description of persistence method and list of file paths where temporary files were stored. Unpatched vulnerability in the PDF viewer is revealed and fixed. A phishing mail subject is added to the watch list in order to track other intrusion attempts of the same campaign. IP addresses of secondary C2 servers that were used to successfully export data to APT actors are blocked.

3 Proposed Approach

When an intrusion is detected, both standard intrusion response procedures and kill chain methodic dictate to isolate the affected systems, collect sources of forensics evidence (e.g., HDD images, log files) for later examination and then perform remediation procedures. To our knowledge, no serious thought has been given to the possibility of studying APT actor behavior on a real compromised system.

We propose *to postpone the remediation and focus on collecting as much indicators* on the already compromised system as possible, in order to maximize the knowledge gain from the APT actor. By allowing the attacker to continue his activity under a close passive surveillance or even during an active tampering with his activity, defenders will reveal more from attacker's knowledge and arsenal, leading to an increasingly descriptive set of indicators. We argue that following a win-win scenario in the short term will result in a win-fail scenario for the defender in the mid/long term.

We want to open a discussion whether and under what conditions it is beneficial for system's owner to postpone system remediation and instead focus on monitoring, effectively changing the compromised system to a live honeypot.

APTs are usually detected and identified during the callback phase or the lateral movement phase. After a careful consideration of the triplet (gain; potential associated risks; costs), decision is to be made whether to stop the attack immediately or let it continue under the increased surveillance. Risks taken into account should be: law and policies, intrusion context, data present on the compromised host, costs of prolonged surveillance and the impact of necessary changes. Regardless of the final decision, sources of forensic evidence for later analysis are always collected. Forensic analysis is performed in parallel to the live system monitoring. Interim monitoring results facilitate the forensic analysis and vice versa.

We propose two stages to the live honeypot – the passive monitoring and the active tampering. During the passive monitoring, defenders focus on learning as much information as possible about the attack without interfering with APT actor's activity. APT actor is misled to believe that his presence in the system has not yet been discovered. We recommend ending this phase after a fixed time deadline or after the attack revealed what type of data (e.g., financial, product documentation, legal documents) was the actual target. Passive monitoring includes but is not limited to:

- Network activity logging both on host and in network (Wireshark, router stats, NIDS logs, proxy logs).
- ACL/filesystem logging (accessed folders, folder listings, created and deleted files).
- Impossible deletion. Any file that is required to be deleted is hidden from the operating system instead.
- Memory dumps of entire host or of selected processes.
- Activation of a collection of low-interaction honeypots to respond to basic network activity.
- System log streaming to a central storage in order to prevent undetectable log file modifications.

During the active tampering defenders create artificial challenges for the attacker to overcome. The goal of defenders is to force the attacker to reveal more from his arsenal (e.g., so far unknown RAT tool, knowledge about internal systems, procedures followed under extreme conditions). Active tampering includes but is not limited to:

- File deletion (e.g., of attacker's temporary files or process binaries). Simulation of activity of external antivirus software. Attacker is forced to use another tool.
- System quarantine, policy hardening. Applying standard tools and policies to block the host from network. Switching the host into a high security mode. Attacker is forced to reveal if he has means to circumvent the limitation.
- Reboot. Attacker is lead to use tools and procedures that are non-volatile. Some attacker actions may not be observable before reboot.
- Network disruption (e.g., rate limiting, gradual IP blocking, TCP maximum segment size limitation). Attacker has to use backup protocols and reveal another part of his control infrastructure.
- Planting baits (e.g., non-essential data, user accounts with various password strengths, encrypted storage with seemingly high value content).

Postponing remediation and close monitoring is a costly action. In order to maintain a reasonable cost/gain ratio, postponed remediation is justifiable only during provably targeted attacks. APTs may be identified from targeted phishing, characteristic behavior (legitimate account misuse, etc.), preliminary analysis that found similarities with previous APT campaigns or from external trusted source (e.g., law enforcement agencies).

4 Properties of Postponed Remediation

4.1 Benefits

B1 – More attack traces acquired. Identification of used tools, procedures followed, methodics, order of steps, employed stealth techniques, employed cryptography/obfuscation, etc.

- Post-cleanup. If the attacker reaches a cleanup phase, comparison of the system state prior to cleanup and post cleanup may reveal unremoved artifacts, which may be later used to detect other systems compromised in the past. To recognize post-cleanup artifact without prior leads is considered extremely difficult.
- High-level time overview of attacker activity. Time characteristics of different phases of attack, temporal order, frequency of attacker interaction in time, duration of campaigns, duration of each phase of the intrusion, etc.

B2 – Discovery of attacker's goals. What data the attacker is after, whether he wants to maintain presence or leave the system in order to minimize traces, what knowledge the attacker possesses from previous campaigns and he plans to use it, etc. Point B2 is a natural outcome of B1.

B3 – Active tampering. Boosts the efficiency of previous benefits, can produce indicators that are not obtainable by any other means. May provide an insight into the scope of intrusion.

4.2 Negatives

N1 – Policies & Law. Institutional regulations or law may require immediate remediation of an affected system. Privacy issues are raised for users who are working with the compromised host. Proceeding with a postponed remediation on systems with customer's or supplier's data requires agreement of all involved parties.

N2 – Attack spread. Attacker may successfully compromise more systems if he is not contained immediately, especially if he was detected soon after the installation phase.

N3 – Increased costs. Costs of security specialist's time (constant observation and necessity to prepare emergency procedures), system user's time and engagement of additional resources are higher than in the case of immediate remediation. No guarantees that there will be more information collected than just through standard forensics methods.

- Destruction. A cleanup stage of intrusion may be designed not to remove just traces of attacker behavior, but the system in its entirety.

5   Open Questions

Q1 – Do filesystems with reversible changes exist? Are they widely used for security and/or data preservence purposes? Filesystems or drivers that can prevent file deletion are known, but their presence can often by detected by an attacker. Regular backup solutions are too cumbersome for malware tracking purposes. Are virtual machines and snapshots a possible solution?

Q2 – How can virtualization make this method easier? Virtual machine introspection techniques enable monitoring of guest system calls, snapshots allow to compare between pre-cleanup and post-cleanup state and virtual switches can easily separate the closely examined network traffic from the rest of network. What other recent virtualization advancements could impact the live honeypot in the near future?

Q3 – When to stop the intrusion? What is the list of conditions and costs that must be always considered for the decision (e.g., personal information in jeopardy, observed attack spreading, criticality of accessed information, monitoring-related costs)? Can the decision be quantified, e.g., with checklists and conditions weights? What roles in organization will likely have to have a word in the decision?

Q4 – Will this method be still effective if the attacker learns about it? The attacker can react by planting dummy traces and baits. Can his behavior in such situation be also considered as attacker profiling? Is it possible to distinguish between true attacker behavior and simulated attacker behavior with anomaly techniques and a preliminary knowledge?

Q5 – Can this method be justified from the legal perspective? Is there a difference between US and EU? Does different rules apply for company data and for personal data of users who are using the computer during their work? What are differences between company internal policies and the law? How the shortest possible time to mitigate the threat clause should be interpreted?

6   Summary

Kill chain is a promising concept to combat Advanced Persistent Threats. As for this concept, the key to a successful defense against APTs is to gain knowledge about APT actors' techniques, tools and procedures. We propose an extension to the kill chain concept which calls for prolonged monitoring of attacker activities. Allowing the attacker to continue with his activities even after he is detected can result in a significant gain – more threat intelligence.

Acknowledgment. Authors would like to express gratitude to the members of Centre for Research on Cryptography and Security of Masaryk University for their valuable ideas and feedback. Special thanks go to Andriy Stetsko, Zdenek Riha and Marek Sys. This work was supported by the GAP202/11/0422 project of the Czech Science Foundation.

References

[BY13]   Bhatt, P., Yano. E.T.: Analyzing targeted attacks using hadoop applied to forensic investigation. In: Proceedings of the Eighth International Conference on Forensic Computer Science (2013)

[FA12]   Frei, S., Artes, F.: Cybercrime Kill Chain vs. Defense Effectiveness (2012). https://www.nsslabs.com/reports/cybercrime-kill-chain-vs-defense-effectiveness. Available 29 May 2014

[HCJA11] Hutchins, E.M., Cloppert, M.J., Amin, R.M.: Intelligence-driven computer network defense informed by analysis of adversary campaigns and intrusion kill chains. Leading Issues in Information Warfare & Security Research, vol. 1 (2011)

[HKP13] Harris, B., Konikoff, E., Petersen, P.: Breaking the DDoS attack chain. Technical report, August 2013

[HP13]   Hewlett-Packard. HP attack life cycle use case methodology, Technical white paper, November 2013. http://h20195.www2.hp.com/v2/GetPDF.aspx. Available 29 May 2014

[ILCP13] Ioannou, G., Louvieris, P., Clewley, N., Powell, G.: A Markov multiphase transferable belief model: an application for predicting data exfiltration APTs. In: 2013 16th International Conference on Information Fusion (FUSION), pp. 842–849. IEEE (2013)

[Man10] Mandiant. M-Trends 2010: The Advanced Persistent Threat, Report (2010). https://www.mandiant.com/resources/m-trends. Available 29 May 2014

[RSA12] RSA. Stalking The Kill Chain, Research note (2012). http://www.emc.com/collateral/hardware/solution-overview/h11154-stalking-the-kill-chain-so.pdf. Available 29 May 2014

[Sec13] Dell SecureWorks. Advanced Threat Protection with Dell SecureWorks Security Services (2013). http://www.secureworks.com/assets/pdf-store/white-papers/wp-advanced-threat-protection.pdf. Available 29 May 2014

Red Queen's Race: APT Win-Win Game
(Transcript of Discussion)

Vit Bukac[✉]

Faculty of Informatics, Masaryk University, Brno, Czech Republic
xbukac@fi.muni.cz

Good afternoon, my name is Vit Bukac, and I came here from Masaryk University and from the company Honeywell. I not will be presenting you a full research, instead I will be presenting an idea. I would like your cooperation in making this idea real and changing it into some working theory. I will be talking about so called advanced persistent threats.

Advanced persistent threats are currently considered one of the most grave threats we can encounter in a classical system security world. These are threats when APT actors, advanced human attackers, penetrate our systems and stay there undetected for a long time. For example, the average time it took to discover an APT attack was 243 days in the last year. APT actors have money, they have knowledge and they have a lot of time. They exploit our systems, they stay in our systems and get everything they need for a prolonged time period. I am talking about targeted events that are going after intellectual property. If APT actors penetrate a pharmaceutical company, they might look for plans of a new drug. If they attack an aerospace company, they may want blueprints for a new airplane. APT actors are using very advanced techniques, such as spear phishing, zero-day exploits, proprietary tools or new attack procedures, because they have money and time to develop them. They are also using stealth techniques, trying to stay under the radar, and modifying their attacks so that they are not discovered by the systems that are used by the company that is the target. For example, if they develop a new kind of malware, they test it against the anti-virus software that is used in that company and modify it, until they are certain it cannot be detected on the day one of the attack.

When we find ourselves in a situation, when these guys are have been detected on our systems, what do we do? That's the first question. Second question is, how to distinguish if this attack is targeted or if it is just a common malware infection. And the final very important question: what lessons we learned? How should we update our systems and how should we alter our procedures? This last question is unfortunately often forgotten.

Let's be honest, APT is basically a buzzword. Kill chain is a term that's being used by security companies for a method that became a weapon of choice against APTs in the last three years. It was created by Lockheed. They had some big issue with APTs, so they developed a new intrusion response model – kill chain. I am proposing an extension to this model.

So what's important about the kill chain? It shows that every APT attack consists of several phases. These phases are subsequent and in order to get to

© Springer International Publishing Switzerland 2014
B. Christianson et al. (Eds.): Security Protocols 2014, LNCS 8809, pp. 62–68, 2014.
DOI: 10.1007/978-3-319-12400-1_8

a next phase, all preceding phases must be completed successfully. For example, if you get to an installation phase it means that there was some kind of reconnaissance when attackers were discovering how they are going to do that attack in the first place, the attack payload must have been prepared and it must have been already delivered to your systems without being detected. At each of these phases we collect indicators of compromise. Indicators are small pieces of information that can be used to describe an attack, separately in each phase. For example, an indicator may be an IP address that was used to during the communication between compromised host and an attacker or it may be a source email address that was used in a phishing email during the delivery phase or it may be an MD5 hash of a file that was installed on our systems during an installation phase. All these simple small pieces of information are used to describe intrusions and their properties.

When you find out that your systems are compromised, the traditional approach is first to stop the intrusion and then go back through the kill chain, tracing all steps that the attacker has taken on affected systems and collecting indicators at each phase.

We propose not to go only backward, but also to go forward. Let me emphasise: when we discovered these attacks, most likely attackers were in our systems for a long time already. They probably already got what they wanted in the first place. So at that point, I really don't think there is much sense to stop them immediately after we found them, because they already got what they wanted. Therefore, we propose to postpone the remediation and play with them a little bit.

This approach is based on the simple idea. We want to find out as much about the attackers as possible and collect as many indicators as possible, in order not to be prepared for an attack that is going on right now, but to be prepared for attacks that will come in the future. Because the attackers will be back. Even if we remove them from our systems right now, they will return sometime in the future.

So this is the basic difference we are proposing compared to the kill chain. Kill chain says what's to be done after they are discovered – trace back. We propose also to go forward. To do that, we think we should certainly monitor the compromised systems. Moreover, we can interact with the attackers. We call this a live honeypot. It's not an exactly correct term, but it's catchy and easy to remember. We image two separate stages: passive monitoring stage and active tampering stage. During passive monitoring we don't want the APT actor to know we have already discovered him, so we limit ourselves only to passive observation. We monitor his network activity by switching routers and intrusion detection systems to a high sensitivity mode. We can monitor filesystem activity, like what files have been created or deleted.

We were considering some kind of impossible deletion, because APT attackers often create temporary files, use them and then delete them. It would be beneficial if we could modify our filesystems to just report the file to be deleted instead of actually deleting it. And we can do all kinds of monitoring such as memory dumping or network activity logging.

After passive monitoring stage an active tampering stage will follow. During this stage we throw obstacles in front of the attacker to force him do something he's not used to do. Something new, which cannot be found through standard forensic methods, because the attacker didn't do that in the past, because he didn't have to. Examples are deletion of a file that the attacker was working with, system security policy hardening, or as simple thing as server reboot, because often attacker's tools and data are stored in a volatile part of the memory only.

I will talk briefly about some benefits we see in this approach and then of course about some negatives.

Frank Stajano: Is this an approach that you have already used, or that you're proposing to use?

Reply: That's a very good question. In my company we encounter APT attacks. Currently, we only go through this passive monitoring stage, because at the time of the attack you usually don't have enough information about the scope of the attack. Therefore, we investigate for some time and once we are fairly certain what has happened, then we remediate. However, until now we didn't employ the active tampering stage.

Saar Drimer: How long do you propose this monitoring to take?

Reply: That's one of the questions for which I am seeking your opinions. We were thinking about a matter of weeks. It should not be proportional to the average length of the attack, because then the negatives, the possible dangers, will be increasing.

Certainly, if we do it for a long time, they may compromise more of our systems.

Timothy Goh: Well there are lots of repercussions for attacks, so that we have to deal with perhaps sometimes publicly. That won't allow you to wait too long, it depends I guess where you are and what kind of attack that was.

Reply: Exactly.

Olgierd Pieczul: I think some of this will be bent on the attacker intent. If the attacker dedicates to disrupt the operations then he might really have succeeded. You can't do this.

Reply: You are absolutely right. However, this is not what APT attackers do. The original problem is to distinguish who is an APT attacker, who really goes after your intellectual property, and who is someone else. It's slightly out of scope of my speech, but I agree with your opinion. I think it's critical for us, because this approach is too costly to do with anyone else than APTs.

Olgierd Pieczul: Passive monitoring, how much passive is it? Someone owns your system and you don't know how much they own it. You start changing the system state to monitoring. Why they wouldn't know that you're monitoring them?

Reply: You can do modifications on systems that you believe are not compromised. In network there are routers, switches, intrusion detection systems, servers and clients. All these systems have different levels of security. We may hope that routers or intrusion detection systems have not been compromised, because they are not the target of these people. By compromising your security systems, they are making themselves more visible. They don't want to do it, so you may pin your hope on that. Otherwise, no, we cannot be sure if the monitoring is actually passive. We just divided this in a way that passive monitoring is something you do that does not directly interfere with the APT actor's actions, while the active tampering is actually doing something to mess with them purposefully.

Frank Stajano: I think you said that it was not in the interest of the attackers to mess around with your intrusion detection because they want to keep a low profile. I question this statement because if they mess around with your intrusion detection so that they are not detected, then that would be in their interest wouldn't it, to try and subvert your security systems so that it looks like they're not there.

Reply: That's true. I am looking at this from the perspective of a really huge company. We have multiple security systems and they are monitoring not only clients and servers, but also each other. So if one of them is behaving differently than it should, it should be observed by some other system. It's not closed system. For example, in an average company you are not relying just on an anti-virus software, because once somebody goes past AV, he's in. So you are using multiple systems that watch each other, and if one of them fails, some other may step in. The standard modus operandi of APT actors is that they will compromise one of your systems, there they will learn legitimate credentials and subsequently they will log onto 2 to 10 more systems. One of them will be the system they are looking for, the system which contains the data and from there they will extract the data. And it doesn't matter if this organisation has 50 computers or 5,000 computers, it's still this small-scale. But I am talking from experience, I'm not talking about how it can be theoretically done.

Simon Foley: What about the analogy of how you deal with a rat infestation? You don't just put poison down in the hope of killing them, you first of all feed them and get them used to coming to the site where you're going to eventually poison them. Apparently this is how you get rid of large rat infestations, so if your attackers are rats.....

Reply: Similar analogy would be to say that you want to feed them first, so you can see how many of them are, to be sure that you killed them all.

Yvo Desmedt: The cuckoo nest, long time ago is such an example. They made, this goes back to the 80s, deliberately a huge file so that it would take them hours to download, and then they basically agreed with phone companies, and so the FBI was able to track from where these attacks originated.

Reply: Yes, this is actually one of the ideas that we also considered, to create a huge file and force them to download it, because then you can trace it through your systems and through their systems. You can cooperate with security companies and with law enforcement agencies.

Yvo Desmedt: This is very old.

Reply: Yes, but it still works, I think it still works.

Hannan Xiao: I think your analogy is very similar to the ancient Chinese art of war. Attract the enemy by using, for example, a pretty woman.

Joan Feigenbaum: Yes, that's the honeypot.

Hannan Xiao: But there is the associated risk. Have you assessed the risk of such an approach? There is an ancient Chinese saying: You'd lose your wife and you'd lose your army and you'd lose the war. So there is a risk associated.

Reply: It is. There are several problems. The first problem is pretty obvious - sometimes you may be forced by law not to do this. For example, usually there is a law clause that mandates to stop any damage being done as soon as possible, to prevent further damage. In the Czech Republic it's a very general clause. You can always argue, that we did this because we want to prevent more damage in the future.

Joan Feigenbaum: Is there an entrapment problem? Might you be considered to have enticed someone to commit a crime who wasn't about to commit a crime, and is that a problem?

Reply: Well it's a question for a lawyer. Personally I don't think so, because we are at the point when we have already discovered someone unauthorised on our systems. I think that to a certain degree it allows us to react in this way, because they already did something. We may leave them space to do something more serious, but they've already committed a crime.

Partha Das Chowdhury: Well a somewhat unrelated incident, there was a case in Nepal, where somebody was accused of not paying a loan to the bank. This guy defended by saying that the bank was always calling him and asking him to take loans, so then this guy took a loan, and eventually didn't pay. So maybe that entrapment thing like, I am into something and then you are enticing me to do more. This case happened and the judge ruled in favour of him and against the bankers.

Reply: I must say, this is a very interesting point of view, I didn't consider that. I think it's linked to something that was said in here before, that first you have to be sure who you are facing. If it is just some script kiddie, someone who is just trying to penetrate your systems, then obviously this could be problematic. But if this is someone who is purposefully targeting your systems and your data, then I wouldn't worry about that. I really wouldn't. I would let the legal department to worry about that. But I think it could be justified even from their point of view.

I will quickly finish the presentation, and then spend time with more questions.

Another obvious problem is the attack spreading. If we leave attackers in our systems for 5 or 6 more weeks, it is possible they will compromise more of our hosts. Fortunately, we observe them closely, so we would probably be able to find the system that they have compromised at that time. Also, we would be able to see the process of compromising new hosts, which would again be an interesting and valuable information, even more indicators. Another obvious problem is an increased cost. We have to dedicate people, we have to dedicate the resources and we also have to modify your procedures, because we must be ready for unexpected situations. In some cases, when attackers gained what they wanted they may decide to wipe systems clean, so we must be ready also for that.

So I will skip this one because we've already talked about that. I have some more questions that you might find interesting. Now is the space to ask more. If you want to send some more questions via email here is my mail address. I promise I will respond to each and every one of you.

Timothy Goh: Do you have an example where future indicators would have helped prevent a further attack?

Reply: Yes. This is based on the similarities between campaigns. Once you observe one campaign, you will find those indicators (e.g., MD5 hashes, domain names, IP addresses, the way how they create phishing emails etc.). Subsequently, there will be another campaign, which will be slightly different. They will maybe use a different mail sender or maybe a slightly different malware with different MP5 hash. But they will probably use at least something that we already know - e.g., domain names, communication infrastructure or they may decide to use the same exploit. So we take all those indicators from one campaign (let's say there will be 30 of them) and observe a new campaign. And If we see that several similar indicators. First, we learn that it's the same APT actor and second, we can predict their next steps. Because if we identify them for example during the delivery phase, then we can stop them and don't allow them to progress any further. All because we've prepared your systems based on the indicators that we collected in the previous campaigns.

Vashek Matyas: I'm realising that actually we have a serious issue here and that's vagueness. We are speaking of "them", but them actually can be someone who's investing their time and effort in developing the access, and then selling the access to somebody else. And then the pattern of use will be completely different between these two groups.

Reply: I relied on the research from Lockheed who addressed this question, I am just extending their research. They claimed that they really experienced first hand situations when they found technical similarities between different campaigns. So your assumption in this context is not valid, because it's really difficult, even for advanced attackers, to change everything, every let's say three months.

Yvo Desmedt: So what's the difference with the usual honeypots?

Reply: Honeypots usually are aimed not at human attackers, but at malware, or automated scripts. The problem with honeypots is that they are low interaction types and high interaction types, but both can be recognized by a knowledgeable attacker. These are people who use remote access tools or scripts on your system, but these are not automated tools, so we are assuming they can go through that. We were thinking about creating a simple honeynet around the identified compromised system to kind of contain it. I don't think the basic idea can be achieved with honeynets, because these attackers probably will be able to identify a honeypot before attacking it, so they will just go somewhere else.

Virgil Gligor: So the idea of kill chain really comes from physical attacks, but it has been used by the military for a long time, as you've heard, perhaps since ancient times. My question is, how successful do you think the users of this methodology have been in the information systems domain, like for example, in the Internet. In other words, does this analogy or metaphor work for us as opposed to the physical attacks, the kinetic attacks.

Reply: I refer back to the paper written by Lockheed.

Virgil Gligor: I'm very familiar with it. I'll say a few words about it, but I'm curious to hear your opinion.

Reply: I like that it's becoming very popular with most of the security companies I come in contact with. Dell, NSS Labs, RSA Security, are also working on this. I believe they are smart people and they are doing something which they believe will work.

Virgil Gligor: Well there is also the sort of herd mentality when all people go in a particular direction because there is no alternative, but not because that direction is definitely proven in any way.

Reply: That's true, I have nothing to comment.

Non-collaborative Attackers and How and Where to Defend Flawed Security Protocols (Extended Version)

Michele Peroli[1], Luca Viganò[2]([✉]), and Matteo Zavatteri[1]

[1] Dipartimento di Informatica, Università di Verona, Verona, Italy
[2] Department of Informatics, King's College London, London, UK
luca.vigano@kcl.ac.uk

Abstract. Security protocols are often found to be flawed after their deployment. We present an approach that aims at the neutralization or mitigation of the attacks to flawed protocols: it avoids the complete dismissal of the interested protocol and allows honest agents to continue to use it until a corrected version is released. Our approach is based on the knowledge of the network topology, which we model as a graph, and on the consequent possibility of creating an interference to an ongoing attack of a Dolev-Yao attacker, by means of non-collaboration actuated by ad-hoc benign attackers that play the role of network guardians. Such guardians, positioned in strategic points of the network, have the task of monitoring the messages in transit and discovering at runtime, through particular types of inference, whether an attack is ongoing, interrupting the run of the protocol in the positive case. We study not only how but also where we can attempt to defend flawed security protocols: we investigate the different network topologies that make security protocol defense feasible and illustrate our approach by means of concrete examples.

Keywords: Security protocols · Defense · Non-collaborative attackers · Attack interference · Attack mitigation · Topological advantage

1 Introduction

1.1 Context and Motivation

Security protocols are often found to be flawed after their deployment, which typically requires "dismissing" the protocol and hurrying up with the deployment of a new version hoping to be faster than those attempting to exploit the

This work was partially supported by the EU FP7 Project no. 257876, "SPaCIoS: Secure Provision and Consumption in the Internet of Services" (www.spacios.eu) and the PRIN 2010-11 project "Security Horizons". Much of this work was carried out while Luca Viganò was at the Università di Verona.

© Springer International Publishing Switzerland 2014
B. Christianson et al. (Eds.): Security Protocols 2014, LNCS 8809, pp. 69–90, 2014.
DOI: 10.1007/978-3-319-12400-1_9

discovered flaw. We present an approach that aims at the neutralization or mitigation of the attacks to flawed protocols: it avoids the complete dismissal of the interested protocol and gives honest agents the chance to continue to use it until a corrected version is released.

The standard attacker model adopted in security protocol analysis is the one of [12]: the *Dolev-Yao (DY) attacker* can compose, send and intercept messages at will, but, following the perfect cryptography assumption, he cannot break cryptography. The DY attacker is thus in complete control of the network—in fact, he is often formalized as being the network itself—and, with respect to network abilities, he is actually stronger than any attacker that can be implemented in real-life situations. Hence, if a protocol is proved to be secure under the DY attacker, it will also withstand attacks carried out by less powerful attackers; aside from deviations from the specification (and the consequent possible novel flaws) introduced in the implementation phase, the protocol can thus be safely employed in real-life networks, at least in principle.

A number of tools have been proposed for automated security protocol analysis (e.g., [1,5,11,13,19,20] to name just a few), all of which follow the classical approach for security protocol analysis in which there is a finite number of honest agents and only one DY dishonest agent, given the implicit assumption that in order to find attacks we can reduce n collaborative DY attackers to 1 (for a proof of this assumption see, e.g., [2]).

In this paper, we take a quite different approach: we exploit the fact that if in the network there are *multiple non-collaborative attackers*, then the interactions between them make it impossible to reduce their attack "power" to that of a single attacker. This paper is based on the network suitable for the study of non-collaborative scenarios defined in our previous works [14,15], in which we introduced a protocol-independent model for non-collaboration for the analysis of security protocols (inspired by the exploratory works [3,4] for "protocol life after attacks" and attack retaliation). In this model: (i) a protocol is run in the presence of multiple attackers, and (ii) attackers potentially have different capabilities, different knowledge and do not collaborate but rather may interfere with each other.

Interference between attackers has spawned the definition of an ad hoc attacker, called *guardian*, as a defense mechanism for flawed protocols: if two non-collaborative attackers can interfere with each other, then we can exploit this interference to neutralize or at least mitigate an ongoing attack (a detailed cost-effective analysis of this approach is left for future work).[1]

There is one fundamental catch, though. We know that a DY attacker actually cannot exist (e.g., how could he control the whole network?) but postulating

---

[1] It is interesting to note how this idea of "living with flaws" is becoming more and more widespread; see, e.g., [9] where runtime monitors are employed to warn users of android applications about "man in the middle" attacks on flawed implementations of SSL. Our approach is also related to signature-based intrusion detection systems, but we leave the detailed study of the relations of our approach with runtime monitors and signature-based intrusion detection systems for future work.

his existence allows us to consider the worst case analysis so that if we can prove a protocol secure under such an attacker, then we are guaranteed that the protocol will be secure also in the presence of weaker, more realistic attackers. A guardian, however, only makes sense if it really exists, i.e., if it is implemented to defend flawed protocols for real, but the attackers and the guardian presented in [14,15] are modeled in order to discover interactions between agents in non-collaborative scenarios rather than pushing for an implementation in the real-world.

1.2 Contributions

Since implementing a guardian with the full power of a DY attacker is impossible, we must investigate ways to make the guardian more feasible. In order to reduce the complexity of the possible implementation of such a defense mechanism, in this paper we relax the notion of guardian and ask him to defend only a subset of the communication channels of the network, which we put under his control.

Furthermore, not being obviously able to know where the competitor is, we investigate where we have to introduce this defense mechanism in the network from a topological perspective, i.e., how the guardian can dominate his competitor(s).[2] Modeling the network as a graph, we study how the topological position of an attacker E and a guardian G, with respect to each other and to honest agents of the protocol, can influence a protocol attack and, thus, the possible defense against it. We define six basic topological configurations and study the outcome of the introduction of a guardian in each specific position. We also introduce the concept of *topological advantage*, which guarantees that the guardian has an advantage with respect to his competitors, and can thus carry out inference on messages in transit in order to detect an ongoing attack and eventually mitigate or neutralize it.

The contributions of this paper thus extend, and in a sense are complementary to, the ones in our previous works [14,15]. In a nutshell: there we discussed the *how* we can defend flawed security protocols and here we discuss the *where*. More specifically, as we will describe in the following sections, in [14,15], we put the basis for the study of the interaction of two attackers in non-collaborative scenarios with the goal of understanding and finding the types of interference the guardian can use, and, in this paper, we give the means to understand how to exploit the interference from a topological point of view, thus bringing the guardian close to real implementation.

1.3 Organization

We proceed as follows. In Sect. 2, we summarize the main notions of attack interference in non-collaborative scenarios. In Sect. 3, we formalize the models of the network and of the guardian, with particular emphasis on the topological advantage that a guardian must have in order to defend against attacks. In Sect. 4,

---

[2] In the following, we focus on one competitor (i.e., one attacker), but it is quite straightforwardly possible to extend our work to multiple competitors.

we discuss, as a detailed proof-of-concept, how we can defend the ISO-SC 27 protocol and summarize the results we obtained for other case studies. In Sect. 5, we briefly summarize our results and discuss future work.

2   Attack Interference in Non-collaborative Networks

2.1   Network Agents

Let *Agents* be the set of all the network agents, which comprises of two disjoint subsets:

- the subset *Honest* of *honest agents* who always follow the steps of the security protocol they are executing in the hope of achieving the properties for which the protocol has been designed (such as authentication and secrecy), and
- the subset *Dishonest* of *dishonest agents* (a.k.a. *attackers*) who may eventually not follow the protocol to attack some (or all) security properties. In addition to being able to act as legitimate agents of the network, dishonest agents typically have far more capabilities than honest agents and follow the model of Dolev-Yao [12] that we summarized in the introduction.

The *knowledge* of an honest agent X is characterized by a proprietary dataset D_X, which contains all the information that X acquired during the protocol execution, and is closed under all cryptographic operations on message terms (e.g., an agent can decrypt an encrypted message that he knows provided that he knows also the corresponding decryption key). D_X is monotonic since an agent does not forget.

2.2   DY Attackers and the Network in a Non-collaborative Scenario

In this paper, we take the non-classical approach that leverages on the fact that the interactions between multiple non-collaborative attackers may lead to interference. We base our work on the network suitable for the study of non-collaborative scenarios defined in [14,15], which we now summarize quickly pointing to these two papers for more details.

Table 1 shows the model that we adopt to formalize a DY attacker E in a non-collaborative scenario in which different attacks may interfere with each other (we restrict the study of this type of interaction to two active attackers but it can be generalized to multiple ones). The knowledge base of E is encoded in the set D_E, whereas D_{net} is the proprietary dataset for the network (we will return to the network model below). The rules in the table describe the operations that an attacker can perform internally, how he can interact with the network and how the system (i.e., the network environment) is configured. It is important to note that the rules in Table 1 are transition rules rather than deduction rules, i.e., they describe knowledge acquisition from a given

Table 1. Dolev-Yao attacker model for non-collaborative scenarios: internal operations (synthesis and analysis of messages), network operations (*spy, inject, erase*) and system configuration (*True-Sender-ID, DecisionalProcess, NetHandler*). *NetHandler* describes the set of attackers who are allowed to spy by applying one of the *spy* rules. We omit the usual rules for conjunction.

Composition:	Encryption:	Projection:	Decryption:
$\dfrac{m_1 \in D_E^i \quad m_2 \in D_E^i}{(m_1, m_2) \in D_E^i}$	$\dfrac{m \in D_E^i \quad k \in D_E^i}{\{m\}_k \in D_E^i}$	$\dfrac{(m_1, m_2) \in D_E^i}{m_j \in D_E^i \text{ for } j \in \{1,2\}}$	$\dfrac{\{m\}_k \in D_E^i \quad k^{-1} \in D_E^i}{m \in D_E^i}$

Inflow-Spy:	*Outflow-Spy*:
$\dfrac{\mu \in D_{net}^i \quad ofInterest_E(X) \quad Y \in D_E^i \quad \psi}{m \in D_E^{i+1} \wedge sender(< X, m, Y >) \in D_E^{i+1}}$	$\dfrac{\mu \in D_{net}^i \quad sender(\mu) \in D_E^i \quad ofInterest_E(Y) \quad \psi}{m \in D_E^{i+1} \wedge Y \in D_E^{i+1}}$

where $\mu = < X, m, Y >$ and $\psi = E \in canSee(< X, m, Y >, i))$

Injection:	*Erase*:
$\dfrac{m \in D_E^i \quad X \in D_E^i \quad Y \in D_E^i}{< E(X), m, Y >\in D_{net}^{i+1}}$	$\dfrac{< X, m, Y >\in D_{net}^i \quad sender(< X, m, Y >) \in D_E^i}{< X, m, Y >\notin D_{net}^{i+1}}$

True-sender-ID:

$$sender(< X, m, Y >) = \begin{cases} E & \text{if there exists } Z \text{ such that } X = E(Z) \\ X & \text{otherwise} \end{cases}$$

DecisionalProcess:

$$ofInterest_E(X) = \begin{cases} true & \text{if } E \text{ decides to pay attention to } X \\ false & \text{otherwise} \end{cases}$$

NetHandler:

$$canSee(< X, m, Y >, i)) = \{Z \in Dishonest \mid Z \text{ can spy } < X, m, Y > \text{ on } D_{net}^i\}$$

operation and a particular configuration rather than the reasoning about "only" the knowledge of the attacker.

As in the classic DY case, an attacker in this model can *send* and *receive* messages, derive new messages by *composing, decomposing, modifying, encrypting/decrypting* known messages (iff he has the right keys), and *intercept* or *remove* messages from the network. An attacker E may also masquerade as (i.e., impersonate) another agent X, which we denote by writing $E(X)$.

The most significant features of the attacker abilities are the two *spy* rules, which formalize the fact that attackers only pay attention to a selection of the traffic on the network (considering only selected target agents):[3,4]

- **Inflow-Spy:** the attacker pays attention to the incoming network traffic of a target agent and saves the identifiers of the sender agents,
- **Outflow-Spy:** the attacker pays attention to the traffic generated by a target agent.

The *target agent* X of the two spy-rules is defined through a decisional process (the function $ofInterest_E(X)$ in Table 1) in which each attacker decides if the traffic to/from the agent X is worth to be followed. This decision is made at run-time when a new agent identifier is discovered over the network (i.e., when a new agent starts sending messages on the channel monitored by the attacker). In this paper, we do not go into the details of how his decision is actually taken, but different strategies might be devised and we will investigate them in future work.

The network net is also formalized through a dataset, D_{net}, which is changed by the *actions* send, receive, inject and erase a message. We write D^i_{net} to denote the state of D_{net} after the i-th action. Messages transit on the network in the form of triplets of the type

$$\langle sender\text{-}ID, message, receiver\text{-}ID \rangle,$$

where, as in the classical approaches, both the attackers and the agents acquire knowledge only from the body of messages, i.e., *sender-ID* and *receiver-ID* are actually hidden to them and only used by the network system. As a consequence of message delivery or deletion, D_{net} is non-monotonic by construction.

In order to regulate the concurrent actions over the network, the model comprises a *NetHandler* whose task is to handle the network by selecting the next action and implementing the dependencies between selected actions and knowledge available to each attacker. That is, *NetHandler*: (i) notifies agents that the state of the network has changed with newly-inserted messages, (ii) polls agents for their next intended action, (iii) selects from the set of candidate actions the one that will be actually carried out, and (iv) informs agents of whether the computation they performed to propose an action is a consequence of a message that they did not have access to (i.e., for these agents a rollback might occur in

---

[3] If an attacker were omniscient and omnipotent (i.e., if he were to control the whole network) then there'd actually be no "space" for another attacker, and thus there'd be no interference. The more "adventurous" reader may want to compare this with the proof of the uniqueness of God by Leibniz, which was based on the arguments started by Anselm of Canterbury and was later further refined by Gödel.

[4] In this paper we only use the *inflow-spy* and the *outflow-spy* filters and not the *restricted-spy* filter used in the previous exploratory works. This is due to the fact that we can certainly know who we want to defend, but we cannot know who the attackers are and we want to have the possibility of intercepting *all* outgoing/incoming messages which leave/come from/to an agent X.

Table 2. The ISO-SC 27 protocol and a parallel session attack against it.

ISO-SC 27 protocol	Attack
(1) $A \rightarrow B : N_A$ (2) $B \rightarrow A : \{\!|N_A, N_B|\!\}_{K_{AB}}$ (3) $A \rightarrow B : N_B$	(1.1) $A \rightarrow E(B) : N_A$ (2.1) $E(B) \rightarrow A : N_A$ (2.2) $A \rightarrow E(B) : \{\!|N_A, N'_A|\!\}_{K_{AB}}$ (1.2) $E(B) \rightarrow A : \{\!|N_A, N'_A|\!\}_{K_{AB}}$ (1.3) $A \rightarrow E(B) : N'_A$ (2.3) $E(B) \rightarrow A : N'_A$

which all knowledge gained since the last confirmed action is deleted from the dataset, and internal operations that have occurred are cancelled).

The outcome of the process governed by the network handler is described through the function *canSee*, which returns a subset of dishonest agents, highlighting the identifier of attackers who can spy "before" the message is erased from D_{net}. In other words, when a message is deleted from the network, the network handler, through the function *canSee*, can decide if an attacker has spied (and saved in his dataset) the message or not. In our previous work we had the possibility of spying a message before its deletion (in this case, the attacker has to decide if the message has been received by the honest agent or deleted by another attacker) but in this paper we relax this assumption and decide that when a message is spied it remains in the dataset of the attacker. The function *canSee* is a configurable parameter of our network and it corresponds to configuring a particular network environment in which the agents are immersed: *canSee* is instantiated by the security analyst at the beginning of the analysis in order to model time-dependent accessibility, strategic decision-making and information-sharing, or to capture a particular network topology (in our framework the function *canSee* is necessary in order to model the topologies that we will introduce in Sect. 3.1).

2.3 Attack Interference (In the Case of the ISO-SC 27 Protocol)

As a concrete, albeit simple, example of security protocol, Table 2 shows the ISO-SC 27 protocol [16], which aims to achieve entity authentication (aliveness) between two honest agents A and B, by exchanging nonces, under the assumption that they already share a symmetric key K_{AB}. Since in the second message there is nothing that assures that the message actually comes from B, the protocol is subject to a parallel sessions attack (also shown in the table) in which the attacker E, who does not know K_{AB}, uses A as oracle against herself in order to provide to her a response that he cannot generate by himself: E masquerades as B intercepting A's first message and sending it back to her in a parallel session (messages (1.1) and (2.1)). When A receives the first message of the protocol from E, she thinks someone wants to talk with her in another instance of the protocol (she does not control the nonce), thus she replies to E generating another nonce N'_A and encrypting it together with N_A (message (2.2)). Now E has got everything he needs in order to complete the attack to the protocol (messages (1.2)). The last message is not mandatory as the session has already been attacked, thus E can omit it (message (2.3)). At the end of the protocol runs, A is fooled into believing that $E(B)$ is B.

If a protocol is flawed, a single DY attacker will succeed with certainty. However, if attacks to the same protocol are carried out in a more complex network environment, then success is not guaranteed since multiple non-collaborative attackers may interact, and actually interfere, with each other. The results of [14,15] show that it is possible, at least theoretically, to exploit interference between two non-collaborative attackers to mitigate protocol flaws, thus providing a form of defense to flawed protocols.

In the case of ISO-SC 27 protocol, which was not studied in [14,15][5], we can identify six cases for the possible interaction between two non-collaborative attackers E_1 and E_2:

1. E_1 and E_2 know each other as honest.
2. E_1 and E_2 know each other as attackers.
3. E_1 and E_2 are unaware of each other.
4. E_2 knows E_1 as honest.
5. E_2 knows E_1 as dishonest.
6. E_2 knows E_1, but he is unsure of E_1's honesty.

The traces corresponding to the interactions of E_1 and E_2 attacking the protocol are shown in Table 3. Attack traces of this type lead to three possible (mutually exclusive) situations: (i) E_1 dominates E_2 (i.e., E_1's attack succeeds while E_2's fails), or (ii) none of their attacks has success, or (iii) both achieve a situation of uncertainty, i.e., they do not know if their attacks have been successful or not.

In order to exploit the interference generated by multiple dishonest agents attacking the same protocol, we can construct an additional, but this time non-malicious, attacker: the *guardian* G.

To define the guardian as a network agent, we refine the previous definition of *Agents* to consider the subset of *benign dishonest agents*, i.e., *BenignDishonest* $\subseteq$ *Dishonest* $\subseteq$ *Agents*, where $X \in BenignDishonest$ means that X has attacker capabilities and may not follow the protocol but he "attacks" with the goal of "defending" the security properties not of attacking them. In other words:

Definition 1 (Guardian). *A guardian is a benign dishonest agent of the network, transparent to the other agents, whose main task is to establish a partial (or total) defense mechanism in order to mitigate (or neutralize) protocol attacks*

---

[5] In [14,15], we analyzed two protocols: (i) a key transport protocol described as an example in [6], which we thus called the Boyd-Mathuria Example (BME), and (ii) the Shamir-Rivest-Adleman Three-Pass protocol(SRA3P [8]), which has been proposed to transmit data securely on insecure channels, bypassing the difficulties connected to the absence of prior agreements between the agents A and B to establish a shared key.

Table 3. Traces for non-collaborative attacks against the ISO-SC 27. Traces are exhaustive: E_1 and E_2 have priority over honest agents. Arrows: relative order between $(2.1')$ and $(2.1'')$ is irrelevant in determining the outcome.

T1: cases 1, 3, 4	T2: case 5

T1: cases 1, 3, 4

(1.1) $A \rightarrow E_{1,2}(B) : N_A$
(2.1) $E_{1,2}(B) \rightarrow A : N_A$
(2.2) $A \rightarrow E_{1,2}(B) : \{\!| N_A, N'_A |\!\}_{K_{AB}}$
(1.2) $E_{1,2}(B) \rightarrow A : \{\!| N_A, N'_A |\!\}_{K_{AB}}$
(1.3) $A \rightarrow E_{1,2}(B) : N'_A$
(2.3) $E_{1,2}(B) \rightarrow A : N'_A$

T2: case 5

(1.1) $A \rightarrow E_{1,2}(B) \quad : N_A$
↓ (2.1') $E_1(B) \rightarrow E_2(A) : N_A$
↑ (2.1'') $E_2(B) \rightarrow A \quad : N_A$
(2.2) $A \rightarrow E_2(B) \quad : \{\!| N_A, N'_A |\!\}_{K_{AB}}$
(1.2) $E_2(B) \rightarrow A \quad : \{\!| N_A, N'_A |\!\}_{K_{AB}}$
(1.3) $A \rightarrow E_2(B) \quad : N'_A$
(2.3) $E_2(B) \rightarrow A \quad : N'_A$

T3: case 2

(1.1) $A \rightarrow E_{1,2}(B) \quad : N_A$
↓ (2.1') $E_1(B) \rightarrow E_2(A) : N_A$
↑ (2.1'') $E_2(B) \rightarrow E_1(A) : N_A$

T4: case 6

(1.1) $A \rightarrow E_{1,2}(B) : N_A$
(2.1) $E_1(B) \rightarrow A \quad : N_A$
+ steps of case 5

at execution time by means of attack-interference in non-collaborative scenarios. G is transparent to honest agents during their execution and becomes "visible" only in the case he has to report an ongoing attack.

3   Modeling the Network and the Guardian

In the previous section, we have seen how the interaction between multiple non-collaborative dishonest agents attacking the same protocol can interfere with both attacks, thus providing a form of defense. As we remarked in the introduction, even if the idea of having a guardian defending honest agents from attacks seems thrilling, the existence of a guardian agent makes sense only with his implementation in the real world. In order to reduce the complexity of such an implementation, we will now investigate where we have to introduce this defense mechanism in the network from a topological perspective (i.e., how the guardian can dominate his competitor(s)). Modeling the network as a graph, we study how the topological position of an attacker E and a guardian G, with respect to each other and to honest agents of the protocol, can influence a protocol attack and, thus, the possible defense against it.

We say that the outcome of the introduction of the guardian on the network for a particular protocol yields a:

– *false positive* if, for some reason, a normal run of the protocol is considered as an attack,
– *false negative* if, for some reason, an attack is considered as a normal run of the protocol,

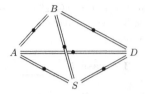

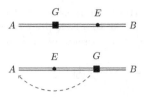

(a) An example of network as a graph; vertices represent agents, edges represent communication channels and the bullets • represent the presence of a DY-attacker E.

(b) Two possible allocations, on a channel between A and B that is controlled by an attacker E, for the guardian G when he defends an honest agent A. For both cases (the above one is implicit), we assume the presence of an authentic and resilient communication channel between G and A (dashed line).

Fig. 1. Model of the network and possible allocations of the guardian on a channel.

– *partial defense* iff it admits false negatives,
– *total defense* iff it does not admit false negatives.

Our objective is to realize a defense mechanism that admits as few false negatives as possible, while limiting also the number of false positives, by investigating the position that gives the guardian a topological advantage (see Definition 4 of defense mechanism and the ensuing Theorem 1).

3.1   A Network for Topological Advantage

We model the network as a graph (an example is depicted in Fig. 1a), where vertices represent the agents of the network and edges represent communication channels (we assume no properties of these channels, which are standard insecure channels over which messages are sent as specified by the security protocols). Since, as we remarked above, it would be unfeasible for the guardian to defend the traffic on all network channels, we investigate which of these channels the guardian should be best positioned on.

Security protocols typically involve two honest agents A and B, who sometimes enroll also a honest and trusted third party S (we could, of course, consider protocols with more agents). As depicted in Fig. 1a, the DY-attacker E is in control of all the communication channels of the network, thus, in the case of a ping-pong protocol between A and B, E controls also the communication channel between A and B. If we were to allocate a guardian G on such a channel in order to defend the honest agent A, it could only be in one of two locations: as shown in Fig. 1b, either the guardian G is between the initiator A and the attacker E, or G is between the attacker E and the responder B. In the following, these two cases will be used as a base of network topologies to be considered during the analysis. We will see in the next section that the guardian should have the possibility of alerting A of the ongoing attack without being detected by the attacker; in such a case (especially as highlighted in the lower topology in Fig. 1b), we thus assume the presence of an authentic and resilient communication channel (confidentiality can be enforced but it is not mandatory) between G and A.[6] In the following, this channel will be omitted from the notation and the figures for the sake of readability.

If the network topologies for two-agent protocols are simple (Fig. 2a and b), for the case where a trusted third party S (or another agent) is present on the network, we have to make some assumptions about the position of the attacker E (the attack power of the attacker is never questioned). In this paper, we consider four main base cases of network topologies for three-agent protocols, where, for every case, we consider which channel(s) the guardian is defending:

- Fig. 2c: the channel between A and S (we assume that the attacker is not present over these channels[7] and the guardian acts like a proxy),
- Fig. 2d: the channel between B and S (this is the specular scenario with respect to the previous case),
- Fig. 2e: A's communication channel (the guardian acts as a proxy for A), and
- Fig. 2f: B's communication channel (the guardian acts as a proxy for B).

These basic topologies abstract the communication channels of a complex network (e.g., a LAN) in a way that permits one to reason about the position of agents without introducing additional parameters in the process (e.g., additional agents that start the protocol at the same time, or multiple network paths relaxed in one link).

In general, we cannot state that a base case is the right one or the wrong one as this actually depends on both the analyzed protocol and the agent we want to defend. In order to implement the right guardian, we should consider the protocol defense possible in each of these cases. We conjecture that all other network topologies with two or three agents can be reduced to the base cases introduced above, but leave a formal proof for future work.

3.2   Network Guardian in Practice

Attacks leverage protocol-dependent features, and thus attack traces always contain particular messages that we can use as signals for ongoing attacks. As messages transit continuously through the network, we assume that the guardian has a way to distinguish them (otherwise, we cannot guarantee any type of defense).

---

[6] This channel could be a digital or a physical channel, say a text message sent to a mobile (as in some two-factor authentication or e-banking systems), a phone call (as in burglar alarm systems), or even a flag raised (as is done on some beaches to signal the presence of sharks). We do not investigate the features of this channel further but simply assume, as done in all the above three examples of runtime guarding (monitoring) systems, that such a channel actually exists.

[7] We do not make assumptions on the real topology of the network between A and S (i.e., there could be more than one channel) but only consider the fact that the communications from E are received by G.

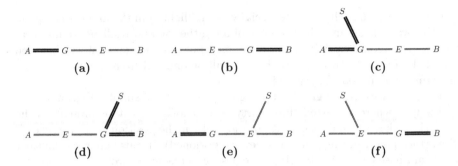

Fig. 2. Base cases of network topologies for protocols between two agents (a, b) and three agents (c, d, e, f). We denote with double stretched lines (in boldface) the channels for which we assume that the attacker is not present.

In order to operate, the network guardian needs to interact with the messages transiting over the network. The two modules that we define in the architecture of the guardian are: (i) the *Identification Module*, and (ii) the *Control Module*. Both modules operate separately, do not interact with each other (even though they share the guardian's dataset D_G), and are meant to (i) distinguish the messages that belong to the protocol[8] that they are defending and (ii) detect ongoing attacks.

These features are achieved by means of two *distinguishers* Δ_{Id} and Δ_C, two probabilistic polynomial time algorithms. Δ_{Id} returns 1 if it believes that a message m belongs to the protocol and 0 otherwise. We use the distinguisher Δ_C in order to detect, from the run of a security protocol $\mathcal{P}$ (identified by the other module), those messages m that are considered *critical*, i.e., that can be used to attack $\mathcal{P}$.

For a concrete example of critical message, we can refer to Table 2. The nonce N_A exchanged in message (1.1) is the first information that the attacker uses in order to perform the reply attack against the ISO-SC 27 protocol, so this message must be considered critical. Even though the nonce is sent as a plaintext, the use of the distinguisher Δ_C overcomes the problem with encrypted messages.

Identification Module. Figure 3a shows the graphical representation of the *Identification Module*. The guardian uses this module, together with the distinguisher Δ_{Id}, to detect those messages m that belong to the protocol and label them as part of $\mathcal{P}$ in the dataset D_G in order to do inference subsequently.

We can see the Identification Module as a finite state machine where the transition from state to state depends on the spied messages. When a message

---

[8] We deliberately wrote "protocol" instead of "protocols" since, for now, we are not going to consider multi-protocol attacks or protocol composition, e.g., [7,10,17]. As future work, we envision a distinguisher able to distinguish between messages belonging to different protocols and thus consider also the attacks that occur when messages from one protocol may be confused with messages from another protocol.

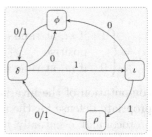

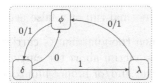

(a) Identification Module: Assuming that m is the message spied from the spy filter, δ is the state where the distinguisher is invoked on input m, ϕ the "forward state", λ the "label state" in which the message m is labeled in the dataset D_G as part of the protocol $\mathcal{P}$.

(b) Control Module: Assuming that m is the message spied from the spy filter, δ is the state where the distinguisher is invoked on input m, ι the state where the attack invariant is invoked on m, ϕ represents the "forward state", ρ the "interference state".

Fig. 3. Identification and Control Modules implemented in the guardian.

m is spied by the spy filter (see Table 1 for the two available spy filters), the Identification Module of the guardian invokes the distinguisher $\Delta_{Id}(m)$ to establish whether the message belongs to the protocol or not.

If $\Delta_{Id}(m) = 0$, the message is not considered useful and the guardian moves to the forward state ϕ, which will let the message go, and subsequently goes back, without checking any condition, to the initial state δ in order to wait for the next message. If $\Delta_{Id}(m) = 1$, then m belongs to the protocol and the guardian moves to the "identification state" λ, where the message is labeled in the dataset D_G. After the message has been labeled, the Identification Module goes back to the initial state δ in order to wait for the next message.

From now on, when we do an operation (spy-filters excluded) on the dataset, we mean (slightly abusing notation) the subset of the labeled messages.

Control Module. Figure 3b shows the graphical representation of the Control Module. The guardian uses this module, together with the distinguisher Δ_C, in order to deal with those messages m that he must control in order to be able to do inference (i.e., check if an attack is ongoing) and eventually interfere with the attacker; we call these messages *critical*.

Once the distinguisher, implemented in the Control Module, believes that m is critical (at time i), the *attack invariant* $Inv(m, i)$ is tested to discover (or exclude) an ongoing attack. $Inv(m, i)$ is a protocol-dependent Boolean condition; formally, it is a first-order logic formula on a critical message of the protocol (which can be straightforwardly extended to a set of messages) tested at time i (i.e., after i actions on the dataset D_{net}; in order to define more complex functions, more than two parameters can be used):

$$Inv(m, i) = \begin{cases} 1 & \text{if } m, \text{ at time } i, \text{ characterizes an ongoing attack or a false} \\ & \text{positive} \\ 0 & \text{if } m, \text{ at time } i, \text{ characterizes a normal run or a false negative} \end{cases}$$

If the computation of the invariant returns 1, then the guardian G carries out the appropriate defense for the attack making the victim abort the current run of the protocol and, eventually, mislead the attacker and/or induce him to abort the attack. We give an example of invariant in Sect. 4.1 when we return to our case study.

When a message m is spied by the spy filter, the Control Module is in the initial state δ, and then the message is passed as input to the distinguisher Δ_C, whose task is to establish whether the message is critical or not. If the result of the distinguisher is $\Delta_C(m) = 0$, the message is not considered critical and the guardian moves to the forward state ϕ, which will let the message go, and subsequently goes back, without checking any condition, to the initial state δ in order to wait for the next message. Instead, if $\Delta_C(m) = 1$, then a critical message has just been distinguished from the others; the guardian moves to the invariant state ι passing the message as input to the attack invariant formula $Inv(m, i)$, whose task is to establish whether an attack is actually ongoing or not (the invariant is computed using the labeled messages in D_G respecting the temporal constraints). If $Inv(m, i) = 0$, then either an attack is not ongoing or a false negative has just happened (i.e., the defense mechanism is partial); thus, the guardian goes to the forward state ϕ, which will let the message go, and subsequently goes back without checking any condition to the initial state δ. Instead, if $Inv(m, i) = 1$ either an attack is ongoing or a false positive has just happened, independently of the used defense mechanism; thus, the guardian moves to interference state ρ to carry out the appropriate countermeasures and subsequently goes back, without checking any condition, to the initial state.

As the Δ_{Id} is needed in order to detect the messages that belong to the protocol $\mathcal{P}$, we envision Δ_C to be useful in the case of protocols with a large number of messages in order to lighten the computation load of $Inv(m, i)$, i.e., we compute $Inv(m, i)$ on a subset of the protocol messages:

$$Critical \subseteq \mathcal{P}_{labeled} \subseteq Messages$$

where $Messages$ are all the messages saved in the dataset by a spy-filter, $\mathcal{P}_{labeled}$ are the messages that Δ_{Id} labeled as part of the protocol $\mathcal{P}$ and $Critical$ are the messages that Δ_C believes may be used to attack $\mathcal{P}$.

3.3 Topological Advantage

To defend protocols against attacks, a guardian should be "near" one of the agents involved in the protocol executions; otherwise the guardian could be useless: if he does not see (and thus cannot control) messages belonging to the protocol in transit from these agents, then he cannot carry out the interference/defense.

Definition 2 (Topological Advantage). *Let $X \in$ Agents be the agent that the guardian $G \in$ BenignDishonest is defending in a particular protocol (with set Messages of messages), and $Y \in$ Agents the other agent. We say that G is in* topological advantage *with respect to the attacker E if*

$\forall m \in$ *Messages.* $\exists i \in \mathbb{N}.$

$\quad G \in canSee(<X, m, Y>, i)) \quad \lor \quad G \in canSee(<Y, m, X>, i)) \quad \lor$
$\quad G \in canSee(<E(X), m, Y>, i)) \quad \lor \quad G \in canSee(<Y, m, E(X)>, i))$

Definition 2 states that for a guardian to be in topological advantage, he must be collocated over the network in one of the configurations of Fig. 2 so that he can spy (and eventually modify) all the transiting messages to and/or from the agent that he is defending, even in the case that they are forged.

In order to define what a defense mechanism is, we have to formalize how an attack can be formalized based on a parametric function that the attacker computes during his execution.

Let $E \in Dishonest$, $X \in Honest$, s be the number of steps composing the attack trace, m_s the message spied over the network or present in the attacker dataset D_E at step s, $Func = \{Erase, Injection, Duplicate, \dots\}$ a set of functionalities that E can use on the messages. Note that the names of the functionalities quite intuitively denote their meaning; not all of the functionalities are used in this paper and many more could be defined. The functionalities in $Func$ have domain in the messages belonging to a given protocol, whereas the codomain is defined as the union of all the possible transformations of the messages in the domain that give (i) messages "acceptable" by the protocol (i.e., that can be sent/received by the protocol's agents) or (ii) an empty message. The codomain is thus a set of messages. We use $func_s$ to denote a functionality in $Func$ used at step s.

Definition 3 (Attack Function). *The attack function $f(m, s)$ selects a functionality $func_s$ to be used on the message m at step s and returns the result of the $func_s$ with argument m ($func_s(m)$).*

As a concrete example, the attack function of the attack in Table 2 is reported in Table 4.

Of course, more complex attack functions could (and sometimes even should) be defined, especially for more complex protocols. Since the attack function is but one parameter, we believe that our definitions and results are general enough and can be quite easily adapted to such more complex functions.

Having formalized how an attack can be seen as a parametric function, we can also assume the existence of an inverse function $f^{-1}(m, s)$ of the attack function (i.e., the function that from a message m such that $m = f(m', s)$, and a step s, computes m'). In this paper, we will not discuss how to formalize the inverse attack function; we leave a definition for future work and for now assume that, during the implementation of the framework, a security analyst can take care of this matter.

Table 4. Example of attack function for a parallel session attack against the ISO-SC 27 protocol.

s	m	$func_s$	$f(s,m)$
1	N_A	Erase	$\emptyset$
2	N_A	Injection	N_A
3	$\{\!\mid N_A, N_A' \mid\!\}_{K_{AB}}$	Erase	$\emptyset$
4	$\{\!\mid N_A, N_A' \mid\!\}_{K_{AB}}$	Injection	$\{\!\mid N_A, N_A' \mid\!\}_{K_{AB}}$
5	N_A'	Erase	$\emptyset$
6	N_A'	Injection	N_A'

Definition 4 (Defense Mechanism). *Let $X \in Agents$ be the agent that the guardian $G \in BenignDishonest$ is defending in a particular protocol (with set Critical of critical messages), let $E \in Dishonest$ be the attacker, and s be the number of steps composing E's attack trace. We say that G is a* defense mechanism *if he knows E's attack function $f(m, s)$ and can compute the inverse function $f^{-1}(m, s)$ in order to enforce the following:*

$$\nexists m \in Critical. \, \forall i \in \mathbb{N}. \, \exists p, j \in \mathbb{N}. \, j > i \, \wedge \, 1 \leq p \leq s \, \wedge$$
$$m \in D_{net}^i \, \wedge f^{-1}(f(m,p),p) = m \, \wedge$$
$$(G \notin canSee(<E, f(m,s), X>, j)) \vee G \notin canSee(<E(Y), f(m,s), X>, j)))$$

If G can compute the inverse attack function, then G has knowledge of the possible attacks against the protocol carried out through the attack function and can detect the critical messages even if the attacker modifies/deletes them.

Thus, we can state the following theorem (which can be quite straightforwardly generalized to multiple attackers):

Theorem 1. *A guardian $G \in BenignDishonest$ is a defense mechanism for an agent $X \in Agents$ in a protocol $\mathcal{P}$, if he is in topological advantage with respect to an attacker $E \in Dishonest$ who is attacking X in $\mathcal{P}$.*

As a proof sketch, let $X \in Agents$ be the agent that G is defending, $Y \in Agents$, $E \in Dishonest$ with attack function $f(m, p)$, $m \in Critical$, f^{-1} known to G, G in topological advantage with respect to the attacker E, s the number of steps composing E's attack trace, and $1 \leq p \leq s$. Then, since $f(m, p) \in Messages$, we have that: $\exists i \in \mathbb{N}. \, G \in canSee(<X, f(m,p), Y>, i)) \vee G \in canSee(<Y, f(m,p), X>, i)) \vee G \in canSee(<E(X), f(m,p), Y>, i)) \vee G \in canSee(<Y, f(m,p), E(X)>, i))$. In order to have a defense mechanism, we have to enforce the following: $\nexists m \in Critical. \, \forall i \in \mathbb{N}. \, \exists p, j \in \mathbb{N}. \, j > i \, \wedge \, 1 \leq p \leq s \, \wedge \, m \in D_{net}^i \, \wedge \, G \notin canSee(<E, f(m,p), X>, j)) \wedge f^{-1}(f(m,p),p) = m$. Since $f(m, p) \in Critical \subseteq Messages$, only $f^{-1}(f(m,p),p) = m$ must be enforced, but it is known to G by assumption.

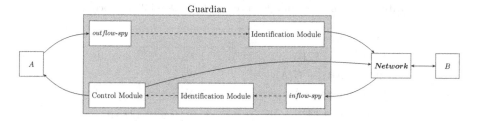

Fig. 4. Guardian configuration for the ISO-SC 27 protocol. With a dashed arrow we describe the fact that the execution flow (not the spied message) continues with the next module.

4   Case Studies

4.1   The ISO-SC 27 Protocol

Even though the ISO-SC 27 protocol is subject to the parallel sessions attack shown in Table 2, we can defend it by means of a guardian G. Since the victim is A, for the defense to be possible, it is necessary that G is in the configuration in Fig. 2a, i.e., between A and the rest of the network agents, so that he can identify/control all of A's incoming and outgoing messages (by Definition 2, in this configuration the guardian is in topological advantage), whereas in the configuration in Fig. 2b he can be completely excluded by an attacker E. In the following, we give as an example the successful case and a brief explanation for the unsuccessful one.

In order to defend the ISO-SC 27 protocol, we have set up the guardian G with the two spy-filters shown in Fig. 4: an outflow-spy filter in order to record in his dataset D_G all of A's outgoing messages, and an inflow-spy filter in order to record and control A's incoming messages.

Even if G does not know the symmetric key K_{AB}, he can become aware that the protocol has been attacked when he spies via the *inflow-spy* filter a message of the same form of the message (1) in Table 2 (i.e., N_A; the guardian knows that the attacker will reply the first message because he knows the attack function of Definition 3) between those that have previously been identified as such: if an attack is ongoing, then the message that has been identified by the Control Module as critical (i.e., is one of the first messages of the protocol) "has already been seen" by G. We formalize this concept by means of the invariant $Inv(m, i)$:

$$\exists m' \in D_G^{i-1}.\ \Delta_C(m) = 1\ \wedge\ \Delta_C(m') = 1\ \wedge\ m = m'.$$

That is, if an attack is ongoing and m is the message spied by guardian's inflow-spy filter, labeled by the Identification Module, and in the Control Module the distinguisher Δ_C believes that it is critical, then the guardian's dataset D_G^i must contain another message m' seen before such that $m = m'$ (the implementation of D_G must be done with respect to the temporal constraints of the invariant Inv, but in this paper we do not discuss the implementation details). Since the

Table 5. Guardian's interference for the ISO-SC 27 protocol.

Interference		
(1.1)	A → E(B)	: N_A
(2.1)	E(B) → G(A)	: N_A
(2.1$_1$)	G(B) → A	: N_{fake}
(2.2)	A → E(B)	: $\{\!\|N_{fake}, N'_A\|\!\}_{K_{AB}}$
(1.2)	E(B) → A	: $\{\!\|N_{fake}, N'_A\|\!\}_{K_{AB}}$
(2.2)	G raises A's flag for abort	

guardian knows that the attacker can use a replay attack, by Definition 4, he has to define the inverse of the attack function as the identity function (the use of the identity function is also reflected in the definition of the invariant).[9]
   Let us assume, following [14,15], that each honest agent defended by the guardian G has a set of flags that G can modify in order to make the agent he is defending abort the protocol. Once he has detected such an ongoing attack, G can defend it carrying out the interference. He modifies the content (i.e., he alters the nonce N_A) of the first message in the parallel session (see Table 5 for the complete execution trace, and Table 6 for the corresponding dataset evolution). At this point, the guardian already knows that an attack is ongoing, but we choose to finish the two sessions of the protocol (G changes A's "abort flag" only at the end) in order to show that we can also deliver false information to the attacker and that the Control Module (shown in Table 6) checks the invariant only once since the replayed message in (1.2) is not seen as critical (i.e., it has not the form of the first message). More specifically, Table 5 shows the interference attack that G can use against the attacker E, and Table 6 the evolution of the dataset and the inference during the protocol execution.
   To measure the defense mechanism implemented by the guardian for the parallel sessions attack against the ISO-SC 27 protocol, we consider false positives and negatives.

False positives: False positives are possible if, after A completes a protocol run as initiator, B restarts the protocol with A (i.e., they change roles) using (in the first message) a nonce N_B that is already contained in G's dataset. If N_B is represented through a k-bit length string, then the probability of this event is equal to the probability of guessing a nonce amongst those belonging to D_G^i (i.e., G's dataset after i actions):

$$Pr[N_B \in_R \{0,1\}^k, N_B \in D_G^i] = \frac{|D_G^i|}{2^k}$$

So, this probability is negligible if k is large enough (e.g., $k = 1024$).

---

[9] Formally, for the ISO-SC 27 we have: $f^{-1}(f(N_A, 2), 2) = f^{-1}(N_A, 2) = N_A$ (where $s = 2$ refers to message (2) in Table 4 or, equivalently, message (1.2) in Table 2).

Table 6. Dataset evolution and inference for the ISO-SC 27 protocol. $\{(x.y)\}$ refers to the message sent in step $(x.y)$ (we omit the repeated messages) and to the configuration in Fig. 2a.

i	Protocol message	D_G^i	Identification module	Control module	
			$\Delta_{Id}(m)$	$\Delta_C(m)$	$Inv(m, i)$
0	–	$\{\ \}$	–	–	–
1	$(1.1)\ A \rightarrow E(B) : N_A$	$\{(1.1)\}$	1	–	–
2	$(2.1)\ E(B) \rightarrow G(A) : N_A$	$\{(1.1)\}$	1	1	1
3	$(2.1_1)\ G(A) \rightarrow A : N_{fake}$	$\{(1.1),(2.1_1)\}$	–	–	–
4	$(2.2)\ A \rightarrow E(B) : \{\!|N_{fake}, N_A'|\!\}_{K_{AB}}$	$\{(1.1),(2.1_1),(2.2)\}$	1	–	–
5	$(1.2)\ E(B) \rightarrow A : \{\!|N_{fake}, N_A'|\!\}_{K_{AB}}$	$\{(1.1),(2.1_1),(2.2)\}$	1	0	–
6	$(2.2)\ G$ raises A's flag for abort	–	–	–	–

False negatives: False negatives are not possible, since not knowing K_{AB} the only way to attack the protocol with the classical attack (Table 2) is to reflect A's messages in a parallel session; but if this situation happens, then the guardian has already seen the message that is coming back to A, and thus he can detect (and afterwards defeat) the ongoing attack. Since G does not admit false negatives for this scenario, G is a total defense mechanism when he is in a topological advantage with respect to his competitor(s), i.e., when he is defending A.

Now that we have seen the successful case, let us focus on the configuration of Fig. 2b. In this configuration, a guardian would not work because B's participation is not mandatory to attack the protocol and thus E can easily exclude G from the run of the protocol; thus there are no false positives and there are only false negatives. In this case, the presence of the resilient channels does not help because G is completely excluded from seeing the execution of the protocol and the attack.

Summing up the analysis of the case study, we have seen how a flawed protocol as the ISO-SC 27 can be defended through the use of a guardian. The first step of our analysis was the attack typically found via model checking and the classical approach. We used the classical attack in order to select the critical messages that the attacker exploits during the attacks. Knowing the critical messages allows us to formalize the invariant, which is also used in order to set up filters and module configurations in the guardian architecture. Finally, we have investigated the different outcomes with respect to the position of the guardian in the network topology.

4.2   Other Protocols

We have applied our approach also to a number of other security protocols. Table 7 summarizes our results, while a more detailed analysis can be found in [18]. For each protocol, in the table we report if the defense is total or partial, which agent is being defended, and the topologies that permit the defense.

Table 7. Other case studies. See [6,8] for details on the protocols.

Protocol	Defense	Agent defended	Topology
ISO-SC 27	Total	A	Fig. 2a
SRA3P	Total	A	Fig. 2a
Andrew Secure RPC	Partial	A	Fig. 2a
Otway-Rees	Total	A	Fig. 2c, e
Encrypted Key Exchange	Total	A	Fig. 2a
SPLICE/AS	Total	A	Fig. 2c
Modified BME	Partial	B	Fig. 2d

In Table 7, we show only the successful results for each protocol in the given task (i.e., defending one of the agents for the corresponding protocol). The outcome of the analysis of these 7 (4 two-agent and 3 three-agent) protocols is quite promising since we have a total defense in 5 cases and a partial defense in the remaining 2 cases.

5   Conclusions and Future Work

Discovering an attack to an already largely deployed security protocol remains nowadays a difficult problem. Typically, the discovery of an attack forces us to make a difficult decision: either we accept to use the protocol even when knowing that every execution can potentially be attacked and thus the security properties for which the protocol has been designed can be compromised at any time, or we do not (generating consequently, kind of a self denial of service). Both choices are extreme, and typically the classical (and conservative) mindset prefers to "dismiss" the protocol and hurry up with the deployment of a new version hoping to be faster than those who are attempting to exploit the discovered flaw.

The above results contribute to showing, we believe, that non-collaborative attacker scenarios, through the introduction of a guardian, provide the basis for the active defense of flawed security protocols rather than discarding them when the attack is found. Regarding the concrete applicability of this approach to security protocols, on one hand, we can use our previous work [14,15] as an approach for discovering how two attackers interact in non-collaborative scenarios and what type of interference the guardian can use, and, on the other hand, in this paper we have given the means to understand how to exploit the interference from a topological point of view, thus bringing the guardian close to real implementation, which is the main objective of our current work.

We are also working on a number of relevant issues, such as how the content of, and the meaning that the honest agents assign to, critical messages may have an influence on the defense mechanisms enforced by the guardian, or such as how to define general attack functions and their inverses. We are also investigating criteria that will allow us to reason about the minimal and/or optimal configurations for protocol defenses. For instance, to show that no further configurations are possible (by showing how m possible configurations can be reduced to $n < m$ base ones, such as the 6 we considered here) or that the considered configuration is optimal for the desired defense (and thus for the implementation of the guardian). It seems obvious, for example, that Fig. 2a is the optimal configuration for defending the initiator A in the majority of two-agent protocols. Similarly, our intuition is that a guardian (with an appropriate defense for a particular protocol) put in configuration of Fig. 2e is also valid for the configuration of Fig. 2c (and similarly for configuration of Fig. 2f with respect to configuration of Fig. 2d).

We envision the some general, protocol-independent results might be possible but that ultimately both the notion (and agents' understanding) of critical message and that of defense configuration will depend on the details of the protocol under consideration and of the attack to be defended against. Our hope is thus to obtain parametric results that can then be instantiated with the fine details of each protocol and attack.

References

1. Armando, A., Arsac, W., Avanesov, T., Barletta, M., Calvi, A., Cappai, A., Carbone, R., Chevalier, Y., Compagna, L., Cuéllar, J., Erzse, G., Frau, S., Minea, M., Mödersheim, S., von Oheimb, D., Pellegrino, G., Ponta, S.E., Rocchetto, M., Rusinowitch, M., Torabi Dashti, M., Turuani, M., Viganò, L.: The AVANTSSAR platform for the automated validation of trust and security of service-oriented architectures. In: Flanagan, C., König, B. (eds.) TACAS 2012. LNCS, vol. 7214, pp. 267–282. Springer, Heidelberg (2012)
2. Basin, D., Caleiro, C., Ramos, J., Viganò, L.: Distributed temporal logic for the analysis of security protocol models. Theor. Comput. Sci. **412**(31), 4007–4043 (2011)
3. Bella, G.: A protocol's life after attacks. In: Christianson, B., Crispo, B., Malcolm, J.A., Roe, M. (eds.) Security Protocols 2003. LNCS, vol. 3364, pp. 11–18. Springer, Heidelberg (2005)
4. Bella, G., Bistarelli, S., Massacci, F.: Retaliation against protocol attacks. J. Inf. Assur. Secur. **3**, 313–325 (2008)
5. Blanchet, B.: An efficient cryptographic protocol verifier based on Prolog rules. In: Proceedings of CSF'01, pp. 82–96. IEEE CS Press (2001)
6. Boyd, C., Mathuria, A.: Protocols for Authentication and Key Establishment. Information Security and Cryptography. Springer, Heidelberg (2003)
7. Ciobâcă, S., Cortier, V.: Protocol composition for arbitrary primitives. In: Proceedings of CSF'10. IEEE CS Press (2010)
8. Clark, J., Jacob, J.: A survey of authentication protocol literature: Version 1.0 (1997)
9. Conti, M., Dragoni, N., Gottardo, S.: MITHYS: mind the hand you shake - protecting mobile devices from SSL usage vulnerabilities. In: Accorsi, R., Ranise, S. (eds.) STM 2013. LNCS, vol. 8203, pp. 65–81. Springer, Heidelberg (2013)
10. Cortier, V., Delaune, S.: Safely composing security protocols. Form. Methods Syst. Des. **34**(1), 1–36 (2009)

11. Cremers, C.J.F.: The Scyther tool: verification, falsification, and analysis of security protocols. In: Gupta, A., Malik, S. (eds.) CAV 2008. LNCS, vol. 5123, pp. 414–418. Springer, Heidelberg (2008)
12. Dolev, D., Yao, A.: On the security of public key protocols. IEEE Trans. Inf. Theor. **29**(2), 198–208 (1983)
13. Escobar, S., Meadows, C., Meseguer, J.: Maude-NPA: cryptographic protocol analysis modulo equational properties. In: Aldini, A., Barthe, G., Gorrieri, R. (eds.) FOSAD 2007/2008/2009. LNCS, vol. 5705, pp. 1–50. Springer, Heidelberg (2007)
14. Fiazza, M.-C., Peroli, M., Viganò, L.: Attack interference: a path to defending security protocols. In: Obaidat, M.S., Sevillano, J.L., Filipe, J. (eds.) ICETE 2011. CCIS, vol. 314, pp. 296–314. Springer, Heidelberg (2012)
15. Fiazza, M.-C., Peroli, M., Vigano, L.: An environmental paradigm for defending security protocols. In: 2012 International Conference on Collaboration Technologies and Systems (CTS), May 2012, pp. 427–438 (2012)
16. ISO: ISO-IEC JTC1.27.02.2(20.03.1.2) entity authentication using symmetric techniques. International Organization for Standardization (ISO) (1990)
17. Mödersheim, S., Viganò, L.: Secure pseudonymous channels. In: Backes, M., Ning, P. (eds.) ESORICS 2009. LNCS, vol. 5789, pp. 337–354. Springer, Heidelberg (2009)
18. Peroli, M., Viganò, L., Zavatteri, M.: Non-collaborative Attackers and How and Where to Defend Flawed Security Protocols (Extended Version) (2014). http://arxiv.org/abs/1405.6912
19. Ryan, P., Schneider, S., Goldsmith, M., Lowe, G., Roscoe, B.: Modelling and Analysis of Security Protocols. Addison Wesley, Reading (2000)
20. Viganò, L.: Automated security protocol analysis with the AVISPA tool. Electron. Notes Theor. Comput. Sci. **155**, 61–86 (2006)

Non-collaborative Attackers and How and Where to Defend Vulnerable Security Protocols (Transcript of Discussion)

Luca Viganò[✉]

King's College London, London, UK
luca.vigano@kcl.ac.uk

Welcome back from the coffee break. Let me start by saying that this is joint work with two PhD students of mine at the University of Verona: Michele Peroli, who is in the audience, and Matteo Zavatteri. In the meantime, I have left Verona and am now at King's College London, but we are still working together of course. I will also mention some of the previous work that we did with Maria-Camilla Fiazza, who is working at the University of Verona. In fact, she is working in robotics. I don't know if I will have time to mention the collaboration that we did in detail at the end of the talk, but I would be most happy to tell you about how we can use at least some of the results that are common to robotics also for security and, in particular, how we can start reasoning about a new paradigm.

Let me tell you about the origins of this work. A few years ago, Michele was working on his Masters thesis and we started reasoning about the fact that we had built a protocol analyser—actually I contributed to building a couple of them—and of course what you typically do with a protocol analyser is you take a protocol, you formalise it (maybe with ProVerif as you heard before, or with AVANTSSAR or with NPATRL, there are dozens of protocol analysis tools) and if you find an attack it's very good news for you because probably you also have a couple of publications in the pipeline, and maybe also some good "scalps under your belt", but still it is a problem for the community. Because what is typically going to happen if you find an attack on a protocol which is widely deployed? For instance, in a project that I led a few years ago, called AVANTSSAR, we found an attack on the implementation of single sign-on deployed by Google: they were selling it for good money but the protocol was attackable with your standard man-in-the-middle attack. We did the responsible thing and notified Google, they asked us for some time before we published the result so that they could fix the protocol, we actually gave them the fix, and after three months they deployed a new version, and asked the users to upgrade to this new version. Fair enough, that's how it works.

But what would happen if somebody found now an attack against TLS[1], or Kerberos, or IPSEC? Typically what you do in such a case is you take the flawed protocol and you throw it away, and you hope that you have a new version ready, and that in the meantime nobody exploits the vulnerability. But what we

---

[1] N.B.: this talk was given before the announcement of the Heartbleed Bug.

© Springer International Publishing Switzerland 2014
B. Christianson et al. (Eds.): Security Protocols 2014, LNCS 8809, pp. 91–99, 2014.
DOI: 10.1007/978-3-319-12400-1_10

started reasoning about is: can we actually "survive" in the meantime? Can we find a way to reason about defending protocols which are vulnerable? Rather than throwing them away (which we will do at some point as of course we don't want flawed protocols to be used indefinitely), can we find a way to somehow keep the flawed protocol working, and buy ourselves time to come up with a new, corrected version? We soon realised that in order to do that, we actually need to change the way we typically think about security protocol analysis. Let me anticipate the idea that I will try to convey: what we need to do is to counter our usual super villains, in particular the Dolev-Yao attacker, who can do everything, well almost everything, by introducing some sort of super hero. If there is a Joker, can we somehow build the corresponding Batman? If you are more inclined to the classics: if there is Lucifer, do we have the Archangel Michael to fight against him? In other words, can we find a way to turn somehow defeat into victory?

In order to do that, we started with what we knew. Take the standard Dolev-Yao attacker, who is very powerful; one can even extend it to reason about cryptography, but I'm not going to talk about cryptography as it is not interesting for the kind of analysis that we're doing. The typical model here is one that tells you that the attacker is the network itself, so you can have all the communication go through the network, and this is actually how some of the protocol analysis tools work: they just model the attacker, they don't care about all the other agents because the attacker is the one handling all the communication in the first place. Actually, the theme of the workshop, "collaborative attackers", at least for the Dolev-Yao attacker, doesn't really make sense, because there are theorems which tell us that if we have n Dolev-Yao attackers that collaborate with each other, then we don't actually need them, one attacker is enough. As a metaphor, you could think about one of the proofs of the existence of God (which is related to this theorem, even though the provers of the theorem didn't know), which relies on the fact that if God is everywhere then there is no space for another god. This is a bad god, the Dolev-Yao attacker, but it's a god who is so powerful that you can just focus on only one.

We asked ourselves the following question: what if instead of collaborating these n Dolev-Yao attackers were actually trying to compete against each other? What happens if they don't collaborate? What happens if we have other attackers out there who are aggressive and do not collaborate with each other? Of course, the argument about the filled-up space doesn't hold anymore, but that was just a metaphor for the theorem, and indeed we had to change our mental model and come up with a new paradigm. We moved from the standard attacker model in which we have A and B, who are honest agents communicating with each other, and the attacker Eve controlling the net, to a model where actually the net is a much more complex thing than the channel or the network controlled by one attacker, because there are different attackers and they are not going to collaborate. So, if you come from the security protocol community, forget the Dolev-Yao attacker model, or actually forget the way you have been thinking about it. The attacker is not the network, the attacker is in the network and there could be other ones.

We formalised all this in our paper, which refers also to a number of previous works. Let me now "conclude" my talk. I have a lot of other slides that I will present, but I will give you the main message now, by saying that actually we found out that if you have two attackers who are non-collaborating they can interfere with each other. We end up with a situation similar to the cold war stalemate, closely related to Nash equilibrium and game theory: if you attack, the risk that somebody else is interfering is so high that it might be worth not to attack in the first place. This is a cool situation if you're trying to save a flawed protocol, because if you can bring the system (or network) to such a point where attacking the protocol does not give the attacker the guarantee of success, then he might think twice before attacking. Moreover, we found out that non-collaborating attackers may not only interfere with each other, but also end up attacking each other. This brings us back to my initial question: if there is an attacker like the Joker, can we build a Batman? We have thus been working on identifying the conditions under which we can build a benign attacker, which we call "guardian", which we can insert into the network to defend a flawed protocol.

Hence, the work that we have been doing and that we are currently still doing, is: given an attack to a protocol can we learn, from the protocol and the attack, how to create a guardian agent that we can put in the network, who will not always of course, but in many cases, ensure that it is not worth for the attacker to attack? Actually, we even have examples (e.g., when carrying out a protocol with a bank) where you can gain profit if the attacker attacks, so you can retaliate and actually gain a lot by counter-attacking. So let me, just for the fun of it, play a video: we are Anne Darrow from the movie King Kong. Anne is the character who is actually trapped on Skull Island, and this, the dinosaur, is the bad attacker. Anne is in trouble because the attacker is much bigger and much stronger, but behold King Kong, a former attacker who has now turned benign and who will fight against the dinosaur and thus defend the honest agent, in this case Anne Darrow, and actually fight against the real attacker. So, Anne can just kick back, relax and enjoy the fight.

This "concludes" my talk: I told you the message, please read the papers, talk to us, we'll be very happy to tell you a bit more. But I'm going to use at least five or so minutes to tell you a bit more about the details, because I'm sure that many of you bought the idea, but there is a fundamental problem: there is a fundamental flaw in what I told you from the beginning, namely, if there is an attacker, can we build a benign guardian agent? But what is this attacker that we're dealing with, what is the Dolev-Yao attacker? It's a fictitious character, it doesn't exist, it's the worst case analysis, there is no attacker online who is able to be the network.

Frank Stajano: The NSA.

Reply: The NSA, true. Then we can talk about Snowden being King Kong and so on. But that's OK, because that's the kind of analysis that we want to do, right? If we validate (where with validate I mean both model checking and testing) our protocol against a Dolev-Yao attacker and we find no attack then we are sure that our protocol is correct, even in the case of real attacks. However, the guardian only makes sense if we can really build it, and that is the difficulty, how can we build a guardian for a protocol? This of course is a very big and difficult research question because, first of all, it will depend on the protocol. Because it is impossible to think of building a guardian who is able to guard, or to defend all protocols. Second, it will depend on the particular attack against that protocol, because there are protocols which have multiple flaws, can be attacked in different ways, and you should tell your guardian what to look for. Third, it will depend on where you actually put the guardian. You cannot put it everywhere, you cannot put it on every laptop, on every device involved in the communication, but you have to put it in a critical point of the network. Hence, there are a lot of research questions, and these start from the fact that we also need to change our mental model about the agents. We cannot use what we used to use, namely that an honest agent is basically an idiot who is just carrying out the protocol as it has been specified, but you need to put more intelligence into honest agents.

Frank Stajano: I like the story, and I would like you to clarify some discrepancies that I can't figure out for myself. At the start you say, OK, you have an attacker, then what if you have several attackers who fought each other? Then you say, now we have an attacker, and we are going to be build a guardian angel who's going to fight the attacker. Now, why would this count as another attacker? You are not going to build something that is going to also attack the protocol are you?

Reply: No, I'm going to build something that is going to attack the protocol in order to defend it. I will give you a brief example in a second.

Frank Stajano: What if it doesn't encounter the other attacker, and it turns out it only attacks the protocol? If you are building something that is attacking the protocol too, how about if the real attacker doesn't turn up today and your thing attacks the protocol? Then you'd feel a bit stupid, right?

Reply: Well, first of all, there is not a 100 % guarantee that you can defend against all possible attacks. Second, the guardian is built to know the attack but not to carry it out (he will not attack the protocol) but rather to thwart it. You have to trust somebody (typically you start from your mother, you trust your mother by definition, although bad surprises can happen), but what we are trying to do is to make the guardian clever and only react to the messages of the attacker, not to the messages of the honest agents, so not give him the possibility to actually attack the protocol. He will, and actually needs to know the attack, of course.

Simon Foley: In that case doesn't the guardian angel then become part of the protocol itself?

Reply: Exactly. It becomes actually part of some of the honest agents executing the protocol, and that's the whole trick to make it implementable, and this is where we don't have a full answer yet. We are working on it, we have some topologies, but this is where the difficulty lies.

Simon Foley: If you were to think of this as a separation of concerns; you're saying, I have my security concern, I have my functionality concern, the protocols and the functionality, but the guardian angel has disappeared.

Reply: Yes and no. It will become clearer later, I hope.

Michael Roe: Is using a man-in-the-middle attach an example of this? You can imagine a security protocol that suffers from a man-in-the-middle attack, but there you use that because you create your own man-in-the-middle, and it goes in and it does some additional change.

Reply: Yes, that would be one of the topologies that you could consider. In fact, in the paper we reference a number of interesting topologies we have been studying (without being complete for now). But let me try to wrap up and tell you a bit more what we have been doing. First of all, as I said, we need to change the agents, but we also need to change the way the network works, because the network is now not going to be necessarily a passive thing, but it will have to coordinate how the messages are being distributed. We're not giving the network any decisional power in the sense that the network will prevent some attacks, or do something else in terms of security, but it will simply need to make sure that the messages are being transmitted between the honest agents and the attackers.

Let me give you one example, which is the BME protocol. I'm not going to describe it in detail and it doesn't really matter; BME stands for Boyd-Mathuria Example, it's one of the examples from their book, and it's a flawed protocol by design, which suffers from a man-in-the-middle attack where the attacker E can jump in-between A and a server and manipulate the way in which the keys are distributed. What we found out is that if we study this and we consider two attackers there are six possibilities, depending on what they know about the other. They know each other as honest, they know each other as attackers, they are unaware of each other, one knows the other one is honest, dishonest or is unsure about it. And in some cases, especially in the case that E_2 knows that E_1 is dishonest, E_2 can intervene: in fact, this partially answers the question before, E_2 may jump into the attack, intercept some of the messages of E_1, and continue the protocol, in such a way that E_1's attack is blocked. There are other situations where E_2 can actually provoke E_1, similar to what is done with honeypots: you can even have situations where you run a flawed protocol and you know that it is flawed in order to counter-attack, and so on. We have been studying all these different possibilities and the result is a table like the one shown on the slide and in the paper, where in some cases we can indeed defend, and in some other cases we don't know, and in some other cases it might work but it depends on a number of factors. We have published some results but in fact our work is still at the beginning because there is a lot to be done in general to make sure that it actually is implementable. We have been investigating how can we come up with something that is concretely realisable, because, as I said before, the Dolev-Yao attacker lives in a fantasy world, and it's OK that he doesn't exist, but the guardian (and this has been for us one of the main problems in having this new paradigm accepted by the protocol analysis community judging from the reviews that we got) must live in the real world, he must be implemented, because what good would it be to know that on paper there is a defence? It doesn't help you, you have to realise it, at least partially.

We realised that we have similar examples in security, although they are not typically used in the security protocol community. For instance, a proxy works in a similar way. The way firewalls work is also similar, they must control some of the packets circulating, and they must react according to the packets, the messages that are being sent.

Let me open now a parenthesis and tell you that another one of the problems that we have is that traditionally our work comes from the symbolic analysis community, and of course we need to go down the levels of the TCP/IP stack and get closer to the real implementation and to the real packets being sent in order to implement the attacker in the first place, so we're also trying to do the mapping as well. There are other similar situations, for instance, in the injection of benignware in the presence of malware. There is a lot of work on mitigating viruses, digital viruses but also physical viruses, human viruses, by injecting another kind of virus that fights it. That's the way our white blood cells work, in a sense, and in fact you can even die of an excess of white blood cells coming back to your question, so it's a difficult system to control sometimes.

Since the guardian cannot control the whole network, we have been carrying out a topological study that, given A, B and the attacker E, identifies where we should put the guardian. There are different topologies we can consider, some of them can bring some results, some of them don't, of course, it will depend on the protocol and on the kind of attack. What we are also working on is trying to generalise this and come up with strategies, which are as little dependent on the protocol and the attack as possible. So, for instance, it would be useful to come up with a guardian that works for man-in-the-middle attacks, whatever the protocol is. I doubt that it can be done in such a general way, but maybe some steps can be achieved.

Another interesting research challenge is communication. Take the first topology on the slide (and in the paper): the communication between the guardian and the agent must be protected, because otherwise E could just try and attack this communication and fool the guardian's work. Hence, we need side channels as additional secure channels. This kind of channel is again not very simple to realise but it exists; that's one of the ideas, for instance, behind two factor authentication and the like, that you introduce an additional channel in the network in order to achieve more security. What we have been doing is to give the guardian a structure of control between the communication of an honest agent and the network. Hence, as Simon was saying, we are enhancing the protocol, in this case enhancing the honest agents with additional information that can help them defend against protocol attacks.

To conclude, the interesting thing for me, and quite surprising, is that a lot of similar work has been done in a completely different context, with a completely different aim, in the robotics community. Basically, in our approach we are starting from attack traces that bring us from the start of the protocol to an attack state, to a more complex environment where there are states where we are not really sure what is going to happen at the end, whether it is an attack, or a defence, or we don't know, to a much more complex and mature view of the protocol from the point of view of the attacker, because if the guardian is there, there are a lot of other possible things that can happen. This is something that the people in robotics and AI have been working on a lot for controlling robots. Very quickly, without going into the details but just to show the similarities, we do have some results where you can actually exploit controller diagrams from robotics in order to guide the actions, to give intelligence to your agents, and in particular to the guardian, and try to control what is happening. You can indeed try and programme an agent controller for a role of a protocol, a controller for a classical attacker, a controller for a competitive attacker, and you end up with something which is again more complex than what we had before, the network, the agents, the flags which are being raised by the attackers, the decisional processes, but also a planner which is learning from the protocol specification, from the agents, and trying to generate a better controller for the guardian agent in order to react to possible attacks and try to defend.

And with this I think I can conclude by mentioning that we need to study also the economics of the whole thing, because we need to check whether it actually makes sense to defend a flawed protocol if the guardian costs much more than what we're trying to defend. That's all I wanted to say.

Peter Ryan: Just playing devil's advocate for a minute, we all teach our students that the classic mistake is to try and patch a security on afterwards, and this seems like a very elaborate way of doing exactly that.

Bruce Christianson: Most of what we teach our students is like that.

Reply: I agree with both of you, in the sense that, yes, it is a very elaborate way to patch a flawed system, but it also starts from the observation that this is how most of the real world actually works. I could have made comparisons with upgrades to your operating system, also Apple a lot but typically Microsoft, because some weird bug has been found; what you do automatically is you click yes, yes, yes, and you hope that they're doing the correct thing, and that it is preventing somehow possible attacks. But yes, I would agree, it's a patch, but this is what we're aiming for, we're not aiming for it to be "the" solution, we're aiming to buy some time until we have the correct solution.

Peter Ryan: Just playing Devil's advocate.

Reply: Sure, but it's a very good point, because also for us it has been an important question, to understand whether we should invest our time on this or not. I mean, it's fun, it's a challenge, it's a pet project, but in the end you also want to get concrete results if possible.

Simon Foley: Let me play devil's advocate as well. It took a while for us to realize that we can't build security into just security kernels but we also have to consider security within applications. Would I be right in saying that your guardian angel, in some sense, is like the network equivalent of a security kernel? In a sense it's enforcing security properties in the same way a conventional security kernel enforces a security property?

Reply: Yes, it's a good metaphor I would say. However, I would say another thing: We're not advocating that you should not do security by design, I mean, I would very much like protocol designers to think about the security from the start, and try to make sure that the protocol is not flawed, however, experience tells us that this is not the case. For instance, we found the attack on Google I mentioned before and we are quite sure that actually the implementation by Microsoft had exactly the same attack, and it is the Needham-Schroeder public key man-in-the-middle attack just rewritten for that protocol. That is on the one hand fascinating for us, because it means there is still a future for security protocol analysis if they do such trivial mistakes, but it is a real problem when it comes to actually selling these things and implementing them. As I said, I think it will be very interesting to come up with a clearer answer, with strategies, but also with the cost benefit analysis, to really understand whether it makes sense, and what it really buys you, and what you can do actually with it in the first place.

Daniel Thomas: How does the guardian that you're using here compare with the kind of tactics you've already used for defending TLS against various attacks like when we found a problem with CBC and so on, and made changes? Are these changes you would add, implementation changes rather than protocol changes? How does that compare, is it the same idea?

Reply: I would say no, in the sense what we're doing here is we're not changing the core of the protocol, we are enveloping, if you can say that, we are putting another layer on top of it. The protocol remains the same so the implementation of the protocol remains the same, you just change the way the agents interact with the network.

Virgil Gligor: You put a wrapper.

Reply: Yes, a wrapper.

Joan Feigenbaum: Encapsulating.

Reply: Thanks! Wrapper or encapsulation, these are the two words I was looking for. We are encapsulating the protocol, we are wrapping it up in such a way that you don't need to change the implementation, you will change it when you have a correct one, but in the meantime you can still use it plus this extra bit.

Virgil Gligor: So it's like Cristo, you put a wrapper.

Reply: We are, yes.

Frank Stajano: Please take one last question.

Alastair Beresford: If it's not going to be a change like a patch to the actual implementation, where is this guardian going to live, I presume he's going to sit on some machine somewhere?

Reply: Yes, this is what I meant, perhaps I was a bit too fast. The topological study aims at ensuring that the honest agents A and B will actually go on and carry out the protocol as it is supposed to be, but we're just going to change the way they connect to the network, by means of the guardian.

Alastair Beresford: So, for example, rather than patching the web browser's TLS implementation, instead you ship an update to the operating system which then tweaks some stuff on its way through to the network, is that the kind of thing?

Reply: It could be, yes. We don't have a definitive answer yet, we have to implement the possible topologies, but that could be a way to realise the defence.

Dieter Gollmann: As I understood the latest TCP implementation attacks they rely on observing the behaviour for very specific messages, by specific message length, and then the wrapper would act, the wrapper make sure that a particular message never gets through to the TLS stack.

Reply: Yes, that would be the goal of our approach. For some protocols and some attacks we know how to do it, for other ones we are still investigating how to best proceed.

Dancing with the Adversary:
A Tale of Wimps and Giants

Virgil Gligor[✉]

Carnegie Mellon University, Pittsburgh, PA 15213, USA
gligor@cmu.edu

Abstract. The long-standing requirement that system and network designs must include accurate and complete adversary definitions from inception remains unmet on commodity platforms; e.g., on commodity operating systems, network protocols, and applications. A way to provide such definitions is to (1) partition commodity software into "wimps" (i.e., small software components with rather limited function and high-assurance security properties) and "giants" (i.e., large commodity software systems, with low/no assurance of security); and (2) limit the obligation of defining the adversary to wimps while realistically assuming that the giants are adversary controlled. We provide a structure for accurate and complete adversary definitions that yields basic security properties and metrics for wimps. Then we argue that wimps must collaborate ("dance") with giants, namely compose with adversary code across protection interfaces, and illustrate some of the salient features of the wimp-giant composition. We extend the wimp-giant metaphor to security protocols in networks of humans and computers where compelling services, possibly under the control of an adversary, are offered to unsuspecting users. Although these protocols have safe states whereby a participant can establish temporary beliefs in the adversary's trustworthiness, reasoning about such states requires techniques from other fields, such as behavioral economics, rather than traditional security and cryptography.

1 Introduction

A system without accurate and complete adversary definition cannot possibly be insecure. Without such definitions, (in)security cannot be measured, risks of use cannot be accurately quantified, and recovery from penetration events cannot have lasting value. Conversely, accurate and complete definitions can help deny any attack advantage of an adversary over a system defender. At least in principle, the seemingly inevitable adversary-defender asymmetry can be reduced and secure system operation achieved. Hence, it seems important to design systems and networks that include such definitions from inception. However, this is unlikely to happen for commodity systems: although security has been recognized to be a fundamental problem, it has always been of secondary importance in the design of commodity systems, and it is very likely to remain that way;

© Springer International Publishing Switzerland 2014
B. Christianson et al. (Eds.): Security Protocols 2014, LNCS 8809, pp. 100–115, 2014.
DOI: 10.1007/978-3-319-12400-1_11

viz., the "axioms" of insecurity [6]. Nevertheless, this fact does not remove the obligation to provide accurate and complete adversary definitions. Adding secure components to insecure commodity systems or networks will continue to mandate it.

Although an adversary's attack advantage cannot be eliminated in large, low-assurance commodity software (i.e., for "giants" [6,12]), it can be rendered ineffective for small software components with rather limited function and high-assurance security properties, which are isolated from giants; i.e., for "wimps." However, isolation cannot guarantee wimps' survival in competitive markets, since wimps trade basic system services to achieve small attack surfaces, diminish adversary capabilities, and weaken attack strategies. To survive, secure wimps must use services of, or compose with, adversary-controlled giants.

In this paper, we propose a structure for adversary definitions that is consistent with those found in other areas of security (i.e., cryptographic schemes, or modes). The proposed structure is desirable. It can yield accurate and complete adversary definitions – just as it does in cryptography – and it is easily adapted for different wimp interfaces, ranging from cryptographic schemes, operating systems, application modules, and human protocols. We argue that accurate and complete definitions yield security properties and metrics, which are useful for the design of wimps. Then we explain why wimps must compose (i.e., "dance") with giants thereby illustrating the paradoxical theme of this workshop, namely the collaboration with the adversary. Finally, we extend the wimp-giant composition metaphor to security protocols in networks of humans and computers where compelling services, possibly under the control of an adversary, are offered to unsuspecting users. These protocols produce value for participants who collaborate. However, they allow malicious participants to harm honest ones and corrupt their systems by employing deception and scams. Yet these protocols have safe states whereby a participant can establish beliefs in the adversary's (perhaps temporary) honesty. However, reasoning about such states requires basic results from other fields, such as behavioral economics, rather than traditional security and cryptography.

2   Accurate and Complete Adversary Definitions for Wimps

Adversary-Controlled Giants. An adversary can be thought of as a program that launches a set of attacks at a system interface under the control of various input commands issued by humans. This implies that, to define an adversary accurately and completely, one must find all adversary-accessible interfaces of all system components, ranging from operating systems and network protocols to all system applications. Then, for each component, one must find all vulnerabilities that could be exploited by an adversary, and all attack strategies to exploit each vulnerability. Furthermore, an adversary could exploit different types of attacks against multiple components of a giant, and thus one must be able to account for all possible attack combinations to obtain an accurate and complete definition; e.g., compose all attack capabilities and strategies. Since giants comprise hundreds of thousands of component interfaces of different sizes and complexity, and tens of million lines of source code, it is highly unlikely that an accurate and complete definition of an adversary will ever be possible. To make things worse, some giant code and interfaces may change faster than the time necessary to complete an accurate adversary definition for it. In short, one can safely assume that *a giant is always part of the adversary definition.* Hence, the only system components that could possibly be defended from adversaries are wimps. Thus, the obligation to provide accurate and complete adversary definitions can be limited to wimps. However, since wimps can be part of different system components, they can have vastly different semantics and thus one needs a fairly general and uniform structure for adversary definitions, since these definitions must compose.

Adversaries in Cryptographic Schemes. A security sub-field that has produced accurate and complete adversary definitions successfully for relatively small modules with precisely specified functions (i.e., wimps) has been cryptography. Although fairly coarse, this analogy is intended to make two points: (1) the structure of the adversary definition in cryptographic schemes serves as a good starting point, given that these definitions have been successfully used in proving properties of encryption/authentication schemes [19]; (2) just as in cryptography, where the adversary definition is part of a cryptographic scheme's specification, the adversary definition can be part of any wimp specification; i.e., for software modules of similar size and complexity.

Security of *cryptographic schemes* is defined in terms of an *attack game*, and a model of *adversary power and privilege.* An adversary can be viewed as the set of possible attacks that can be launched against the *scheme.* Informally, each attack consists of a triple: an adversary's *goal*, set of *capabilities*, and *strategies* that exploit capabilities to reach the goal. In encryption schemes, the scheme's interface comprises an encryption, and possibly a decryption oracle, and the goal may be distinguishability of ciphertexts leading to leakage of plaintext information. In authentication schemes, the interface is to an authentication-tag generation and a verification oracle, and the adversary's goal is to forge a plaintext or an authentication tag that passes the verification-oracle's check. Capabilities represent the adversary's ability to obtain verifiable, predictable, known, or chosen plaintext from the system or network – as needed – and invoke an oracle. Attack strategies include launching adaptive, interactive, or concurrent attacks; e.g., exercising both choices of plaintext and ciphertext to break plaintext secrecy or create ciphertext forgeries.

The adversary *power* (e.g., polynomially bounded/unbounded, deterministic/randomized program, types of operations and their speed and storage requirements) and *privileges* (e.g., access to an oracle's entry points, ability to selectively specify input data, and invoke a single oracle or more) specify how an adversary plays the attack game; e.g., whether the adversary can exercise a particular game strategy. Capturing *all* attack strategies is important because otherwise one can-

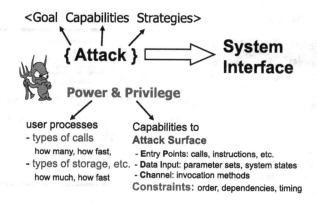

Fig. 1. Simple attack-definition template

not produce encryption or authentication schemes that demonstrably counter all attacks; e.g., provably support indistinguishability properties in encryption or unforgeability properties in authentication for different types of attack capabilities.

Structure of Wimp Adversaries. A similar adversary structure as that used for cryptography schemes can be applied to other types of wimps. As in cryptography, the adversary can be defined as the set of all possible attacks that can be launched at a wimp interface. In addition to the typical call interface, a wimp's interface must account for all sources of input; e.g., memory state, I/O devices, initial system state. As in cryptography, the adversary is a program, or a set of programs, that executes instructions based on inputs it receives from its users and/or other attack programs. However, the goals and capabilities of an attack game will be different, and so will the strategies. Nevertheless, just like in cryptography, we can define the attack game via <goals, capabilities, strategies> triples at different wimp interfaces. We also define the adversary's computationally bounded power and privileges in an analogous manner. For example, the adversary power includes a specification of how many end-hosts and processes operate the attack, how fast processors need to be, how much and what type of storage areas are needed, and what types of communication media and how much bandwidth are required. The adversary's power would have to be polynomially bounded – just as is done in complexity-based cryptography – since these wimps may use cryptographic schemes whose adversary is assumed to be bounded.

Figure 1 illustrates the template for an attack definition whereas Fig. 2 summarizes the use of the template with two attack examples. The size and complexity of the Xenix Kernel are not intended to approximate those of a wimp and are used only for illustrative purposes. In the attack of Fig. 2(a), the *attack goal* is to invoke the internal function *panic* of the Xenix operating system kernel [8] via unprivileged system calls and crash the system repeatedly, thereby causing persistent denial of service for system users. The *attack capabilities* comprise

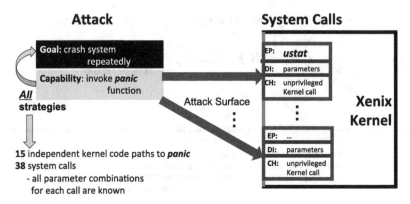

a) A Large-Surface Attack

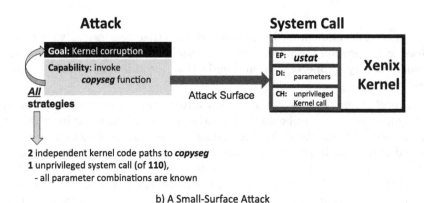

b) A Small-Surface Attack

Fig. 2. Attack examples

access to 38 of 110 system calls and the *attack strategies* are all call-parameter combinations that trigger a crash. In a practical sense, the adversary's capabilities and strategies represent a measure of an attack's surface [9,15].

The power and privileges of the adversary are fairly common; i.e., the adversary is an unprivileged user-level program that invokes unprivileged kernel calls. In this example, there is no call ordering, timing or dependency constraint on call capabilities that are left unknown after source-code analysis of the kernel. This requires both control-flow analysis to identify all the 15 independent flow paths that lead to the *panic* function, and information-flow analysis to identify all call-parameter values and combinations thereof that activate these flow paths. In this example, the integrated (control and information) flow analysis reveals *all* strategies (i.e., kernel calls and call-parameter combinations) the adversary can employ to crash the system repeatedly. At the time of this analysis, the security properties of the Xenix kernel did not counter the activation of any of the 15 independent code paths that led to the panic function invocation.

In contrast with Fig. 2(a), which illustrates a large-surface attack, Fig. 2(b) illustrates an attack that has a small surface, which can be easily countered in practice, once discovered. The *attack goal* is to invoke the internal function *copyseg* of the Xenix kernel via an unprivileged system call with a parameter combination that enables overwriting adversary-selected values in kernel space, thereby corrupting kernel operation. The *attack capabilities* comprise access to a single system call and the *attack strategies* all call-parameter combinations that cause a kernel overwrite. The adversary is an unprivileged user-level program that invokes unprivileged kernel calls. Integrated flow analysis on source code indicates that there are two independent flow paths to *copyseg*, and thus the strategy space (i.e., kernel calls and call-parameter combinations) is limited, although additional flow-path activations are possible using privileged calls (which Fig. 2 omits). At the time of this analysis, the security properties of the Xenix kernel did not counter the activation of any of the two independent code paths.

Examples of small attack surfaces whose exploitation is via *probabilistic strategies* also exist. Typical examples are the so-called *time-of-check-to-time-of-use attacks*, which attempt to exploit specific vulnerable time windows in system implementation; e.g., the *binmail* attack [2] where the goal of the adversary is to get root privilege using a strategy that exploits a small time window in file (un)linking. This attack uses conventional capabilities and unprivileged system call invocation.

Attack Composition. To obtain a desired capability, an attack A may require a capability provided by meeting the goal of attack B, and this leads to the notion of *attack composition*. Attack composition requires that (1) the adversary capabilities, power, and permissions necessary for attack B do not conflict with (e.g., exclude) the other capabilities needed by A, and (2) the strategies used by B do not conflict with those of A. For example, in many business applications, if the success of attack B requires a capability to access an accounts payable application, then adversary launching attack A cannot obtain a capability for issuing purchase orders. Or, if launching attack B requires root permissions, then launching a successful attack A from the unprivileged mode is ruled out. Also, if the strategy employed by attack A's requires timely program execution, executing attack B's strategy must exclude crashing the system.

In attack composition, the goal of B may represent a capability needed by multiple attacks – not only by A – and this leads to (directed) *attack graphs*. That is, a node of an attack graph comprises the triple <goals, capabilities, strategies>, adversary power and privileges, and an edge connects the goals of descendant nodes to the capabilities needed by their ancestors.

We note that, even when instances of attack graphs are (directed) trees, these trees are different from those often illustrated for the past two decades [1, 16, 24, 25], in at least three ways. First, each node defines the attack game, adversary power, and privileges, and hence it captures *all* attack execution strategies and capabilities needed, including their ordering, dependencies, and timing. Second, adversary privileges include a security boundary, or attack surface specification, whose size and complexity is minimized by wimp definitions; e.g., all entry points required and input parameter combinations to exploit capabilities. Third, attack nodes offer a direct way to measure security strength, as explained below.

Our notion of the attack graph also differs from that of the more recently defined but more limited notion of the "kill chain" [10]. While the reconnaissance, weaponization, and delivery steps of a kill chain correspond to the notion of a set of capabilities to an attack surface discovery (i.e., entry-point, malicious data input, and delivery channel), the exploitation, installation and execution steps capture only a single attack strategy, instead of *all* strategies as required by our attack node.

We stress again that our attack structure is intended for the accurate and complete definition of wimp adversaries. Even if this structure may be applicable to giants in principle, it is unlikely that such definitions can be used in practice due to giants' inherent size and complexity.

3   Wimp Security Properties and Metrics

Accurate and complete attack definitions imply that a defender can design security properties to counter those attacks, and implicitly deny the adversary's (asymmetric) advantage. Some properties may deny certain attack strategies and/or capabilities and hence the adversary cannot reach his/her goal. Other properties may deter the adversary from using specific strategies or capabilities; e.g., by audit, by increased workload. Yet others may limit the attack's success; e.g., the defender may recover secure system states thereby forcing the adversary to retry the attack (and eventually get discovered); or undo the effects of an attack that corrupts system memory states.

Since an adversary attack comprises a program executing in response to user input commands, an adversary's *attack behavior* can be viewed as sets of instruction-execution traces. Attack behaviors can be countered by defining wimp interfaces, which restrict or block some execution traces whenever the adversary attack invokes a wimp. Hence, just as in cryptography, the adversaries' attack behavior becomes part of a wimp's definition, and a wimp's security properties become *negations* of adversary attacks. For notational simplicity, we denote the set of properties that counter an attack A by $\overline{A}$.

In turn, security properties can yield basic metrics of security. For example, we say that attack $A \Longrightarrow$ attack B if all security properties that counter attack B also counter attack A. For example, this relation is required when attacks A and B compose, and is strictly weaker than composition. Like composition, it is reflexive, anti-symmetric, and transitive. Attack A $\not\Longrightarrow$ attack B if not all security properties that counter attack B counter attack A. This relation captures cases when attack B can be used by, but is not necessary for, attack A or when the two attacks do not compose. Using these relations we can then define the notions of attack "dominance $(>)$," "equivalence" $(\Longleftrightarrow)$, and "incomparability" $(\Longleftrightarrow\!\!\!\!/)$ as follows. Attack $A >$ attack B, if attack $A \Longrightarrow$ attack B, and attack B $\not\Longrightarrow$ attack A. Attack $A \Longleftrightarrow$ attack B if attack $A \Longrightarrow$ attack B and attack $B \Longrightarrow$

attack A. Equivalence captures, for instance, cases when the same ("copycat") attack is launched against different instances of the same wimp in different systems. Attack equivalance differs from attack "isomorphism"($\sim$) where we say that attack $A \sim$ attack B if they have the same goals, capabilities and strategies, except that they refer to different types of wimps. Attack A $\not\leftrightarrow$ attack B if attack A $\not\Rightarrow$ attack B and attack B $\not\Rightarrow$ attack A. Incomparability captures many attack differences including attacks whose goals differ, others whose capability sets differ, and finally those whose strategies differ.

The dominance and incomparability relations naturally lead to partial orders on adversary attacks and hence to *basic* security metrics. It follows that without accurate and complete adversary definitions one cannot define accurate and complete security properties, and without such properties one cannot obtain basic security metrics. Incomplete adversary definitions (e.g., traditional "attack trees" and "kill chains") would not do. It also follows that precise security metrics require wimp definitions and separation from giants, since giants are part of the adversary. Of course, other relations among attacks exist and can be used to define a much richer set of metrics. An orthogonal set of basic metrics arises from (partial) orders among the different types of security-property assurance and assurance evidence.

Using accurate and complete definitions, one can then use traditional proof techniques to perform different types of attack reductions and compositions for different types of wimps. For example, one can formally verify that a wimp has security property $\overline{A}$ in the presence of adversary attack A launched by a giant, as follows. First one verifies $\overline{A}$ assuming that the wimp is isolated from the giant. Then one verifies that the micro-hypervisor (i.e., a basic wimp) supports application wimp isolation [17] and cannot be bypassed by an attack B launched by the giant; i.e., the micro-hypervisor has security property $\overline{B}$. Finally, one proves that if the micro-hypervisor has property $\overline{B}$, then the wimp has property $\overline{A}$ when compiled and registered with the micro-hypervisor and invoked using it. In short, one is able to provide compositional, composability, and additivity proofs, in Rushby's verification terminology for separation kernels [20].

4   Wimps' Dance with Giants

There are many examples of wimp interfaces where it is possible to define all attack strategies for simple goals and small sets of capabilities. Such adversary definitions are not intended scale to the size of commodity systems, compose across networks of services, nor retain their usefulness when new applications are installed. For commodity systems, only incomplete definitions (e.g., traditional attack trees and kill chains) derived from hacking exercises (e.g., red teaming, penetration testing) have been practical to date. Reactive countermeasures to individual attacks, or piecemeal security, is all we could deliver for commodity systems and networks in the past.

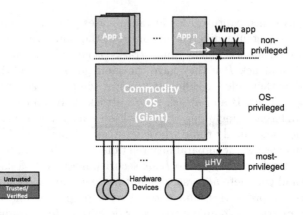

Fig. 3. A wimp-giant isolation architecture based on a micro-hypervisor

How can we do better in the future? A wimp-giant isolation architecture provided by a micro-hypervisor, which operates at a higher privilege level than the giant and hence is isolated from it, is illustrated in Fig. 3. Will wimp-giant isolation be sufficient for accurate and correct adversary definitions, demonstrable security properties, and sound security metrics in practice?

The answer to this questions is decidedly negative. Wimps must compose (i.e. "dance") securely with giants for at least two reasons. First, secure wimps must use services provided by adversary-controlled giants and share platform resources (e.g., I/O, physical memory) with them. This can happen only after wimps efficiently verify the results of those services [29], and the initialization of platform resources in a secure (e.g., malware-free) state [26]. Second, secure wimps could help insecure giants restrict their own (adversary) behavior in specific ways; e.g., prove that certain malicious behaviors are not perpetrated by a giant. For example, wimps have been used to protect cryptographic libraries and key management subsystems against giant misbehavior [17,28], and can also be used to protect application-level reference monitors and cryptographic protocols [6].

The fact that wimp survival depends on collaborating with adversary-controlled giants appears to be paradoxical: wimps can counter all adversary attacks, but only if they use adversary-controlled services from which they have to defend themselves; and to prove that they have not behaved maliciously in certain applications, giants must rely on secure wimps whose operation they attack.

Using Giant Services. To retain all their security properties with reasonable assurance and not become insecure giants, wimps will have to trade very basic system services for small attack surfaces, diminished adversary capabilities, and weak attack strategies. For example, wimps typically lack persistent memory, file system and directory services, network protocols, trusted paths to humans, and isolated I/O services needed to protect applications; see Fig. 4. Placing such

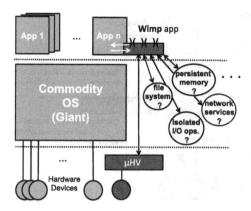

Fig. 4. Examples of missing services from both wimps and micro-hypervisor

services in a trustworthy computing base (e.g., in the micro-hypervisor) to serve wimps would be inadvisable. Trusted computing bases would become bloated, unstable, and devoid of security assurance; e.g., they would often include code of diverse and sometime uncertain origin, such as device drivers.

Note that a different choice of service placement was made in Lampson's *red-green machine* [13]. The red-green machine actually separates *two giants*: an untrustworthy (red) one from a less untrustworthy (green) one. The green giant is a carefully configured, maintained, and connected full-service machine. Although this type of separation can certainly be attained in practice, it does require a trusted-path mechanism to enable careful users to determine the machine they talk to; viz., CMU's Lockdown system [23]. Since the green giants are self-contained, trustworthy red-green communication, and use of the red machine's (efficiently verifiable) services by the green one, is rare. In contrast with wimps, defining and countering all attacks against the green machine remains a daunting and likely unattainable goal.

In principle, one does *not* need to lump services needed by wimps in a green machine. Efficient verification of some system-service results, which enables service implementation in red giants, has been known for over three decades; e.g., cryptographic verification of page integrity [4] and implementation of virtual memory services outside a security kernel in an untrusted operating system. Other efficiently verifiable services, which require only minimal trusted base support, have been proposed more recently; e.g., persistent wimp memory [21], and selected kernel functions for on-demand isolated I/O channels [29]. A wimpy I/O-kernel is illustrated in Fig. 5.

Sharing Platform Resources with Giants. Wimp sharing of commodity platform resources with giants is both useful in practice and fundamentally necessary. It is useful for resources that can be isolated from giants, such as I/O channels and devices, and made available to wimps on-demand. This enables wimps to use only the devices they need and when they need them. Thus, wimps need not

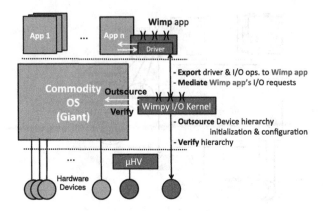

Fig. 5. Wimpy-kernel architecture for on-demand isolated I/O services

include nor rely on unnecessary I/O services, which would dramatically increase their exposure to attacks from giants. However, sharing I/O devices with giants requires wimps to verify the integrity of device firmware and initialize devices to known secure (e.g., malware-free) states after giant use [14,27].

Sharing a hardware platform with the giant is unavoidable for most wimps when dedicated hardware (e.g., co-processors) is unavailable – a common case on commodity platforms. For example, the most basic system wimp, the micro-hypervisor, shares the CPU, memory, and some basic (e.g., DMA) devices with the giant. How can one be sure that giant-inserted malware in memory and device controller firmware does not corrupt the micro-hypervisor *before* the micro-hypervisor boots? To detect and/or prevent this from happening, one needs to introduce the notion of the *verifiable boot*, whereby the micro-hypervisor boots only in a malware-free device state. The notion of verifiable boot is stronger than both *trusted boot* and *secure boot* [18]. Neither trusted nor secure boot provides assurance of malware absence in the *entire device* – not just in directly-addressable processor memory [26] – at boot time and immediately thereafter. Whether the giant infects devices with malware later would become less relevant for a wimp that is able to re-initialize devices that are shared with a giant to a known secure (e.g., malware-free) state on-demand.

It is worth noting that implementing the notion of the verifiable boot on a commodity platform would enable a user to reset a platform to a malware-free state, and a micro-hypervisor and application wimps to execute in an *untampered* execution environment. Furthermore, *on-demand verifiable boot* would enable a user to ensure that application wimps can restart in a malware-free state in the, hopefully unlikely, case of successful penetration by giants. In this case, the giants would be forced to dance "FlipIt" [3] with wimps.

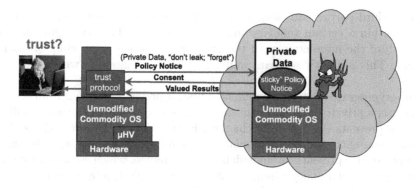

Fig. 6. An interactive trust protocol: sending private data to a giant

5   Wimps and Giants in Networks of Humans and Computers

There is an intriguing but limited similarity between wimp-giant collaboration on commodity platforms and *interactive trust protocols* [7,11] between ordinary users and web services. For example, interactive trust protocols (1) produce value for participants who cooperate; (2) potentially allow malicious participants (i.e., giants) to harm honest participants (i.e., wimps) by employing deception and scams; and yet (3) may have safe states whereby an honest participant can establish beliefs in a malicious participant's temporary trustwothiness, even if traditional security and cryptography techniques cannot be employed. Like in the typical wimp-giant collaboration, interactive trust protocols offer attractive and compelling web services to users. However, dissimilarities are equally evident. Unlike the wimp-giant collaboration on commodity platforms, where a wimp *never* engages services of giants unless it can verify the results of those services, ordinary users can seldom verify the results produced by adversary-controlled services and defend themselves against attacks. Nevertheless, interaction between honest but unsuspecting users and adversaries is desirable, if safe. Such interaction can lead to new trust relations to be formed and potentially can create new value. Safe protocol states can, in principle, provide credible evidence that the adversary-controlled service isn't harming an unsuspecting user. Here, again, the attack definition would benefit from specifying a wimp-giant security game, including the <goals, capabilities, strategies> triple and a model of the adversary's power and privilege.

In the protocol illustrated in Fig. 6, a user delegates her rights to a client-machine wimp, which executes the steps of a trust protocol with an adversary-controlled service; i.e., a giant. The wimp agrees to provide the user's private data, for example personal indentification information, to the giant in exchange for results the user deems to be valuable; e.g., personalized ads, live news, weather and traffic reports. It cryptographically seals a personal privacy policy (i.e., a "sticky") notice onto the private data specifying that they must not be leaked to third-parties and "forgotten" as specified; i.e., erased from the giant's storage within a certain time/use limit or on-demand. The cryptographic seal and much of the interaction with the web server is done via a wimp on user's machine. This a giant's software would be unable to interfere with the user's actions.

The cryptographic seal has a dual role: first, it prevents the giant from accessing the user's private data unless the giant consents to abide by the user's policy; second, it prevents the user from changing her mind, adding more policies after the giant consents, and then complaining about policy violations. This phase of the protocol represents an undeniable fair exchange, which secures a consent (by the giant) and a policy commitment (by the wimp) thereby assuring mutual accountability. However, mutual accountability does not guarantee giant compliance with the user's privacy policy. The wimp has no way to control the giant's operation and enforce non-leakage and timely data erasure. So why would a user output her user's private data to the giant? Clearly, the user must establish "output trust" in the giant. How could that happen?

First, the user can decrease the risk of giant leakage by *anonymizing* her identity and network address, and ensure that her anonymous identity is *unlinkable* to any other identity she may have used in the past. The user can always change her anonymous and unlinkable identity to reduce the damage caused by giant-saved and leaked private data. Second, the user must ensure that the giant's service is regulated by legal statutes, and thus a non-compliant but accountable giant may be punished. Third, the user could obtain recommendations attesting to the giant's trustworthiness and reputation ratings, which may increase the user's beliefs in giant's trusworthiness in abiding by the user's privacy policy.

Individually, none of the three components of trust establishment between the wimp and the giant offers absolute guarantees of policy compliance by the giant. First, anonymous and unlinkable identities cannot prevent a powerful giant from collecting large amounts of data regarding this user's behavior and linking her identities via *behavioral correlations*. Second, accountability may not necessarily guarantee punishment under the legal statutes and punishment may not necessarily deter a non-compliant giant. However, the user's aversion to betrayal by the giant may be reduced considerably. Third, recommendation systems and reputation ratings can only capture past evidence of trustworthiness but do not necessarily guarantee present or future honest behavior. Nevertheless, research in behavioral economics and practice suggests that all three measures are often sufficient for trust establishment. For this reason, the wimp-giant collaboration suggested by this example may not be as dangerous as anticipated despite the wimp's inability to verify the giant's future actions.

6   Summary

In this paper, we argue that accurate and complete adversary definitions are necessary if the asymmetric advantage of an attacker over a defender is to be eliminated. However, such definitions are likely to be possible only for "wimpy" software components. We provide a structure for accurate and complete adversary definitions for wimps, which was inspired from similar definitions in cryptography. These definitions yields basic security properties and metrics, and are instrumental in providing security assurance for commodity systems. Although the wimp isolation from giant software components becomes necessary for obtaining such definitions in practice, it is insufficient for wimp survival. To survive in commodity markets, secure wimps must compose with insecure giants. We illustrate a safe way to compose a wimpy I/O kernel with a commodity operating system, and extend the wimp-giant composition metaphor to interactive trust protocols in networks of humans and computers.

Acknowledgments. This paper benefitted from discussions and joint work with Min Suk Kang, Miao Yu, Jun Zhao, and Zongwei Zhou. Their insights are gratefully acknowledged. This work was supported in part by the National Science Foundation (NSF) under grant CCF-0424422 and a gift from Intel Corporation at CyLab. The views and conclusions contained in this document are those of the author and should not be interpreted as representing the official policies, either expressed or implied, of any sponsoring institution, the U.S. government or any other entity.

References

1. Amoroso, E.G.: Fundamentals of Computer Security Technology, pp, 15–29. Prentice-Hall (1994) ISBN0131089293
2. Bishop, M., Dilger, M.: Checking for race conditions in file accesses. Comput. Syst. **9**(2), 131–152 (1996)
3. van Dijk, M., Juels, A., Oprea, A., Rivest, R.L.: FlipIt: the game of "Stealthy Takeover." J. Cryptology **26**(4), 655–713 (2013). (also in IACR Cryptology ePrint Archive, Report 2012/103, 2012)
4. Gligor, V.D., Lindsay, B.G.: Object migration and authentication. IEEE Trans. Softw. Eng. **SE–5**(6), 607–611 (1979)
5. Gligor, V.D.: On the evolution of adversary models in security protocols (or Know Your Friend and Foe Alike). In: Christianson, B., Crispo, B., Malcolm, J.A., Roe, M. (eds.) Security Protocols 2005. LNCS, vol. 4631, pp. 276–283. Springer, Heidelberg (2007)
6. Gligor, V.D.: Security limitations of virtualization and how to overcome them. In: Proceedings of the 18th International Workshop on Security Protocols (SPW-18). LNCS, Cambridge University, UK, vol. 7061. Springer, March 2010
7. Gligor, V., Wing, J.M.: Towards a theory of trust in networks of humans and computers (transcript of discussion). In: Christianson, B., Crispo, B., Malcolm, J., Stajano, F. (eds.) Security Protocols 2011. LNCS, vol. 7114, pp. 223–242. Springer, Heidelberg (2011)
8. Gupta, S., Gligor, V.D.: Experience with a penetration analysis method and tool. In: Proceedings of the 1992 National Computer Security Conference, Baltimore, Maryland, pp. 165–183 (1992)
9. Howard, M., Pincus, J., Wing, J.M.: Measuring relative attack surfaces. In: Lee, D.T., Shieh, S.P., Tygar, J.D. (eds.) Computer Security in the 21st Century, chap. 8, pp. 109–137. Springer, New York (2005)

10. Hutchins, E.M., Clopper, M.J., Amin, R.M.: Intelligence-driven computer network defense informed by analysis of adversary campaigns and intrusion Kill Chains. In: Proceedings of the 6th Annual International Conference on Information Warfare and Security, Washington, DC (2011)
11. Kim, T.H.-J., Gligor, V., Perrig, A.: Street-level trust semantics for attribute authentication (transcript of discussion). In: Christianson, B., Malcolm, J., Stajano, F., Anderson, J. (eds.) Security Protocols 2012. LNCS, vol. 7622, pp. 96–115. Springer, Heidelberg (2012)
12. Lampson, B.W.: Software components: Only the giants survive. In: Computer Systems: Theory, Technology, and Applications, pp. 137–145. Springer, New York (2004)
13. Lampson, B.W.: Usable security: how to get it. Commun. ACM 52, 25–27 (2009)
14. Li, Y., McCune, J., Perrig, A.: VIPER: verifying the integrity of peripherals firmware. In: Proceedings of the ACM Conference on Computer and Communications Security (2011)
15. Manadhata, P.K., Karabulut, Y., Wing, J.M.: Report: measuring the attack surfaces of enterprise software. In: Massacci, F., Redwine Jr., S.T., Zannone, N. (eds.) ESSoS 2009. LNCS, vol. 5429, pp. 91–100. Springer, Heidelberg (2009)
16. Mauw, S., Oostdijk, M.: Foundations of attack trees. In: Won, D.H., Kim, S. (eds.) ICISC 2005. LNCS, vol. 3935, pp. 186–198. Springer, Heidelberg (2006)
17. McCune, J., Li, Y., Qu, N., Zhou, Z., Datta, A., Gligor, V., Perrig, A.: TrustVisor: efficient TCB reduction and attestation. In: CMU-CyLab-09-003, March, 2009. (also in Proceedings of the IEEE Symposium on Security and Privacy, Oakland, CA, May 2010)
18. Parno, B., McCune, J.M., Perrig, A.: Bootstrapping trust in commodity computers. In: Proceedings of the IEEE Symposium on Security and Privacy, May 2010
19. Rogaway, P.: On the role definitions in and beyond cryptography. In: Maher, M.J. (ed.) ASIAN 2004. LNCS, vol. 3321, pp. 13–32. Springer, Heidelberg (2004)
20. Rushby, J.M.: Separation and Integration in MILS (The MILS Constitution). Technical report, SRI-CSL-TR-08-XX, Feb 2008
21. Parno, B., Lorch, J., Douceur, J., Mickens, J., McCune, J.: Memoir: practical state continuity for protected modules. In: Proceedings of the IEEE Symposium on Security and Privacy (2011)
22. Vasudevan, A., Chaki, S., Jia, L., McCune, L.J., Newsome, J., Datta, A.: Design, Implementation and Verification of an eXtensible and Modular Hypervisor Framework. In: Proceedings of the IEEE Symposium on Security and Privacy (2013)
23. Vasudevan, A., Parno, B., Qu, N., Gligor, V., Perrig, A.: Lockdown: a safe and practical environment for security applications. In: CMU-CyLab-09-011, 14 July 2009. (Also in Proceedings of TRUST, Vienna, Austria, 2012)
24. Schneier, B.: Attack trees. Dr. Dobb's J. 24(12), 21–29 (1999)
25. Weiss, J.D.: A system security engineering process. In: Proceedings of the 14th National Computer Security Conference, Baltimore, Maryland (1991)
26. Zhao, J., Gligor, V., Perrig, A., Newsome, J.: ReDABLS: revisiting device attestation with bounded leakage of secrets. In: Christianson, B., Malcolm, J., Stajano, F., Anderson, J., Bonneau, J. (eds.) Security Protocols 2013. LNCS, vol. 8263, pp. 94–114. Springer, Heidelberg (2013)
27. Zhou, Z., Gligor, V., Newsome, J., McCune, J.: Building verifiable trusted path on commodity x86 computers. In: Proceedings of the IEEE Symposium on Security and Privacy (2012)

28. Zhou, Z., Han, J., Lin, Y.-H., Perrig, A., Gligor, V.: KISS: "key it simple and secure" corporate key management. In: Huth, M., Asokan, N., Čapkun, S., Flechais, I., Coles-Kemp, L. (eds.) TRUST 2013. LNCS, vol. 7904, pp. 1–18. Springer, Heidelberg (2013)
29. Zhou, Z., Miao, Y.: Dancing with giants: wimpy kernels for on-demand isolated I/O on commodity platforms. In: Proceedings of IEEE Symposium on Security and Privacy, Oakland, CA (2014)

Dancing with the Adversary:
A Tale of Wimps and Giants
(Transcript of Discussion)

Virgil Gligor[(✉)]

Carnegie Mellon University, Pittsburgh, PA 15213, USA
gligor@cmu.edu

The work reported here is based on some research that I have done with my students Min Suk Kang, Miao Yu, Jun Zhao, and Zongwei Zhou. The title of this presentation, "Dancing with the Adversary," is a take off on a paper[1] which will be presented at this year's IEEE Symposium on Security and Privacy.

Motivation. What does it mean for a defender to "dance" with an adversary, and what motivates the defender to do so? Briefly, it means that the defender both receives services from and provides services to an adversary. Since both the defender and adversary are programs, the dance is a safe program composition across a protection interface so that neither loses from it. In fact, if we choreograph the dance correctly, both parties will be better off than before the dance. Often a dance is motivated by necessity, sometimes by perceived value and usefulness, and sometimes merely because the defender wants to test the behaviour of the adversary.

To choreograph the defender-adversary dance one needs a definition of the adversary, and not just any definition. One needs a complete and correct definition. Nothing else will work. If one uses an incomplete or incorrect definition, the adversary will end up having an advantage over the defender, and this will give rise to the so-called "inevitable" asymmetry between a defender and an adversary. Fundamentally, this asymmetry need not exist at all in computer systems and network security, contrary to popular belief. The asymmetry arises only when one does not have, or does not use, a complete and correct definition of one's adversary. To understand the reason for this we need to ask ourselves a simple question: What's a security property? Informally, a security property is a negation of an adversary's behaviour. Hence, in principle, if one has a correct/accurate definition of *all* adversary's behaviours, one automatically also has the definition of *all* security properties that counter those behaviours, and one is done. The adversary has no (e.g., the first mover) advantage over the defender.

In theory, we already know how provide such definitions. In arguing this point, I will refer to an analogy with adversary definitions in cryptography (e.g., in cryptographic schemes) where accurate and complete definitions are the norm.

---

[1] Zongwei Zhou, Miao Yu, and Virgil Gligor. Dancing with Giants: Wimpy Kernels for On-demand Isolated I/O. In Proceedings of the IEEE Symposium on Security and Privacy, May 2014.

© Springer International Publishing Switzerland 2014
B. Christianson et al. (Eds.): Security Protocols 2014, LNCS 8809, pp. 116–129, 2014.
DOI: 10.1007/978-3-319-12400-1_12

In practice, however, the situation is a lot more complicated than this, largely due to the large size and complexity of the code used in the commodity computer systems and networks we use, which prevent us from defining the adversary completely and correctly. You might remember that in my presentation here in 2010, I argued that there will always be large software components in commodity systems (i.e., the "giants") whose security properties are not understood by most users; viz., my Axiom 2 there. [Butler Lampson makes a stronger statement when he says that among software components *only* the giants survive, and I believe he's right.] Often giants include components of diverse origin, whose security properties - and hence adversary definition – are often unknown. For these reasons, accurate and complete definitions will always be impractical for large commodity systems.

Joan Feigenbaum: So could you be a little more specific about what you mean by specifying an "adversary behaviour," because at least in the theory of cryptography that I'm most familiar with, you don't specify an adversary behaviour, you put a limit on the adversary's resources.

Reply: That's right, one captures all possible behaviours.

Joan Feigenbaum: Of any adversary.

Reply: Yes. We need *all* adversaries behaviours, since they define *all* attack strategies possible against a particular target, just as cryptographic proofs do. My use of the term "adversary behavior" comes from formal methods where program behaviours are defined as predicates on program traces, and sometimes on sets of traces. As in cryptography, the adversary is a program, or a set of programs, so, in principle, the notion of adversary behavior makes sense here.

Joan Feigenbaum: But it is something other than saying any probabilistic polynomial time adversary, or something like that?

Reply: My view of the adversary, which I will present a bit later, is consistent with that in cryptography, which was in fact my inspiration for adversary definitions. As illustrated in the accompanying paper, adversary programs can have probabilistic behavior, just as in cryptography, and are polynomial-time.

Frank Stajano: So maybe I misunderstood you but I'd rather you set me right before the rest of the talk. At some point I believe you said something along the lines of complete and correct definitions are very difficult to do, and if we could do complete and correct specification of the adversary, we'd be done. Well, you can define the adversary, but this doesn't mean you have a solution for that, so why would you be done?

Reply: In principle, if one has a complete and correct definition of the adversary, one can negate it and obtain all the security properties one needs. Implementing those properties in a practical system is a different story.

Peter Ryan: Bolt in on afterwards ...

Reply: Right, and we can all retire then.

In the case of giants, an adversary always has an advantage over a defender, and for this reason I consider giants to be adversary controlled. In contrast, complete and correct definitions are always possible for what I call the "wimps." Wimps are comparatively small, relatively simple, functionally limited components, whose behaviour is well understood. In other words, one can define and verify *all* their security properties, which are defined as a negation of adversary behaviors. I stress that this is possible only for wimps. Both complete and correct adversary definitions and formal verification of security properties are expensive processes and hence only applicable to small and simple programs; e.g., currently well under twenty thousand lines of code. And, of course, I don't mean formally verifying a *simple property* of a large program; e.g., a million lines of code giant via model checking, which is certainly possible now[2].

Peter Ryan: Maybe this is a stupid question, but what is a *commodity* system?

Reply: A commodity system is a system that is not merely commercially available but is also so inexpensive that almost everyone uses it; e.g., Windows, Linux on a PC or phone. As in most industries, these systems are developed for very competitive mass markets, where a producer can never afford to build formally verified operating systems and applications[3]. In contrast, one can find niche markets, such as aerospace and defense markets, where building verified separation kernels and secure applications makes economic sense. These would *not* be commodity systems in my definition, however.

So basically the adversary need not have an advantage over the defender when the defender is a wimp. However, wimps are unlikely to survive in competitive markets, and the reason for this is that they lack very basic services. Wimps are small and simple: they might not even have persistent memory, a file system, virtual memory, network services, and on-demand I/O; viz., Fig. 4 of the accompanying paper. Well, so what can they do? As it turns out, not a lot. In contrast, giants are well endowed, and as Butler points out, they are the only software components that survive. Paradoxically, if secure wimps are to survive, they have to use insecure giants, in other words, they have to compose or dance with them. They have to evolve with giants, or else they will not keep up with rapid innovation in giants, and will eventually disappear.

Hence my main theme is that wimps have to dance with giants. So if one wants to have security in commodity systems, one will have to rely on wimps, and if one wants security to survive, one has to compose wimps with giants. Otherwise, we will not have security in commodity systems. Again, I'm not talking about niche systems. This is the whole point of this presentation. From here on I'm going to give you examples of why the wimp-giant composition is useful, in fact often necessary. I will say a few words about adversary definitions,

---

[2] Hao Chen, Drew Dean and David Wagner. Model Checking One Million Lines of C Code. In Proceedings of the 11th USENIX Security Symposium, pages 171–185, San Diego, CA, February 2002.

[3] Virgil Gligor. Security Limitations of Virtualization and How to Overcome Them. In Proceedings of the 18th International Workshop on Security Protocols (SPW-18), Cambridge, UK, March 2010, LNCS vol. 7061, Springer Verlag.

and maybe compare attack definitions with the more traditional attack trees and kill chains, about which you heard this morning.

A Collaboration Example. Here is an example of how to support wimps and compose them with giants. Figure 3 of the accompanying paper provides a simplified view of the micro-hypervisor that we built at CMU CyLab, called TrustVisor[4]. This was followed by another micro-hypervisor, which is now available as open source code, called XMHF[5]. These are not virtualising hypervisors and they operate under an unmodified operating system. They enable one to isolate well defined, small and simple modules in applications, and even in the commodity operating systems.

However, we quickly realized that wimp isolation was insufficient because wimps lack basic services. All other mechanisms that support fine-grain wimp isolation (e.g., hypervisors for virtual machine isolation) share this drawback. Hence one has to be able to compose the small isolated wimps with systems that support useful but perhaps insecure services. The alternative to composition, namely adding services that wimps lack to the micro hypervisor, is not going to be helpful because all the formally verified properties of micro-hypervisors, such as memory integrity, will disappear when one adds services such as file systems, networking, and on-demand I/O. This is also true for ordinary hypervisors, security kernels, and separation kernels.

Hence a question arises regarding how one could provide a very simple I/O service to application wimps; for example, a USB service that is isolated from that of the commodity operating system and handles wimps' I/O with an application device inserted in the USB slot. Adding a USB sub-system would more than double the size of our micro-hypervisor (i.e., XMHF), and increase its complexity to the point that its formally verified properties become invalid. Adding interrupt handling would also add concurrency, which would complicate significantly any effort to redo those proofs.

Instead of adding the USB subsystem to the micro-hypervisor, we designed another wimp, which we called the "wimpy kernel," to provide on-demand isolated I/O channels to application wimps; viz., Fig. 5 of the accompanying paper. The wimpy kernel relieves the micro-hypervisor from doing any I/O whatsoever, so it does not have to support more than one or two devices; e.g., a DMA device. However, to be wimpy, this kernel must outsource some USB functions to the unmodified commodity OS, namely those whose results it can verify efficiently. In short, the wimpy kernel must dance with the giant OS.

Note that some functions, and in fact entire services, could be easily outsourced to a giant since their results can be verified efficiently; e.g., an application wimp

---

[4] Jonathan McCune, Yanlin Li, Ning Qu, Zongwei Zhou, Anupam Datta, Virgil Gligor, and Aadrian Perrig. TrustVisor: Efficient TCB Reduction and Attestation. Technical Report, CMU-CyLab-09-003, March, 2009. (also In Proceedings of the IEEE Symp. on Security and Privacy, Oakland, CA, May 2010.)

[5] Amit Vasudevan, Sagar Chaki, Limin Jia, Limin Jonathan McCune, James Newsome, and Anupam Datta. Design, Implementation and Verification of an eXtensible and Modular Hypervisor Framework. In Proceedings of the IEEE Symposium on Security and Privacy, 2013.

can outsource its files to an untrusted file system, its virtual memory to an untrusted virtual memory system. In 1979[6] we showed how to this when we attempted to define authenticated encryption and message authentication codes that would enable us to outsource objects to insecure operating system components and verify their properties upon object return. Clearly, a wimp can use cryptographic techniques to outsource objects and verify whether they are authentic when they return to the wimp. Unfortunately, this cannot be done in the case of the USB services. Instead, we had to select particular USB subsystem functions that can be outsourced such that their results could be verified first efficiently, and here I mean fast, and second with simple code.

However, result verification for outsourced functions is not always possible because, as illustrated in our SPW 2011 paper[7], one quickly encounters NP-complete and even undecidable verification problems. In the USB case we reduced the size of a typical USB service of twenty thousand lines of source code to less than three thousand lines in the wimpy kernel. I am cheating a bit here because some of the code size reduction was in fact done by exporting some USB service code to the application wimp (e.g., drivers). Hence, not all savings could be attributed to the wimpy kernel's composition with the giant operating system. Nevertheless, the savings derived from the dance were massive.

Micah Sherr: So you're decreasing the size of the code by outsourcing some of the USB function to the giant. Is that what you're doing?

Reply: Yes, we are outsourcing some functions of the USB, such as device hierarchy initialization and configuration, since the wimpy I/O kernel can verify the results of those functions very fast, and with very few lines of code. Consequently, the complexity of device hierarchy and configuration management can remain in the giant.

As mentioned already, we did a bit more than outsource-and-verify, but this example aligns better with the workshop theme. The bottom line is that the wimpy-kernel dance with the giant becomes necessary, because otherwise we couldn't formally verify the wimpy kernel functions, and in fact we couldn't even compose the wimpy kernel with the underlying micro-hypervisor.

A Different Collaboration Example. Suppose that a client browsing various services on the Internet is asked by a service to outsource personal data to the service in exchange for some free service, personalized ads, live news, weather and traffic reports. This is an *interactive trust protocol*[8] between ordinary users

---

[6] Virgil D. Gligor and Bruce G. Lindsay. Object Migration and Authentication. In *IEEE Transactions on Software Engineering, SE-5*, No. 6, 1979, pp. 607–611.

[7] Virgil Gligor and Jeannette Wing. Towards a Theory of Trust in Networks of Humans and Computers. In Proceedings of the 19th International Workshop on Security Protocols (SPW-19), Cambridge, UK, March 2011. LNCS 7114, Springer Verlag.

[8] Tiffany Hyun-Jin Kim, Virgil Gligor, and Adrian Perrig. Street-Level Trust Semantics for Attribute Authentication. In Proceedings of the 20th International Workshop on Security Protocols (SPW-20), Cambridge, UK, April 2012, LNCS 7622, Springer Verlag.

and web services in the sense that it (1) produces value for participants who cooperate; (2) allows malicious participants (i.e., services) to potentially harm honest participants (i.e., unsuspecting user of Fig. 6) by employing deception and scams; and yet (3) might have safe states whereby an honest participant can establish beliefs in a malicious participant's temporary trustworthiness. Like in the typical wimp-giant collaboration, interactive trust protocols offer attractive and compelling giant services to wimps. Unlike the wimp-giant collaboration on commodity platforms, ordinary users can seldom verify the results produced by adversary-controlled services and defend themselves against attacks.

Now suppose that the Federal Trade Commission (FTC) in the United States, or the equivalent in the European Union, regulates service providers such as Google, Facebook, Amazon, or Microsoft, asking them to abide by any policy restricting the use of personal data specified by users; e.g., not to distribute user data to third parties without explicit data-owner consent; not to track user actions without consent; and erase user personal data upon request. In other words the FTC and like-minded organizations start paying attention to user privacy. How can users take advantage of that?

Suppose that we have a protocol between some wimp running on the client machine that can attach a policy specification to an object that contains its user's private data. We call this policy a "sticky policy" because it cryptographically affixes the policy specification to the object containing private information. When the service receives the object containing the private data and sticky policy, it can only access the data if it replies that it agrees to abide by the sticky policy.

How could the user know whether the service will keep its agreement and abide by the policy; and how does the service know that the user, or the client-machine wimp, does not change the policy specification after receiving the agreement and frame the service to the regulatory agency by claiming non-compliance? This dilemma is resolved by an undeniable fair-exchange protocol that provides *mutual accountability* between the user and the service; i.e., the user has the service's consent to respect the sticky policy and at the same time the service has the user's commitment not to change her policy and frame the service. The intent of mutual accountability backed by regulation is to deter both parties from reneging on their agreement. Also note that the user's wimp ensures that the service cannot corrupt the user's policy specification by inserting malware on the user's machine, and ensures that the undeniable fair exchange protocol is executed correctly on the user's machine. Unfortunately, accountability is not necessarily sufficient for enforcing regulation (i.e., punish violators), and punishment does not always deter. Hence, the user must establish a limited degree of trust in the service before personal data disclosure.

To establish a limited trust, users only need to employ mechanisms that help (1) decrease their betrayal and risk aversions in interactive trust protocols where they can be cheated, and (2) build their beliefs in the trustworthiness of the service. Betrayal aversion is decreased by accountability mechanisms and regulation here, and risk aversion by users employing anonymous credentials that are unlinkable with previous credential uses. The service need not know the users' true identity to deliver the promised functions and abide by the sticky policy. And finally, users can increase their belief in the trustworthiness of services, by relying on recommendations and reputation rankings for the service. If trust is increased to the point of user-service collaboration, value will be created for both users and services and everybody wins.

Overview of Adversary Structure. Now I would like to move on to the last part of my talk and I hope I have another ten minutes or so, to return to the definition of adversary for wimps, which I promised in my answer to Joan's question a little earlier. Recall that the challenge was to define adversaries completely and correctly. I argue that one can use a similar structure for an adversary definition as that used for the adversary in cryptographic schemes (aka., modes); i.e., the set of all possible attacks against a security interface, where an attack is defined as a *security game* and a model of *adversary power and privileges*. Of course, there will be some differences between adversary definitions in cryptography and in operating systems and applications, but the overall structure is similar. Briefly, the security game comprises the triple <goals, capabilities, strategies>. In crypto schemes the attack goals might be to distinguish encryptions, forge authentication tags, or forge ciphertext. Capabilities may be provided by chosen plaintext, chosen ciphertext, known plaintext, predictable plaintext, verifiable plaintext, and the ability to invoke oracles; i.e., the crypto schemes interface. Attack strategies include launching adaptive, interactive, or concurrent attacks; e.g., exercising both choices of plaintext and ciphertext to break plaintext secrecy or create ciphertext forgeries. The adversary *power* (e.g., polynomially bounded/unbounded, deterministic/randomized program, types of operations and their speed and storage requirements) and *privileges* (e.g., access to an oracle's entry points, restrictions on oracle invocations, ability to selectively specify input data, and invoke a single oracle or more) specify how an adversary plays the attack game. Capturing *all* attack strategies is important because otherwise one cannot prove that all attacks are countered.

A similar adversary structure can be used for operating systems and application wimps; viz., Fig. 1 of the accompanying paper. For example, one defines the adversary of all possible attacks at a wimp interface. One also defines an attack as the triple < goals, capabilities, strategies >, but here the element of the triple are different in nature. Of course, this is impractical for commodity systems and applications but it is always practical for wimps. Why? Because we can make the wimp interfaces very small, we can reduce their attack surfaces, we can limit their functions such that all adversary strategies are also limited.

In the accompanying paper I give two examples of how one defines these attacks completely in terms of goals, all capabilities, and all strategies and the type of analysis required to provide such definitions. The key observation is that the size of the adversary attack surface, namely the capabilities for a wimp interface, can be reduced until *all* strategies can be analyzed. In the first example, the goal of the attack is to invoke the internal function *panic* of the Xenix operating system kernel via unprivileged system calls and crash the system repeatedly, thereby causing persistent denial of service for system users[9]. The *attack capabilities* comprise access to 38 of 110 system calls and the *attack strategies* are all call-parameter combinations that trigger a crash. Here, the adversary is an unprivileged user-level program that invokes unprivileged kernel calls. This attack is illustrated in Fig. 2a) of the accompanying paper.

The second example illustrates an attack that has a small surface, where the *goal* is to invoke a different internal function *copyseg* of the Xenix kernel via an unprivileged system call with parameter combinations that enable overwriting adversary-selected values in kernel space, thereby corrupting kernel operation. The *attack capabilities* represent accesses to a single system call and the *attack strategies* all call-parameter combinations that cause a kernel overwrite. The adversary is, again, an unprivileged user-level program that invokes unprivileged kernel calls. The attack strategies are much more limited than in the first example reflecting the benefit of a much smaller attack surface; i.e., there are two independent flow paths to *copyseg*, and thus the strategy space (i.e., kernel calls and call-parameter combinations) is limited. This attack is illustrated in Fig. 2b) of the accompanying paper.

How does our attack structure compare with the more traditional attack representations? Remember that the adversary can be viewed as the set of all attacks. There is some very good work done in this area starting with J. D. Weiss[10], Ed Amoroso[11], and Bruce Schneier[12], and continued by Sjouke Mauw[13] and his students who use attack-defence trees, which are very good tools to have. However, these attack definitions are not particularly useful for our purposes; i.e., for wimps. First, our structure captures *all* attack execution strategies and capabilities needed, including their ordering, dependencies, and timing. Second, adversary privileges include attack surface specification, whose size and complexity is minimized by wimp definitions; e.g., all entry points required and input parameter combinations to exploit capabilities. Third, attack nodes offer a direct way to measure attack/security strength; e.g. partial orders on attacks and corresponding security properties. Nevertheless attack trees are fine tools and perhaps could be enhanced in the future and become useful for our purposes.

---

[9] Sarbari Gupta and Virgil D. Gligor. Experience with a Penetration Analysis Method and Tool. In Proceedings of the 1992 National Computer Security Conference, Baltimore, Maryland, pp. 165 - 183.

[10] J.D. Weiss. A System Security Engineering Process. In Proceedings of the 14th National Computer Security Conference, Baltimore, Maryland, 1991.

[11] Edward G. Amoroso. *Fundamentals of Computer Security Technology*. Prentice-Hall, 1994, pp, 15–29, ISBN0131089293.

[12] Bruce Schneier. Attack Trees. In *Dr. Dobb's Journal,* v. 24, n. 12, December 1999, pp. 21–29.

[13] Sjouke Mauw and Martijn Oosdijk. Foundations of Attack Trees. D. Won and S. Kim (Eds.), Proc. of the ICISC 2005, LNCS 3935, Springer Verlag, pp. 186–198.

Now you heard this morning about Lockheed-Martin's kill-chain method[14], this also partially maps into our attack structure for wimps. The reconnaissance, "weaponization," and delivery steps of a kill chain correspond to the notion of a set of capabilities to an attack surface discovery; i.e., entry-point, malicious data input, and delivery channel. However, the exploitation, installation and execution steps capture only *a single* attack strategy, instead of *all* strategies as required by our attack structure. This maybe the case because this method is intended for attacks where the adversary has an asymmetric advantage as in large commodity systems and is not intended to be used as a defense tool for wimps.

In summary, if wimps must be composed with giants, we need to correct and complete adversary definitions of the giants' attacks against the wimps. Without such definitions, giants are going to step on wimps' toes and the dance will be short lived. I extended the wimp-giant metaphor to the level of interactive trust protocols between humans where I would like to pursue, for example, automatic detection of scams, deception, and manipulation. In the face of the sophisticated adversaries that we have right now on the Internet, we really are all wimps. This completes my presentation.

Rafi Yahalom: In your privacy example earlier, which is fascinating and provides a lot of food for thought, what was the wimp? Was it the user specifying the privacy policy?

Reply: Yes. The wimp was the user's delegation to an isolated client-side program that executes the steps of the trust protocol with the the remote-service giant; viz., Fig. 6 in the accompanying paper). The client-side wimp ensures that the user's privacy policy regarding personal data is neither corrupted by someone who subverted her commodity operating system nor is misused (e.g., distributed or retained without permission) by the giant. So the user's privacy policy is protected by the client-side wimp. And, as a matter of fact one can even empower the user to verify that the client-side wimp, which attaches her policy to her private data, is present on her machine. She can do that using a verifier device (not shown in Fig. 6), which runs an attestation protocol that proves the presence of both the micro-hypervisor and privacy wimp. In the case of the remote service, the user has to establish a trust relationship, which would assure her that the service abides by her privacy policy.

Rafi Yahalom: Couldn't you achieve a similar result in this example with just traditional security policy for the adversary?

Reply: Well, when you refer to a traditional security policy, do you mean a policy enforced by a security kernel and the like?

Rafi Yahalom: A privacy policy, sorry.

---

[14] Eric M. Hutchins, Michael J. Clopper, and Rohan M. Amin. Intelligence-Driven Computer Network Defense Informed by Analysis of Adversary Campaigns and Intrusion Kill Chains. In Proceedings of the 6th Annual International Conference on Information Warfare and Security, Washington, DC, 2011.

Reply: It depends ... A traditional privacy policy will most likely not work. Let me give you an example. First, the traditional "notice-and-consent" policy won't work, because in protocol with the remote service the user is giving the notice regarding her privacy policy to the remote service, which would have to consent; i.e., this is notice-and-consent *in reverse*. Second, the user's policy has to be specified and attached to her personal data in a protected subsystem under user's control, and commodity systems and applications cannot enforce her control. Such control would require that we built special systems, namely non-commodity or niche systems, to enforce our policies. Those will probably work, but they won't make any difference in practice. We want to deal with commodity systems, not with niche systems. So that's why I answered "it depends:" if a client-machine system enforces such policies it's not going to be a commodity system. In a commodity system one has to add security, most likely via wimps that compose with the commodity system. This is fundamental shift from the early security theory, which emphasized that security must be built from ground up[15]. That theory is what most still believe, and I consider that to be a very useful theory, but again, only for specially-built, niche systems, not for commodity systems, which we all use.

Micah Sherr: So, to go back to your last example, you have a micro kernel in your USB example that's using work done by the giant.

Reply: No, the wimpy kernel does that.

Micah Sherr: Sorry, the wimpy kernel. I was wondering if you could characterise what types of features that are offered by the commodity operating systems are efficiently verifiable. I'm not a crypto person, but my understanding of proof of work, and other things like that, is that they are expensive.

Reply: Right. My initial answer is: I wish I knew all types of operating systems functions that are efficiently verifiable. I think we need more research for that. My second answer is: I know how to verify that a fully untrusted giant carried out a certain computation correctly, using the notion of the verifiable computation[16]. However, this works only when a wimp has the luxury to specify its own computation, encode it as a garbled circuit, homomorphically encrypt it, and outsource it to the giant. The point here is that one doesn't want to do that here; i.e., a wimp doesn't want to build, encode, and encrypt its computation. Instead, a wimp wants the giant to do all the work, and then just verify the result, which is a very different problem. In fact, in such a setting, verification may quickly lead to co-NP complete problems, if not to undecidable problems, as mentioned earlier. So my initial answer was not facetious. The verifiable

---

[15] Jerome H. Saltzer and Michael D. Schroeder. The protection of information in computer systems. In *Proceedings of the IEEE*, Vol. 63, No. 9, pp. 1278–1308, September 1975.

[16] Rosarion Gennaro, Craig Gentry, and Bryan Parno. Non-Interactive Verifiable Computing: Outsourcing Computation to Untrusted Workers. In Proceedings of CRYPTO 2010, Springer Verlag, August 2010.

computation theory, while holding great promise in many applications, is not applicable everywhere.

Micah Sherr: But if I may rephrase my question a little bit, in the USB example how much, or what else, what other functions of an I/O implementation can be outsourced?

Reply: In other words, what other types of I/O functions could be implemented by the wimpy kernel using the outsource-and-verify method? We have an implementation for PCI subsystem support, so if you take USB and PCI you've got over 70 % of all the character-oriented I/O. We do not have, and do not advocate, implementations of record-oriented I/O in the wimpy kernel. For example, record-oriented I/O such as that needed for file systems or virtual memory, could be easily outsourced directly by wimp applications as I mentioned already, using authenticated encryption. Hence these functions need not be in the wimpy kernel at all. However, most users need isolated I/O using character-oriented devices whose I/O subsystems (e.g., PCI, USB) have large bodies of code, which could be outsourced to giants.

Dieter Gollmann: Your comparison with cryptography strikes me as very interesting. In cryptography, we would not enumerate what the attacker is about to do. We bound how much the attacker can do. We get proofs that are called "security proofs," but those I've seen are only reduction proofs obtained under convenient assumptions. I'm getting papers saying, "this is an assumption that is now well accepted," so our new protocol using it must be secure. And I think you get different guarantees on the micro-hypervisor. At some point, you will have to model the wimpy-kernel interface, namely the operations the user can invoke. I'm thinking now also of the work on API attacks. One can easily get into undecidable problems, if one is not careful. In theory, one can get proofs that say "this is not possible" without any assumptions.

Reply: As far as I am concerned, there isn't a difference between "this is not possible," and "this is possible only with negligible probability," *in practice*. Here is why.

Dieter Gollmann: Reduction proofs don't give you local ability. They only give you local ability under the assumption that something unknown cannot happen.

Reply: Yes, but formal-method proofs also make assumptions about things that cannot happen, which are often even more questionable. So I don't think there is an advantage there over complexity-based cryptography.

The reason why I think that there is no difference in practice between the two statements is because the weaker guarantees offered by reduction proofs are usually *not* the weakest link in security. Remember the weakest-link story of the two hunters and the bear? The first hunter asks the second hunter: "In case you shoot and do not kill the bear, can you outrun the him?" And the second hunter replies: "I don't have to outrun him. I only have to outrun you." The idea is that if one makes the adversary's life hard enough using crypto-style primitives (i.e., complexity-based crypto adversaries, not information theoretical ones, which are unbounded), the adversary will move and attack a weaker link; i.e., the bear will get the slower second hunter. We usually aim to design security architectures that send the adversary into somebody else's backyard. We are not looking for perfection, but only for good enough security; namely, for correct and complete adversary definitions and corresponding security properties for wimps, while giants will most likely remain the weaker links. However, since wimps' functions are of limited use, we try to make wimps useful by composing them with giants. That's my message.

Rafi Yahalom: How do you define useful, how can you prove that you have made progress?

Bruce Christianson: It is sometimes much easier, as you said, to verify that a result is correct than to obtain the result.

Reply: So where do we stand now in terms of wimps and giants? There is a couple of research projects that formally proved source-code level properties of micro-hypervisors and also micro-kernels, so progress is being made there; e.g., these wimps are well under twenty thousand lines of code. Progress is being made in the sense that we can add formally-verified isolated wimps to a commodity operation system (i.e., to a giant) without changing the existing code of that system. As I argued here in 2010, one can select modules of an application and encapsulate them as wimps. Of course, one would have to recompile the application to do that, but that's the only modification one has to make ot it. The recompiled modules are then registered with the micro-hypervisor.

What type of modules would we encapsulate in wimps? Crypto libraries, certificate management code of CAs, ACL managers. All can make their services available to giants. Nevertheless there is a long way to go in making wimps useful, but there is progress. For example, in 2011, Bryan Parno and his colleagues at Microsoft Research showed how to build persistent memory for wimps. Why do we need that? Giants manage wimp memory, and hence they could attack wimps by retrieving old versions of memory. Wimps would otherwise be unable to detect this attack, since do not have state. In 2012, we added trusted path between a few user devices and wimps using a micro-hypervisor and bypassing the commodity operating system. And very recently we added on-demand isolated I/O channels for USB devices to wimps. Also, we know how to provide file-system networking services for wimps. We built a wimp-based key management system, called KISS, which we presented last year atTRUST[17]. So progress is being made.

By the way, I think that you will see versions of these ideas in commodity systems within the next few years. People have already started seeing that building wimp isolation in operating systems and applications is a fairly useful approach. They don't necessarily use our micro-hypervisors, but at least they recognise the

---

[17] Zongwei Zhou, Jun Han, Yue-Hsun Lin, Adrian Perrig, and Virgil Gligor. KISS: "Key it Simple and Secure" Corporate Key Management. In Proceedings of the 5th International Conference on Trust and Trustworthy Computing (TRUST), London. 2013.

need to isolate pieces of application code and encapsulate them without touching the commodity operating system (i.e., the giants), or other applications. So that's really the point here. Giants shall remain giants. Without them, wimps won't survive in competitive marketplaces. And history actually has proven that.

Joan Feigenbaum: I have a question for Dieter. So what is your objection to unproven assumptions? Is it that you don't believe the assumptions, or that you don't think in whole structure of proof: if the following assumption is true, then a certain class of attacks won't work. What is it that you don't like about this?

Dieter Gollmann: It's not about not liking, it's about uncertainty to getting a different type of guarantee. In one case you get a guarantee based on a favourite assumption, and in the other case you get a guarantee without any additional assumption. That is the price you pay for having a more powerful attacker, and being not forced to enumerate precisely the steps the attacker is allowed to perform.

Reply: Yes, but all formal methods have used reduction proofs.

Dieter Gollmann: Is this [a] proof?

Reply: In cryptography most proofs employ different types of reductions. Formal methods might use fewer reduction proofs, but basically most security proofs in layered systems include reductions because the security of higher layer services always depends on that of the lower-layer services. In the case of wimp applications and wimpy kernel, the security properties of the wimp apps depend on those of the wimpy kernel. Proofs are of the form: if the wimpy kernel is secure against adversary A, then the wimp app is secure against adversary B. In essence this is a reduction proof. Whether the wimpy kernel is secure against A depends on the security of the micro-hypervisor, and so on. At some point below the micro-hypervisor we start making assumptions about hardware security without offering any evidence for their soundness.

Despite such assumptions, there a proof advantage in using only the micro-hypervisor, wimpy kernel, and wimp apps over reduction proofs for application security that must include *every layer* of the operating system. That is, in traditional system security one starts with the security kernel, then one builds the file system, directory service, networking layers and so on, and proofs of application security must include the proofs of *all* layers below. In contrast, using micro-hypervisors and wimpy kernels composed with commodity operating systems (i.e., insecure giants), one only needs to add security properties "on the side" to the giant (as shown in Figs. 3, 4 and 5 of the accompanying paper), bypassing many layers of giant code. My first point is that we need to have a uniform way to define the adversary attacks, and hence security properties, such that the security of wimp apps will need to be reduced *only* to those of the wimpy kernels and micro-hypervisors. The latter two will depend on very few lower-level assumptions; e.g., about the hardware and verifiable boot; viz., accompanying paper. In contrast, the traditional layer-by-layer security proofs that start with a security kernel never worked for application security in commodity systems because there were too many complex layers between the kernel and applications. We have never completed the many layer-by-layer proofs.

My second point is that we can make the adversary definition an integral part of wimp security, just as in cryptography - a field that has been very successful in making adversary definitions an integral part of a scheme/protocol security. Why not learn from success? And why should we not apply similar techniques to all system interfaces that are exposed to an adversary?

And, yes, there are practical problems with *some* reduction proofs in cryptography. In fact, I was just talking to Yvo [Desmedt] about this danger of adapting asymptotic properties derived by non-tight reduction proofs[18],[19] to block-oriented symmetric ciphers. For such properties, the key and block lengths of block ciphers must be increased to compensate for non-tightness and yet these parameters cannot be easily changed except once every twenty to fifty years, when standards change. Hence, the requirement of increasing the security parameter to decrease the adversary's advantage and account for the non-tightness is rather impractical. This is one of the reasons why Bellare and Rogaway[20] introduced the *concrete* approach to the definition for cryptographic schemes.

Nevertheless, there is value in defining the adversary. If one doesn't define the adversary, there is no security problem to solve, and collaboration with the adversary (i.e., this workshops theme) would not be possible.

Frank Stajano: OK, that sounds like a good note on which to conclude.

[18] Virgil D. Gligor, Bryan Parno, Ji Sun Shin. Network Adversary Attacks against Secure Encryption Schemes. Technical Report CMU-CyLab-10-001, January, 2010.
[19] Sanjit Chatterjee, Alfred Menezes, and Palash Sarkar. Another look at Tightness. In IACR Cryptology ePrint Archive 2011: 442 (2011).
[20] Philip Rogaway. On the Role of Definitions in and Beyond Cryptography. In Proceedings of ASIAN, pages 13–32, 2004.

Better Authentication: Password Revolution by Evolution

Daniel R. Thomas[(✉)] and Alastair R. Beresford

Computer Laboratory, University of Cambridge, Cambridge, UK
{daniel.thomas,alastair.beresford}@cl.cam.ac.uk

Abstract. We explore the extent to which we can address three issues with passwords today: the weakness of user-chosen passwords, reuse of passwords across security domains, and the revocation of credentials. We do so while restricting ourselves to changing the password verification function on the server, introducing the use of existing key-servers, and providing users with a password management tool. Our aim is to improve the security and revocation of authentication actions with devices and end-points, while minimising changes which reduce ease of use and ease of deployment. We achieve this using one time tokens derived using public-key cryptography and propose two protocols for use with and without an online rendezvous point.

Keywords: Authentication · Public-key cryptography · Passwords · One time token

1 Introduction

Text-based passwords, passphrases or PINs are the dominant method of authenticating users today. They are used to establish the identity of an individual to an *end-point*, by which we mean either: a local physical device controlled by the user, or software running locally on it (local end-point); or a service available over a network (remote end-point). With the rise of the Internet, and particularly the Web, the number of remote end-points has risen dramatically with the average user managing 25 web accounts in 2007 [13]. Similarly, as ubiquitous computing takes hold, the number of devices individuals carry or use has increased along with the number of local end-points. Rather than sharing access to one home PC, many users now have multiple desktops as well as a laptop, tablet and smartphone. These all need lots of credentials – shared secrets – not just to access apps on the device or remote services but networks too. For example Fig. 1 shows the distribution of credentials for non-open WiFi networks that we found from the 8622 devices in the Device Analyzer project. Many users have more than 5 sets of wireless credentials and some have more than 40.

Passwords or PINs are popular because they are easy to use (incorrectly) and easy to deploy [7]. They are also popular because they are the incumbent technology: application developers believe they know how to deploy password

© Springer International Publishing Switzerland 2014
B. Christianson et al. (Eds.): Security Protocols 2014, LNCS 8809, pp. 130–145, 2014.
DOI: 10.1007/978-3-319-12400-1_13

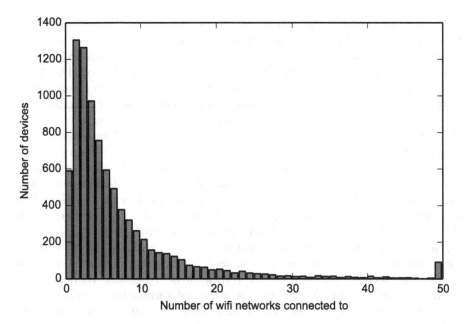

Fig. 1. Number of WiFi credentials (WEP, WPA etc.) used while Device Analyzer [32] was installed on 8622 devices (only counting if they participated for at least a week) devices which never connected to any wireless networks not counted. Data collected between 2011 and 2014.

authentication securely, and users know what a password is and do not need any new hardware as almost all devices requiring authentication today have a (soft) keyboard to enter numeric or textual data. It has also been speculated that authentication by passwords is popular because it conveys a sense of exclusivity and membership, and is therefore attractive to businesses which otherwise do not need to authenticate individuals [6].

We cannot remember strong passwords without strong incentives and good technical understanding of what is required [1]; attributes which the vast majority of users (quite reasonably) lack. As a result, the use of passwords for authentication has always been problematic because individuals choose weak passwords and reuse passwords across security domains. These two weaknesses mean that brute-force attacks are possible, and the compromise of one end-point or device with credentials compromises another end-point or device. More recently, as the number of passwords and devices with credentials has increased, the revocation of passwords in the event of loss is becoming both increasing difficult and increasingly important. Since passwords represent a shared secret, the loss of a device means that many passwords across many end-points and devices need to be reset. Can you remember all the passwords you would need to reset if you lost your smartphone? What would be the effect on your access to your remaining devices and end-points if you did so?

Whilst the use of passwords for authentication has remained largely unchanged for 40 years, there have been two important changes which have been widely adopted and deployed. Firstly, on the end-point side, different password verification functions have been used from DES Crypt [21] through MD5 to SHA512 and scrypt [24]. Secondly, on the user side, the automation of password management, in the form of keychains, browser features and general password managers, has become popular. In a survey of password behaviour [26], 28 % of respondents said they always use a "remember my password" function, and 70 % have made use of such a feature. Unfortunately popular password managers do not address important security issues: they allow users to input weak passwords which can also be shared across multiple domains (though many offer the facility to generate them), and they do not address the issue of revocation. Some also do not deal with backup and frequently do not encrypt the password database making it vulnerable to theft (for example if the user does not select a master password).

In this paper we explore the extent to which we can address three issues with passwords today: the weakness of user-chosen passwords, reuse of passwords across security domains, and the revocation of credentials. We do so while restricting ourselves to (i) changing the password verification function on the server, (ii) introducing the use of existing key-servers, and (iii) providing users with a password management tool. Our aim is to improve the security and revocation of authentication actions with devices and end-points, while minimising changes which reduce ease of use and ease of deployment and so make this a practical system.

2   Design Overview

Our approach is similar to Monkeysphere (Sect. 4.1) in that we intend to replace password-based shared secrets with public-key cryptography. Our design operates in a similar manner to a password management tool, such tools are widely deployed and familiar to many users. This has the advantage that existing software stacks, which assume the existence of a secret encoded as a string, continue to function provided the underlying verification function is modified.

Our design makes use of three components: key-servers, devices with keys and end-points. Our Key-servers would maintain an auditable append-only log[1] of public-keys and associated fingerprints (hashes), revocation certificates and signatures. Personal devices each have a public/private key pair for every identity and publish their public-keys on key-servers.

Users authenticate themselves to end-points by using a device with keys they control which is not an end-point. Authentication between the device with keys and the end-point takes place over an established secure channel (e.g. physical proximity or TLS) and requires a single message generated by the device to be delivered to the end-point (e.g., by typing).

---

[1] Existing key-servers do not maintain auditable append only logs.

2.1   Threat Model

Informally our adversary has the following abilities. Information sent and received from the key-servers can be observed, tampered with or dropped. Information sent over the channel between the device and end-point cannot be observed or tampered with. End-points in multiple security domains can be compromised by the adversary. Under those constraints an adversary should not be able to authenticate to any end-points in domains without compromised end-points. A compromised end-point should only be able to authenticate as the user to other end-points in that domain if the user attempts to authenticate to that end-point (unlike with shared secrets where end-points can pretend to be any user to other end-points).

2.2   Key Distribution

A diagram showing the different actors in the key distribution is given in Fig. 2.

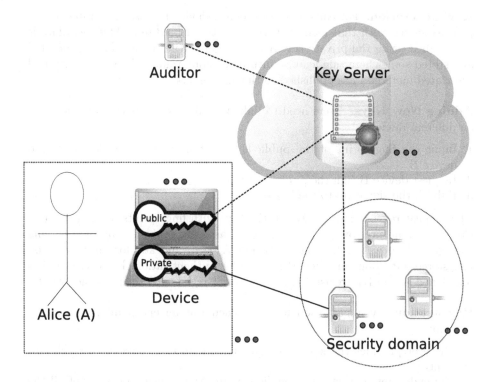

Fig. 2. Each user has a device(s) with a keypair(s). The public-keys, signatures and revocation certificates are published to the key-server(s) which maintain an append-only log, which is audited by the auditor(s). The key fingerprints are registered with the security domain(s) which can then subscribe to the key-server(s) and authenticate users using a one time token.

A user is a person who has personal computing devices, such as a smartphone, a tablet, a laptop, a desktop or a smartwatch.

A user may have multiple unlinked identities, perhaps one for their legal identity 'Joe Bloggs' another for when anonymous 'A. N. Other' and another for secret activity 'James Bond'. For each identity on each device the user can generate a public/private key pair to use for authenticating that identity using that device.

These public-keys are distributed to key-servers. Key-servers do not need to be trusted to provide integrity or authenticity as all their actions can be audited as all the data they store is public and signed. For example a Certificate Transparency [19] style system could be used.

Users need to authenticate within many different security domains. At home they need to authenticate to their own systems, with others at work, online they need to authenticate to many mutually untrusting online providers such as identify providers, banks and governments. These security domains have many end-points at which authentication can be required.

Key Generation. For each identity on each device the user generates a key-pair associated with that identity with a creation timestamp. This metadata is then signed using the private key. A revocation certificate should be generated and stored somewhere safe against future key compromise. The public key and associated metadata are published to the key-servers.

Adding New Keys. Users need to link the public-keys for the same identity on different devices:

1. Input the fingerprint of the public-key for that identity on device A into device B
2. Request device B sign the public-key input
3. Publish the signature to the key-servers

Then repeat reversing A and B. All the keys with fingerprints in the transitive closure of signatures by one key are treated as being equivalent by the verifying end-point. Hence if A has signed B and A is a valid key for authentication (registered with domain) then B is valid for authentication. However if B has not signed A and B is registered (and A is not registered) then A is not valid.

Registration. At registration for this scheme at an end-point in a security domain:

1. The user provides the key fingerprint for one of their keys for the relevant identity.
2. The end-point requests that public-key and the transitive closure of all the public-keys signed by the corresponding private key as being equivalent keys.
3. The end-point stores the fingerprints of all these public keys as being those supplied at registration by the user after confirming this with the user.
4. The security domain registers with the key-servers to be told about any relevant new signatures or revocations on these keys.

Revocation. When a key-pair needs to be revoked then the adversary may have the key-pair and the legitimate user may not have it. If the legitimate user still has the key-pair then they can issue a new revocation certificate specifying the date when the key-pair was compromised. Then any signatures or authentication attempts made using that key-pair after that date are invalid. Otherwise they can publish the revocation certificate generated originally, invalidating all signatures made with that key. Hence the importance of the end-point at registration following the transitive closure of signatures by the given key, as this prevents the user losing all access when later revoking that key. Additionally a valid uncompromised key-pair can be used to sign a modification to the revocation certificate specifying a later date when this should apply, however this key must still be valid even if the revocation were applied at the original revocation date, so that an adversary cannot publish a modification which moves the revocation date later after compromising the key.

Since the public-keys and signatures are published to an auditable append-only log with timestamps, the adversary who has compromised a key cannot produce signatures with dates in the past as they will only appear in the log after their real creation date.

Thus an adversary can only push the revocation time earlier, invalidating valid signatures and so while they could perform a denial of service, they could not authenticate as the user. They also cannot cause key-pairs which they have not compromised and which were valid at registration to be invalidated.

2.3   Simple One Time Token Authentication Protocol (SOTTA)

We propose the simple one time token authentication protocol (SOTTA). We assume that the end-point is already authenticated to the user, e.g. by physical proximity or Transport Layer Security (TLS) (for all the flaws of the CA hierarchy [9]). We also assume that they are communicating over a secure channel resistant to man in the middle (MITM) attacks.

To ensure that tokens valid for one domain are not valid for use at other domains we include the domain's name (such as a DNS domain name) D in the token. To ensure that tokens are fresh without having specific shared state we incorporate a timestamp.

Notation (in the style of the BAN logic [8]):

- K_X is the public-key associated with the identity X and K_X^{-1} is the private key for X.
- I is the time interval in which a token is valid.
- t is the current epoch time on Alice's (A) device's clock, t' is end-point's (server, S) time.
- The floor function $\lfloor t \rfloor$ quantises a time to the system's quantum Q (e.g. one minute).
- The $\|$ operator concatenates the octets of its arguments each preceded by its own length represented as 4 bytes, big-endian.
- $\{y\}_{K_X^{-1}}$ denotes the signature of y with X's private key.

The initial state for authentication is:

- Alice (A) has a device with K_A, K_A^{-1} and a clock synchronised to within Δt of UTC.
- The end-point (server, S) in domain with name D has K_A and a clock within $\Delta t'$ of UTC.
- $|\Delta t - \Delta t'|+$ transmission delay $< I$
- A has a secure connection (provides confidentiality and integrity) to S which authenticates S

Then A can authenticate to S in one step by sending its name A and a one time token o:

$$A \to S : A, \{D||\lfloor t \rfloor\}_{K_A^{-1}} \tag{1}$$

S knows D and assumes its time t' is within I of t (even after the transmission delay) and has received the one time token o from A. It can then check whether:

$$\exists t_c . t' - \frac{I}{2} \le t_c \le t' + \frac{I}{2} \bigwedge t_c \bmod Q = 0 \bigwedge \mathrm{verify}(D||t_c, o, K_A) \tag{2}$$

That is, is there a candidate time t_c within $\frac{I}{2}$ of S's clock t' which causes the one time token o to verify. If I is for example 5 system quanta, then S must perform at most 5 verifications before rejecting an authentication attempt. Hopefully usually only one verification would be required if S picks the order to verify t_c's in carefully (most likely first). It does not require much storage for S to check that it has not seen this token before, since tokens expire quickly.

While in many circumstances a password-manager style application could be used to input o, in some cases the user must still type the password. Hence the size $|\{D||\lfloor t \rfloor\}_{K_A^{-1}}|$ is important as this may have to be typed in by the user. This size is determined by the signature algorithm used.

2.4 Signature Algorithm

User text entry of random strings is a low-bandwidth channel with a high error rate and so we want the signature size to be as small as possible. Table 1 gives the number of characters required for different bit lengths with different encodings. With symmetric key-based signatures a client can provide a truncated signature to a server and the server can still verify it by computing the signature and truncating it. With public-key cryptography the server cannot generate a signature, only verify signatures and so the client must send the full signature. For 128 security bits a 3072 bit RSA [27] key is required [2] and even for 80 security-bits a 1024 bit RSA key is required (and that could be brute forced). With RSA the signature length is the same as the key length and 1024 bits takes 172 Alphanumeric[2] characters to represent, which a user will not be willing to type in. DSA[3]

---

[2] [A-Za-z0-9].

[3] DSA is broken if the random number used for nonces is biased which is problematic as frequently devices have bad random number generators that would leak the private key [15].

(and ECDSA) [12] need signature lengths four times the security-bits size and so need 320 bits for 80 security-bits or 512 bits for 128 security-bits which takes 54 and 86 Alphanumeric characters respectively.

Table 1. Encoding sizes for different bit lengths

Bits	Bytes	Numeric [0-9]	Alphabetical [a-z]	Alphanumeric [A-Za-z0-9]	Algorithm
32	4	10	7	6	
64	8	20	14	11	
80	10	25	18	14	
128	16	39	28	22	
160	20	49	35	27	
256	32	78	55	43	Minimum
320	40	97	69	54	BSL?
512	64	155	109	86	DSA
1024	128	309	218	172	
3072	384	925	654	516	RSA

Table 2. Bits required for different signature schemes for different numbers of security-bits

Scheme	80	112	**128**	256
RSA	1024	2048	3072	15360
DSA	320	112	512	1024
BSL	171 [5], 160 [3]	224 [3]	256 [3]	640 [17]
Minimum	160	224	256	512

There are shortened signature schemes for DSA [22,23,25] but they seem to use message recovery which does not help as the message is implicit and so only the signature needs transmission. We are also suspicious of such schemes as the DSS clearly states that the ephemeral key k used in the signing process must be cryptographically random and secret [12], indeed leaking any bits of it progressively compromises the private key [15].

The BSL signature scheme [5] provides signature lengths approaching the theoretical minimum of twice the number of security-bits but is not widely deployed. The theoretical limit for a hash function is double the number of security-bits because of the birthday problem. A comparison of the signature lengths of different schemes is given in Table 2.

There are other schemes: NTRUSign was broken in 2012 [11]. Lamport signatures [18] could be used but would need a different scheme with one public-key chain per domain which would make scalability harder. Schnorr signatures [29] have similar properties to DSA but are less widely used.

Ideally we would like a public-key signing scheme with a signature size providing at least 112 security-bits[4] using fewer than 256 bits in total (43 Alphanumeric characters) but there is no widely used scheme with this property – BSL might be a suitable candidate. The user can type the signature in on each authentication but we can also input it either by automatically inputting it (Sect. 2.5) or by using online assistance (Sect. 2.6). Typing it in is a fall back option if more user friendly methods are unavailable.

2.5   Automatic Entry (AOTTA)

If the device containing the keys is the same device as the one where the token needs to be input (e.g. if the keys are on a smartphone and authentication to a website through the mobile browser is being attempted) then the token can simply be copied – as with passwords and password-managers. If the device containing the keys emulates a keyboard (e.g. using Bluetooth) to the machine into which the token needs to be input, then when the user pushes a button on the device the token can be automatically typed. If the device containing the keys has a screen and the end-point where the token needs to be input has a camera then a QR code could be used. Alternatively audio networking could be used if the device has a speaker and the end-point has a microphone [20].

2.6   Online Assisted One Time Token Protocol (OOTTA)

When both the device with the keys and the end-point are online then they can rendezvous and authenticate with a short token s transmitted locally; this is shown in Fig. 3. Data about a device's preferred rendezvous point can be associated with the public-key and so does not need to be input. All that needs to be input is the identity of the user A and a random token s which can be low entropy. Then Password Authenticated Key Exchange (PAKE) protocols (Sect. 4.2) such as J-PAKE [14] or SPEKE [16] can be used to generate a shared key between the device with the keys and the end-point. Since this shared key is authenticated by s the device with the keys can perform the simple one time token authentication protocol (SOTTA) (Sect. 2.3) over a connection encrypted and authenticated with the shared key with the same result as before.

To analyse the latency and steps in this protocol more precisely we will use J-PAKE and assume that messages must be forwarded via a relay (R)[5] as the user device and the end-point may not be able to communicate directly due to network address translation.

First A must send the random short secret to the end-point (S) over the existing channel e (e.g. keyboard).

$$A \overrightarrow{e} S : s \tag{3}$$

---

[4] NIST minimum number of security-bits to 2030 [2].

[5] We are going to ignore TCP handshakes here and retransmissions as these are implementation details (we could implement this with UDP).

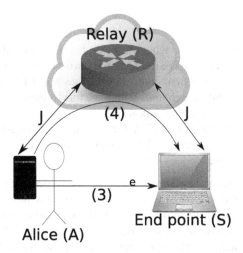

Fig. 3. Architecture of OOTTA: the existing channel is labelled 'e' and communication via the relay is set up using J-PAKE 'J'

Then concurrently A and S each send a message and a response to each other via the relay according to the J-PAKE protocol [14]. Then they can both compute session key $\mathcal{K}$ and confirm it with another request and response.

At this point A and S share a session key $\mathcal{K}$ which they can use for authenticated encryption (denoted $E_{\mathcal{K}}(x)$) and which has the same properties as the original secure channel e (such as physical proximity) in terms of integrity, confidentiality and the authenticity of S to A. It remains to authenticate A to S which we can do using the SOTTA protocol encrypted with $\mathcal{K}$.

$$A \rightarrow S : E_{\mathcal{K}}(\{D || \lfloor t \rfloor\}_{K_A^{-1}}) \qquad (4)$$

Since the first two pairs of messages are sent concurrently, the total time spent transmitting messages over the network is five times the time it takes to send a message from A to S via the relay R or 2.5 RTTs which equates to about 1 second in the worst case.[6]

2.7 Deployment

In practice we would expect large technology companies and perhaps internet infrastructure organisations such as ICANN to run key-servers (Google has already indicated a willingness to run a Certificate Transparency server which is a similar service). Relays could be self hosted or run by technology companies interested in increasing lock-in for their users. End-points range from desktops, laptops and other local devices through to servers running websites of all descriptions. Devices containing private-keys could be dedicated hardware, or commodity smartphones, desktops or laptops.

---

[6] A and S adjacent and R on the opposite side of the world.

3   Evaluation

Many different authentication schemes have been proposed to replace passwords. Bonneau et. al. [7] have conducted an exhaustive survey of authentication
schemes which we will not repeat here. It proposes the UDS framework criteria
for evaluating authentication schemes which we use to evaluate our proposal and
defines the terms in *italics* which follow.

In the following we will use OTTA for our proposal in general, SOTTA for
the simple manual input case, AOTTA for the automatic entry case and OOTTA
for the online assisted case.

Usability: OTTA is *Memorywise-Effortless* as users do not need to remember
any secrets. It is *Scalable-for-Users* as it can be used for hundreds or thousands
of domains without an additional burden on the user (they might need to input
the domain name into their device once per domain but this still scales). It
is not *Nothing-to-Carry* as the user must carry a device with keys. It is not
Physically-Effortless as the user must type something in. It is hard to evaluate
Easy-to-Learn without a real system to test against. It could be *Efficient-to-
Use* for AOTTA and OOTTA. It should be *Infrequent-Errors* for OOTTA and
for AOTTA. It is *Easy-Recovery-from-Loss* as multiple working devices with
independent keys are supported and so backups can be taken.

Deployability: OOTTA is at least as *Accessible* as passwords. It is *Negligible-
Cost-per-User* as we assume users will already have a 'suitable' device such as a
smartphone or laptop and the security domains do not need additional hardware
or other per user costs. A dedicated device might provide better security but is
not necessary. It is not *Server-Compatible* as some changes would be required
at the server end to support it. However it would be compatible with existing
users still using passwords as it just requires different treatment of the received
token. It is *Browser-Compatible* as the browser only sees a text password input,
protocol logic is at the end-point and in the device with keys. It is not *Mature*
as it has not been implemented. It is *Non-Proprietary* using known algorithms
and protocols not encumbered with patents.

Security: OTTA is *Resilient-to-Physical-Observation* as tokens are only valid
once and for a short period. An attacker could observe a token and type it in
faster than the user but this would only be valid once. Domains should ensure
that they request a new token when an authenticated client attempts to add a
new key (as with passwords). It is *Resilient-to-Targeted-Impersonation* as it
relies on randomly generated keys. It is *Resilient-to-Throttled-Guessing* and
Resilient-to-Unthrottled-Guessing as the keys would need to be brute forced
and that should require 2^{128} work (depending on the security parameter). It is
not *Resilient-to-Internal-Observation* at least not if the device with the keys is
not a dedicated device that cannot acquire malware. It is *Resilient-to-Leaks-
from-Other-Verifiers* as the verifier has nothing that can be used to impersonate
a user to a different verifier. It is *Resilient-to-Phishing* as a phishing site can
only obtain a one time token which would have to be used in real time (the definition of *Resilient-to-Phishing* excludes this and we assume a secure connection

to the end-point which authenticates it). It is not *Resilient-to-Theft* in general as we place no restriction on the devices that could be used. If users use strong security to protect their device such that data on it cannot be accessed then they would have this benefit. There is *No-Trusted-Third-Party* since bad key-servers can only compromise availability and many key-servers can be used safely and audited. It is *Requiring-Explicit-Consent* as a user must select which domain they want to authenticate to and then type something/press a button. It is very much not *Unlinkable* as one (set of) public-key(s) is used for all domains: the tokens themselves cannot be used for linking.

4   Related Work

Password managers exist that generate unique passwords for each site, but so far they have not been popular. For example, PwdHash [28] automatically generates secure passwords by hashing a user-supplied master password with the domain name of a website but has only been downloaded over 100,000 times since 2009.

If end-points supported multiple passwords then a different password could be specified for every (device, end-point) pair but this would not scale with hundreds of end-points and many devices as each password would have to be manually configured. A single dedicated hardware token such as a Pico [30] could be used but this could still be compromised and hence a revocation and resetting of credentials protocol would be required. Additionally someone would need to pay for this new hardware token. A password manager could be used to store one strong password per security domain (e.g. identity provider, work, home) but then this needs to synchronise the secrets between several devices. The compromise of any one device would result in the passwords needing to be reset for all domains. Secure synchronisation is not trivial though there is work on plausible solutions [31].

There are shared secret schemes with better resistance to brute force attacks and weak choice of passwords such as the one time password scheme used by Google's Authenticator [7, p. IV.I.5] or RSA tokens [7, IV.H.1] – but they have the same scalability problems as passwords.

SSH can use public-key cryptography to authenticate users to the server and the public-key can be distributed to many end-points. Monkeysphere solves the difficulty of revocation and distribution of new keys in that situation.

4.1   Monkeysphere

Our original motivation for developing SOTTA was to extend our existing scalable distributed authentication mechanism for our servers, which use Monkeysphere and SSH, for the cases where networking on the VM was broken or physical connection to a server was required. Monkeysphere[7] solves the key

---

[7] http://web.monkeysphere.info/

distribution and revocation problem for SSH[8] by using GPG/PGP with its key-server infrastructure to perform fast revocation. The user provides the domain administrator with a user id (uid) for their keys and the administrator signs the keys they have verified (e.g. in person) with a key trusted by the domain. Then the machines can automatically fetch all the keys which match the uid and verify them using a domain key. Those which verify can then be used to login. The key pair for SSH is embedded as a GPG subkey in the main GPG key and then SSH public-key authentication proceeds as normal with the public subkeys from the verified GPG keys being added to the relevant `authorized_keys` file.

In our group there are two domain administrators who sign the Monkeysphere enabled GPG keys of users that are then used to authenticate to our machines.[9]

4.2 Password Authenticated Key Exchange (PAKE)

Passwords are low entropy secrets, and they have no resistance against brute force offline attacks where the number of guesses an attacker has is unlimited. However low entropy secrets can be secure against online attacks where an attacker has a limited number of guesses. Unfortunately encryption, decryption and signing expose the key used to perform the cryptographic operation to offline brute force attacks and so high entropy keys are required. Password Authenticated Key Exchange (PAKE) schemes use a low entropy password to authenticate a high entropy key which two parties have generated (e.g. by using Diffie-Hellman (DH) key exchange [10]). A secure PAKE scheme only reveals to the two parties whether they have the same password on each run of the protocol. So each party knows how many times the protocol has been run and can refuse to participate in future.

J-PAKE [14] is a PAKE scheme which uses DH key exchange and is the only such scheme with a security proof and no known issues, however it is also relatively new (2011). The first such scheme was EKE [4] (1992) but some flaws have been found in it [14]. SPEKE [16] (1996) appears to be better but still has flaws allowing more than one guess of the password on each run [14]. Both EKE and SPEKE have been patent encumbered which has reduced adoption. Hence we consider only J-PAKE for use in our protocol.

5 Discussion and Conclusion

The system proposed in this paper could be implemented and make use of existing infrastructure. As with Monkeysphere we want to perform authentication, using a specific GPG subkey, perhaps with some additional associated data (the relay information for OOTTA). Then we can perform distribution of the public-keys and associated data in the background using higher bandwidth internet links on a periodic basis. Verification can be performed at registration by supplying a

---

[8] It also aims to augment/replace the CA hierarchy for TLS but that is not our focus.
[9] The source code is available https://github.com/ucam-cl-dtg/dtg-puppet/.

uid (e.g. 'Daniel Robert Thomas <drt24@cam.ac.uk>') and a key fingerprint (e.g. '5017 A1EC 0B29 08E3 CF64 7CCD 5514 35D5 D749 33D9'). The supplying of the key fingerprint allows the key to be automatically signed, and subsequent keys can be verified by: (i) signature of an existing key, (ii) inputting the key id within an existing login session, or by (iii) signature of one of the domain admins. Since all the keys are synchronised via the key-server network, it is possible to audit which keys are being circulated for different uids and which keys have signed them. So it would be easy to offer users a service which would tell them about new keys with one of their uids and keys that were signed with their keys so that signing of malicious keys can be detected and the keys revoked.

We have assumed that it is possible for users to have 'password manager' style programs, for the 'password' verification function to be changed and that the GPG key-servers can be used in backwards compatible ways for new purposes. We assume this since, unlike most aspects of password-based authentication, all these things have changed before. Crucially, our proposal does not alter the input and transmission of 'passwords' through the system and therefore any change made to the server is limited to modifying the verification function.

We described a protocol that allows users to authenticate to end-points with a single message that can be generated on a device they already have without requiring input to the device. This is backwards compatible with passwords, except for a change to the password verification function, which improves deployability. This provides good usability when the token can be input automatically (SOTTA) or when the user's device and the end-point both have an internet connection (OOTTA). This system could realistically be used to replace passwords in many circumstances, particularly when bootstrapping or when resolving failures. In the past, password authentication has evolved through changes in the verification function and the introduction of password managers. We hope this system will provide better authentication by evolving those parts of password authentication that have been shown to evolve in the past.

Acknowledgement. Frank Stajano, Nicholas Wilson, Oliver Chick, Andrew Rice, Markus Kuhn, Robert Watson, Joseph Bonneau and Bruce Christianson all provided useful feedback on various versions of this idea.

References

1. Adams, A., Sasse, M.A.: Users are not the enemy. Commun. ACM **42**(12), 40–46 (1999). doi:10.1145/322796.322806
2. Barker, E., Barker, W., Burr, W., Polk, W., Smid. M.: SP 800–57 Recommendation for Key Management - Part 1: General. In: NIST Special Publication, pp. 1–142 (2007)
3. Barreto, P.S.L.M., Naehrig, M.: Pairing-friendly elliptic curves of prime order. In: Preneel, B., Tavares, S. (eds.) SAC 2005. LNCS, vol. 3897, pp. 319–331. Springer, Heidelberg (2006)

4. Bellovin, S.M., Merritt, M.: Encrypted Key Exchange: Password-Based Protocols Secure Against Dictionary Attacks. In: IEEE Security and Privacy, Oakland, California, pp. 72–84. IEEE, May 1992. doi:10.1109/RISP.1992.213269, ISBN: 0818628251

5. Boneh, D., Lynn, B., Shacham, H.: Short signatures from the Weil pairing. J. Crypt. **17**(4), 297–319 (2004)

6. Bonneau, J., Preibusch, S.: The password thicket: technical and market failures in human authentication on the web. In: The Ninth Workshop on the Economics of Information Security, WEIS (2010)

7. Bonneau, J., Herley, C., van Oorschot, P.C., Stajano, F.: The quest to replace passwords: A framework for comparative evaluation of web authentication schemes. In: IEEE Symposium on Security and Privacy (2012). doi:10.1109/SP.2012.44

8. Burrows, M., Abadi, M., Needham, R.M.: A logic of authentication. In: Proceedings of the Royal Society A: Mathematical, Physical and Engineering Sciences 426.1871, pp. 233–271, December 1989. doi:10.1098/rspa.1989.0125, ISSN: 1364-5021

9. Clark, J., van Oorschot, P.C.: SoK: SSL and HTTPS: revisiting past challenges and evaluating certificate trust model enhancements. In: IEEE Symposium on Security and Privacy 2013, pp. 511–525 (2013). doi:10.1109/SP.2013.41

10. Diffie, W., Hellman, M.E.: New directions in cryptography. IEEE Trans. Inf. Theory **22**(6), 644–654 (1976)

11. Ducas, L., Nguyen, P.Q.: Learning a zonotope and more: cryptanalysis of NTRUSign countermeasures. In: Wang, X., Sako, K. (eds.) ASIACRYPT 2012. LNCS, vol. 7658, pp. 433–450. Springer, Heidelberg (2012)

12. FIPS 186-3: Digital Signature Standard (DSS). In: National Institute of Standards and Technology (NIST) (2009)

13. Florêncio, D., Herley, C.: A large-scale study of web password habits. In: Proceedings of the 16th International Conference on World Wide Web. Banff, Alberta, Canada. ACM, pp. 657–666. (2007). doi:10.1145/1242572.1242661, ISBN: 9781595936547

14. Hao, F., Ryan, P.Y.A.: Password authenticated key exchange by juggling. In: Christianson, B., Malcolm, J.A., Matyas, V., Roe, M. (eds.) Security Protocols 2008. LNCS, vol. 6615, pp. 159–171. Springer, Heidelberg (2011)

15. Howgrave-Graham, N.A., Smart, N.P.: Lattice attacks on digital signature schemes. Des. Codes Crypt. **23**(3), 283–290 (2001). doi:10.1023/A:1011214926272

16. Jablon, D.P.: Strong password-only authenticated key exchange. ACM SIGCOMM Comput. Commun. Rev. 26(5), 5–26, October 1996. doi:10.1145/242896.242897, ISSN: 01464833

17. Koblitz, N., Menezes, A.: Pairing-based cryptography at high security levels. In: Smart, N.P. (ed.) Cryptography and Coding 2005. LNCS, vol. 3796, pp. 13–36. Springer, Heidelberg (2005)

18. Lamport, L.: Constructing digital signatures from a one-way function. Technical report. SRI International, pp. 1–7, October 1979

19. Laurie, B., Langley, A., Kasper, E.: RFC6962: Certificate Transparency. Technical report IETF, pp. 1–27, June 2013

20. Madhavapeddy, A., Sharp, R., Scott, D., Tse, A.: Audio networking: the forgotten wireless technology. In: Pervasive Computing, pp. 55–60, July 2005. doi:10.1109/MPRV.2005.50

21. Morris, R., Thompson, K.: Password security: a case history. Commun. ACM **22**(11), 594–597 (1979). doi:10.1145/359168.359172

22. Naccache, D., Stern, J.: Signing on a postcard. In: Frankel, Y. (ed.) FC 2000. LNCS, vol. 1962, pp. 121–135. Springer, Heidelberg (2001)

23. Nyberg, K., Rueppel, R.A.: Message recovery for signature schemes based on the discrete logarithm problem. Des. Codes Crypt. 7(1-2), 61–81 (1996). doi:10.1007/BF00125076, ISSN: 0925-1022
24. Percival, C.: Stronger key derivation via sequential memory-hard functions, May 2009. http://www.unixhowto.de/docs/87_scrypt.pdf. Accessed 07 January 2014
25. Pintsov, L.A., Vanstone, S.A.: Postal revenue collection in the digital age. In: Frankel, Y. (ed.) FC 2000. LNCS, vol. 1962, pp. 105–120. Springer, Heidelberg (2001)
26. Riley, S.: Password security: What users know and what they actually do (2006). http://usabilitynews.org/password-security-what-users-know-and-what-they-actually-do/. Accessed 07 January 2014
27. Rivest, R.L., Shamir, A., Adleman, L.: A method for obtaining digital signatures and public-key cryptosystems. Commun. ACM 21(2), 120–126 (1978). doi:10.1145/359340.359342, ISSN: 00010782
28. Ross, B., Jackson, C., Miyake, N., Boneh, D., Mitchell, J.C.: Stronger password authentication using browser extensions. In: Proceedings of the 14th USENIX Security Symposium, pp. 17–31 (2005)
29. Schnorr, C.-P.: Efficient identification and signatures for smart cards. In: Brassard, G. (ed.) CRYPTO 1989. LNCS, vol. 435, pp. 239–252. Springer, Heidelberg (1990)
30. Stajano, F.: Pico: no more passwords!. In: Christianson, B., Crispo, B., Malcolm, J., Stajano, F. (eds.) Security Protocols 2011. LNCS, vol. 7114, pp. 49–81. Springer, Heidelberg (2011)
31. Thomas, D.R., Beresford, A.R.: Nigori: Secrets in the cloud (2013). http://www.cl.cam.ac.uk/research/dtg/nigori/. Accessed 2013
32. Wagner, D.T., Rice, A., Beresford, A.R.: Device Analyzer: Large-scale mobile data collection. In: Sigmetrics, Big Data Workshop. ACM, Pittsburgh, June 2013

Better Authentication Password Revolution by Evolution (Transcript of Discussion)

Daniel R. Thomas[✉]

University of Cambridge, Cambridge, UK
daniel.thomas@cl.cam.ac.uk

Reply: This is a crazy idea that I had after last year's Security Protocols Workshop.

The problem is that passwords are a rubbish way of authenticating, and there has been a lot of work trying to deal with this. One of the problems is that if you have a shared secret scheme then you need a different secret for every pair of things. For every user they need a different secret per thing they are authenticating to. If they have several of devices then they need one set of these per device as well, so that if one of them is compromised then you don't lose everything. However revocation and key management are then difficult. The problem with passwords is that you still have to use them because lots of things require a password input, and it's hard to change that.

Our idea is to generate a one-time token, which is like a password, and goes into a password field. If we generate this using public-key cryptography then we don't have any shared secrets. Then all we need to change is the verification function. The machine configuration is public then you can say, these are the keys to use, and it will just work without needing any setup of secret material. Then compromise doesn't mean you lose anything because you can just build a new machine.

The inspiration for this comes from two projects: The Monkeysphere project, which does SSH public-key management for use on servers, and which we use in our research group to manage authentication to all our servers. Google Authenticator, which is a popular one-time token authentication system.

Passwords don't scale, and this is problematic. We have lots of servers and lots of virtual machines and want to be able to authenticate to them. But we don't want the compromise of any one machine, to mean that all our machines are now compromised because you can brute-force the hash. We tried managing different passwords for different machines for a while, but you end up with lots of emails saying, 'your password for this machine is $foo', and it just doesn't work. The problem then is, if you don't have a password for a machine, then there comes a situation where you need to log into it, not over the network when you can use SSH public-keys, but physically, because you're not quite as good a sysadmin as you thought you were and you've broken the networking.

We use XenCenter, which is a Xen management client to manage our virtual machines. When we try to log into the console of a virtual machine, it requires a password. The only way to login is to boot it into single user mode by changing

© Springer International Publishing Switzerland 2014
B. Christianson et al. (Eds.): Security Protocols 2014, LNCS 8809, pp. 146–153, 2014.
DOI: 10.1007/978-3-319-12400-1_14

the kernel options, so that `init=/bin/bash` and rebooting, which is tedious, but at least you can do it at your desk. However with physical machines, we have to go to the server room and try to login to a machine that, again, doesn't have a password, so you have to reboot it and press escape at the right point in the boot cycle, and it's just a bit tricksy. So we want a solution that works even when we don't have networking working.

We want to replace passwords, so we need some of the properties that passwords have. We want to be able to put it into a password field, but we can also use existing devices. When passwords were originally devised then you didn't have devices that could do public-key cryptography in your pocket, and some of the ideas hadn't been invented yet. We're going to use some devices that we already have, some public-key cryptography, and then be able to do things we couldn't do before.

Over the last 40 years or so some things about passwords have changed. Hash functions were invented, and they got harder to compute so slowed down brute-force attackers. Web browsers have had password managers, they remember your password for you, and that makes some things slightly less painful. Kerberos, uses servers and does some cryptography, maybe that makes things a bit better, but that only really works within one domain. Inside one organisation we can do Kerberos, but it's much harder to do Kerberos to authenticate you to everything, because it's just not set up to let you do that.

In our proposed scheme there are a three things that we need to change. First we replace the hash function that takes your password, and checks the hash with a verification function which does something more complicated. Second we have a new password manager, which stores some secrets. Third we have some slightly updated public-key infrastructure, but we're modifying existing things that are already around.

Figure 2 from the paper is a design overview. The precise details of how signatures work and are published to the key-server are important and complicated and in the paper. The key-servers provide an auditable append only log which is signed by the key-server. In a similar manner to certificate transparency. We don't have to trust this key-server very much because we can check that it's doing the right thing, and if it lies to anyone then everyone can tell. We have auditors that will check this. So the key-server has stores the public-keys and the signatures on them. A security domain is, for example, a department, or the University, or your bank, or the government, organisations which are managed by different groups of people. Obviously there are lots of all of these things, so there will be lots of key-servers, lots of people auditing them. People have lots of devices, and there are lots of people. There are servers or end-points in the domains, and they can register with the key-server to subscribe to information on keys with this user id. The user, when they register with the security domain, specifies their public-key(s), and then later on when they want to authenticate they just need to send them this one-time token.

The dotted lines on Fig. 2 indicate the transmission of public-key information and the solid line indicates the transmission of one-time tokens over pre-existing a secure connection. The one-time tokens are generated using the private-key, and verified using the public-key.

The basic protocol is Alice sends a message to the server, containing her username, and just the signature on the domain and quantised timestamp. We don't send what the domain is or what the timestamp is, because that's implicit in the fact that the end-point knows it's domain and it has a vaguely similar time. We are quantising to the nearest minute, and then checking the nearest five or ten minute intervals either side of that. We are trying to reduce the amount that needs to be typed at the password prompt as you don't want this to be very long.

Bruce Christianson: What is going to be typed into the password prompt?

Reply: The one time token, a signature on the domain and timestamp.

Frank Stajano: Is this a truncated or the full version of the signature?

Reply: It has to be the full signature because it's a public signature, you can't truncate it and still verify it.

Bruce Christianson: So you're looking at elliptic curve or something?

Reply: Yes, but that doesn't necessarily buy you all that much either.

Bruce Christianson: No, and you need a confounder in there as well as just the domain and time. Otherwise the attacker could just use a random choice and apply the public-key until they get a match on the end bits.

Joseph Bonneau: Could be a randomised signature scheme.

Reply: Yes, we're thinking of a randomised scheme like DSA. If it was not built in we would need to add it.

This is an example of this authentication in practice. We have the username, which is nice and short, and then we have this 86-character long signature, this is the length of a DSA signature encoded in alphanumeric form. It takes about one minute 20 s for me to type this in, and I got to about here, and I thought that was an L and actually it's an I, so I got it wrong as well. It's not necessarily the best scheme. I think Joe might know some of the work that's going on in the modern crypto list[1] about usability studies for how you input lots of random data in a way the user can verify or maybe type in. There is nothing published on it yet.

We can look at different signature schemes and how long they take to encode. Table 1 shows how many characters in different formats you need to encode different numbers of bits. There are problems with DSA that if your randomness isn't quite random when you're making signatures, then you leak the private-key, so we'd prefer to avoid using DSA at all. But the problem is that RSA, then requires 516 characters to type in, which far too long, with low probability of successful input. There is also the BSL scheme, which is from Dan Boneh and friends, but that's not been widely used, and I found it difficult to find precisely

---

[1] https://moderncrypto.org/

how many bits it would actually require for 128 security-bits. The minimum number of bits is 256, because of the birthday problem for hash functions you need twice as many bits in the signature as security-bits. Since all of this could be brute-forced as the public-key is available, we need to have that level of protection.

Joseph Bonneau: So 128 security-bits, normally people use that because it's fairly conservative, and if you're dealing with something humans have to type you could be more aggressive.

Reply: We could carefully bring it down, perhaps to 112 security-bits.

Joseph Bonneau: If you bring it to 80 security-bits for most people's personal accounts that is still far too expensive, and it's half the typing.

Bruce Christianson: But remember I don't care which user I login as, I just need to find an account of someone I can login as.

Alastair Beresford: It depends on what machine you're protecting.

Reply: When you're specifying a new scheme you want to pick some safe defaults, people will only ever use the defaults. We pick one that no-one's going to break ever, then we won't need to upgrade later. However we might want to pick a smaller one in this case. If you're handing out a public-key to anyone who wants it then you need your key and the signatures not to be brute-forceable.

Tim Goh: If the concern is producing a valid signature what about adding a reverse a channel. You explicitly prevent the offline attack by giving a small nonce in the message. Some existing secure systems do this by making you input a nonce displayed on the screen into the device before it generates the token.

Reply: If you have a reverse channel you can do some of these things, but since we want to preserve the work flow with passwords then we can't have a reverse channel. A reverse channel might put some additional constraints on what kind of device you need to have, as you need to be able to input stuff as well as output it. There are definitely trade-offs here, but we want to go for the most universally deployable solution so this is what we have to do.

We have a long random string to input, but computers are good at automated tasks like inputting text, so if the device you have is a phone then it can pretend to be a Bluetooth keyboard. Or if storing the key on the device you are using to authenticate with you can just copy and paste. Or you can use QR codes, audio networking, or something else, and maybe that would make this more feasible.

Our other idea applies if both ends of the authentication have networking. The properties of the channel that you're using to send the token over are important, it authenticates the thing you're authenticating to. With a keyboard plugged into a server, you know you're talking to that server with no man in the middle. We want to preserve the properties of that channel. But we also might have an online channel we can use for doing the heavy lifting of moving bits.

We are going to use the J-PAKE protocol which was presented a few years ago at the Security Protocol Workshop. It is a password authenticated key exchange protocol that takes a short token with not very many bits and produces a strong key that we can use for an encrypted channel, with same properties as the original channel. J-PAKE uses a Diffie-Hellman scheme which generates a shared key, then combines this with the short token to generate the key used. If anyone is man-in-the-middling they will end up with the wrong key, and have start again from the beginning. To brute-force J-PAKE you have to get the user to type in the different short token a hundred million times. Once we've got this channel set up, then we can just do as before and send the signature across. At this point we also already know Alice's username because that's gone out across the original channel as well.

Our assertion is that this is a deployable system which could use in practice without too much difficulty. Monkeysphere uses the PGP infrastructure (key-servers) that already exists. While we might want a slightly more clever key-server that has this auditable property, and can provide us with some stronger guarantees about when things happened in a way that we can check and verify. But we could with only a small loss of usability use existing servers. Then various people already run those kind of servers. In terms of auditors, people like the EFF already check lots of certificate authorities to see whether they're behaving properly, if we design it so it's easy to verify maybe they can do quite good job of verifying. With several organisations doing that, maybe you trust one of them enough to rely on it.

In terms of what we're authenticating to, there are lots of different kinds of servers that we could use this for. Since it's entirely backwards compatible in terms of the user interaction, then maybe you can just change your backend system to allow this mechanism, and they can just tick a box in their settings saying, 'I would like to use one-time token authentication, and this is my public-key', and it would just work without interfering with existing users, making this incrementally deployable. People have lots devices, which can do this kind of stuff, and there are geeks around to be first adopters. There aren't many people using Monkeysphere at the moment, but there are some people. In terms of relays, which you might need to punch through NAT, then we can encode the information about the relays that a user is using with the public-key, so that can be distributed through the same channel. But who might run those things? If you care about user identity because you're user is your product, then you might run a relay service for them to increase lock-in into your services. There are people to do all of the roles that we need.

In conclusion, we can replace passwords using publicly verifiable one-time tokens, which only use public data. We can maybe make this easier to use by automatically inputting the token, or by using some online assistance. Then we can just use existing public-key infrastructure, and it should all work.

Bruce Christianson: Is it my imagination, or do I still have to remember a password to do J-PAKE?

Reply: No, because you're given a random short token of six characters.

Alastair Beresford: You have to remember between seeing and typing.

Reply: Six characters fits in your working memory but 86 characters doesn't.

Bruce Christianson: So roughly how long is what I have to type in to the keyboard now given that you've eliminated all the other attacks and driven the guessing attacks on-line, roughly how many characters do I need to type in for the actual verifiable one-time token.

Reply: So if we're using BSL then that's 54 characters-ish, though there wasn't a paper that said, this many bits for, 128 security-bits.

Bruce Christianson: The attacker can't do a brute-force attack online anymore can they?

Alastair Beresford: Yes, so what the online relay thing did was just to cut the number of characters you have to type in, assuming that both machines can rendezvous at some point.

Reply: The public-key is still distributed so you could still brute-force the public-key. The idea is that you publish your public-key there and you will then get that.

Bruce Christianson: But I never see what the signature actually was?

Reply: No, but you know what the format is so you can still make one if you know what the protocol is.

Bruce Christianson: But that's encrypted under a key that's as long as I like?

Reply: Yes, so the signatures are all sent over encrypted, or in other ways secure channels that authenticate the end-point, so you only need to authenticate the user. Either it's a keyboard that you're typing it in on, or you're trying to authenticate to a website using SSL, and OK, SSL isn't very good, but it's as good as we've got at the moment and so we'll live it.

Ross Anderson: Well if you're disregarding an active man-in-the-middle attack, then surely it's sufficient to just have the implementation on your phone, and I pick up my phone and I say to it, phone authenticate me to cl.cam.ac.uk, and it sends a signed timestamp to that machine and we're done.

Reply: Yes, exactly, that's what the automatic entry does, it puts this in the right place automatically.

Ross Anderson: So you don't need new hardware or anything like that, it's just a phone app?

Reply: Yes, or a browser extension, or whatever.

Alastair Beresford: So the keyboard typing in is a fallback in the case where you've got nothing else available to use, rather than Daniel looking puzzled at a machine in a server room with no passwords at all on it.

Bruce Christianson: But again, if I'm only going to have to do this about as often as I currently have to reboot a machine with the escape key held down, this is clearly an improvement.

Joseph Bonneau: So this is maybe kind of left field, but one thing that's a little odd here is that logging into a server is no longer deniable, they have non-repudiable proof for every time that you've logged in the history. Because you're signing the time and the domain that you want to login.

Bruce Christianson: Servers cannot impersonate their clients.

Reply: Yes, because it's public-key based rather than shared.

Joseph Bonneau: Yes, I suppose it's kind of interesting that they can provide proof under a court order of every time that you've logged in. Currently a lot of services can and do, do that, but you can also deny it.

Reply: Well you can claim that your device was compromised.

Bruce Christianson: Well it's quite easy if you're about to do a high value transaction you can say you need to login to the green zone to do this, and you prove that you did.

Frank Stajano: Well if the way you can deny it now, you say, well but someone else also got my password, you can also say, someone has got my private-key, right.

Joseph Bonneau: Well you could deny it that way, or you can say the server has just modified their logs, because they know the password too.

Frank Stajano: But if you really had to deny it couldn't you say someone else stole my private-key, or something.

Joseph Bonneau: Yes, although then the banking industry will say then, you've been negligent.

Virgil Gligor: In the UK, but not in the USA.

Joseph Bonneau: I'm not sure it's an interesting property either way, or which way we want, but it's an interesting change to password authentication that is non-repudiable proof of every time you've logged in.

Alastair Beresford: Well particularly because time is also wrapped up inside the signed thing, it's kind of locked away there.

Joseph Bonneau: Have you considered unlinkability between different domains so that all the different domains can't tell that they have the same, presumably the public-key is owned by one person and then they create accounts with all these different places.

Reply: The device can have multiple public and private-keys, and then you can have one per identity that you want to be separate, so if you want to unlink things then you can say, I will have two different keys, are you the right one depending on what I need to authenticate to.

Bruce Christianson: This is an old idea, Bruno Crispo and I, put forward in a previous workshop[2], but actually there's no reason why you have to share

---

[2] See LNCS 2133, pp. 182–193.

public-keys across all the clients, given the clients have to remember one key for everything they want to log into, you might as well have a unique public/private-key pair for every client who logs in. It solves your repudiation problems, it doesn't make key management much harder, and in your architecture that's actually wise.

Frank Stajano: And that's what Pico also does.

Bruce Christianson: Yes. We stole your idea and published it ten years earlier.

Tim Goh: I'm not sure if this is addressed in the paper but how do you bootstrap keys onto a fresh server machine?

Reply: Either when you originally register, or where you have an existing session and you're setting this up for the first time, you provide the public-key identifier. Then the server goes and fetches the public-key and any ones that are signed by that key, and then it has an initial set of keys that were valid originally when you first set this up. Assuming that session is then good we can use that to deal with problems later. So if a key is later revoked, one of the properties of the append only auditable log, is that an attacker can't use a key to sign, saying, 'I've signed another key five years ago and therefore that key is valid', because it will be later in the append only log. So an ordering is imposed by that, meaning an attacker can only cause denial-of-service by saying, this key was compromised before he compromised it. Obviously you can't prevent an attacker saying that they compromised their key before they did, because then you can't say they compromised it when they did. However we can make it so that they can't produce something that's valid in the past, hence any keys that weren't compromised can still be used.

Tim Goh: So the compromised scenario I was thinking of specifically here was what happens if you have a limited number of key-servers and are bootstrapping the entire protocol, and an attacker takes down the key-servers, how do you bootstrap 40,000 machines.

Reply: You cache the public-key information, if you've already had a user before, then it's fine, and you can configure new key-servers. If all the key-servers are down then you can't add new users until you get some new key-servers, or deal with the revocation and so on, but hopefully you can have enough different, independent ones then, they're not all going to be down at once for that long.

Simon Foley: If you're logging into a machine to fix its networking, you have to have logged in before?

Reply: It needs to have had network before, or you need to have put the cache, in the initial build image, it must have at some point had access the data.

Tim Goh: This, seems to break the everything is broken, I'm going to take the password off the envelope on the machine, and get physical access scenario.

Reply: But it will give you something else you can type in instead, and you don't need envelopes. Assuming it's had network before, but not a prior login.

Collaborating with the Enemy
on Network Management

Chris Hall[2], Dongting Yu[1], Zhi-li Zhang[4], Jonathan Stout[3],
Andrew Odlyzko[4], Andrew W. Moore[1], Jean Camp[3],
Kevin Benton[3], and Ross Anderson[1]([⊠])

[1] University of Cambridge, Cambridge, UK
Ross.Anderson@cl.cam.ac.uk
[2] Highwayman Associates, Leatherhead, UK
[3] University of Indiana, Bloomington, IN 47405-7000, USA
[4] University of Minnesota, Minneapolis, MN 55455, USA

Abstract. Software Defined Networking (SDN) deconstructs the current routing infrastructure into a small number of controllers, which are general purpose computers, and a large number of switches which are programmable forwarding engines. It is already deployed in data centres, where it offers considerable advantages of both cost and flexibility over a switching fabric of traditional routers. Such applications have a single controlling organisation and issues of trust between subdomains do not really arise. However for SDN to fulfil its potential, it is necessary to design and develop mechanisms for smart networks with mutually mistrustful principals.

In an earlier paper, we used as an example an airport where we might have 100,000 staff working for 3,000 different firms which include not just competitors but also organisations in a state of conflict (for example, El Al and Iran Air). That paper discussed using hierarchical control structures to delegate trust with mechanisms focussed on preventing denial-of-service attacks, with the assumption that confidentiality and integrity would be provided by the principals at higher layers. But this turns out to be a quagmire. Can you run your app and your enemy's app on the same controllers of the same fabric, and get a passable separation of behaviour on private networks that run over the same switches? And can all this be done without a trusted root anywhere?

This paper reports a project to build a test environment that adapts Quagga so that a software defined network can be automatically configured using information learned from BGP. Our Quagga for SDN Module, "QuaSM", is designed to support the use of SDN in three further use cases: in a network exchange point, in an organisation seeking to join up two or more SDN islands using an existing BGP fabric; and in security research on virtual networking.

1 Introduction

At this workshop in 2013, we discussed the security of software defined networking (SDN) [1]. SDN is a new approach to network management, which grew out

© Springer International Publishing Switzerland 2014
B. Christianson et al. (Eds.): Security Protocols 2014, LNCS 8809, pp. 154–162, 2014.
DOI: 10.1007/978-3-319-12400-1_15

of earlier research into active networks [2]. It separates the control plane and data plane so that forwarding is done by simple but fast hardware, while the control logic is offloaded to commodity PCs [3]. These PCs calculate and install logic on forwarding devices, which inspect the headers of incoming packets and follow forwarding rules specifying where and how each packet is to be forwarded. The behaviour of the network (i.e. what the network does with all the packets it receives) is defined by the sum of all forwarding rules in all forwarding devices. Instead of using vendor-supplied code, operators can now use any software of their choice as the control plane, with sufficient freedom in deciding how the overall network behaves and how each forwarding device reacts to particular packets. SDN is gaining traction in industry because of simpler network management and reduced capital expenditure.

In conventional routed networks, each router has a control plane and a data plane, which in large routers are manifestly separated. However, in a router the local control software constructs forwarding rules based on its local view of the state of the network and its local configuration. Routers are configured in a variety of ways and have a variety of features to control the construction of forwarding rules — depending on the make and model of the router and, in larger routers, the hardware configuration. The control plane in a routed network is fragmented. The behaviour of the network depends on all routers having a sufficiently good view of the state of the network and each one being configured to construct the required forwarding rules. Routers talk a variety of routeing protocols to learn and distribute network state, but the information available to each router is limited by the routeing protocol. Given the limited capabilities of routers that manufacturers provide and the complexity of the task, the effectiveness of the configuration is limited.

In contrast, an SDN control plane may be integrated and largely independent of the underlying forwarding devices [4]. The revolution here is that the management of the network is "top down"; the network's policies may be fed down into the control plane, which will construct the forwarding rules — depending on the state and topology of the network — which in turn are fed down into the forwarding plane. This is the fundamental difference with a conventional routed network, which is managed "bottom up"; there the routes are managed individually, with the intention that the emergent behaviour of those independent actors will meet the network's requirements. Furthermore, the capabilities of the (open) control plane are a "simple matter of programming", unconstrained by current routeing protocols and liberated from today's tightly bound control/forwarding (closed) devices. This should lead to rapid advances in control software, as was envisaged by McKeown et al [5].

The separation of forwarding also opens the way for innovation and competition in the hardware-intensive world of the forwarding device. The immediate effect is a reduction in capital costs, which already attracts interest. Further, "middle-boxes" such as firewalls, load-balancers and intrusion-detection systems are significant parts of most networks. These devices comprise both specialised control software and specialised forwarding hardware. Assuming that forwarding devices become more general and more powerful, middle-box functions may well be absorbed into and distributed across the SDN, which could simplify and reduce costs. Further, where firewalls in an existing network are choke points, an SDN might in theory mobilise the entire network to repel unwanted packets.

Thrilling though innovation and cost saving in the data plane may be, the real revolution that SDN drives is the revolution in network management. Most SDN deployments today are in the data centre, where many tens of thousands of servers are connected by thousands of switches, in a largely switched (rather than routed) network [6]. Here the key advantages of an SDN are that the management of the network can be more effectively automated, improving the efficiency of the network, increasing the speed and ease of implementing changes, and reducing operational costs. Switched networks are straightforward, the switches are told what to do and they do that — the problem is that changing the network means telling the switches to do something different. Switched networks will guarantee that the configured capacity is available between two points while everything is working; the problem is that they do not automatically respond to failures. Yet modern data centres use large numbers of commodity PCs rather than small numbers of expensive mainframes, and the key enabling technology is automated failure recovery. Firms like Google pioneered computing platforms that recover more or less seamlessly from the loss of a single hard drive, or a whole PC, or a rack, or even an entire data centre; automating the control plane for the vast switched networks in such centres is both necessary and revolutionary.

The next step is to take SDN beyond the closed environment of a data centre. At a carrier, for example, it can also improve the efficiency, increase the speed and ease of implementing changes, and reduce operational costs. Centralising the control plane of a large network allows it to be managed as a whole (top down). To support this, the control plane must keep track of the state of the whole network, so that the automated-decision making processes can, guided by the configuration, program the data plane to fulfil the operator's requirements to the greatest extent possible, given the state of the network at the time. This vision of complete control of the network is seductive and compelling. Clearly, however, no large real-world network is going to be controlled by a single, all-seeing, all-knowing controller device. In a data centre the SDN control plane may be implemented that way (with suitable provision for fail-over), but beyond that we must expect it to be a distributed system, perhaps based on a distributed database of configuration and network state. The control plane may be implemented as a hierarchy of systems (as we described in our 2013 paper [1]), with local systems making decisions for the local network, and regional or global systems making higher level, larger-grain decisions. The argument for SDN is that once liberated from today's routers, whose function is based on the network and computing resources of the 1970's, the control plane can be transformed.

Currently, routers keep track of the state of a network using internal routeing protocols (notably OSPF, IS-IS and iBGP). These protocols provide each router with a view of the network which is more or less complete (at least locally) and more or less timely. In an SDN we may expect this information to be maintained at the logical centre of the network, so these protocols are likely to be casualties of the SDN revolution.

Externally, where different operators' networks are connected, the routers speak eBGP, the de facto routing protocol of the Internet, to each other. There is clearly no likelihood of eBGP being sent to *Madame la Guillotine* in the near future, so if only as a transitional measure, we need to consider how to use BGP as a component of an SDN control plane.

2   QuaSM

Our Quagga for SDN Module, or 'QuaSM', is being produced as part of a DARPA seedling project. It is designed to provide a component for use in an SDN control plane.

A BGP router accepts routes advertised to it by its "neighbours". Each route comprises a "network prefix" and a set of "attributes". Each route represents an undertaking from the advertiser of the route that it will forward packets destined for the IP addresses given by the prefix towards their destination. The receiver of a route will examine it and decide whether to include it in its "Local Routeing Information Base" (Loc-RIB) as a candidate for selection, and in the process may modify some attributes. The router will select the route which it considers to be the best of the available candidates. That route will be installed for use in the router's forwarding hardware, and will be advertised to the router's neighbours. (This is not a complete description of BGP, but is sufficient for our discussion.)

Underlying the way that BGP works is the assumption that the BGP process is making routeing decisions on behalf of the device it is running on. Where relevant, the selection process will consider the device's place in the network, so the "network cost" of using a given route from the perspective of the router will be taken into account. The notion of network cost of a route is defined by its operator, and usually includes factors such as the number of hops and preference derived from business relationships.

For an SDN control plane BGP needs to be lifted out of individual routers, and become part of a logically (if not actually) centralised system. So a key part of QuaSM is to separate out the network cost considerations and to allow for multiple, parallel selection processes. A network of any size will generally comprise a number of Points of Presence (PoPs) connected together. A PoP may be a large data centre or may be a router or two connecting to customers or other networks. QuaSM views the underlying network as comprising a number of "route-contexts", and runs a separate selection process for each one. Where network cost is relevant when choosing between routes for use by devices in route-context 'C', then if route '1' is via a neighbour in route-context 'A' and route '2' is via a neighbour in route-context 'B', then the network costs of getting from 'C' to 'A' and from 'C' to 'B' are taken into account. In a given network each PoP might be treated as a route-context. A cluster of small PoPs might be treated as a route-context; a really large PoP might be treated as more than one. The essence is that a collection of devices may be lumped together in a route-context when it makes sense for QuaSM to make the same decision for all of them, which means that the network cost between these devices is, effectively, zero. Another perspective is that routeing decisions optimise network cost over route contexts rather than over individual nodes or routes.

QuaSM manages BGP conversations with other BGP speakers, accepts routes from neighbours, maintains the usual Route Information Bases, makes the usual BGP routeing decisions (but one for each route-context), and announces routes to neighbours. The routes announced to neighbour 'C' will be those selected for the route context in which the connection to 'C' is made. The interface between QuaSM and the rest of the SDN control system includes a means to configure the BGP processing, a means for BGP to discover and be told about network costs (using an "infinite" cost to signal loss of connection), and a means for BGP to pass the selected route (one for each route context) to the rest of the SDN.

All of this is recognisably BGP. In this form QuaSM can be dropped into an SDN control plane as a straightforward replacement for an existing BGP mesh, where it manages all the eBGP connections and replaces all the iBGP ones. The interface between QuaSM and the rest of the SDN can be extended, first so that more of the information learned by BGP is available to the control plane, and second to augment or replace the selection process. Further work may well be needed to scale this approach up for large networks. As for SDN in general, for large networks it may be necessary to subdivide the network and perhaps create a hierarchy.

Another possible application for QuaSM is the use of BGP to tie islands of SDN together. In this case the QuaSM instance in one SDN island would be talking iBGP to instances in other SDN islands, and perhaps to the rest of the network's iBGP mesh.

The flexibility of SDN and operator-run code also allows for a smooth transition in the event we find ourselves connecting a traditional BGP network to an SDN-for-BGP network. The SDN part, being newer than traditional BGP, can understand and talk in the protocol language in a backwards compatible manner. Since no flag day will happen in which everyone on the Internet updates their routing software simultaneously, the ability to manage a transition stage well is crucial to the deployment of a new technology.

3   SDN and Security

An SDN control plane will comprise control and forwarding elements connected by some control network. It is clearly essential to ensure that those elements and that network cannot be suborned or prevented from working. Where the control network is separate and self-contained (as, perhaps, in a data centre), that may suffice. The use of TLS and some means of distributing the necessary certificates may suffice in the more general case, though the network might wish to give priority to control traffic where it shares bandwidth with other traffic. Those are issues which affect the security of the inner workings of the SDN, which are essential to ensure that the network is not disrupted by an enemy, but are not related to collaborating with the enemy.

Across the data plane a network will carry all sorts of traffic, but not all traffic will be welcome in all parts of the network, and some traffic may not be welcome at all. Some traffic may be welcome in limited amounts. As noted above, current firewalls, load-balancers, intrusion detection systems and so on are "point solutions". For them to be effective, network engineers must ensure that any traffic which may be suspect will pass through the required middle-boxes, and that all middle-boxes are configured correctly. This is inevitably in tension with the need to avoid or mitigate service-denial attacks[1]. The ability to specify traffic rules centrally, and leave the system to decide where and how to implement those rules, may transform a network's ability to control the traffic it carries. This could be done with existing middle-boxes: the SDN control plane could take responsibility for directing packets through the required middle-boxes. Given a way to program those middle-boxes, the control plane software could automate their configuration as well; it's worth noting that if the control plane is compromised then the middle-boxes can be avoided. When sufficiently capable and powerful general-purpose forwarding devices become available, the programming of traffic control rules may be simplified. In short, the greater control and automation implicit in SDN can transform a network's ability to manage collaboration with the enemy in handling packets. However the control plane itself is of necessity trusted, so it must run on a trustworthy platform.

Network Ingress Filtering (BCP38/RFC2827 and 2267 before it) has been recommended practice for some 15 years, but is not commonly implemented. If all networks policed incoming packets, and rejected those with spoofed source addresses, then some forms of Denial-of-Service attack would be impossible and others at least traceable to their source. Unfortunately, policing incoming packets is not straightforward and there is the usual lack of incentive to overcome that. Greater automation does not solve the incentive problem, but could make the implementation straightforward, and perhaps reduce costs to the point that it becomes the default option.

Security concerns with BGP are not new. A more secure form of BGP has been at least fifteen years in the making. The latest and one that is most likely to see real world deployment, is BGPSEC, which has spawned some 22 RFCs in the last two years, though the "BGPSEC Protocol Specification" is still in draft form. BGPSEC sets out to secure the BGP AS_PATH attribute, so as to make it possible to detect most forms of path tampering. However, BGPSEC does not address "route leaks", which are the most common way of disrupting global routeing; nor does it mitigate those attacks that do not require a forged AS_PATH. The processor and memory requirements projected for BGPSEC are well beyond the capability of current routers, even high-end million dollar devices. Furthermore,

---

[1] Firewall rules are not straightforward, and it may be necessary to configure each firewall differently: where not all the firewalls in the network are of the same make and model; or where for performance or other reasons not all rules for the network can be installed in every router; or where the rules for different parts of the network simply aren't the same; and so on.

the security economics of deployment are difficult, as the protocol's benefits are more global than local.

Lifting BGP out of routers may yet prove to be the most practical way to implement BGPSEC. Bringing the BGP routeing information and decision making into the light will also allow for innovation in the verification of the information and allow other sources of information to influence route selection. A useful analogy might be drawn here with authentication, where for years researchers at this workshop (and elsewhere) have focussed on password verification protocols. Nowadays, user authentication is becoming a 'Big Data' service; firms such as Google, Facebook and Microsoft see billions of authentications a day and are far better placed than individual e-commerce websites to spot an account compromise. Large-scale analytic techniques can also be used for network security tasks, once a suitable platform can be deployed. Further improvements to the security of inter-domain routeing need not then take another fifteen years!

Integrating the information learned by BGP with the rest of the SDN network state can allow the control plane to create low level forwarding rules consistent with the high level routeing. For example, packets sent to a given neighbour should be destined for addresses which the neighbour has announced valid routes for, and those addresses only. Conversely, packets received from a given neighbour should only have source addresses for which the neighbour has announced valid routes.

In addition, most network failures at present result from operator error, as traditional routers are managed using 1970s-vintage command-line interfaces; these do not support such desirable features as atomic updates and managed rollbacks. Worse, the router vendors have all customised the commands slightly making it easy for even experienced operators to make mistakes. Modern user interfaces with proper tools can improve reliability and usability as well as security.

4   Latency Rains on Parade?

The "logically centralised" SDN control plane appears to promise the nirvana of complete, automatic control of the network. Instead of having to guess how a network of independent routers will respond to changes in traffic or link or equipment failure, the SDN control plane, armed with perfect and complete knowledge will re-optimise the network.

The most obvious issue with this is latency. In a global network, a device in Sydney is 150 ms from London, as the packet flies. So a network event in Sydney would take at least 150 ms to be registered in London, and any network changes would take at least 150 ms to make their way back. This does not make obvious sense. In fact, when it comes to latency, engineering reality is often very much worse than the limits set by physics, and the main reason is the needless introduction by engineers at many levels in systems and networks of mechanisms that introduce unnecessary delay [7]. Locating controllers at such a distance from the switches they drive may degrade telepresence and other services that require interactivity [8].

Scaling and latency point towards the need for an SDN to be subdivided. Latency points to a subdivision on a geographical basis, so that local decisions can be made locally. Unsurprisingly, perhaps, this returns the SDN to some of the problems with existing routed networks, where latency and information skew cause, transient, routeing issues. How very large networks will solve these issues remains to be seen. So far there have been some proprietary solutions; Google's implementation is described at [6].

5   The Research Opportunities

Software defined networks are the new cutting edge of networking innovation. They are widely deployed in large data centres, where they first save cost by replacing expensive routers with commodity hardware, and second provide resilience by supporting intelligent failover to replace failed machines or racks. Deployment is starting in Internet exchange points (we have worked with one IXP in developing the BGP-for-SDN module software) [9]. The next likely target after that is in corporate networks, which already have islands of SDN that they wish to link up; and in large carriers, where the driver will be saving labour costs. More complex multitenanted networks, such as the airport example discussed in [1] here last year, may follow.

SDN technologies have the potential to deliver much more secure networks, by making practical the deployment of security protocol suites such as BGP SEC; by enabling network-wide monitoring, analytics and control in order to deal with the threats that BGP SEC ignores; and by allowing specific services such as intrusion detection, DDoS prevention, firewalls and indeed interception to be re-engineered as network applications. This creates a lot of scope for creative innovation in defence, and (it must also be said) in attack. As much of the design and development work for large-scale SDN remains to be done, there is an opportunity for security researchers to get involved in time to make a difference.

We have therefore been developing (in the context of a DARPA seeding project) a Quagga SDN Module, QuaSM, that enables researchers and developers to carve out the BGP functions from an SDN network for the purposes of experimentation and testing [10]. This will enable SDN to build on the existing BGP mechanisms for negotiating the details of transit and peering between mutually distrustful parties. By using BGP as a scaffolding, we can not only build the next generation of production systems for slightly more complex and decentralised environments, but provide a platform on which researchers can experiment with novel trust mechanisms for virtual networks. Once we have two separated networks that interoperate using BGP, we can also test two logically separate networks that interoperate using BGP while running on the same switch fabric. It will then be possible for security researchers to play network games by combining ideas from DDoS, red pill/blue pill, concurrency/API and all sorts of other attacks, to determine empirically whether a network can obey the maxim 'hold your enemies close'.

Acknowledgement. The work described in this paper was funded under DARPA BA 12-29 FA8750-13-2-0023, 'Hardening the next generation control plane', whose support is gratefully acknowledged.

References

1. Yu, D., Moore, A.W., Hall, C., Anderson, R.: Authentication for resilience: the case of SDN. In: Christianson, B., Malcolm, J., Stajano, F., Anderson, J., Bonneau, J. (eds.) Security Protocols 2013. LNCS, vol. 8263, pp. 39–44. Springer, Heidelberg (2013)
2. Feamster, N., Rexford, J., Zegura, E.: The road to SDN: an intellectual history of programmable networks. In: Queue, vol. 11, no. 12, pp. 20–32, December 2013
3. Limoncelli, T.: OpenFlow: a radical new idea in networking. In: Queue, vol. 10, no. 6, pp. 40–46, June 2012
4. Caesar, M., Caldwell, D., Feamster, N., Rexford, J., Shaikh, A., van der Merwe, J.: Design and implementation of a routing control platform. In: NSDI 05, pp 15–28 (2005)
5. McKeown, N., Anderson, T., Balakrishnan, H., Parulkar, G., Peterson, L., Rexford, J., Shenker, S., Turner, J.: OpenFlow: enabling innovation in campus networks. ACM SIGCOMM Comput. Commun. Rev. **38**(2), 69–74 (2008)
6. Jain, S., Kumar, A., Mandal, S., Ong, J., Poutievski, L., Singh, A., Venkata, S., Wanderer, J., Zhou, J., Zhu, M., Zolla, J., Hölzle, U., Stuart, S., Vahdat, A.: B4: experience with a globally-deployed software defined WAN. In: SIGCOMM 2013. http://cseweb.ucsd.edu/~vahdat/papers/b4-sigcomm13.pdf
7. Cheshire, S.: Latency and the quest for interactivity. http://www.stuartcheshire. org/papers/LatencyQuest.html
8. Geelhoed, E., Parker, A., Williams, D., Groen, M.: Effects of latency on telepresence. Hewlett Packard technical report 120, June 2009. http://www.hpl.hp.com/ techreports/2009/HPL-2009-120.pdf
9. Gupta, A., Shahbaz, M., Vanbever, L., Kim, H., Clark, R., Feamster, N., Rexford, J., Shenker, S.: SDX: a software defined internet exchange. Georgia Institute of Technology, SCS technical report; GT-CS-13-06 (2013). https://smartech.gatech. edu/handle/1853/49629
10. Hall, C.: quagga.euro-ix. https://github.com/GMCH

Collaborating with the Enemy on Network Management (Transcript of Discussion)

Ross Anderson[1](✉) and Chris Hall[2]

[1] University of Cambridge, Cambridge, UK
[2] Highwayman Associates, Leatherhead, UK
Ross.Anderson@cl.cam.ac.uk

[RJA]: This talk is about collaborating with the enemy. Last year at the Protocols Workshop we talked about software defined networks, and this is an exciting new technology which is being deployed in data centres. The idea is that you can take a router which costs a million dollars and you can split it up into a commodity PC running some control software, and a number of switching cards that are also commodities. And you can potentially make a whole lot of stuff software that up to now was custom Cisco stuff or Juniper stuff, and not very accessible. This has got traction because if you are someone like Google you could save an enormous amount of money on all the routers in your data centres. The question is whether you can do something more interesting and exciting with it, and use it in more difficult environments. Last year we talked about whether you could use software defined networks in a complex multi-tenanted environment, like Heathrow, where you have got over a hundred thousand badged staff working for three thousand different companies. How do you manage all the cross-domain trust issues involved, if you have got both El Al and Iran Air among your tenants at your airport?

We figured that this was going to be a very, very hard problem to solve, so what we try and solve first is a slightly easier problem: how you run SDN in a big company. The sort of company that we might be talking about is somewhere like Deutsche bank, or Goldman Sachs, where you might have tens of thousands of employees over fifty countries, peering with the Internet at perhaps twenty exchange points. And if you've already got some islands of SDN in your network, how do you join them all up together in a way that makes sense, and in a way that's reasonably secure? Another application is what happens in an internet exchange point, such as Linx in London, where various ISPs from Britain come together and peer. There you've got some quite complex networking requirements, and there are various ways in which you could make the world an awful lot better if you could do much of the route management in software.

So last year we decided that we would actually build some software to try and make this work, so we could experiment with it. The guy who's been leading the software development task is Chris Hall, so I'm going to hand over to him for the next 20 min to describe what he did.

[CH]: Before going on to talk about this software I thought we'd have a quick slide to explain what software defined networking is. Most people start with the separation of the control plane and the data plane, but it's a lot more

© Springer International Publishing Switzerland 2014
B. Christianson et al. (Eds.): Security Protocols 2014, LNCS 8809, pp. 163–171, 2014.
DOI: 10.1007/978-3-319-12400-1_16

revolutionary than that. The three key points are first that the forwarding plane is programmable, so the forwarding rules are installed automatically under program control from the control plane. The second key thing is that now the network operator is managing their network top down, so they specify from the management systems what they want. The control layer takes that and a view of the current state of the network, and then automatically installs forwarding rules in the layer below to do what the operator wants. And the third key thing is that the control plane now has an overall view of the network, and can take whole network decisions on behalf of the network.

So you'll notice that there are no routers in our software defined network, and I'll talk about that more in a second. The other thing that you see in many networks these days are many middleboxes – firewalls, load balancers, intrusion detection systems, traffic shapers, all kinds of stuff. In a software defined network you can integrate all of that functionality and embed it in the whole control plane and forwarding plane, so you don't need to have specialised boxes to do all this work. And so instead of your firewalls being isolated pockets of resistance to bad stuff travelling round your network, the whole network could be mobilised to do these functions. Another example is DDoS using NTP which was in the news recently. Network ingress filtering is well known to be a possible way of reducing these sorts of attacks, but nobody implements network ingress filtering because it's hard work, and all the incentives are pointing in the wrong direction. Now software defined networking can't change those incentives, but it can perhaps automate the whole process of network ingress filtering so that it becomes the default option.

So in what we may now call sniffily a conventional routed network, your network consists of lots of routers connected together, which talk to each other, and as we can see here, already separate the control plane and the forwarding plane. So what it is exactly about SDN which is quite so revolutionary? Well when you've got lots of routers your control plane and your forwarding plane are fragmented across your network, and each router is making decisions on its own for itself using only local knowledge. And each router has to be configured individually, so your network is now operated bottom up rather than top down. And frankly it's all really rather hard work. Further, what you can do in your network is constrained by what the router manufacturer can provide to you, because these are all closed, completely closed systems. So with a software defined network we can open everything up, and we can do new things which we previously could not do.

What I've talked about so far fits neatly with the major current application of software defined networks, which is data centres. If we're going to go further than that then we need some more stuff in our SDN, and so we go to the opposite extreme now of inter-domain routing, the mother of all 'collaboration with the enemy' in the internet; and BGP, which is the daddy in this particular area. So here we have our example network AS2529 connected to a number of other networks, and to do all the magic it speaks BGP to those networks – specifically external BGP, or eBGP – and then inside the network it talks iBGP in order to distribute the routes. Now BGP has a bunch of well-known problems which I'm not going to rehearse, which in our SDN perhaps we can open up and apply novel solutions to.

So how are we going to get our SDN and BGP to cooperate? Straightforwardly, we need a sub-layer of our control plane which is going to talk BGP to outside world, and which is going to exchange information with the rest of the control plane. That's what I've suggested on this slide. Now the slide actually seems to suggest that the routing element – the bits which are doing BGP – would be entirely separate from the rest of the control plane, but that's not really to be taken literally. I imagine that the software would be integrated into the rest of the control plane. So what this is doing is lifting BGP up out of the routers and liberating it so that we can do new and interesting things with it. And furthermore we can use BGP to contribute the information that it's learning into the whole network state that the control plane has.

So this is what BGP does currently, and the diagram here shows the processing for an individual prefix where this BGP speaking box has a bunch of neighbours providing it with routes. In this case we've got four routes for our prefix P, those routes come in, are stored, and go through a bunch of in-filters into the local RIB where they become candidates for selection, they're selected, and the best group is then installed in the router's local forwarding hardware, so in the line cards within the router. And this is actually a strong built-in assumption with BGP, that the BGP process is making selections of routes for the local device, something which is not going to be true for our SDN as you'll see in a minute. And then having selected the best route then that route is then advertised to all the peers on the other side passing out through a bunch of outbound filters.

Now the in-filtering and the out-filtering are what implement what is grandly called routing policy inside these routers. And one of the things you could do with the inbound filtering, for example, is to change the local preference on routes before the route goes through as a candidate for selection. This is not a very subtle way of directing the selection process, which goes through those properties there in order. And also configuring all of those in-filters for 500,000 odd possible prefixes, if you've got 30, or 40, or 50 peers for a given router, you've got 220 or something order routers across your network, all of which have to be configured individually, this is all hard work, and even once you've done it the selection process is not terribly subtle. You'll notice that the network metric down there is very low in the pecking order, so everything else has to be equal before it even considers the network metric. This is particularly a pain with internal BGP, iBGP, and one of the reasons why one would be quite keen to get rid of iBGP if one only could.

So now if we imagine our AS2529 now re-implemented as a software defined network, you'll see that we've replaced all the routers by various amounts of forwarding engines, and control plane engines, and in the middle we have our routing engine doing all of the BGP work on behalf of the entire network. So now all of those eBGP sessions we showed before are now being tunnelled back into our central BGP processor, which is going to make routing decisions. We've also shown here that this particular network has presence in London and in

Amsterdam, and shown that for our favourite prefix, prefix P, we've got routes from three of our neighbours, two in London, A and D, and one in Amsterdam, H. So it's fairly clear that on behalf of the network in Amsterdam it would be nice if our central device here selected route H for use in Amsterdam, and selected either A or D in London. So for our central SDN BGP we need a BGP which is capable of making multiple routing decisions in the context of the devices for which it is making those decisions. And this I happily called a route context. So here we have straightforwardly two route contexts, London and Amsterdam, and we want our routing engine to make different decisions for those two contexts.

And then this is the BGP process extended to do that. So now instead of one lot of candidates and one selection process, we've got one lot of candidates, and the selection process per route context. And instead of sending the selections down to the local routing hardware, selections are being sent into the control plane. The software that I've been working on does pretty much this, and is intended to be a component of the larger software defined network in the control plane. It's got the input and the output, in order to do different route policy for each route context, there's an additional filter like the in-X filtering, which is done on a per route context basis. And clearly there's more work going on in here depending on the number of route contexts you're supporting in your centralised VPN engine, but not all the work is actually multiplied up by the number of route contexts, just parts of it, which is cheering in a way.

Now this is all still recognisably BGP using filters and so on. Once we got to this stage we've lifted the BGP up out of the router and into the central place, then that becomes 'a simple matter of programming', as we say, to replace the in-filtering and whatnot in the selection process with something which is altogether more cunning, and may give us information beyond the stuff that BGP is gathering from the outside world, perhaps implementation systems, time-of-day routing, quality-of-service routing, all kinds of things can now be built into this, since we've liberated the BGP processing out of the routers.

So as an example of this in action, there's a small IXP in New Zealand which is running OpenFlow switches and their own custom control layer to operate the exchange. So this, if you're not familiar with internet exchange points, an internet exchange point is basically a big switch to which the clients all connect and can send the packets to each other. Most exchange points these days run a thing called a route server which helps new clients connect into the exchange, so that instead of having to establish a BGP connection to every other existing member of the exchange, a new client connects to the route server, and that broadcasts its routes to everybody, and send everybody's existing routes to it, and it's immediately then connected to the outside world.

So what the guys in New Zealand have is a custom control plane above the OpenFlow switches, and they also connect the OpenFlow route server into the control plane. And now what it does is that the switch, instead of allowing any packet at all to be directed at a client server, the default state now for the switching infrastructure is that client Z receives no packets at all. When client Z announces a route through the route server, the route server sees it, sends the message down to the control plane and says, 'he's announced this prefix', it says up the required flow route, and that prefix, the package can now be directed to client Z for that prefix, and only for that prefix, which is kind of cool, integrating the information all the way up the BGP plane, right the way down the forwarding route automatically. And I think it's a fine example of automation, which is the real power of software defined networks.

But nothing is for nothing, as they say, and the obvious problem with centralising the BGP processing for a large network is that it introduces new and interesting forms of latency. In particular, there's no real way of telling how long it's going to take for routes given by BGP to make their way through the control layer, and to be actually implemented as forwarding rules down in the forwarding plane, and how long that's going to take compared to the advertisement of routes which are saying 'that this is the state of our network' – so a potential inconsistency between routes advertised and routes actually implemented, a truth-in-advertising problem with the first water.

Now BGP, I have to say, is full of all sorts of latencies, it's a very slow thinking protocol. The standard requires, for example, once you've announced a route for prefix P you have to wait at least 30 s before you advertise another route for that prefix. So BGP is slow already, but we're used to that. These latencies are new, and may be interesting, or they may not. It's an interesting problem.

[RJA]: So one of the things that we've been doing with Dongting is looking at how various new and interesting types of service denial attack might come out once you start building this new extra network which links up your route server and your various controllers and switches. So some interesting issues arise out of this from the protocol designer. To sum it up, we got a number of issues with the BGP protocol. Now BGP is not secure, there's a secure version of it being designed – BGPSEC. There are NSA people on the committees, so given the Snowden revelations people may not believe BGPSEC to begin with. But even if it does work and gets introduced, it only signs static data, and so it can introduce fragility. And it doesn't assure all the things that we might like to; you've got assurance in one direction of packet flow but not in the other. And there are some fairly large holes in it so that. For example, if you see a route that's signed by somebody, you can sign it too and pass it on. So the sort of attack that we saw with Pakistan Telecom announcing routes for YouTube, is still perfectly possible with BGPSEC deployed.

So here's an example of a protocol, a security protocol that's about to be deployed, which isn't going to do all the work that's required of it, so you need extra stuff. You need extra smart software, which will take the BGPSEC signatures as only one input out of many into the actual routing decisions. And as Chris said, you might be using reputation, time of day, all sorts of big-data analytics to actually make your routing decisions. Now this is reminiscent of one or two other things we've seen in the protocol space. For example, in EMV, in the old days either your PIN was correct or not, and if it was correct you got the money from the cash machine, and if it wasn't you didn't. Nowadays there tend to be big data analytics in banks, and usually they will go with the result of a PIN verification, but sometimes they won't. Sometimes you can put in the wrong PIN and still get your money if all the other analytics come up with green lights, OK? And this is something that traditional protocol designers find a little bit 'thrill making'. (laughter)

Well the point of this is that in the future, at the very core of the network itself, with the core routing protocols that make everything work, there are strong incentives for people to move to technologies which will similarly take a much more holistic view of what's going on. And the reasons for this, as Chris said, are: we want to coordinate the policy centrally; we want to be able to replace iBGP, that's the version of BGP which is used within an organisation; and so on. So instead of simply driving our forwarding by routing information, which is either there or not there, in future we want to do it by a whole network, which means that you verify routes by multiple means, and you can upgrade your software presumably fairly frequently. This will give you the ability to respond to attacks, vulnerabilities, and so on, in the normal way that we are used to it in the world of software as opposed to the world of protocols.

Now one of the things that we talked about I think two years ago was the incredible difficulty that you have of changing a protocol if it's vulnerable. People had remarked, for example, that with TLS, when somebody comes up with a new timing attack, or whatever in TLS, you can't change it at both ends because it's a two-sided market and the deployed base of servers is too great, and the deployed base of clients is too great, so you end up doing one-sided fixes. Well a world in which you have got this extra software there, is one in which some fixes can be deployed very much more easily than in the past. And hopefully you can get local incremental benefit, because you're not just changing all your TLS clients in order to benefit the servers, or vice-versa – you are actually fixing your corporate network so that it's less likely to get attacked. So the incentives in the medium term may line up a little bit better. And of course, as David Wheeler used to be a regular at these events, I can't avoid making David's comment that in computer science we solve all problems by introducing another layer of abstraction. So that is in effect what this new SDN software is going to do.

So what are the industrial and research implications? Well Chris has been writing a version of Quagga, which takes out the BGP part from the rest of it, so that you have got space to play between the routing and the forwarding there. And that was supposed to be finished at the end of the year with our project, but it will probably ship about sometime next month, and that will give people interested in SDN security here something to play with, so we can start looking at what sort of other things are needed there. Such playing around as we've done up till now has indicated that you get all sorts of really interesting new service-denial attacks if you don't do this right. But hey, we're going to have to get the software and start playing with it before we can move onto the next stage.

Anyway, if there's any questions? The hard ones are for Chris.

Virgil Gligor: So I have a question about deployment. How do you plan to deploy it, and how do you integrate it with all BGP, which is our adversary you like to trust?

[CH]: Well the code I've been working on, as I said, is intended to be a component that you fit in as a module into your control plane software.

Virgil Gligor: Right, so it will co-exist with the current BGP.

[CH]: Yes, so it will talk straightforward BGP to anything that you've connected to, so left and right it's talking standard BGP to whatever, but up and down, down into, from the BGP's perspective, down into the control plane there's a bunch of new interfaces for shipping information that way, and for getting network information back up into the BGP.

Virgil Gligor: So the idea is that if this is indeed better it will take over the world slowly, if it's not, it will be localised to data centres and the like.

[CH]: Well you can use this to implement your own network as an SDN talking standard BGP to everybody else's network, which are still legacy stuff. You can use it to construct islands of SDN within your network, because you can actually use this to talk iBGP between islands of SDN control systems, so you can use it in a number of different ways.

Andrew Moore: It's worth observing that BGP sees an enormous amount of use internally in large organisations that are effectively an isolated installation. It's one deployment strategy that essentially every large University in the UK is able to do BGP and run it entirely in its own router.

[RJA]: And there are many other applications. I mean, at a meeting I was at in London yesterday there was a chap talking about the problems of protecting industrial control systems, and indeed if you do have a large electricity or petrochemical installation running protocols that have got no authentication at all, then how do you perimeterise it robustly? One of he ways of doing it is by completely taking over the corporate network in a way that gives you much more fine-grain control than before. So there's another possible deployment scenario for something that lets you throw out iBGP, and replace it with something that you've crafted yourself.

Virgil Gligor: That is an interesting thought with one exception, the people who run large industrial control systems don't usually want to touch this stuff. they worry about the application layer, and they use commodities of all sorts underneath. So that may be a little bit of a harder sell, but I could see the benefits of using it in that domain.

[RJA]: Well at present people basically re-perimeterise using fancy specialised firewalls. The point is that once this kind of software becomes mainstream in five or 10 years time, then there will be a competitor to that particular suite of products.

Bruce Christianson: And in particular where you've got something that has to play well with others, the firewall option really is a heavy burden. This plays much more nicely with others, with the traditional components.

Tim Goh: With regard to your earlier latency issue, has there been any consideration of protection similar to link protection since you have a global view of the entire network. Do you do something similar to BGP L(ocal) P(rotection) or MPLS TE, i.e. you install a successor route that is likely to be functional during failure?

[CH]: Well current networks also suffer from lots of different sorts of latencies already so.

Tim Goh: And MPLS fast reroute is particularly effective in internal outages. It's something that is likely to converge before standard IGP convergence.

[CH]: Yes, of course, you can pre-compute fallback paths and all that stuff, so clearly you could do that in your SDN.

Tim Goh: It seems to be in a better position to do this than standard MPLS?

Andrew Moore: Sure thing, I mean, this is one of the more elegant parts, because you're actually in the element that is effectively running at layer 2 and layer 3 you can do all of the things that layer 2 currently do to short circuit recovery, and you get all of the layer 3 policy mechanic as well. So in fact one of the issues that shows up in a VPLS TE is that sometimes the recoveries are invalidated with a BGP policy, and you can actually force an enforcement through, all the way through from the top to the bottom, both for the primary and the recovery parts.

[RJA]: And of course once you can go across layers you've got all sorts of magnificent new security vulnerabilities opening up.

Bruce Christianson: How easy is it to replicate function at layer 3? I'm thinking first of all about resilience of failure, and secondly about reducing latency where you've got very large geographical spread.

[CH]: Right, OK. I think that as far as your SDN replacement for your existing routed network dealing with those issues is deemed to be 'a simple matter of programming'. So rather than try to implement solutions to those things in the protocols, and get distributed routers talking to each other to try to overcome these things, you've moved all of your control plane into a nice central place. And now you manage your resilience by having hot spare backups, all of the standard software techniques used to achieve those things. You kind of simplify the network protocol's business by taking all of that stuff out and doing it at a different level in your software system. With all the routing information that BGP is gathering you can consider that to be essentially a database, and you can then use database replication techniques to do your resilience, and your backup, and your redundancy, and so on.

Bruce Christianson: Yes, it's a question of just how much volatile state that central database needs to have.

[CH]: Yes, and that's a good question, and it's going to be interesting. SDN can't solve all the problems immediately.

Bruce Christianson: Oh no, but it moves it around to somewhere where you can actually see it and get at it.

[CH]: Absolutely, yes.

[RJA]: Well I suspect it's unrealistic to expect that the whole of Level 3's network will be run off one PC sitting in Virginia somewhere, right? So realistically what you might expect is that a network the size of the University of Cambridge might have one route controller, with one backup, but with larger operations you would instead use SDN to divide things into route context islands, if you like. And then you end up having to spend the next ten years developing a whole suite of protocols, which enable the more intelligent controllers to talk to each other by means of some kind of negotiation. And of course this enables you to bring in many, many techniques, and many, many new threats too from agent-based stuff to API security, to all the good things that we've seen over the last 20 years. So there's significant amounts of work to be done in this space if this is the direction that technology takes.

Bootstrapping Adoption of the Pico Password Replacement System

Frank Stajano[✉], Graeme Jenkinson, Jeunese Payne, Max Spencer,
Quentin Stafford-Fraser, and Chris Warrington

Computer Laboratory, University of Cambridge, Cambridge, UK
{frank.stajano,graeme.jenkinson,jeunese.payne,max.spencer,
quentin.stafford-fraser,chris.warrington}@cl.cam.ac.uk

Abstract. In previous work we presented Pico, an authentication system designed to be both more usable and more secure than passwords. One unsolved problem was that Pico, in its quest to explore the whole solution space without being bound by compatibility shackles, requires changes at both the prover and the verifier, which makes it hard to convince anyone to adopt it: users won't buy an authentication gadget that doesn't let them log into anything and service providers won't support a system that no users are equipped to log in with. In this paper we present three measures to break this vicious circle, starting with the "Pico Lens" browser add-on that rewrites websites on the fly so that they appear Pico-enabled. Our add-on offers the user most (though not all) of the usability and security benefits of Pico, thus fostering adoption from users even before service providers are on board. This will enable Pico to build up a user base. We also developed a server-side Wordpress plugin which can serve both as a reference example and as a useful enabler in its own right (as Wordpress is one of the leading content management platforms on the web). Finally, we developed a software version of the Pico client running on a smartphone, the Pico App, so that people can try out Pico (at the price of slightly reduced security) without having to acquire and carry another gadget. Having broken the vicious circle we'll be in a stronger position to persuade providers to offer support for Pico in parallel with passwords.

1 Introduction and Motivation

For normal people, passwords are a pain. Their inadequacy in terms of both usability and security has been repeatedly pointed out [1,4]. As people must now handle dozens of accounts, passwords are a solution that can no longer scale. Yet passwords continue to dominate as the well-entrenched incumbent because, from the viewpoint of the verifier, they beat every alternative hands down when it comes to ease of deployment [3].

Pico [11], which we briefly describe in Sect. 2, is our ambitious long-term project to replace passwords with a more usable and more secure system that

© Springer International Publishing Switzerland 2014
B. Christianson et al. (Eds.): Security Protocols 2014, LNCS 8809, pp. 172–186, 2014.
DOI: 10.1007/978-3-319-12400-1_17

will not require you to memorize any secrets[1]. In its quest to explore the entire solution space for the best possible solution in terms of usability and security, Pico is a clean-slate redesign that explicitly gives up on compatibility with passwords. It is immediately clear that, in the short term, this choice will harm Pico's deployability. Our rationale is that, in the long term, passwords will become so blatantly unacceptable that the world will eventually demand something better; and, by then, Pico will have undergone several cycles of prototyping and testing and will be ready for adoption as a user-friendly, secure and technically sound solution that both users and service providers consider an improvement.

Having said that, in order to be ready for adoption when the time comes, Pico has to be taken seriously by the stakeholders, both on the client side and on the server side. For this reason, while we continue to investigate and develop the architecture without considering ourselves constrained by backwards compatibility, we also intend to provide a plausible migration path from the current password-dominated scenario to a future one in which Pico has replaced passwords. Charting this path is the topic of this paper.

The main obstacle to widespread adoption of Pico is a classic vicious circle (Fig. 1). Organisations that authenticate their users with passwords are reluctant to change their servers to support an unfamiliar and unproven system, especially if it also requires outfitting every user with a physical gadget at non-zero unit cost. People, on the other hand, will be understandably reluctant to acquire, carry and use a new authentication gadget, even if genuinely easier to use than passwords, if it does not work with the services to which they wish (or need) to authenticate. Our strategy involves disrupting this vicious circle in several places. Where circular dependencies prevent users from adopting Pico before servers have adopted it and vice versa, in this paper we present software modules we have developed to break such dependencies.

Our first contribution, on the client side, is the "Pico Lens" web browser add-on, described in Sect. 3: when you view a website through the Pico Lens,

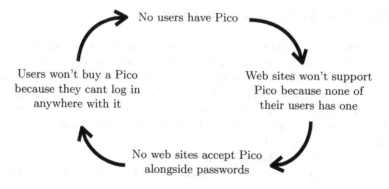

No users have Pico

Users won't buy a Pico
because they cant log in
anywhere with it

Web sites won't support
Pico because none of
their users has one

No web sites accept Pico
alongside passwords

Fig. 1. The vicious circle opposing Pico adoption.

---

[1] The project's website, http://pico.cl.cam.ac.uk/, contains a brief introductory video, the original paper, a FAQ and other resources.

it appears Pico-enabled even if it isn't, so that you may authenticate to the website using your Pico device rather than by typing your password. This breaks the vicious circle for users because it allows them to use a Pico and reap most of its usability benefits even before their favourite websites start offering native Pico support. In turn, once enough people adopt Pico for its convenience, website operators have more of an incentive to support the full Pico authentication system alongside traditional password login.

Our second contribution, on the server side, is the "Pico Verifier" plugin for Wordpress[2], described in Sect. 4. It breaks the vicious circle for content providers because it allows webmasters of Wordpress-based websites to make their site Pico-enabled simply by installing the plugin, without any development effort. This plugin also provides a reference implementation of the server side, for webmasters who might wish to develop a Pico-enabled version of their non-Wordpress website.

Our third contribution, on the client side, is the "Pico Prover" app for Android smartphones, described in Sect. 5. This software breaks the vicious circle for users because it allows them to use their existing smartphone as a Pico device, without having to buy (or carry) any extra hardware. The Pico Prover app can to authenticate to both natively Pico-enabled verifiers and to non-Pico-aware websites viewed through the Pico Lens, so it lets users reap many of the usability and a few of the security benefits of a real Pico without any significant investment. If they like the user experience (which, by releasing the app early, we can refine and enhance while taking into account the feedback of many users in a crowd-sourced fashion), they may wish to upgrade to a dedicated Pico, which will eventually be smaller, simpler and more secure. The Pico Prover also provides a reference implementation for the client side.

After a brief overview of the Pico system in Sect. 2 to make the presentation self-contained, the rest of this paper describes each of these three contributions in greater detail.

2   The Pico Architecture in Brief

The Pico system consists of the Pico device itself (a small, dedicated and tamper-resistant hardware authenticator the size of a pedometer or a car key fob), acting as the prover, and a back-end acting as the verifier. Even though the technical contributions described in this paper focus on the use-case of web authentication, in which the verifier is a website, in the general case any entity that authenticates its users (whether with or without passwords—think of car keys) could be augmented with a Pico back-end.

Pico relies on a multi-channel authentication protocol [14] in which an additional channel (acquisition of a QR code [7] in the current implementation)

---

[2] According to W3techs statistics (http://w3techs.com/technologies/overview/content_management/all/), as of February 2014, Wordpress is the most widely used Content Management System on the web, being used by 21.5 % of all websites and by 60.0 % of all websites that use a content management system.

conveys the user's intent to authenticate to a designated verifier. The verifier signals that it supports Pico authentication by displaying a Pico visual code, perhaps alongside the conventional login prompt for user name and password. The human prover signals her intent to authenticate to a particular verifier by acquiring the verifier's QR code with her Pico device. This action initiates the execution of the Pico authentication protocol, which mutually authenticates the verifier to the Pico and the Pico to the verifier.

In the current implementation the Pico system uses the SIGMA protocol [8] for mutual authentication and generation of a symmetric session key. The Pico prover and back-end verifier create digital signatures to prove ownership of a public key, which is their long-term public identity. Pico has adopted the "I" variant of the SIGMA protocol [8], in which the verifier must authenticate its identity to the prover, before the prover reveals its identity to the verifier, preventing any privacy loss to verifiers presenting "counterfeit" visual codes. To protect the user's privacy further the Pico uses a different key pair for every account so that colluding verifiers cannot link accounts belonging to the same user. A run of the SIGMA protocol also yields a fresh symmetric session key, which the Pico and verifier use for continuous authentication.

In some cases, for example when logging into a local computer or when opening a Pico-enabled door, the Pico prover device talks directly to the Pico verifier that displays the QR code directly. In other cases, though, most notably when logging into web sites, a third device is involved: when you authenticate to a website with your Pico, you actually access your account for that website through the web browser of your normal computer. In such cases the website provides the authenticated Pico with a "session delegation token" (a cookie) that the Pico then transfers to the web browser to delegate[3] the session it has authenticated[4].

When the verifier is remote, as in the case of a website, the Pico needs a connection to the Internet and a connection to the user's web browser so that the Pico can transfer the session delegation token to the web browser after authenticating. In our implementation as of March 2014 the Pico connects to the user's computer via a Bluetooth Personal Area Network (PAN) and tunnels out to remote services via this interface as well so that Pico doesn't need to have its own Internet connection via WiFi or via a mobile phone network.

Pico offers continuous authentication, whereby the Pico device authenticates to the verifier at regular intervals without user intervention, so long as the Pico remains unlocked and in proximity of the computer running the web browser. The verifier may thus keep the session open for as long as necessary but close it immediately when the user is no longer present, minimising the window of vulnerability during which another person could hijack the session if the user

---

[3] Delegation is a process whereby a principal authorises an agent to act on its behalf by transferring a set of rights.

[4] The session delegation protocol used by Pico is described in further detail in our other paper "I bought a new security token and all I got was this lousy phish— Relay attacks on visual code authentication schemes", also in these proceedings.

left the terminal unattended. In the current prototype we detect proximity with a heuristic based on Bluetooth signal strength, though in the future we plan to adopt a more secure distance bounding protocol [5,6].

As with any token-based authentication method, the Pico system must protect the token against misuse by others who might find or steal it. In our design this is achieved through the Picosiblings mechanism [11,12]: the Pico device locks up (with its credentials encrypted), pauses the continuous authentication of any active session, and stops authenticating new sessions whenever it cannot sense the "aura of safety" around its owner. The "aura" is defined by the proximity of a sufficient number of other electronic devices (the Picosiblings) worn by that person. A biometric sample and a connection to a home server also act as special Picosiblings that offer additional protection properties and allow remote revocation. Because this Picosibling-based locking mechanism is independent of the normal operation of the Pico device and, particularly, of the "vicious circle of adoption" alluded to above, it will not be discussed further in this paper.

The credentials stored in the Pico device are backed up automatically, in encrypted form, whenever the Pico is plugged into its docking station for recharging. Backup, too, despite being a fundamental component of the Pico architecture, is independent of the "vicious circle of adoption" and will not be discussed further in this paper.

3   The "Pico Lens" Firefox Add-On

The "Pico Lens" is a web browser add-on that rewrites websites on the fly to make them appear as if they support Pico alongside password authentication. The Pico Lens detects web pages containing login forms and adds a Pico visual code to them, alongside the existing username and password fields, so that Pico users have the option of authenticating with their Pico instead of typing their password.

Although the underlying methods used by the Pico to authenticate to Pico-enabled and only *Lens-enabled* websites are quite different, our aim was to make the user experiences as similar as possible. The end result in both modes of operation is the same: the user's web browser receives a session cookie granting access to the user account. Behind the scenes, however, what happens is rather different.

3.1   Pico Authentication

For comparison, authentication to a fully Pico-enabled website (that is, a website that supports the real Pico authentication protocol) is described by the following sequence of events.

1. The user, whose web browser has a Pico add-on installed[5], navigates to a login page.
2. The login page includes a visual code encoding the public key of the service. If the full Pico Lens add-on is installed, it detects that the website is Pico-enabled (for example through a `pico-enabled` HTML `meta` tag.), and refrains from rewriting the page.
3. The user scans the visual code with their Pico.
4. If the user has multiple accounts for the website, they select one from the list displayed by the Pico. If the user only has a single account for the website, as is common, this step is skipped.
5. The Pico and the website mutually authenticate.
6. The website sends the Pico a fresh session delegation token, which for a web authentication takes the form of a set of cookies and a URL.
7. The Pico sends the session delegation token to the local terminal via the Bluetooth PAN.
8. The Pico add-on causes that browser to navigate to the URL contained in the session delegation token.

When a website is not Pico-enabled, the Pico Lens add-on allows the user to follow the same work flow, despite the differences in the underlying mechanism.

1. The user, whose browser has the Pico Lens add-on installed, navigates to a login page.
2. The Pico Lens detects a login form on the page, and displays an authentication visual code containing the domain name of the website (Fig. 2).
3. The user scans the code with their Pico.
4. If the user only has a single account with the website, as is common, this step is skipped and the Pico proceeds to mutually authenticate the website. Otherwise the user selects an account for the website from the list displayed by the Pico (for each account the Pico device holds the username/password credentials used to authenticate).
5. The Pico internally loads, fills in and submits the login form using its stored username/password credentials for that account, tunneling an end-to-end HTTPS connection to the website through the Bluetooth PAN established with the local computer.
6. The Pico receives the website's response to the form submission and creates a session delegation token consisting of any cookies set in the response and the address it was redirected to.
7. The Pico sends the session delegation token to the user's computer via the Bluetooth PAN. In the web browser, the Pico Lens installs the set cookies and follows the redirect, so that the user is logged in.

---

[5] To perform Pico authentication with a Pico-enabled website, the Pico Lens, which rewrites legacy login pages to add a QR code to them, is clearly not required; however, *some* Pico browser add-on is still needed for receiving session delegation tokens from the Pico device.

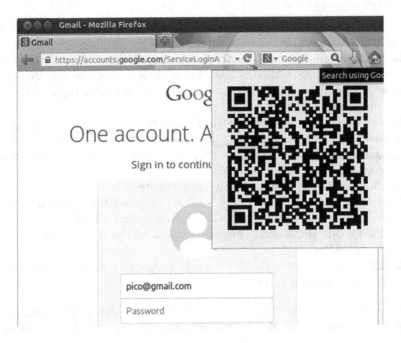

Fig. 2. QR code presented by the Pico Lens add-on for authentication to a website that does not natively support Pico.

3.2   Pico Lens Pairing

Before a user can log into a Lens-enabled website with their Pico, they must store on in its encrypted storage their account credentials for that site and the Pico must learn how to fill out the login page on behalf of the user. The interaction is somewhat different to the "pairing" interaction with a Pico enabled site. Assume the user already has a password-based account with the web site and now wants to be able to log in with their Pico when viewing the site through the Pico Lens.

1. The user, whose web browser has the Pico Lens add-on installed, navigates to a login page.
2. The Pico Lens add-on detects a login form on the page and thus rewrites the page[6] to display an "authentication" visual code containing the domain name of the web page (Fig. 2).
3. The user, having not yet stored any credentials to their Pico for this website, ignores this first QR code, types their username and password in the login form and submits it as if without Pico.

---

[6] The Pico Lens at this stage has no idea that this is going to be a first-time pairing rather than a regular login, so it behaves exactly as in the previous case.

Fig. 3. Dialogue presented by the Pico Lens add-on after a login form is submitted.

4. The Pico Lens add-on detects the form submission, captures the name-value pairs being submitted, and offers to save these credentials on the user's Pico (Fig. 3), much as an in-browser password manager[7] would.
5. The user accepts this offer and the add-on displays a "pairing" visual code containing the submitted credentials[8], as well as the domain name of the website.
6. The user scans the visual code with their Pico.
7. The user confirms the pairing details and the username and password credentials are saved in the Pico's encrypted database, with the website domain as their lookup key.

3.3 Pico Lens Design Trade-Offs and Future Work

The current implementation largely mimics existing in-browser password managers but is still a work in progress at the time of writing. Design decisions still to be finalised, possibly with the help of user studies, include at least the following.

First, we could do better in step 6, security-wise, by encrypting the username and password to the Pico before encoding them into the QR code; but we'd need some key for encrypting the message from Lens to Pico, and what would be the most usable way of establishing that[9]?

---

[7] We call "password manager" a piece of software that records username-password pairs on behalf of the user and supplies them to verifiers as appropriate, saving the user from having to remember and retype them. A password manager may be a standalone program or it may be integrated in a web browser. Password managers may store their database locally or in the cloud, and in cleartext or in encrypted form. The latter case provides greater security but requires entering a master password.

[8] The pairing code is currently unencrypted. If the visual code is observed during the account pairing, the attacker gains the user's password for that website.

[9] Bearing in mind scenarios in which one Lens serves several Pico devices, as when several family members use the shared tablet in the living room.

Second, we might consider using radio rather than the visual channel in step 6, sparing the user from having to scan a visual code, although there may be technical difficulties on platforms where the add-on is not allowed to open a socket.

Third, instead of making it the responsibility of the user to choose a suitably strong password, the Pico itself might choose a random password as hard as the website's policy will allow, to ensure greater randomness than can be expected by letting a human choose a secret [2]; the difficulty there being that the Pico would have to be informed about the constraints imposed by the website's password policy (e.g. certain characters disallowed, password length not to exceed some limit, etc.)[10] or discover them by trial and error.

We assume that many web users will already be familiar with the concept of a password manager since most modern web browsers incorporate one that pops up and offers its services when appropriate. An *encrypting* password manager, even though it stores your passwords on your computer thus exposing them to network intruders[11], offers a significant improvement in both security and usability compared to plain passwords because it allows you to use stronger passwords that are all different and that you don't have to remember nor retype. The fact that Pico can be seen as a portable password manager will allow users to mentally associate the former to the latter, making it easier for people to adopt Pico because they won't have to form a totally new mental model for it.

In contrast to a password manager, the username-password pair is stored not on the computer running the web browser but within the encrypted storage of the Pico (just as the private-key cryptographic credentials would be in the fully-Pico-enabled use case [11,12]) making the credential more strongly protected against network attacks than with the in-browser password manager. Although the implementation is very different, we are keen to maintain consistency in the user's mental model ("it's my Pico that holds my credentials") between the two cases of visiting a Pico-enabled website and visiting a legacy website through the Pico Lens.

The Pico visits the target website's login page independently from the web browser, rather than sending the password to the web browser; therefore, if the terminal is compromised, only individual session cookies can be compromised, rather than the long-term password. In this respect, too, the Pico Lens is a security improvement on existing password managers.

The Pico Lens add-on cannot provide continuous authentications for non-Pico-aware websites because, in order for continuous authentication to work, the back-end must accept "pause" and "resume" methods for the session, besides the standard "start" and "stop". A session that has been paused is inactive

---

[10] It would be nice if websites published their password policy in a uniform machine-readable form; and even nicer if they imposed no upper bounds on making passwords arbitrarily long and complicated. As argued by Bonneau and Preibusch [4], websites that impose such limits probably do so because they are not hashing their passwords.

[11] A risk that is greatly reduced with Pico, which is a dedicated device not intended to run other software.

but retains its state; this must be explicitly supported by the back-end verifier. A session with a non-Pico-enabled website can only be either "logged in" or "logged out".

In our current implementation the Pico connects to the user's computer via a Bluetooth Personal Area Network (PAN) and tunnels out to remote services via this interface. Setting this up is, whist reasonably straightforward, is non-trivial. Further work is required to ensure that the solution is easily deployable by geeks and grannies alike. Since presenting this work at the SPW in March 2014 we have been working on replacing the Bluetooth PAN with a web-based rendezvous point. Whilst introducing the need to securely pair the Pico and web browser, removing the dependency on Bluetooth significantly simplifies deployment of the solution.

The current Pico Lens add-on implementation is a technology demonstrator of the core insight that we can offer users the Pico experience even before their favourite websites are Pico-enabled. For actual deployment, though, we may have to revisit some of our implementation choices; the leading browser is now Chrome[12] rather than Firefox, although their add-on architectures are rather similar.

4   The "Pico Verifier" Wordpress Plugin

Wordpress, originally a blogging platform, is currently the leading content management system on the web[13]. Our "Pico Verifier" plugin for Wordpress implements the back-end side of Pico for any website running Wordpress. It allows users to log into the website using the genuine Pico protocol (not a simulation, as would be the case with the Pico Lens) while of course still allowing traditional password-based authentication.

With the Pico Verifier plugin installed on a Wordpress website, the login page is modified to include a Pico visual code, alongside the usual username and password prompt. Unlike the visual codes added by the Pico Lens, the ones the Wordpress plugin adds are in the HTML returned by the web server. The Pico visual code contains the name, address and public key of the website (see Fig. 4).

To authenticate to the Wordpress website, the user scans this QR code with her Pico. Provided the Pico is already paired with her user account on the website, the Pico then initiates the mutual authentication protocol of Sect. 3.1 with the website's Pico verifier (also provided by our Wordpress plugin). If authentication is successful, the Pico verifier returns to the Pico a session delegation token, which the Pico uses to delegate its authority to the web browser as discussed in Sect. 2.

Users can create a Pico-enabled account by scanning another visual code (similar to the one shown in Fig. 4) which the plugin adds to the Wordpress

---

[12] As of January 2014, Chrome holds 55.7 % market share, with Firefox a distant second at 26.9 %, according to W3schools statistics (http://www.w3schools.com/browsers/browsers_stats.asp).

[13] See footnote 2.

```
{
    "serviceName": "Some Wordpress Blog",
    "serviceUri": "http://someblog.com/pico:8080",
    "servicePublicKey": "MFUw...iC8U",
    "signature": "MEAC...9uGn",
    "TYPE": "KeyAuthenticationVisualCode"
}
```

Fig. 4. Example visual code added to the login page by the Wordpress plugin.

account creation page. The plugin also adds a "Pico" section to the Wordpress account management page. Here users can unlink a Pico which is already linked with their account and a QR code is added to allow the user to link a new Pico. For administrators, new Pico-related settings are added to the site's settings page.

Normally, once mutually authenticated, the Pico and the service execute a continuous authentication protocol over the established secure channel. When the Pico is out-of-range of either its Picosiblings or the terminal, the session is first paused and then eventually terminated. Terminating a session is straightforward. Pausing is more difficult, as Wordpress wasn't designed with pause/resume in mind, and this feature isn't currently provided by our plugin.

To experience a Pico compatible Wordpress blog requires that both websites and web visitors install and configure some software. The demands placed on the website are relatively modest—to install our Pico Verifier Wordpress plugin. In contrast, each user (prover) is required to install and setup multiple pieces of software (browser add-on, Bluetooth device driver etc.) and to provide network connectivity between the Pico, their computer and the website. Our future work includes simplifying these requirements in order to make Pico easier to deploy.

5   The "Pico Prover" Android App

It seems prudent that an authentication token holding all your login credentials should not be a general-purpose computing platform, with unfettered networking facilities, on which users merrily install arbitrary code of dubious provenance [9]. For this reason (as well as to be simple and easy to use) the Pico client is ultimately intended to be a dedicated single-purpose hardware device rather than a smartphone app. However, users tend to be extremely reluctant to carry one more device. And a smartphone can already simulate, if not the form factor, at least most of the intended functions of a Pico. It therefore seems reasonable for us to release a smartphone app that will allow users to try out the Pico functionality at no cost—without having to acquire a physical Pico (which we haven't yet built anyway) nor having to carry one around (assuming they'd already carry their smartphone regardless). While they're trying out Pico, users may still retain traditional passwords for the few accounts they consider most valuable and only use Pico for their more numerous lower-value ones. The risk introduced by the possibility of their long term credentials being exposed by malware on the smartphone is therefore limited.

We consider a dedicated tamper-resistant hardware token and the use of a consumer computing device such as smartphone as being at opposite ends of a design spectrum. Within this spectrum there are several other interesting options, such as the use of a Trusted Execution Environment (TEE). A TEE is an isolated execution environment in which sensitive or security enforcing functions can be executed. The Protection Profile for TEE—produced by the Global Platform collaboration—targets the Common Criteria Evaluation Assurance Level EAL2 ("Structurally tested"). Thus an implementation of the Pico Prover App using this technology would offer security benefits over a basic smartphone app.

Despite TEEs based on ARM's TrustZone technology being present in over 100 million handsets, the software running in the isolated environment has, until recently, been tightly controlled by handset manufacturers. With the advent of the Samsung S4 the TEE has been opened upeta third party developers and this trend is likely to continue.

Despite the security benefits provided by a TEE, ensuring a trusted path to the user is a significant residual problem: malware can't access the data segment of the TEE-secured Pico Prover app, but it could simulate its screen. Because Pico does not require the user to remember or enter secrets, such concerns are somewhat mitigated. However, careful thought is needed to ensure that a malicious app can't trick the user in some elaborate way or abuse the API between the rich and trusted side to extract sensitive data such as keying material. A detailed analysis of Pico executing within a TEE on a smartphone would make interesting future work.

During the transition phase, the smartphone app will support both the native Pico protocol and also the Pico Lens protocol. Therefore, an important constraint placed on the Pico Lens solution is that it should be as usable as the native Pico. Distributing the Pico Prover as a free app allows us to crowd-source feedback about the usability of the solution and ensure that we are meeting this goal.

6   User Acceptance

To date the security and usability benefits of Pico have only been considered by technologists [3]. The Unified Theory of Acceptance and Usage of Technology (UTAUT) [13] applies to technology adoption the ideas of the more general Theory of Planned Behaviour (ToPB) from social psychology. The UTAUT model postulates that a user's intention to adopt a new technology is driven by four constructs:

Performance Expectancy
  The root component of which is *perceived usefulness*.
Effort Expectancy
  The root component of which is *ease of use*.
Social Influence
  Similar to *social norms* in the ToPB model.
Facilitating Conditions
  Objective factors that influence the *ease of adoption* of the technology.

As users often hold inaccurate notions of security and of the importance of security measures [1,10], the stated security benefits need to be reconciled with the benefits that end users perceive Pico to offer. However, without a working implementation and more importantly without compatible services to log into, validating these benefits would be tricky. In our initial work we have focused on providing "Facilitating Conditions" that allow us to perform large scale user studies to validate Pico's assumed benefits.

The solutions presented in this paper allow Pico to be adopted by a broad user community and used with legacy services based on password authentication. The insights gained from users adopting Pico in a day-to-day setting will highlight what we got wrong and inform changes to our design. Reporting and acting on these findings is a significant and exciting part of the future direction of the Pico project.

7   Conclusions

We still believe that, in our quest to produce a more usable and more secure password replacement, it would be a mistake to limit our horizon to solutions that are compatible with passwords: it may well be that better solutions exist beyond that horizon, and we want the freedom to explore those regions of the design space too.

On the other hand, we fully realise that a realistic solution requires a plausible path to deployment and that, when encouraging major players to adopt Pico, we cannot act as if passwords weren't already a strongly entrenched incumbent. The vicious circle undeniably exists: websites won't have any incentive to support Pico authentication until users already have Pico devices, and users won't have any incentive to get a Pico unless it works with their websites of interest.

Our strategy is therefore to break this vicious circle in several places. We have shown how the Pico Lens browser add-on allows users to reap the benefits of a Pico device even before the websites support it. We have shown how the Pico Verifier website plugin allows webmasters (of Wordpress sites) to support Pico at no development cost. And we have shown how the Pico Prover smartphone app allows users to try out Pico for some of their accounts without having to buy anything or carry any additional gadgets.

A significant advantage of this bootstrapping strategy is that allows us not to compromise on the purity of the Pico design: the clean-slate Pico is incompatible with passwords, but the solutions presented above are stepping stones that bridge this compatibility gap because they interwork with both legacy passwords and Pico, thus allowing for a transition phase.

Our next step will be more organisational than technological: we need to get the website operators on board—especially the big ones. If we can demonstrate that a critical mass of users finds the Pico Prover app and the Pico Lens add-on to be more usable than passwords (and we'll have to work hard at simplifying the installation process) we'll be in a good position to persuade the big players that it's worth supporting Pico as an alternative authentication method. This will in turn attract more users and we'll finally move from a vicious to a *virtuous* circle.

Acknowledgements. We gratefully acknowledge the European Research Council for funding this research under grant 307224.

We also thank Roel Peeters *et al.* for their independent implementation of Pico and for sharing pre-publication drafts of their work "Towards Building the Pico: The Security Perspective" (still in submission at the time of writing), from which we adopted the SIGMA-I protocol for mutual authentication.

References

1. Adams, A., Sasse, M.A.: Users are not the enemy. Communications of the ACM **42**(12), 40–46 (1999). http://doi.acm.org/10.1145/322796.322806
2. Bonneau, J.: Guessing human-chosen secrets. Ph.D. thesis, University of Cambridge, May 2012. http://www.jbonneau.com/doc/2012-jbonneau-phd_thesis.pdf
3. Bonneau, J., Herley, C., van Oorschot, P.C., Stajano, F.: The quest to replace passwords: a framework for comparative evaluation of web authentication schemes. In: Proceedings of the 2012 IEEE Symposium on Security and Privacy, SP '12, pp. 553–567. IEEE Computer Society, Washington (2012). http://dx.doi.org/10.1109/SP.2012.44
4. Bonneau, J., Preibusch, S.: The password thicket: technical and market failures in human authentication on the web. In: WEIS 2010 (2010)
5. Brands, S., Chaum, D.: Distance bounding protocols. In: Helleseth, T. (ed.) EUROCRYPT 1993. LNCS, vol. 765, pp. 344–359. Springer, Heidelberg (1994)
6. Hancke, G.P., Kuhn, M.G.: An RFID distance bounding protocol. In: Proceedings of the First International Conference on Security and Privacy for Emerging Areas in Communications Networks, SECURECOMM '05, pp. 67–73. IEEE Computer Society, Washington (2005). http://dx.doi.org/10.1109/SECURECOMM.2005.56

7. ISO: Information technology–automatic identification and data capture techniques–QR Code 2005 bar code symbology specification. ISO 18004:2006, International Organization for Standardization, Geneva, Switzerland (2006)
8. Krawczyk, H.: SIGMA: the 'SIGn-and-MAc' approach to authenticated Diffie-Hellman and its use in the IKE protocols. In: Boneh, D. (ed.) CRYPTO 2003. LNCS, vol. 2729, pp. 400–425. Springer, Heidelberg (2003)
9. Laurie, B., Singer, A.: Choose the red pill and the blue pill: a position paper. In: Proceedings of the 2008 Workshop on New Security Paradigms, NSPW '08, pp. 127–133. ACM, New York (2008). http://doi.acm.org/10.1145/1595676.1595695
10. Sasse, M.A., Brostoff, S., Weirich, D.: Transforming the 'weakest link' - a human/computer interaction approach to usable and effective security. BT Technol. J. **19**(3), 122–131 (2001). http://dx.doi.org/10.1023/A:1011902718709
11. Stajano, F.: Pico: no more passwords!. In: Christianson, B., Crispo, B., Malcolm, J., Stajano, F. (eds.) Security Protocols 2011. LNCS, vol. 7114, pp. 49–81. Springer, Heidelberg (2011)
12. Stannard, O., Stajano, F.: Am I in good company? A privacy-protecting protocol for cooperating ubiquitous computing devices. In: Christianson, B., Malcolm, J., Stajano, F., Anderson, J. (eds.) Security Protocols 2012. LNCS, vol. 7622, pp. 223–230. Springer, Heidelberg (2012). http://dx.doi.org/10.1007/978-3-642-35694-0_24
13. Venkatesh, V., Morris, M.G., Davis, G.B., Davis, F.D.: User acceptance of information technology: toward a unified view. MIS Q. **27**(3), 425–478 (2003). http://dl.acm.org/citation.cfm?id=2017197.2017202
14. Wong, F.-L., Stajano, F.: Multi-channel protocols. In: Christianson, B., Crispo, B., Malcolm, J.A., Roe, M. (eds.) Security Protocols 2005. LNCS, vol. 4631, pp. 112–127. Springer, Heidelberg (2007). http://www.cl.cam.ac.uk/fms27/papers/2005-WongSta-multichannel.pdf, updated version in IEEE Pervasive Computing 6(4), 31–39 (2007)

Bootstrapping Adoption of the Pico Password Replacement System (Transcript of Discussion)

Frank Stajano[✉]

University of Cambridge, Cambridge, UK
frank.stajano@cl.cam.ac.uk

I spoke about Pico in 2011 at this workshop. This is not about how to build it, but how to *bootstrap adoption* of the Pico password replacement system. All the researchers in the Pico team who have contributed to this work, whose names are on this opening slide, are here today. In 2011 Pico was just a dream and I'm very glad now to have been able to recruit people that made this into something real that we want people to actually use.

Eliminating passwords has now become even more of an imperative because passwords are really impossible to deal with, at least in the way that we present them to a normal human being:

"Pick something you can't remember, then don't write it down",

as Mikko Hypponen once overheard and tweeted[1]. If you get hacked after not actually following these impossible instructions then you get the blame. Is this a fair thing? I don't think it is. We technologists should offer people something they can actually do. Passwords are pathetic from the viewpoint of usability, they are also not very good in terms of security, and so we need to improve on that. So this is why I came up with Pico.

For those of you who were not here in 2011, we have made a little movie to show you what this is about.

Readers of these proceedings are encouraged to watch the 7-min video on our web site, http://pico.cl.cam.ac.uk, *because we are not reproducing a transcript of the movie here.*

This is an envisionment video, of course: the device shown is not the real Pico but merely Graeme's highlighter marker! We showed you how we envisage Pico will work when we finally build it.

However, we've got a problem: compatibility. I said we wanted to be bold and explore the whole solution space. Imagine a Venn diagram with three nested sets. The innermost one is passwords. The one that encloses it is the set of password-replacement solutions that are still *compatible* with passwords, so you have some hope of actually working with what exists today. However, around it, there is a much bigger set: a solution space of systems that might replace passwords but are *incompatible* with them. Not many researchers go there, but I wanted to make sure we are not missing out on something good that only exists over there.

Pico doesn't constrain itself to the inner sets. This gives us great intellectual freedom but of course it also means that Pico is incompatible with what currently

---

[1] https://twitter.com/mikko/status/102984155809333248

© Springer International Publishing Switzerland 2014
B. Christianson et al. (Eds.): Security Protocols 2014, LNCS 8809, pp. 187–196, 2014.
DOI: 10.1007/978-3-319-12400-1_18

works today. When you have a Pico—that's great!—what do you want to do with it? You want the freedom of not having to type a password every time you log into Google, or into Amazon, or into Expedia, or into whatever else you use—but you can't, because, at least today, these sites are not Pico-compatible! They don't even know that Pico exists.

We have essentially a "vicious circle of adoption": this is our big problem. Nobody has a Pico because we haven't built it yet, and this means that websites won't support Pico because none of their users have one. No website accepts the Pico alongside passwords, and therefore this means that users have no incentive to buy a Pico, because they can't use it to log into any site that they might actually want to visit. As a consequence, no users have a Pico, and we have this vicious circle. Today's presentation is about the work we have been doing to *break* this vicious circle.

We have developed several pieces of software in order to break this circle in three different places. So we're going to talk about three pieces of software. The first is the Pico Lens, a plugin for your browser that displays the websites as if through a magic lens that makes them appear as if they supported Pico even though they don't. So it's no longer the case that "no websites accept Pico alongside passwords" because, if you look at them through the Lens, then suddenly they *do* accept Pico. The second is the Pico Prover App for smartphone, which is essentially a version of the Pico gadget as an app. This *(tongue in cheek)* is evil! I said from the start in 2011 that that's not the way it should be done, because your smartphone contains software you download from strange places thinking it's as good as Angry Birds, and instead it's probably malware, and you don't want to have all your login credentials sitting next to that malware, so from the security viewpoint you are in a state of sin if you make a Pico app. But, on the other hand, if you are trying to break the vicious circle, the advantage of making a Pico app on the phone is that the user doesn't have to buy a Pico because they already have the smartphone; perhaps even more importantly, the phone is something they already carry: we don't have to persuade them to bring along another gadget. So, this way, they get a Pico-equivalent device in their hands, relatively painlessly. The third piece of software we developed is the Pico Verifier plugin for Wordpress-based websites. This means that websites don't need to invest in a major software development effort to support Pico because, so long as they are running Wordpress (and 60 % of the websites that are run on a content management system are Wordpress-based), then they can just adopt our Wordpress plugin, and they will automatically support Pico without effort.

So let's have a look at these one by one. The Pico Lens is, as I said, a browser plugin such that, if you visit a website that doesn't know anything about Pico, when you look at it through the lens it appears as Pico enabled, and you can interact with it with your Pico and it works.

Joseph Bonneau: Is it technically a plugin or an extension? A plugin is like Flash, it can read your hard drive.

Reply: The Firefox APIs have changed recently: technically these days it's called an add-on. The API that we wrote for originally, when we starting doing the

Lens, has also changed and has been deprecated. Chris can give you all the details offline if you wish. Anyway, to explain the Pico Lens and also to demonstrate the Pico App on the phone, we prepared another small video.

The video, not transcribed here, showed the then-current prototype of the Pico App on the Android smartphone logging into two non-Pico-aware sites, Gmail and LinkedIn, through the Pico Lens in the Firefox browser on the laptop. It also demonstrated the initial pairing phase between a new site and the Pico.

Let me point out the crucial difference between the previous video and this one. The previous video, which we did in December 2013, was an envisionment of what we wanted to do. This other video, from a few days ago... OK, it's completely flawed, there's a bunch of stuff that we want to change, but this actually *works*, we built some software to implement this. This is tremendously exciting! We can break the vicious circle by releasing this app and this add-on and letting people use the Pico system even *before* the big websites start to support it. With this, we are independent of everybody else having said yes to Pico. We can all start using it as soon as possible.

In developing this browser plugin (I'll keep calling it a plugin even though that may no longer be the most technically appropriate term) we had to face some interesting design decisions. We imagined: let's make the plugin in such a way that the site seen through the lens is as similar as possible to the real site. To do that, we would have had to basically use the same protocols as the Pico device would use with a real Pico-compatible website. Normally the real website offers its public key in a certificate, which is in this QR code; then, from that, a channel is established between the site and the Pico, and so on. Now, if the Lens plugin were to generate a public key for the site on its own (a key which, of course, the real site doesn't know about), and offer that to the Pico device when scanned, then who would have the secret key for that public key? Not the real site, because Google or LinkedIn or Expedia doesn't know that we are doing Pico. So the key would have to reside in the plugin itself, but that's dumb: what happens if you visit the same web site through another computer (with its own Pico-Lens-equipped browser)? You'd get a different public key for this website. So this doesn't work. Then we thought that maybe we can have some back-end, say http://mypico.org, that holds the master copy of all these fake key pairs generated by the plugins, and then all your plugins on various computers could synchronize through that back-end. But we didn't really like having this trusted third party somewhere in the network and having to depend on http://mypico. org being up 99.999 % of the time. We'll never have the same number of nines as the big websites like Google and it would be painfully embarrassing if your authentication (to an unrelated place) failed because our site was not up at the time.

So, how does this work now? In a way that is rather more convoluted. In fact, we do something different when the Pico talks to the Lens plugin as opposed to a real Pico-enabled website, so we have to maintain different strategies for the two cases. The Pico device has a direct connection to the website; it may be tunnelled through the terminal, but the Pico talks to the website over an end-to-end-encrypted SSL channel, and it does its own login, by sending the password; then it obtains a cookie, which it then transfers to the plugin in the web browser. The Pico transfers this credential just for that session, so it doesn't actually even tell your password to your browser, unlike what happens with a password manager in the browser, where the password manager knows your password and sends it to the website you visited. In this case the password is in your Pico device, and the Pico device gives the password directly to the website at the other end, receives a cookie and passes this cookie as a kind of session credential to your browser, which then logs in. And then, if the browser is compromised, you've only lost that cookie, as opposed to having lost the password. So, in some sense, this is slightly more secure than using the password manager in your browser, even though conceptually it is very similar.

Virgil Gligor: What if you lose the Pico (or phone) that has the initial password?

Reply: You have two concerns: one is confidentiality and the other is availability. As far as confidentiality goes, the device is locked. The Pico hardware device is designed to have all its storage encrypted; otherwise, with the Pico app, you rely on whatever protection your model of phone gives to all of the private data it stores locally. For the availability aspect, as shown in the first video, you have a backup: in the case of the hardware version of Pico, every time you recharge it, it gets backed up automatically. In the case of the software version we have something equivalent: whenever it learns a password for a new site, it automatically does a backup to the cloud, so there's a forcing function that doesn't depend on you taking backups personally. And then you can always just buy a new phone, reinstall the Pico app and restore your credentials on there.

Virgil Gligor: Do you mean the passwords?

Reply: Yes: in the case of non-Pico-enabled sites seen through the Pico Lens, your credentials would be your passwords. (Otherwise, for proper Pico-enabled sites, they'd be your private keys.) It's a similar situation if you have on your laptop a password manager storing all your passwords, and you lose your laptop. You can restore from the backup after buying another laptop. Hopefully your laptop had full disk encryption so the guy who stole it cannot access all your passwords. The same situation, really.

Alastair Beresford: You might be able to sell a USB charger that actually also does enough actual stuff, over either ADB (Android Debug Bridge) or perhaps just the protocol for sharing data from USB storage, to do the backup bit.

Reply: Yes. The interesting thing about this is that the original design that is already in the 2011 paper said that whenever you recharge the Pico, it takes a backup; and I thought I was very clever because nobody ever does "backup", but everybody does "recharge", so I got the backups for free. But now, if Pico becomes as an app on the phone, then we cannot guarantee that people will recharge the phone through that gadget you're mentioning, even if we build it, so it doesn't have the same "forcing function"[2] property as the original solution. The original design is all very nice but, if we are also distributing a Pico app, we have to find some other way to make sure that the backup is taken, because people won't necessarily be using our docking station or your USB charger for the recharge—they might just charge the phone with any random USB cable, because that's all they have to hand. What we are doing for the Pico App is that, anytime the Pico goes online to talk with a site, once it has done its bit, since it has network connectivity it can also do a cloud-based backup. We've been talking to Ben Laurie about various things and he suggested that we use his Nigori[3] for doing the backing up that the docking station would do. This is a possibility and we'll consider it.

OK, so that was the Pico Lens. In the second video, you've also seen the Pico Prover App on the smartphone. The prototype just recently started working and what we need to do now is to make it practical to use. We claim that Pico will be easier to use than passwords; at the moment it isn't, and it's a bit slow, but the technical mechanics of it are there, and it's exciting to login with it! I repeat, this second video is not Hollywood, these were the real Google website and the real LinkedIn website. We have to deal with the same issues as the normal password managers in the browser: you have to write ad-hoc code for many special cases because there isn't really an API for logging into a website by machine. You have to catch many variations in web page design, things that people do in different ways, and hope that you cover enough cases. Even the in-browser password managers who have been at it for years sometimes get it wrong, so of course we are getting it wrong a lot more; but these are the real websites, we are not faking the back-end.

Ultimately we want Pico to be a single-purpose trustworthy hardware device: it does nothing else, it doesn't have other software running on it that can become malware, you have no reason (and no way) to install other stuff of dubious provenance, and there is hardware security to protect storage and to provide a trusted path between the user and the display and the application. However it is very hard to make people buy a new gadget and it is even harder to make people *carry* a new gadget, even if the gadget were free. It's kind of miraculous that people have been converted to carrying a mobile phone: almost everybody carries a mobile phone nowadays. But it's a really tough uphill struggle to make people carry one more thing, so it's much easier to get this Trojan horse on a piece of software, on something that they already carry. (Of course I am saying things in jest: my marketing department, if I had one, would tell me that I should never use such tainted language to describe our wonderful software! The Pico App is in no way a Trojan horse, it's a marvellous gift that will make people wonder how they could ever live without it before.)

We suggest you start by using the Pico App on your smartphone only with sites that don't require extreme security. Most of the websites that you visit and type passwords into don't really need super-high security: they're not all

---

[2] In the interaction-design sense of a behaviour-shaping constraint.

[3] http://www.links.org/files/nigori-overview.pdf

the same as your online banking and you can get away with some low-grade password. Well, you could easily use Pico for these sites while you are not yet sure whether you trust Pico or not.

Our third piece of software is the Pico Verifier backend for Wordpress sites. We chose Wordpress because it's used by 20 % of all sites and, as I said, by 60 % of the sites that are based on a content management system. In this slide you see what a Wordpress blog looks like when you enable the Pico plugin: next to the username and password prompt that you're familiar with, you also get a QR code. If you scan it (assuming you already have an association with that blog) then you get in. How do you make the association if you don't have one? You just log in with your normal password account and, on the settings page in the blog, you will get another QR code which, if you acquire it, will form a pairing between your Pico and your account in the blog. From then on, you can log in with Pico.

What is the socio-economic context in which we are trying to get Pico deployed? Remember the famous saying that "nobody ever got fired for buying IBM"; well, it's similar here: nobody ever got fired for using passwords to authenticate users. We have an incumbent in this field (passwords) that is going to be pretty difficult to displace, because it's what everybody else does, and there's no reason to do things differently, and there's a very big "activation energy" barrier to overcome. As I said, it's also very hard to persuade normal human beings to carry another gadget. When talking to banks and insurance companies we also discovered another barrier to overcome: they worry that they ought to be able to sue someone if the system doesn't work or gets hacked. If someone *sells* them a password-replacement solution, then they can sue them if it doesn't work. But if Pico is an open system they wonder: Where is my recourse? Who bears the liability? If this is something anybody can build and implement, how will we manage the risk of not being sure if this is going to work?

There's another potential issue, which is something we have seen in the history of our industry at the end of the last millennium. As you may remember, Sun came up with the Java programming language—an open, standard language that anybody could use or implement. Microsoft in response implemented a version of Java that worked better with Microsoft products: they did that by introducing some additional instruction that only the Microsoft Java Virtual Machine implemented. Sun got really upset because Microsoft's incompatible version threatened their "write once, run anywhere" vision. And Microsoft was so big, with their widely deployed base of Windows, that, if they changed the JVM, then for most people it was going to be just the Microsoft Java that worked well, not the real Java. Sun sued them in 1997 for 35 M$, and they settled out of court after several years. We don't want something like that to threaten the universality of Pico, either: this would be the dystopian scenario of one big web company making their own incompatible version of Pico so that they "own" it and control it, and this bastardized Pico becomes the de facto standard just because they're big.

And then, another issue: where's the incentive for people who might manufacture the hardware Pico? There isn't a lot of money in a very low-margin product like this, so you only have an interest after you are sure that there is a market of billions of people who actually want a Pico.

I am very happy that I got this team of people who are making this dream a reality, and especially that we found a strategy that does not pollute our dream. We are not compromising our design by trying to be compatible with passwords as a prerequisite, and yet we can still allow early adopters to enjoy the Pico benefits.

What next? First of all, try the Pico app and the Pico Lens for yourself, as soon we release it, which we hope will be soon. If you are a user, tell us what it would take you to use Pico for authenticating. If you are a representative of a company that uses passwords to authenticate its millions of users, then what would it take *you* to adopt Pico? This slide shows a paper design, by some of our undergraduates, of what the Pico hardware might look like. This final slide lists all the people who have worked on Pico so far, including the members of the team, who are here, and the past and present project students, one of whom one is here as well. Thank you very much.

Ross Anderson: The last time I bought a £10 mobile phone, it was being subsidised from their anticipated future sales of minutes, because it was locked in. And similarly, at an RSA conference three years ago (I think it was), I got hold of one of these VeriSign Identity Protection devices, which is a one time authentication token that they give away free. Their business model is that they charge 10 cents or 20 cents per authentication to the websites which use it. Their clients are typically people like stockbrokers, who place a significant value of risk, but are not big enough in terms of number of users to roll out their own custom authentication infrastructure.

Reply: It is true that in the past the £10 phones were subsidised by network operators selling you minutes. Nowadays, however, this is a £10 phone that I bought in Tesco, SIM-unlocked. I just paid £10 for it and nobody tied me to any contract. So, once the market is big enough, there is obviously enough money to be made just by selling you the £10 phone. I want to figure out how can we get to that stage with Pico.

Bruce Christianson: You start with drug dealers!

Rubin Xu: For the Pico Lens, presumably for some web sites you still need the users to remember their password to periodically refresh their authentication cookies?

Reply: Well, not quite. The Pico does it for them. Every time you log in via the Lens, your Pico sends the password directly to the real website; it just doesn't send it to the browser.

Rubin Xu: I thought you said the Pico doesn't remember your passwords.

Reply: The full Pico protocol uses public key crypto and uses no passwords at all. However, when the Pico device (which in this case is the Pico App on your phone) accesses a site through the Pico Lens, it has to use (and remember) your password instead, because the site itself doesn't know about the public keys of the true Pico protocol. The Pico just doesn't tell your browser the password; instead, it talks to the website directly and tells the website the password. When the website replies with an authentication cookie, the Pico gives the authentication cookie to your browser, so that the browser can actually have the session.

Unidentified Audience Member: You pass along this cookie through some different channel?

Reply: Yes. *(Draws a diagram on the flip chart and refers to it.)* This is the website, this is your terminal that contains your browser, this is your Pico device (which in the video was on your phone), this is the internet, and the terminal connects through the internet to the website, and the Pico talks to the terminal with some short-range radio channel. The Pico can tunnel through the terminal or it could, by connecting to the internet on its own, talk to the website directly.

We already have to have this local connection from Pico to browser for reasons that will become clearer in Max's talk, so through this connection we tunnel a direct connection from Pico to website, through which the Pico does a login as if this were a web browser on its own. And then, when it gets a cookie, it gives it to the browser, which then uses it in a connection that is somehow faked, because it was established by the Pico, but which the browser pretends is its own.

Virgil Gligor: Couldn't this be subject to a relay attack?

Reply: That's going to be the subject of the next talk!

Bruce Christianson: Do you have a plan to break the new vicious circle which you've got now, where people won't buy a Pico because they've already got a mobile app that does it, and websites won't implement Pico because their users can just use the Pico Lens?

Reply: The fact that people might just be content with a mobile phone is a matter of where your personal security trade-off is. If you're sufficiently paranoid that you want to have something more secure than a smartphone app, then, for what we hope will eventually be the £10 of today's low-end mobile phone, you can buy yourself a gadget that's stronger security-wise, besides being easier to use because it's dedicated rather than general-purpose. Concerning web sites, if you use the Pico Lens you're getting some of the benefits of Pico, but not all of them, especially on the security side. If you're a website and you are fed up with all the security problems of passwords and having to deal with all the incidents, then you really benefit, in security, if your customers switch to using Pico, especially if they already have a Pico for other reasons anyway.

Joseph Bonneau: This is a follow-up on what Bruce is saying. It seems like one of the security benefits, to a website, of supporting Pico, is that, for example, it would prevent phishing. But that's only a benefit if users were sometimes willing to type the password and still remember it. But, if they're doing that, then it implies there is some usability benefit why they would occasionally want to type the password themselves at other terminals or whatever.

Reply: I am not sure I fully understand the question. The sort of patch that we are deploying now (the Pico Lens) is something that you, as a user, adopt because you get many of the usability benefits of Pico, but not all the security benefits.

Joseph Bonneau: What I'm saying is: take any security benefits from switching from the phone-based sort-of-fake Pico without the website support to a full Pico, one of which would be phishing resistance. Aren't these benefits already granted even with the fake Pico Lens, assuming that users no longer type the password?

Reply: Not quite. The Pico Lens still relies on the website accepting normal replayable static passwords, which is what it sends behind the scenes. So most of the inherent security flaws related to the use of replayable static secrets (that can be overheard and then replayed, or leaked at the far end and so forth) are still there. Even if the user never types a password, the website could still get hacked and lose the (hopefully hashed and salted) password file, for example.

Rafi Yahalom: I was wondering: for the smartphone manufacturers, what would they have to implement at the infrastructure level to have the Pico application be enough? Is there any chance of that happening?

Reply: The smartphone manufacturers are already doing things such as using ARM's TrustZone for separating apps within the phone. The thing that is still missing is a trusted path from the user to the app. Right now, you can't easily tell if another app puts up a screen that looks like another's. Even though the malicious app cannot access the data of your good Pico app, the malicious fake app can still look like the Pico and trick you into doing things, and that's something that's missing.

Virgil Gligor: So you need a Wimp!

Max Spencer: Bruce mentioned a "new vicious circle" where there's no incentive for the service providers to adopt the full Pico protocol: well, actually there is! The way the Pico Lens works is that it takes the username and password that you previously typed and tries the login form again; it's not like a bank login where I have to have my little separate token: there, the Lens clearly wouldn't work. So, if there is now this positive spiral where people have Picos and use them for all the services that do support them, then there's pressure on the more security-conscious services (like banks) to adopt the full protocol so that they become Pico-compatible, given that people are now in the trend of wanting to use it.

Partha Das Chowdhury: For the Pico mobile, does the phone company need to implement any Picosiblings?

Reply: You raise a good point. At this stage, the smartphone prototype we are deploying doesn't have all the locking mechanisms that we described in the original paper. We are just implementing the interaction between the Pico device and the remote site, while relying on whatever the phone does to lock itself. This could be the usual PIN, the usual squiggle, the fingerprint recognition if you have the latest iPhone that costs £500 and so forth. But that's of course not the full design. Would the phone app also implement the Picosiblings? It depends on how much we separate the two parts of Pico (interaction with the verifier vs locking of the Pico token). If the phone did the Pico-style locking, it would also have to talk, locally, to your Picosiblings; maybe not all phones will have hardware that can do that.

Partha Das Chowdhury: In the actual implementation, what's the right number of Picosiblings you will have?

Reply: For now we can only guess. We'll have to determine the most appropriate number through user trials once we build prototypes of that hardware.

I Bought a New Security Token and All I Got Was This Lousy Phish—Relay Attacks on Visual Code Authentication Schemes

Graeme Jenkinson, Max Spencer[(⊠)], Chris Warrington, and Frank Stajano

Computer Laboratory, University of Cambridge, Cambridge, UK
{graeme.jenkinson,max.spencer,chris.warrington,
frank.stajano}@cl.cam.ac.uk

Abstract. One recent thread of academic and commercial research into web authentication has focused on schemes where users scan a visual code with their smartphone, which is a convenient alternative to password-based login. We find that many schemes in the literature (including, previously, our own) are, unfortunately, vulnerable to relay attacks. We explain the inherent reasons for this vulnerability and offer an architectural fix, evaluating its trade-offs and discussing why it has never been proposed by other authors.

1 Introduction

We consider a relatively new class of web authentication schemes, currently attracting significant academic and commercial interest, which we refer to as *visual code authentication schemes.* A user may log into a website which supports such an authentication scheme by scanning a visual code, such as a Quick Response (QR) code [13], using their hand-held authenticator device, henceforth *scanner.* The scanner is generally a smartphone, but might be a dedicated hardware gadget. The user carries their scanner at all times, or at least whenever they might want to authenticate to a website; the scanner may have a mechanism to prevent its misuse if lost or stolen. Our own Pico system [20] is of course in this class too.

Such schemes are interesting because they have some important usability benefits which passwords do not; specifically, there is nothing for users to remember or type[1]. Furthermore these schemes are resilient to conventional phishing[2] because the long-term secrets never leave the scanner and so an attacker cannot trick the victim into revealing them. However, visual code authentication schemes present a new risk. Because the information in a visual code is not human-readable, and visual codes are easily relayed, a user may be tricked into scanning a visual code displayed outside its intended context.

---

[1] Cfr. definitions of *Memoryless, Scalable-for-Users* and *Nothing-to-Type* in the Usability, Deployability and Security (UDS) framework of Bonneau *et al.* [2].

[2] As defined in the UDS framework [2].

© Springer International Publishing Switzerland 2014
B. Christianson et al. (Eds.): Security Protocols 2014, LNCS 8809, pp. 197–215, 2014.
DOI: 10.1007/978-3-319-12400-1_19

We have surveyed a range of schemes currently in the literature, some commercial [4,7] and some academic [11,20,21]. We find there are significant structural similarities between the schemes and that they all are[3] susceptible to attacks in which the victim inadvertently authenticates a session for the attacker.

This paper makes the following contributions:

- We show that the architecture of many visual authentication schemes currently in the literature leaves them inherently vulnerable to attacks that relay the visual code, allowing an attacker to gain control of sessions authenticated by other users.
- We present our proposed solution, *session delegation*, now adopted by Pico, which uses an additional communication channel to prevent the aforementioned relay attacks, and discuss why no other scheme has adopted anything similar.
- We discuss extensions to our session delegation protocol and some alternative means of mitigating these attacks, while considering their impact on the usability, deployability and security of the system.

2   Visual Code Authentication Schemes

All of the schemes surveyed offer a similar user experience and share some crucial architectural features. In this section we describe these commonalities and then review the individual schemes in more detail.

2.1   User Experience When Authenticating

When a user visits a website in their web browser, the login page includes a visual code, possibly alongside a traditional username and password login form. In order to login, the user scans the code with their scanner, which authenticates to the website identified by the visual code. After the scanner has authenticated on the user's behalf, the web browser receives a *session cookie* which grants access to the user's account through their browser.

The scanner is responsible for the generation and retention of all keys and secrets. As a result, using the scanner with arbitrarily many accounts and services does not require additional cognitive (and in particular memory) effort on the part of the user.

2.2   Protocol

Crucially, these authentication schemes must also be able to authorise a web browser running on a different host than the scanner. We call this process *browser authorisation*. Without this ability users would be restricted to logging into, and using, websites only on their scanner. But it is this crucial feature, and the

---

[3] Or were, in the case of Pico.

common approach taken by the surveyed schemes to provide it, that leads to the security vulnerabilities we describe in Sect. 3 below.

The schemes surveyed use differing protocols for the actual authentication between the scanner and the website. However, we found extensive similarities between the mechanisms used to perform the browser authorisation and, below, we show a generalised version of the overall protocol, to which the concrete implementations can all broadly be mapped[4]. Figure 1 shows the sequence of messages sent between the user's web browser, B, their scanner, S, and the website, W.

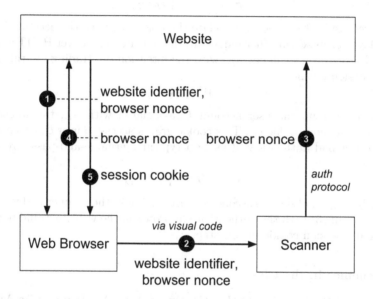

Fig. 1. Generalisation of the flawed browser authorisation protocol used by the reviewed visual code authentication schemes. The figure shows how a session cookie, c_U, for user U is installed into their browser B.

1. The user navigates to the login page of a website W in their web browser B. The login page returned by the website includes a visual code containing the website's address (or identifier) W and a fresh *browser nonce*, n_B. Note that the request and response are performed over HTTPS and therefore encrypted under a TLS session key, K_{BW}.

$$W \rightarrow B : \quad \{W, n_B\}_{K_{BW}}$$

---

[4] At least as far as we can infer—some schemes have not openly published a complete specification.

2. The website address W and browser nonce n_B are transferred to the scanner, S, when the user scans the visual code on the website's login page.

$$B \rightarrow S: \quad W, n_B \quad \text{(visual channel)}$$

3. The scanner authenticates to the website using a scheme-specific authentication protocol. The website looks up the user account, U, associated with the identity authenticated by the scanner. Subsequently, or as part of the authentication protocol itself, the scanner securely sends the browser nonce to the website.

$$S \rightarrow W: \quad \{n_B\}_{K_{SW}}$$

The website is then able to associate the nonce n_B with the account U.

4. The browser makes another request to the website, again over HTTPS, which includes the browser nonce n_B, with the intention of "trading in" this nonce for a session cookie.

$$B \rightarrow W: \quad \{n_B\}_{K_{BW}}$$

5. After looking up the user account U associated with n_B, the website W returns a session cookie c_U. This cookie grants access to user U's account, as if the user had authenticated using a typical username-and-password-based scheme.

$$W \rightarrow B: \quad \{c_U\}_{K_{BW}}$$

If the browser had sent its second request (4) before the scanner had validated the nonce in (3) with the authentication protocol, the website would not have granted a session cookie in this step.

2.3 Schemes in the Class

Method and System for Authenticating a User by Means of a Mobile Device (2009). This patent [4], held by GMV Soluciones Globales Internet S.A., describes a visual code authentication scheme in which users authenticate to remote services with a trusted application running on a mobile phone.

In this scheme the user selects the service to authenticate to by acquiring a visual code displayed by an untrusted device. The visual code contains both a random challenge and an identifier of the service to authenticate to. On scanning the visual code the mobile device creates a response to the challenge by signing it with a private key. The scheme uses Identity Based Encryption (IBE) allowing the response to be verified using the user's public identity such as an email address.

In common with the other schemes described here, the scheme links the login session on the untrusted device with the scanner's response using the random challenge contained in the visual code. Thus, this random challenge is directly equivalent to the browser nonce shown in Fig. 1.

Snap2Pass. Snap2Pass [8] is a visual code authentication system for web applications in which users authenticate using a smartphone application.

In this scheme the user selects the service to authenticate to by acquiring a visual code displayed by an untrusted device. The visual code contains both a random challenge and an identifier of the service (the relying party) to authenticate to. On scanning the visual code, the mobile device creates a response to the challenge comprising of the HMAC-SHA1 hash of the entire challenge message using a pre-shared secret as a key. The provider verifies this responds and, if successful, the browser session is authenticated with the appropriate account.

The challenge nonce (sometimes referred to as a session key) in the visual code is directly equivalent to the browser nonce. Snap2Pass explicitly acknowledges that it does not mitigate active man in the middle attacks such as those discussed in this paper.

Pico (2011). Stajano's Pico [20] is a visual code authentication scheme intended for a dedicated hardware device, although it could also be implemented, trading off security for convenience, as an application running on a smartphone[5]. Pico also includes a novel locking mechanism dependent on the proximity of a number of other, smaller devices referred to as *Picosiblings*, as well as on proximity detection between the user's Pico and their web browser (or rather the computer it is running on), allowing the user's session to lock automatically when they are away.

A prototype of the Pico system has been developed by Fu [9] and it uses a *sessionID* in the visual code that is directly equivalent to the browser nonce above.

tiQR (2011). van Rijswijk's tiQR [21] is a prototype smartphone-based visual code authentication system. The scheme uses the OAuth Challenge Response Authentication (OCRA) [18] protocol to authenticate the user to services. The user has a four-digit PIN, in addition to a secret held by the phone, for logging in to each of their accounts.

In this scheme the visual code contains a random challenge that is directly equivalent to the browser nonce.

Login Using QR Code (2012). This patent [7], held by eBay Inc., describes an authentication scheme that uses a visual code authenticator to broker secure log-ins to websites from devices that may be insecure. The scheme uses a trusted application, running on the mobile device to authenticate to a single third-party Identity Provider (IdP).

The contents of the visual code displayed on the untrusted device are passed to the IdP by the authenticator. The contents of the visual code are encrypted and can only be read by the IdP. Upon validating the contents of the visual code, the IdP issues a challenge to the trusted device, such as requesting a password.

---

[5] As already envisaged in the original paper [20] as well as in our other paper in these proceedings, "Bootstrapping adoption of the Pico password replacement scheme".

Once the user has authenticated, the IdP informs the relying web service which maintains an association between the QR code contents to active login sessions. The relying web service then updates the status of that login session.

The information contained in the visual code is sent from the IdP to the website to identify the authenticated web session. Although the description given in the patent [7] is a bit vague and obscure, it seems reasonable to assume that this data is somewhat analogous to the browser nonce.

QRAuth (2013). Howard's QRAuth[6] [11] is a research prototype visual code authentication system with significant similarities to Pico. The authenticator has a shared secret for each service, unlike Pico which uses asymmetric cryptography and QRAuth uses a mobile application rather than a dedicated hardware device as the visual code authenticator.

In this scheme the *login identifier* is directly analogous to the browser nonce.

Secure Quick Reliable Login (2013). Another recent smart-phone-based scheme is Secure Quick Reliable Login (SQRL), proposed by Gibson [10]. Visual codes used in the SQRL scheme contain a URL which includes a *session id* and points to an authentication service. The SQRL app signs this URL and then sends the signature to the authentication service over HTTPS. It uses a different public-private key pair for each service but, unusually, these key pairs are not stored, but are derived from a master secret and master password when needed. The system specifies a revocation protocol to be used when a SQRL device is lost or stolen.

The *session id* contained in the URL in the visual code is directly equivalent to the browser nonce.

3   Attacks

3.1   Core Vulnerability

Visual codes are not human readable; so, whilst acquiring a visual code reflects the user's intent to authenticate, it is unclear to the user what they are authenticating *to*, or whether the information in the visual code is fresh. Although the visual channel itself can reasonably be assumed to be unmodifiable, the user's web browser is not a trusted display. Specifically it does not prevent *relayed* visual codes from being displayed.

The attacks we describe below all exploit the same core vulnerability. In all cases the attacker (who uses browser B') seeks to obtain a cookie, c_U, which will give them access to victim U's account for a given website W.

---

[6] There is also a commercial mobile application [12] of the same name, but it is equivalent to a password wallet and bears only a superficial resemblance to the other schemes discussed here.

For each attack, the attacker makes a request to W and gets back a visual code containing $W, n_{B'}$ (see step 1 in the description of the protocol above).

$$W \rightarrow B' : \quad \{W, n_{B'}\}_{K_{B'W}}$$

The attacker then relays this visual code and convinces the victim to scan it, thereby causing the user's scanner to authenticate to W and link U's account with $n_{B'}$ (see steps 2 and 3 above). Note that the relayed channel may or may not be re-encrypted, depending on the mode of the attack.

$$B' \rightarrow B : \quad W, n_{B'} \quad \text{(relay)}$$

$$B \rightarrow W : \quad W, n_{B'} \quad \text{(visual channel)}$$

Finally the attacker's browser can send $n_{B'}$ back to W, trading it in for the session cookie c_U they want (see steps 4 and 5 above).

$$B' \rightarrow W : \quad \{n_{B'}\}_{K_{B'W}}$$

$$W \rightarrow B' : \quad \{c_U\}_{K_{B'W}}$$

The details of how an attacker might relay a visual code and convince a user to scan it with their visual code scanner device are given below. None of these attacks involve the attacker modifying the contents of any visual code[7], only relaying them to trick victims into authenticating sessions they did not intend to. We show how two well-known types of attacks, phishing and mafia fraud, are even more insidious when applied to visual code authentication schemes.

Perhaps surprisingly, proponents of several of the schemes surveyed claim that resilience to phishing is one of their key security benefits; moreover, the Usability-Deployability-Security evaluation framework [2] for web authentication schemes does not penalize schemes that are only vulnerable to more elaborate real-time man-in-the-middle or relay attacks (*cfr.* the definition of its *Resilient-to-Phishing* benefit). However, while this definition is appropriate for the schemes presented in Bonneau *et al.*'s evaluation, it fails to tell the whole story for visual code authentication schemes.

3.2   Phishing with Visual Codes

In a traditional phishing attack, the victim unwittingly divulges their password to an attacker, who pretends to be or represent a website the victim trusts. The use of a scanner appears to offer some protection against phishing because the secrets used to authenticate the user are contained within the scanner and are unknown to the user and, depending on the specific authentication protocol, might even never leave the scanner. While these secrets can be revealed by physically compromising the device, this is an altogether different type of attack which doesn't scale. An attacker can only physically compromise a single device

---

[7] It would still be prudent to sign the contents of visual codes to prevent such attacks.

at a time, with significant effort, rather than attack many of them in parallel over the net.

However, an attacker is able to convince the victim to *use* their scanner and an attacker is able to relay a specific visual code over various communications channels, including email. For example, the attacker could send an email to the victim, purporting to be from their bank, claiming they need to scan a code to "validate" their scanner. When the victim does so, they authenticate the nonce in the visual code which the attacker knows and relayed (see n'_B above), and the attacker can now trade this nonce in for the user's session cookie. (We might view this as an instance of the "chosen protocol attack" [14].)

A visual code phishing email may come with the usual carrots ("you will be entered into a prize draw") and sticks ("your account may be locked") to persuade the victim to comply. However, there are several reasons why it would be more difficult for a user to spot a visual code phishing attempt, making the new attack more insidious. In a traditional phishing attack, the victim must either reply to the attacker's email, in which case the attacker must disclose an email address they control; or the victim must enter their password into a form on a fake version of the trusted website, which the attacker must provide. With a visual code phishing attack, neither is required of the attacker: the victim can scan the visual code right in their email client, thus contacting the legitimate website directly, and needn't reply to the attacker in any other way. By the same token, no "suspicious address" (email or web) will be found in the email that an alert user could spot to detect the fraud.

Furthermore, it is important to see that the victim's scanner also does not contact any server controlled by the attacker; the scanner really does authenticate to the website the phisherman is impersonating. If the scanner prompted the user for confirmation before each authentication, it would still not defend against this type of attack because the website identified by the visual code and contacted by the scanner for authentication is "correct"; the victim *wants* to authenticate to it. Any existing training the user may have received, to check for the right website address or the HTTPS padlock, is useless here, even if followed to the letter.

In light of this attack, the only advice that users could be given is that they should never scan a visual code contained in an out-of-band communication, such as an email, and they should only scan visual codes found on websites that they trust. But it is well known that reliably authenticating the website to the user is a hard, unsolved problem.

Besides, users may be accustomed to scanning visual codes with their smartphone for other purposes than authentication; therefore they are unlikely to appreciate the difference between scanning an authentication visual code and a visual code on an advert. Furthermore, there are additional attacks if users trust websites which are not trustworthy and then do not pay full attention to all confirmation messages the scanner might present to them.

3.3   Mafia Fraud with Visual Codes

A "mafia fraud" relay attack against a visual code authentication systems results from users trusting an untrustworthy (mafia-operated, in the canonical example) website. The mafia fraud, as first described by Desmedt *et al.* [6], is a type of man-in-the-middle attack in which a challenge from the verifier is relayed without modification, in real time, to an honest prover. The man-in-the-middle then transmits the honest prover's response back to the verifier as shown in Fig. 2.

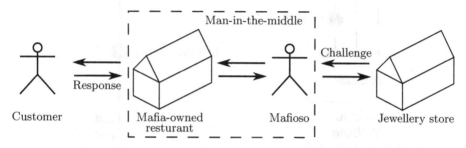

Fig. 2. Anatomy of a mafia fraud. The honest customer thinks they are paying for their meal, but is actually being tricked by the mafia into buying them some jewelry.

A mafia fraud with a visual code authentication system is slightly different because the response of the user, or rather the user's scanner, goes directly to the verifier, but the structure of the attack is otherwise the same.

As an example, consider a discussion forum website. This is a low-value site that the user trusts sufficiently to read discussion threads and sometimes post comments. If the user logged in to the forum with a username and password it would be difficult for the malicious site operator to trick the user into authenticating to the forum using their credentials for another high-value website, such as their online banking website[8]. However, with a visual code authentication system, only the non-human-readable visual code tells the scanner which website to authenticate to. The user may not detect the substitution, by the malicious operator, of a visual code for the forum with one from their online banking website.

If the consequences of such an attack were simply that the victim authenticates to a different website to the one they intended, then the advantage that a malicious actor gains is modest. However, as with the phishing attack above, the attacker can record the browser nonce, n_B, contained in the visual code, before relaying the code to the victim U and later trade this nonce in to obtain a session cookie c_U granting them access to the victim's account. Figure 3 shows the sequence of messages sent when such a mafia fraud attack is carried out.

Any attacker could start up their own malicious website to perform this kind of attack, or they could hijack another website with existing users. In either case

---

[8] Unless of course the victim uses the same password on every site.

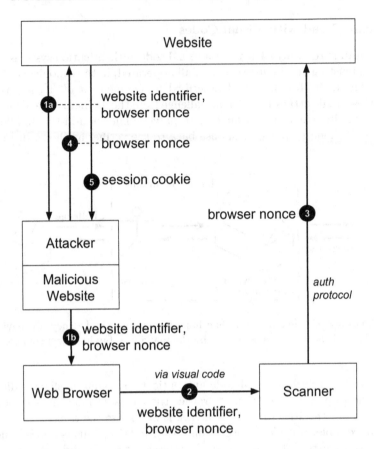

Fig. 3. Relay attack on the flawed browser authorisation protocol shown in Fig. 1. Figure shows how the attacker obtains a session cookie, c_U, for user U using a malicious website they control.

they could try to avoid detection by launching the attack only a fraction of the time, so that users would assume any discrepancy was the fault of their scanner rather than the malicious website.

The key difference between this mafia fraud attack and the previous phishing attack is that the user is not tricked into thinking that the attacker represents someone else. This means the user has an opportunity to spot that something is wrong if their scanner asks them to confirm the authentication and tells them the service that the visual code identified. However we do not think highly of protection techniques that dump back on the user the actual onus of checking. Users are conditioned by false alarms to accept or override such warning messages indiscriminately. Furthermore, because the user wants to log into the malicious website, which they trust and which they may have logged into successfully many times before, they are unlikely to be looking out for any discrepancies.

4 Solutions

4.1 Session Delegation

We call "session delegation" our proposed solution to prevent these types of attacks. Instead of having the website W initially send the browser B a browser nonce n_B, which the browser can later "trade in" for the session cookie c_U after the authentication has linked n_B with a user's account U, we propose passing c_U from the website to the browser via the trusted scanner. In order to do that we need a new channel from the scanner to the browser and furthermore we propose this new channel be authenticated and encrypted, so that a scanner may only delegate to a browser with which it has previously established a trusted pairing.

A visual code authentication scheme that requires this new channel with these constraints suffers from reduced deployability, which may be why the schemes surveyed do not do so. In our ongoing work to improve deployability of this solution we are developing a *rendezvous point*. Provided that browser and scanner have an Internet connection, the rendezvous point allows them to communicate even when their net connection is heavily restricted by NATs and firewalls. We also present a fallback mechanism for the protocol so users can still log in when the browser they are using cannot be modified to carry out the cryptographic pairing procedure.

First we describe the session delegation protocol in more detail. Figure 4 shows the sequence of messages sent when the session delegation protocol is used.

1. The user navigates to the login page of a website W in their browser B. The login page returned by the website includes a visual code containing the websites address (or identifier) W, but now no browser nonce.

$$W \rightarrow B : \quad W$$

2. The website address W is transferred to the scanner S when the user scans the visual code on the websites login page:

$$B \rightarrow S : \quad W, B \quad \text{(visual channel)}$$

3. The scanner authenticates to the website, W. There is no longer a nonce to send at this stage. The website looks up the user account, U, associated with the identity authenticated by the scanner. The website creates the session cookie c_U and returns to the scanner:

$$W \rightarrow S : \quad \{c_U\}_{K_{SW}}$$

4. Via a new authenticated and encrypted channel, the session cookie c_U is transferred to the browser. c_U grants access to user U?s account through the browser as previously.

$$A \rightarrow B : \quad \{c_U\}_{K_{AB}} \quad \text{(new channel)}$$

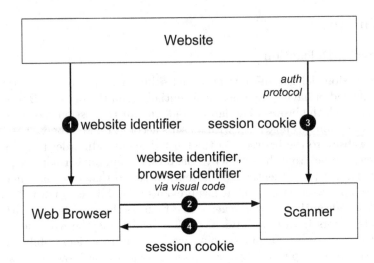

Fig. 4. Our proposed browser authorisation protocol: session delegation. Figure shows how a session cookie, c_U, for user U is installed into their browser.

The New Channel. Our session delegation protocol shown in Fig. 4 imposes two requirements: first, there must exist a new channel from scanner to browser[9] in order to transmit message 4. Second, this channel must be authenticated and encrypted.

We have built prototypes using two different types of channel: one using a local Bluetooth link and another using the Internet. The former does not require the scanner to have its own Internet connection, reducing its hardware requirements, but it imposes requirements on the hardware of the host on which the web browser is running. For the second type, the Internet-based channel, we implemented a HTTP-based rendezvous point in the public Internet. In an ideal world, the browser would simply put the IP address of its host into the visual code and the scanner could connect to that, but this is not possible for all browser-scanner pairs due to NATs and firewalls.

To use our rendezvous point, the web browser first makes request for a "channel" and the server responds with a URL of the form:

```
http://rendezvous.example.com/channel/<channel-uuid>
```

The browser includes this URL in the visual code, and the browser and scanner may subsequently write to this channel by making HTTP POST requests and read from it by making GET requests.

We suggest that this new channel should be authenticated and encrypted so that a cookie sent over it cannot be eavesdropped and an attacker cannot have a scanner return a cookie to *their* web browser, B', simply by getting a

---

[9] The existing visual channel from browser to scanner is of course unsuitable because it is unidirectional in the wrong direction.

user to scan a code containing B''s identity and address. In other words, the scanner must only send cookies to those browsers which can prove ownership of a private key corresponding to an identity the scanner trusts. Our suggestion is that before step 4 above, the authenticator and the browser carry out a mutual authentication protocol, such as the SIGMA protocol [15], which has the side-effect of generating a session key, K_{AB} thereby providing the authentication and encryption simultaneously.

For the trusted browser to authenticate some identity to the scanner they must have previously "paired". This pairing could be done through a menu in the browser which causes the browser's full public key to be displayed to the scanner in a visual code.

Increasing Deployability: Fallback Mode. Unfortunately, if the new channel is to be authenticated and encrypted, the user's web browser requires modification, harming the deployability of the system by removing the *Browser-Compatible* UDS benefit [2]. The browser must be able to receive cookies over an encrypted channel and install them as if they had been set by the website directly. This is possible using a browser addon, but installing such an addon will not be possible for all users in all situations. We propose a fallback mechanism, transcription of a URL, to be used in these, hopefully rare, circumstances.

When the website W returns cookie c_U to the scanner (see step 3 above), it also returns a special single-use login URL, l_U, which is of the form:

$$\texttt{https://<domain-of-W>/?<nonce>}$$

The website links the nonce in l_U with U, such that opening the URL in a web browser will cause the corresponding cookie c_U to be installed. So if the scanner is unable to write the cookie back to the browser automatically because the latter is unmodified and/or no channel is available, the scanner can instead display the login URL l_U for the user to transcribe into the browser's address bar manually and after another round-trip to W the cookie is installed. In effect the user themselves takes on the role of the new required channel. Clearly this impacts on usability, notably compromising the *Physically-Effortless* and *Infrequent-Errors* benefits of the UDS framework [2]. From a usability perspective typing out l_U, which must contain an unguessable random nonce, is at least as difficult as having to type a password, but it is just a fallback to save the user in rare cases and there is still nothing for the user to remember.

The benefit of using a login URL which is typed directly into the browser's address bar, is that it's hard to send the nonce to the wrong person. Browser B making a request to a URL of the above form, is effectively the same as:

$$B \to W : \quad \{n\}_{K_{BW}}$$

Crucially the URL contains the nonce to send, n, the website to send it to, W, and the protocol to use, HTTPS, which provides the encryption under K_{BW}. If instead the user were asked to transcribe a single-use password into some specific form field on the website's login page, an attacker could coerce the user to enter it into a form field on their own fake login page (using traditional phishing techniques) and then forward it to the real site[10].

Session Gifting Attack. Unfortunately, introducing this fallback mechanism introduces a new vulnerability[11]. An attacker, U', can use their scanner to obtain a fallback URL $l_{U'}$ and then get a victim to open it, leaving the victim with a cookie $c_{U'}$. In other words, the attacker *gifts* the victim a session for an account they (the attacker) control, just by having them open $l_{U'}$. If a user did not notice this, they might divulge sensitive information, such as credit card details, which would later be accessible to the attacker.

To defend against such attacks we augment the new session delegation protocol with something similar to the "browser nonce", n_B, from the original (flawed) protocol above (see Sect. 2.2).

When the user navigates to the login page of the website, the website installs a fresh "browser identifying cookie", c_B, in the user's browser, B. This browser ID cookie will automatically be sent back to the website with each future request until it is deleted. The value of c_B is also included in the visual code and thus reaches the scanner. The scanner sends c_B back to the website when it authenticates, allowing the website to form a link between c_B, and the session cookie c_U and login URL l_U it returns.

Now, whenever a browser makes a request to a login URL, the website simultaneously receives the nonce in the URL, and any browser ID cookie previously set for that browser. The website can check if the correct browser ID cookie is included in any such request before granting session cookie c_U.

With this countermeasure, the session gifting attack is no longer possible. The attacker may acquire the fallback URL $l_{U'}$, but if the victim opens it they will not be granted cookie $c_{U'}$, because their browser doesn't have the required browser ID cookie.

4.2 Other Solutions

It may be argued that the challenges in the visual code should only remain valid for a limited period to reduce the window of vulnerability. However we consider this to be merely an implementation feature that does not fundamentally address the underlying security issue. The attacker can relay the visual code more quickly, perhaps requesting it on-demand, or they can relay the same code to many targets simultaneously to improve the chances of a catch before it expires.

Trusted Visual Code Display. An alternative solution to attacks where the visual code is relayed from one site to another would be to extend the trusted computing base to include the browser. In such a scheme the browser, or browser addon, verifies that the domain of the website presenting the visual code matches

---

[10] It would still be possible for attackers listen for nonces by typosquatting on domains similar to the domain of a popular website W.

[11] We thank Olgierd Pieczul for pointing this out during the workshop.

the website identifier or address being transmitted to the scanner in that code. Unfortunately we deem this to be a non-solution for several reasons.

It is not in general possible for the web browser to tell when it is displaying a visual code. An attacker clearly wouldn't helpfully tag their relayed visual codes to make them easier for the browser to find, so it would have to run a detection algorithm on every displayed image. But then an attacker might not use an actual embedded image, but create a visual code by arranging other HTML elements[12].

Alternatively, the browser could provide a special trusted display area specifically for visual codes somewhere in the chrome of the browser window and offer some kind of API to allow websites to have visual codes for their own domain displayed there. However this does not prevent other visual codes being displayed in the normal, non-trusted browser window and experience with mechanisms such as the HTTPS padlock shows that such signals are not fully understood by users. A user may not understand the difference between a visual code in the trusted display area and one in the normal web page.

Furthermore visual codes might be present in any number of other locations including physical locations; we already discussed an email-based session phishing attack above. There is no way that everywhere a visual code is displayed on-screen, or printed, can be trusted.

Secure Bookmarks. As the session phishing attacks presented in this paper rely on the user scanning a relayed visual code, they can, of course, be prevented using a different sort of authentication scheme which doesn't use visual codes. In a secure bookmarks scheme, such as Phoolproof [19], a hardware authenticator device, analogous to our scanner, holds all the keys and secrets and authenticates to websites on behalf of the user. When using a secure bookmark system, the user is responsible for manually selecting the website they wish to authenticate to.

While such a system is resilient to session phishing because it doesn't use any kind of browser nonce, it does require a channel from the authenticator device to the web browser, just like a scanner using our session delegation protocol, and thus faces the same deployability issues. The secure devices have a similar role in both types of scheme, namely that of brokering a session between the browser and the website. One usability benefit of visual code authentication schemes over secure bookmark schemes is that they do not require the user to select the website and browser they want to broker a session between because both are identified in the visual code.

5   Related Work

Desmedt *et al.* [5] introduces the term mafia fraud in the context of a mafia owned restaurant (cfr. Fig. 3). In this paper we appropriate the term mafia fraud to describe the similar attack in which the visual code is relayed unchanged by

---

[12] For example the qrcode.js library (https://github.com/davidshimjs/qrcodejs) uses the new HTML5 canvas drawing element.

an active man-in-the-middle. It is clearly impossible to relay the visual channel undetectably between the web browser and the scanner. And whilst it is possible to relay the channel between the scanner and website, the use of SIGMA-I ensures that the attacker gains no benefit for doing so.

Beth and Desmedt [1] seek to mitigate relay attacks by enforcing a maximum round-trip time of a challenge-response protocol. Brands and Chaum [3] refine the technique and make it robust, introducing the first distance-bounding protocol. But distance-bounding does not relay attacks; rather, it solves the simpler problem of ensuring that the prover and verifier are located within a specified distance bound. However, when authenticating to web services, physical proximity is irrelevant because the honest prover could be in a different country or continent from the verifier. Furthermore, an honest user may wait an indeterminate amount of time before scanning a visual code even after it has loaded.

Parno, Kuo and Perrig's "Phoolproof Phishing Prevention" [19] uses a trusted mobile device to mutually authenticate with remote services from an untrusted terminal, the main objective being to prevent or limit the efficacy of phishing attacks. In this scheme the user selects a web service to authenticate to from a secure bookmark on the trusted authenticator device. A secure session is then brokered between the web service and the untrusted terminal by the trusted authenticator device. While Phoolproof is not a visual code authentication scheme, it does require a channel from the authentication device to the browser, like the scanner does when using our session delegation protocol; the comparison between the two is therefore instructive.

Mannan and van Oorschot [17] define a protocol, MP-Auth, for user authentication and secure financial transactions from an untrusted device with assistance of a trusted mobile device. Although not a visual code authentication scheme, MP-Auth shares many architectural similarities with such schemes. MP-Auth does not seek to address the fundamental security weakness of passwords, nor does it reflect the realities of modern mobile phone platforms where malware is common. And so, whilst MP-Auth is not vulnerable to the relay attacks presented in this paper, it does not offer the security and usability benefits of visual code authentication schemes.

Laurie and Singer [16] argue that it is impossible to have a system which is both general-purpose and trustworthy. Furthermore, they define the requirements for a trusted device, referred to as the Neb, that may be used to authenticate online transactions. This is relevant to the decision as to whether the scanner should be a dedicated device or a smartphone application.

6   Conclusion

We presented the first comprehensive analysis of visual code relay attacks on the emerging class of authentication schemes in which users login to websites by scanning a visual code. We identified a variety of schemes in this class and highlighted their common features. In particular we generalised the protocol they all use to authorise a web browser running on a separate host. We found that all of the currently proposed schemes that we reviewed are vulnerable to attacks in which the visual code is relayed.

We have presented examples of such attacks and discussed the architectural reasons for the vulnerability. Such attacks are worrying because the attacker does not have to modify any visual code and the user's scanner authenticates to a trusted website. In particular, if the user's scanner acted according to specification there may be a burden of proof on the user to prove that any resulting transactions were fraudulent[13].

We reject claims that these attacks can be mitigated by requiring the user to carry out manual checks or using a trusted display. The root cause of this vulnerability is the use of a browser nonce which the browser obtains at the start of the protocol and then "trades in" for an authorisation cookie, c_U, once the scanner has, independently, authenticated user U. Our proposed solution, the session delegation protocol, allows authorisation of the web browser without the use of a browser nonce. Instead, the website sends the session cookie to the browser, via the trusted scanner, only *after* the authentication has taken place.

The cost of that solution is the need for an authenticated and encrypted communication channel from the scanner to the browser. We have explored the use of a local radio channel (Bluetooth) and a connection via the Internet, assisted by a rendezvous point. In either case, modification of the browser is required which harms the deployability of scheme, which is perhaps why none of the schemes surveyed adopted a similar approach. However, we have provided a fallback mechanism for the occasions when browser modification is not possible.

The class of visual code authentication systems seemed a promising contender for replacing passwords but that critical and seemingly inherent vulnerability present in all past implementations made it not credible. By allowing ourselves to consider more fundamental changes to the architecture (such as the inclusion of another channel from scanner to web browser) rather than being constrained by backwards compatibility, we have found a way to stop an array of session phishing attacks. Now we can move forward by selecting the most appropriate trade-off between usability, deployability and security.

Acknowledgments. We gratefully acknowledge the European Research Council for funding this research under grant 307224.

We also thank Olgierd Pieczul for pointing out the login gifting attack during the workshop.

References

1. Beth, T., Desmedt, Y.G.: Identification tokens – or: solving the chess grandmaster problem. In: Menezes, A., Vanstone, S.A. (eds.) CRYPTO 1990. LNCS, vol. 537, pp. 169–176. Springer, Heidelberg (1991)

---

[13] The real problem instead being that the specification was wrong, in so far as the scheme is vulnerable to relay.

2. Bonneau, J., Herley, C., van Oorschot, P.C., Stajano, F.: The quest to replace passwords: a framework for comparative evaluation of web authentication schemes. In: Proceedings of the 2012 IEEE Symposium on Security and Privacy, SP '12, pp. 553–567. IEEE Computer Society, Washington (2012). http://dx.doi.org/10.1109/SP.2012.44

3. Brands, S., Chaum, D.: Distance bounding protocols (extended abstract). In: Helleseth, T. (ed.) EUROCRYPT 1993. LNCS, vol. 765, pp. 344–359. Springer, Heidelberg (1994)

4. Cobos, J.J.L., Hoz, P.C.D.L.: Method and system for authenticating a user my means of a mobile device. Patent filed 17 September 2009, published 4 September 2012

5. Desmedt, Y.G., Goutier, C., Bengio, S.: Special uses and abuses of the fiat shamir passport protocol. In: Pomerance, C. (ed.) CRYPTO 1987. LNCS, vol. 293, pp. 21–39. Springer, Heidelberg (1988). http://dl.acm.org/citation.cfm?id=646752.704723

6. Desmedt, Y.G., Goutier, C., Bengio, S.: Special uses and abuses of the fiat shamir passport protocol. In: Pomerance, C. (ed.) CRYPTO 1987. LNCS, vol. 293, pp. 21–39. Springer, Heidelberg (1988)

7. DeSoto, D.B., Peskin, M.A.: Login using QR code. Patent filed 15 February 2013, published 22 August 2013

8. Dodson, B., Sengupta, D., Boneh, D., Lam, M.S.: Secure, consumer-friendly web authentication and payments with a phone. In: Gris, M., Yang, G. (eds.) MobiCASE 2010. LNICST, vol. 76, pp. 17–38. Springer, Heidelberg (2012)

9. Fu, H.P.: Pico: no more passwords! Msc thesis, University of Leuven, Flanders, Belgium (2013). https://www.cosic.esat.kuleuven.be/publications/thesis-232.pdf

10. Gibson, S.: Secure quick reliable login. https://www.grc.com/sqrl/sqrl.htm, October 2013. Accessed 6 Nov 2013

11. Howard, A.: QRAuth. Bsc. thesis, Bournemouth University, Bournemouth, UK (2012). https://www.grc.com/sqrl/files/Adam-Howard-FYP-Dissertation.pdf

12. Computing Objects Inc.: QRAuth. http://www.computingobjects.com/qrauthinfo (2012). Accessed 13 Nov 2013

13. ISO: Information technology–automatic identification and data capture techniques–QR Code 2005 bar code symbology specification. ISO 18004:2006, International Organization for Standardization, Geneva, Switzerland (2006)

14. Kelsey, J., Schneier, B., Wagner, D.: Protocol interactions and the chosen protocol attack. In: Christianson, B., Lomas, M., Crispo, B., Roe, M. (eds.) Security Protocols 1997. LNCS, vol. 1361, pp. 91–104. Springer, Heidelberg (1998). http://dl.acm.org/citation.cfm?id=647215.720386

15. Krawczyk, H.: SIGMA: the 'SIGn-and-MAc approach' to authenticated Diffie-Hellman and its use in the IKE protocols. In: Boneh, D. (ed.) CRYPTO 2003. LNCS, vol. 2729, pp. 400–425. Springer, Heidelberg (2003). http://dx.doi.org/10.1007/978-3-540-45146-4_24

16. Laurie, B., Singer, A.: Choose the red pill and the blue pill: a position paper. In: Proceedings of the 2008 Workshop on New Security Paradigms, NSPW '08, pp. 127–133. ACM, New York (2008). http://doi.acm.org/10.1145/1595676.1595695

17. Mannan, M.S., van Oorschot, P.C.: Using a personal device to strengthen password authentication from an untrusted computer. In: Dietrich, S., Dhamija, R. (eds.) FC 2007 and USEC 2007. LNCS, vol. 4886, pp. 88–103. Springer, Heidelberg (2007). http://dl.acm.org/citation.cfm?id=1785594.1785610

18. M'Raihi, D., Rydell, J., Bajaj, S., Machani, S., Naccache, D.: OCRA: OATH Challenge-Response Algorithm. RFC 6287 (Informational), June 2011. http://www.ietf.org/rfc/rfc6287.txt

19. Parno, B., Kuo, C., Perrig, A.: Phoolproof phishing prevention. In: Di Crescenzo, G., Rubin, A. (eds.) FC 2006. LNCS, vol. 4107, pp. 1–19. Springer, Heidelberg (2006)

20. Stajano, F., Stajano, F.: Pico: no more passwords!. In: Christianson, B., Crispo, B., Malcolm, J., Stajano, F. (eds.) Security Protocols 2011. LNCS, vol. 7114, pp. 49–81. Springer, Heidelberg (2011). http://dx.doi.org/10.1007/978-3-642-25867-1_6

21. Van Rijswijk, R.M., Van Dijk, J.: Tiqr: a novel take on two-factor authentication. In: Proceedings of the 25th International Conference on Large Installation System Administration, LISA'11, p. 7. USENIX Association, Berkeley (2011). http://dl.acm.org/citation.cfm?id=2208488.2208495

Relay Attacks on Visual Code Authentication Schemes (Transcript of Discussion)

Max Spencer[✉]

University of Cambridge, Cambridge, UK
ms955@cam.ac.uk

My name is Max and I've been working on the Pico project with Frank and the rest of the team since last summer. We've just been hearing about some of the deployability advances we've been making with Pico, but I'm going to be talking about some security properties of Pico and similar schemes. Specifically I'm going to be talking about a type of relay attack one could carry out on such schemes, were they in common use, and how we've changed the way that Pico works to address this threat.

I'm going to be talking about both Pico and other so-called visual code authentication systems. So first let's be clear about what such a system is. They make use of a hand-held authenticator device, henceforth *scanner*. The scanner may be a smartphone with a specific app installed, or a dedicated hardware device, as Pico is envisaged to be. Services display visual codes, such as QR codes, to users when they can login with their scanner and *to* login the user simply has to scan and acquire this code. Their scanner goes off and does its authentication with the service, and the user is logged in. Some schemes are limited to just providing authentication in the context of like the web, but some proposed schemes like Pico are more ambitious, aiming to get rid of passwords in a wider range of contexts.

Here are some examples of such schemes. There's Pico of course, there's a scheme called Snap2Pass, which is a Stanford research project, there have been some Open Source projects such as SQRL and tiQR and there have been some patents as well. Those have much more boring names.[1]

All of these schemes have to solve the same problem. When a user wants to login to a service, for example Gmail, they often want to be logged in the web browser on their computer, rather than being logged in on their scanner device. Using their scanner they acquire the code and the device goes off and authenticates to Gmail and the authentication succeeds and that's fine. But now at this point the user's web browser is still unknown to Gmail; Gmail needs some way to link the scanner and the web browser together. So, how do we go about doing that?

Well one way of solving this problem is to include a nonce in this QR code. This is the solution adopted by all of the aforementioned schemes, with the exception, now, of Pico, since we've changed the way it works. When the scanner, scans the code it gets a nonce, and when it authenticates, it authenticates a tuple

---

[1] "Method and System for Authenticating a User by Means of a Mobile Device (2009)" and "Login Using QR Code (2012)".

B. Christianson et al. (Eds.): Security Protocols 2014, LNCS 8809, pp. 216–220, 2014.
DOI: 10.1007/978-3-319-12400-1_20

of that nonce and the user's ID. The web browser where the QR is displayed also knows the nonce and so at some later time it can send that nonce to Gmail. Because of the scanner previously associated the nonce with a user ID a session can be started for the appropriate user account.

That seems OK and this is *a* solution. The key benefit of this is that no communication channel between the scanner and the user's web browser is required, so that's good. However, it leaves the system vulnerable to attacks where the attacker relays the visual code. So again using Gmail as an example, I as the attacker load up the Gmail login page and get a QR code (with a nonce), and then if I can get any other Gmail user to go and scan that code and authenticate with it, then I'm in possession of a nonce which I can *trade in* for a session that's authenticated by that user. That's pretty bad.

Let's just see a really naïve, simple example of how such an attack could be formulated, just to kind of flesh the idea out a bit. Our attacker has his own personal computer and he's the, rather untrustworthy, operator of some game website, somegame.com. Our victim happens to be a user of somegame.com, and they've logged in there using a visual code authentication system successfully, many times previously. They also happen to have a bank.com online banking account. To carry out the attack our attacker goes to the bank.com login page, takes the QR code and publishes it on the login page of somegame.com. Our victim comes along, scans the code on somegame.com, but their scanner authenticates to *bank.com* instead, and they've authenticated their ID with the nonce which is also in the possession of the attacker, who can just send that off to bank.com, and get logged in as our victim. This is a really crude example but, I'm sure you can see how this could be automated and carried out on a larger scale.

So what can we do to prevent such an attack? One simple mechanism which has good deployability, because it doesn't require any additional channel between the scanner and the browser, is prevention through confirmation. There's a point after the QR code has been scanned, but before the authentication has taken place, where the user can, if prompted by their device, spot the discrepancy between the website that *they* think that they're logging into, and the website identified by the QR code. That is, the scanner can pop up a box whenever the user scans a code saying "do you want to authenticate to bank.com?", and if that isn't what they were expecting the user can prevent any authentication from going ahead.

The problem with this is that if the user is in a hurry, and lets say they've authenticated to somegame.com 200 times before and never been a problem, they may just quickly just click continue, without doing the check. Maybe they're doing something and they're in a rush, and they just don't read the message properly.

This prevention mechanism kind of becomes useless when the attack is combined with traditional phishing techniques. So say you received an email, apparently from bank.com, and you're told that you've got to scan this code to make sure you don't lose all your money because there's been some kind of security breach etc. Well if you scan the code now, the scanner asks "do you want to authenticate to bank.com" and yes, yes you do, that's exactly what the email was telling you to do, so the confirmation step is innefectual here. With these phishing emails it's kind of worse than before when they were after your passwords. There's no like dodgy link to click, it's not asking you to reveal any secret, or anything like that, so all the previous training that people have received with regards to phishing of passwords is of little use now. So prevention through confirmation is not looking great.

Another idea is trusted display of QR codes. This means that in the user's web browser there's some sort of special zone on the screen where the web browser will display login QR codes, if they are for logging into the same site as that which the user is currently viewing *and*, importantly, they won't display any other QR codes there. The user is told to only login by scanning codes in that special zone, which would be somewhere outside the area that a web page could put an image. The attacker cannot relay a code into the special zone, but there's no way that the browser can stop a web page just putting a QR code somewhere else. It seems likely that at least some proportion of users wouldn't understand the distinction between a QR code that's in that special zone and a QR code that's elsewhere, and so they could still be tricked into scanning a relayed code anyway.

Another slightly different type of system is a secure bookmark system, which is not a visual code authentication scheme, but it does still use a hand-held authenticator. In such a scheme a user has a list of accounts or services they can log into stored on their device, and they have to pick the one that they want first, rather than scanning a code. So they necessarily can't be tricked into authenticating to the wrong thing which is good, but such a system requires a channel between the authenticator and their computer. With that channel we think that we can come up with a better solution for visual code authentication systems, which we call *session delegation*.

Let's look at our Gmail example again to see how Pico works with session delegation. Before we had the nonce starting in the QR code, then going to the device, and then going to Gmail when the authentication happened. Then at some later time, it was sent to Gmail again by the web browser. What we propose is still using the nonce, but having it move around in a different manner. It is generated at random by Gmail when the scanner authenticates and Gmail associates the nonce with the authenticated user ID. The nonce is sent back to the device, which then sends it back to the browser, which can then send it to Gmail to get a session where the authenticated user is logged in. For web applications, the nonce could be contained in a URL, so that the browser just has to make a request to the URL for the nonce to be sent back to the issuing website.

Unfortunately, as well as having the actual communication channel, you now need a plugin to receive that nonce URL and do something useful with it, like making a request to it. But we've got an OK fallback channel here, namely the user! Because the nonce is just a URL, your Pico can helpfully say "Please go to example.com/login/abc123" and you have to type out that address, but it's still better than being locked out, or having to remember a fallback password which you haven't used in six months.

So I'll just summarise and then I'll hopefully have some questions. There's this class of schemes and they QR codes which contain nonces to allow the verifier to link requests from the user's main computer and their scanner device. This makes them vulnerable to a type of relay attack where the QR code and the nonce it contains is copied by the attacker, effectively extending and eavesropping the visual channel. Our solution involves changing the way that this nonce moves around, but this requires a new communication channel from the scanner device to the user's computer.

That's the end of my main slides, I have some extra slides, that I can go through, but first I'll invite some questions.

Bruce Christianson: You said that your proposed solution is for the nonces to originate at the site, such as the bank, and then come to my mobile phone. What do I experience as that's happening, do I as the user have to do anything to cause that to happen?

Reply: No, we hope that from the user's perspective everything would appear the same. Pico carries out its authentication protocol with the website, and the last message it receives from the website contains the newly generated token with the nonce.

Joseph Bonneau: So your experience is joy and tranquillity.

Olgierd Pieczul: So did you consider a *session gifting attack*[2], the attack where someone gets a nonce and authenticates a session using their device, but then gets someone else to use that session, without realising. The victim might start sending emails containing sensitive information, or, for example, they might add their credit card to the attacker's PayPal account.

Reply: This seems like a good point, but no I hadn't considered that.

Alastair Beresford: So in this scenario the attacker would have to have a connection to the victim's terminal?

Olgierd Pieczul: No, because I as the attacker end up with a nonce URL token which will log the victim in as me if they open it.

Reply: Yes you're right, the URL token is a link to an account that you want me, the victim, to access. If you can get my browser to open that URL, in any way, and I don't notice that it's not my account, then yes, that attack is still viable in this formulation.

Olgierd Pieczul: So the solution to that is to have something like a cookie upfront so you check the cookie and the nonce, maybe that's enough?

---

[2] The term originally used by Olgierd was something like "login seizure attack", but it wasn't clear from the audio exactly what he'd said and we couldn't find references to anything of this name. We decided to pick a new, more descriptive, term for it when writing the paper and it has been changed here for consistency.

Reply: So your suggesting sort of combine combining how it worked before with our new session delegation method. Yes that's interesting.[3]

Chris Warrington: Do you lose the transcription fallback though? You can't expect a normal person to go ahead and enter a whole cookie manually into their browser's cookie store.

Reply: But I think the suggestion is that the cookie is loaded into your browser when you first access the login page, and then it's necessarily sent back when you make the second request.

Dongting Yu: Would it be possible for the Pico device to only send its authentication message to a website once it verifies that it is the same website as claimed in the QR code? That way you could stop the attacker from presenting the QR code for a different website.

Reply: The problem is that from the Pico's perspective is that it doesn't know which website you were intending to authenticate to. The QR code is just copied straight from the correct website's login page and the Pico is communicating with the real back-end for that website. So from its perspective it is sending its authentication and the nonce from the QR code (in the original, flawed mode of operation) to the right place. The problem is that it's opaque to the user, the user can't tell that the place it's sending it to is not what they're expecting, or that someone else is in possession of that nonce, which is really the crucial part of the attack.

---

[3] We thank Olgierd for pointing out this vulnerability and proposed solution. We discuss this in more detail at the end of Sect. 4.2 in our paper.

Censorship Resistance as a Side-Effect

Henry Tan and Micah Sherr[✉]

Georgetown University, Washington, DC, USA
msherr@cs.georgetown.edu

Abstract. This position paper presents the following thought experiment: can we build communication protocols that (1) are sufficiently useful that they achieve widespread adoption as general-purpose communication mechanisms and (2) thwart censorship as a consequence of their design? We posit that a useful communication platform that is inherently resistant to traffic analysis, if widely adopted and *used primarily for purposes not related to censorship circumvention*, may be too politically and economically costly for a government to block.

1 Introduction

The privacy enhancing technologies community has proposed a number of systems for circumventing government censorship, some of which (notably, Tor [3]) are in active use today. Many existing approaches construct *covert communication channels* that are hidden from the censor's view. For instance, Infranet [4] constructs a covert channel using sequences of seemingly "benign" HTTP requests, Collage [2] embeds messages in images uploaded to sites that host user-generated content, and *decoy routing* techniques such as Telex [17] hide requested URLs in SSL/TLS handshakes. More recently, a number of *traffic shaping* approaches have been proposed (e.g., SkypeMorph [8] and Freewave [6]) that attempt to conceal covert channels by either tunneling them within permitted protocols or changing their traffic patterns to cause them to appear as benign streams.

While the above techniques certainly make censorship more difficult, their security properties are not currently well-understood. In particular, a knowledgeable and powerful censor could potentially defeat such measures by applying steganographic detection techniques [9], enumerating the location of decoy routers [10], and/or leveraging machine learning-based traffic analyzers to perform traffic classification (cf. [14–16]).

Fully understanding the security of existing censorship resistant techniques is an open question that we do not address in this paper. In this position paper, we posit that the security analyses of censorship circumvention systems will likely follow the typical security "arms race" in which discovered vulnerabilities are followed by proposed fixes. Arguably, given the asymmetry between the adversary (e.g., a nation state with centralized control over the nation's communication architecture) and the user of the anti-censorship system (e.g., a dissident who is dependent on the monitored network infrastructure), the advantage in this arms race likely lies with the censor.

© Springer International Publishing Switzerland 2014
B. Christianson et al. (Eds.): Security Protocols 2014, LNCS 8809, pp. 221–226, 2014.
DOI: 10.1007/978-3-319-12400-1_21

This paper takes the position that rather than existing as a standalone system, censorship-resistance should be a __characteristic__ of a widely fielded and general-purpose communication platform. That is, we assert that it is more difficult for a censor to block a ubiquitous and widely-used communication protocol than a niche application designed solely to circumvent censorship. Our goal is to avoid the censor vs. anti-censorship arms race by instrumenting a reliable and high-performance communication primitive that we hope will be widely deployed, *not* used primarily as an anti-censorship apparatus, but that is inherently difficult to surveil and block as a natural consequence of its design.

Paradoxically, to be effective as an anti-censorship technology, such an architecture should achieve widespread adoption for purposes *unrelated* to censorship circumvention. If the primary purpose of the architecture is censorship circumvention, the cost to the adversary of barring access to protocols built using the architecture is low. However, if the architecture is also regularly used for business and commerce, blocking an otherwise useful tool that has widespread adoption may be too politically and economically costly for a censor. To this end, the architecture must both encourage general purpose usage and be competitive with existing methods of communication.

2   Censorship-Resistant Communication Architectures

We consider two parties, Alice and Bob, who want to communicate with each other over the Internet. Eve, the censor, observes and controls all packets going to or coming from Alice. Alice is motivated to prevent Eve from discovering that she is attempting to communicate with Bob. We assume that Bob is outside of the censor's view.

To facilitate its general use as a communication platform and not just as a censorship countermeasure, our architecture should provide benefits over direct IP communication. Below, we briefly outline general-purpose centralized (Sect. 2.1) and decentralized (Sect. 2.2) architectures that enable efficient and reliable communication and are also resistant to censorship.

2.1   Centralized Architecture

We observe that, in principle, anti-censorship can be straightforwardly achieved by using a trusted third party to bridge a connection between Alice and Bob, so long as the censor does not block access to the third party. The third party server, which we call the *broker*, maintains full control of the communication network and manages key distribution and status information. We assume that users know the public key of the broker and can hence communicate privately with it. Users upload their public keys to the broker and are required to register with the broker before they can participate in the network. The broker serves as a relay for all communication between clients.

To achieve end-to-end communications privacy, Alice and Bob can query the broker for the other party's public key (certificate) and communicate privately over SSL/TLS, using the broker as an intermediary (i.e., a router). Importantly, messages should be protected using SSL/TLS with the broker so that the censor cannot discover with whom Alice is communicating.

We emphasize that *such a rendezvous mechanism also enhances reliability* since it enables two parties to communicate even when direct IP communication is not available (e.g., when the receiver is behind a firewall or NAT and cannot accept incoming connections). A broker with sufficient resources to provide high bandwidth, low-latency communication between nodes could encourage widespread utilization of the service. Importantly, since Bob's identity is encrypted and (by assumption) Bob is located outside of the censor's view, then the censor cannot distinguish between streams that should be subject to censorship and those that should not. That is, it is left with the choice of either blocking access to the broker—and hence "censoring" *everything*—or permitting all traffic. If sufficiently widely adopted for business and commerce, we posit that the financial cost of blocking the service may outweigh the adversary's desire to censor.

We note that such a centralized architecture is feasible even at large scale, as is illustrated by Google's Voice and Hangout services. However, a centralized design comes with the obvious weakness of having a single global point of failure: should the centralized service be compromised by the censor, attacks such as monitoring, eavesdropping, and censorship become much easier to perform. As indicated by the Snowden documents, governments can (and do) leverage the centralization of existing communication systems (e.g., Skype, Facebook, Google, etc.) to focus their surveillance efforts, with or without the cooperation of the operators of the centralized systems [5].

2.2   Distributed Architecture

We briefly sketch a distributed communication protocol that is performant, has several potentially useful advantages over direct IP communication, and is naturally resistant to monitoring and censorship. Since a major goal of *censorship-resistance by side-effect* is to gain widespread adoption of our protocol, we aim to support a variety of network applications (e.g., voice-over-IP, file transfer, interactive messaging, etc.).

Our protocol makes use of a fully decentralized directory service that supports put(key, value) and value ← get(key) semantics. A standard DHT (e.g., Chord [12]) that supports low-cost lookups is a reasonable implementation. When *nodes* (potential communicants) come online, they register by putting their public key as well as a *contact point* into the decentralized directory, keyed by a unique identifier (UID) such as a hash[1] over their email address. To anchor trust in the system, public keys could be signed by peers, creating a social web of trust similar to that used by PGP/GnuPG. Additionally, decentralized certificate verification techniques (e.g., Google's Certificate Transparency [7]) that rely on append-only data structures may provide useful protections.

---

[1] The use of the hash function provides some privacy protections, since it makes it more difficult to cull email addresses and network locations from the directory.

If a node can receive network communication—e.g., it is not behind a firewall, proxy, or NAT—then it advertises its network address as its contact point. Otherwise, the node (i) chooses a peer as a rendezvous point (RP) and sets its contact point to be the RP's UID, and (ii) creates a TLS connection to its RP.

When a node, Alice, wants to send a message to a node Bob, it queries the directory to discover Bob's contact point and public key. (We assume Alice has apriori knowledge of Bob's UID/email address.) If the contact point is a network address, then Alice initiates direct communication; otherwise, Alice must iteratively query the directory until she learns of an appropriate rendezvous point for Bob. Using the public keys retrieved from the directory, Alice initiates a TLS connection to Bob or Bob's rendezvous point (or the rendezvous point's RP, etc.). In the latter case, Bob's RP relays the communication (again, using a TLS connection) to Bob.

Our envisioned protocol supports *explicit redirection*—the metadata of a message may contain instructions to forward that message to another party. Since messages are encrypted in TLS, this permits a form of onion routing [13] similar to that used by Tor [3].

The above RP and redirection schemes provide useful reachability properties: Alice can contact Bob, regardless of their network locations. That is, Alice can initiate a connection to Bob, even if Bob is behind a firewall or NAT, eliminating the need to develop specialized NAT piercing techniques. In addition to enabling anonymous communication, explicit redirection also improves reachability and reliability, since traffic can be easily rerouted around network failures. And importantly, by adopting the above protocol, developers do not need to build their own directory services, significantly decreasing development time.

To provide high-performance messaging, our protocol can natively take advantage of previously proposed network performance optimization techniques. For examples, the protocol could apply pre-fetching techniques such as SPDY [11] to request multiple objects (e.g., elements of a webpage) in an initial request, reducing the number of roundtrips and significantly shortening latency. Our protocol could also borrow techniques from resilient overlay networks [1] and exploit triangle inequalities in the network underlay to decrease end-to-end latency and potentially improve goodput.

We argue that the above design—while admittedly far from complete—provides useful properties to application designers, and has the potential to significantly decrease development time. Although the protocol is *not* robust against blocking (in particular, an adversary can prevent access to the directory service), its use of encrypted payloads and potential redirection makes it difficult for an adversary to discern the endpoints and content of an intercepted communication. The censor thus has to choose between preventing all use of the protocol or allowing the protocol's use. If the protocol is sufficiently advantageous to developers and is widely adopted by a variety of network applications, then the adversary may be forced to forgo censorship.

3   Conclusion

This paper proposes two general-purpose communication protocols that inherently resist censorship. To motivate adoption *even when censorship resistance is not a goal*, our protocols are generally useful: they allow peers to communicate when direct IP connections are unsupported (e.g., due to a firewall, proxy, or NAT), and they provide message confidentiality through end-to-end encryption. This paper argues that if such communication designs are widely used, then censors must choose between significant "overblocking" (thus incurring high political and potentially economic costs) and allowing unfettered access to information.

Acknowledgments. This work is partially supported by NSF CAREER CNS-1149832 and NSF grants CNS-1064986, CNS-1204347, and CNS-1223825. The findings and opinions described in this paper are those of the authors, and do not necessarily reflect the views of the National Science Foundation. Additionally, this material is based upon work supported by the Defense Advanced Research Project Agency (DARPA) and Space and Naval Warfare Systems Center Pacific under Contract No. N66001-11-C-4020. Any opinions, findings and conclusions or recommendations expressed in this material are those of the author(s) and do not necessarily reflect the views of the Defense Advanced Research Project Agency and Space and Naval Warfare Systems Center Pacific.

References

1. Andersen, D.G., Balakrishnan, H., Kaashoek, M.F., Morris, R.: The case for resilient overlay networks. In: Workshop on Hot Topics in Operating Systems (HotOS) (2001)
2. Burnett, S., Feamster, N., Vempala, S.: Chipping away at censorship firewalls with user-generated content. In: USENIX Security Symposium (USENIX) (2010)
3. Dingledine, R., Mathewson, N., Syverson, P.: Tor: the second-generation onion router. In: USENIX Security Symposium (USENIX) (2004)
4. Feamster, N., Balazinska, M., Harfst, G., Balakrishnan, H., Karger, D.: Infranet: circumventing web censorship and surveillance. In: USENIX Security Symposium (USENIX) (2002)
5. Gellman, B., Soltani, A.: NSA Infiltrates Links to Yahoo, Google Data Centers Worldwide, Snowden Documents Say, The Washington Post, 30 October 2013
6. Houmansadr, A., Riedl, T., Borisov, N., Singer, A.: I want my voice to be heard: IP over Voice-over-IP for unobservable censorship circumvention. In: Network and Distributed System Security Symposium (NDSS) (2013)
7. Laurie, B., Langley, A., Kasper, E.: Certificate Transparency. RFC 6962, Internet Engineering Task Force (2013)
8. Moghaddam, H.M., Li, B., Derakhshani, M., Goldberg, I.: SkypeMorph: protocol obfuscation for tor bridges. In: ACM Conference on Computer and Communications Security (CCS) (2012)
9. Provos, N., Honeyman, P.: Detecting steganographic content on the internet. Technical report 01-11, Center for Information Technology Integration, University of Michigan (2001)

10. Schuchard, M., Geddes, J., Thompson, C., Hopper, N.: Routing around decoys. In: ACM Conference on Computer and Communications Security (CCS) (2012)
11. SPDY: An Experimental Protocol for a Faster Web. http://www.chromium.org/spdy/spdy-whitepaper
12. Stoica, I., Morris, R., Karger, D., Kaashoek, M.F., Balakrishnan, H.: Chord: a scalable peer-to-peer lookup service for internet applications. In: Conference on Applications, Technologies, Architectures, and Protocols for Computer Communications (SIGCOMM) (2001)
13. Syverson, P.F., Goldschlag, D.M., Reed, M.G.: Anonymous connections and onion routing. In: IEEE Symposium on Security and Privacy, Oakland (1997)
14. White, A.M., Snow, K., Matthews, A., Monrose, F.: Phonotactic reconstruction of encrypted VoIP conversations: Hookt on fon-iks. In: IEEE Symposium on Security and Privacy, Oakland (2011)
15. Wright, C.V., Ballard, L., Coull, S.E., Monrose, F., Masson, G.M.: Spot me if you can: uncovering spoken phrases in encrypted VoIP conversations. In: IEEE Symposium on Security and Privacy, Oakland (2008)
16. Wright, C.V., Ballard, L., Monrose, F., Masson, G.M.: Language identification of encrypted VoIP traffic: Alejandra y Roberto or Alice and Bob? In: USENIX Security Symposium (USENIX) (2007)
17. Wustrow, E., Wolchok, S., Goldberg, I., Halderman, J.A.: Telex: anticensorship in the network infrastructure. In: USENIX Security Symposium (USENIX) (2011)

Censorship Resistance as a Side-Effect
(Transcript of Discussion)

Henry Tan and Micah Sherr[(✉)]

Georgetown University, Washington, DC 20057, USA
msherr@cs.georgetown.edu

This is a thought experiment, which is a euphemism for a half-baked idea, that my wonderful grad student, Henry Tan, and myself have come up with over the last few months. To provide some context, the talk is really about censorship and unblockability, so I'll start by describing what I mean by that. Suppose we have some user, Alice or Bob, and unfortunately he or she is located in some network that is controlled by a censor. So you can imagine, for example, they're in China or Iran, which allows them to access some sites, but there are other sites, like for example, Twitter, which are deemed inappropriate, and therefore are blocked by the censor. So our goal, like much work in censorship and unblockability, is to allow the user in this restricted regime to be able to communicate with whatever website or service he or she is trying to access. In other words, we're trying to make it indistinguishable from the censor's perspective as to where they are going.

We have two goals, and I'm going to state them fairly informally. The first is *privacy*—we want to prevent the censor from determining both the content of what's being communicated, and also the destination, so this is privacy over both data and the metadata. And the second is *unblockability*, and in the context of this talk when I speak of unblockability what I mean is I want to make it costly or expensive for the censor to block access to a particular service. I don't necessarily want to make it impossible for the censor to do so, because the censor, at least in my scenario, controls the network, so the censor can do something like what was done in Egypt where they just shut off the entire network infrastructure. So we can't defeat against this: this isn't a talk about anti-jamming, all we're trying to do is make it expensive for the censor to go ahead and block communication.

So let me give a very high level overview of my talk. I'm going to try and make the case in the first part of my talk that censorship resistance, if you look at the techniques that exist today, is very much an arms race between the people who want to enable access for people who are censored to censored sites, and the censor; and this is a back and forth game that's played, and I'll show some evidence that this is actually going on; but I think fairly intuitive that this is what is happening. And we tend to lose when the adversary (and by we I mean the people who are trying to build these censorship resistant systems) is powerful. So when the adversary is something like a nation state, or someone

---

Talk presented by Micah Sherr.

© Springer International Publishing Switzerland 2014
B. Christianson et al. (Eds.): Security Protocols 2014, LNCS 8809, pp. 227–238, 2014.
DOI: 10.1007/978-3-319-12400-1_22

who controls the infrastructure, or the communication network, the adversary has a big advantage over the person who is using that infrastructure.

So the somewhat controversial thought experiment that we're proposing is whether or not we can achieve censorship resistance, not as an artifact of a particular protocol that's designed to be censorship resistant, but rather by building communication protocols that have really nice communication features in terms of performance and reliability, and build them such that they're used for purposes not related to censorship resistance but also have censorship resistant properties. Because they are useful as general communication protocols, they will then become so ubiquitous and popular that it becomes too expensive for a censoring country to block it—because it's used for things like voice communication and commerce. And so we think the answer is a qualified maybe, but only if the services' main features are unrelated to censorship circumvention.

This is kind of a wide move from what's currently done, which is to concentrate on systems that specifically achieve censorship circumvention. We're doing the opposite—we're building something that is high-performance, and oh, just so happens to have censorship circumvention. And the idea again is that we hope the censorship-resistant protocol will be used first primarily as a good communication paradigm, or service, picked up, widely deployed. If sufficiently widely deployed, it'll have the property that it's expensive for the censor to curtail.

So there are a lot of techniques that deal with censorship circumvention, and when you talk about anonymity, which is related to the concept of unblockability, the first things that comes to mind is Tor. I'm not going to really go over how Tor works, but at a very high level you have a client who contacts a directory, and from that directory the client learns a bunch of potential relays through which she can relay her traffic, anonymously through Bob. Layered cryptography prevents an adversary who doesn't have a global view of the network from figuring out where Alice is going. The problem with Tor, at least in the original Tor design, when it comes to unblockability, is that it's easily blockable. And the reason is that since Alice discovers these relays by consulting a directory service, every client has to be able to talk to those directories in order to know which relays are available through which it can send its communication. So clearly someone who works for the great firewall of China can sit there, immediately download the same list, and then just add it to their firewalls rules in order to block Tor.

Tor knows this, and what they've done is they've come up with a workaround called Tor Bridges. A Tor bridge is exactly the same thing as a Tor relay, the only difference being that rather than have the relay publicly advertised, it's not publicly advertised. The idea behind bridges is that the client obtains one of these bridge addresses using some out-of-band mechanism, enters the network address and the public key of the bridge, and then can use that to connect (to literally *bridge*) into the Tor network. The adversary doesn't have this information about the bridge, and doesn't know that the traffic is being routed through Tor, and therefore doesn't block it.

The problem with this technique is that there is no user identification when the Tor Project gives out these bridges, so if you're a dissident you can request a bridge by sending a message through gmail to the Tor Project, the Tor Project will say, here's a bridge, don't tell anybody about it. The problem there is that if you instead you work for the great firewall of China you can do the exact same thing, and there is nothing that the Tor Project can do to distinguish between the people who really want this in order to bridge to the Tor network, and the people who are trying to just enumerate all the bridges. And because there are only a thousand or so bridges in existence today, and I think it's estimated that there are 100,000 people who work for the great firewall of China, it's very easy and trivial for them to enumerate all the bridges and then just block them. So this is a technique that doesn't work particularly well.

There is also related work in covert channels and steganography. Nick Feamster came up with an approach in 2002 called Infranet, where you embed your requests inside of an HTTP request. There's later work also by Nick and his students in 2010 where instead of doing it in text, which is very low bandwidth, you embed it in pictures of cats that you upload to some file-sharing site, using the site essentially as a drop-box. There's even more recent work in this area that you can also perhaps categories as being steganographic, but it's called decoy routing, and the idea here is that you use entropic portions of the TLS handshake, and what I mean by that is, portions of the TLS headers that are supposed to be random bits, and instead of putting the random bits you embed a secret that's read by some router on a path between the user and some benign site that you're allowed to visit. Some actual internet router receives this, decodes the secret message, and then routes the message to the encoded URL rather than the overt URL. And again it uses steganography because you're hiding the message in plain sight.

So the problems with these techniques is that, again, steganograghy is an arms race. There's work at CCS a few years ago, enumerating decoy routers, and how this technique may be flawed, although I'm told that there is subsequent work that says that's actually harder than previously. But again, this is at best an arms race back and forth between defenders and attackers.

There's also a lot of current work where you try to make your traffic look like something that's not blocked. For example, in the context of Tor bridges, rather than making your traffic look like the Tor protocol, which is the default, you make it look like something else. This is done by changing its characteristics to appear to the censor to be something like Skype, and Skype is a good choice because it allows a lot of bandwidth.

Relatedly, there's a great attack paper in last year's Oakland, where they really tear these types of techniques apart. The hard part for doing this type of "morphing" is that you need to implement all aspects of the protocol that you're mimicking, and it turns out that that's incredibly difficult to do. For example, Skype uses UDP, and if a packet gets lost all hell breaks loose. If you look at the traffic traces you have a huge burst of packets as they try to renegotiate audio/video codecs. If you're pretending to be Skype you're not going to exhibit that behaviour, which makes you stick out tremendously. So it turned out to be very easy to identify these mimicry type techniques.

And lastly there's a technique Nikita and his students introduced called Freewave, which is a really interesting technique where you tunnel IP traffic inside of an actual Skype message. This is not "try to look like Skype"; instead, it's "I build essentially a software and modem on both sides of the communication, and I encode my raw bits as audio signals, I send that through Skype". These modulated audio signals are decoded on the other side back into binary. This doesn't suffer the parroting effects that I mentioned in the previous slide, because it perfectly mimics the correct application behaviour because it is actually running over Skype. It's a fairly promising approach. It also happens to be something that Henry and I were working on, and were coding up at the time that Nikita published his paper, so thank you very much for scooping us.

But there are a few problems with it. Obviously it allows only limited bandwidth, at least for audio communication. It's probably vulnerable to traffic analysis in the sense that if you are familiar with Fabian Monrose's and Charles Wright's attacks against encrypted Skype traffic (where they'd look at the sizes of encrypted packets to determine the language being spoken), it's probably much easier to do these style attacks against Skype traffic that's not carrying audio but instead are just carrying random binary packets. And finally

Frank Stajano: You could conceivably go one step further instead of just making a modem you could make something that makes it look like words. At lower bit rate of course.

Reply: Yes, you could probably combine these techniques by morphing it to look like an actual audio, and then relay it over Skype. That's an interesting idea.

Frank Stajano: In the limit you could say the words one and zero.

Reply: Yes, that's right.

Joseph Bonneau: That's not perfect either, you could make it so that the audio is just people saying "one" and "zero", but people never actually speak that way, so you're just pushing the steganography further and further.

Reply: Well you could have a conversation in English to encode a zero or French to encode a one, but yes, I agree that this is an arms race where the users get lower and lower bandwidths.

Joseph Bonneau: It's a pretty slow channel.

Reply: It's a very slow channel. There are also potential legal issues. Skype is already involved with the Snowden leaks, but they probably don't want to necessarily have their system be taken over by people who are exploiting it ala Freewave to bypass censors. So I imagine that their fix might be to change their acceptable user policy, and just say, you can't do this, and that might be their defence.

Nikita Borisov: So are these issues kind of fundamental to the whole approach that you're considering, because if you're building a system where the purpose was specifically not subverting censorship, then when users use it to subvert censorship, then they are also violating the AUP.

Reply: There's a subtle difference. We're not proposing a communication system, we're proposing a communication set of primitives, like a programming library, that different applications can use. One of these applications can be "let's get through a censorship system". So in other words, building protocols specifically for censorship resistance may be a losing battle. The reason why it may be a losing battle is that there are asymmetric resources between the user and the censor, and this is something that Virgil talked about yesterday in a different context. But here there really is some fundamental asymmetries, one of which is that the censor runs a country, or the telecommunication services in that country, and the activist or the user can't see what's going on in that larger view, all they can see is what's going on in their local network.

The adversary has a lot more control over the infrastructure. The adversary—the censor—has a lot more computational resources. And, if you're targeted, it can throw a lot of cycles at you to do some sort of analysis like the attacks that Fabian and his group came up with for analysing Skype traffic.

Nikita Borisov: Could I question this assumption a little bit, just because the adversary does have a lot of computational resources but they also have the problem of scale. So in some sense the amount of computation you can put in a protocol that is, from your computer, is much larger than the computation of let's say a great firewall of China would be able to deploy per connection.

Reply: Sure. I agree with you that that you could certainly make it so that the asymmetry goes in the other direction; crypto does that by having trapdoors.

Bruce Christianson: That's assuming the censor distributes their resources evenly.

Nikita Borisov: Right, yes.

Micah Sherr: In the case we're discussing, the censor is trying to censor the traffic on a nationwide scale. If they are specifically targeting the censorship against small groups of people, then, yes, this is a valid concern.

There are additional points of asymmetry between the censor and the activists. Take the specific example of Tor bridges in China, where there are a lot more resources in terms of the firewall reacting and probing attempted users of bridges than the activists have. And finally, there are asymmetric human resources: the activist is essentially off by him or herself for the most part, whereas the censor may have hundreds of thousands of people working 40 hours a week on building a censorship system.

There's evidence to support that this arms race exists: you can look at the Tor metrics project, which has a lot of fascinating graphs on users who use Tor, aggregated by country, so you can see, for example, that in 2009 during the Iranian uprising, there was a huge uptake in Tor use, and then immediately crashed down as the internet was shut off. As you can see, sometime in early 2013 the Iranian government clearly started censoring Tor, and gradually Tor is making some inroads there. When you look at data from bridges, which are specifically designed to get around censorship and blocking, you see spikes going in both directions, which basically again highlight the fact that this is an arms race back and forth, where Tor makes an advance to make the system unblock-able, and that advance is then countered by some specialized DPI system.

In this talk, we're proposing to avoid the arms race entirely. Our solution can be summed up in kind of one word, which is, to cheat. We cheat by changing the game and its assumptions. We don't build an anti-censorship protocol. Instead what we do is we change everything else. We introduce new communication protocols that are censorship resistant, but the primary purpose of which is not censorship resistance.

I know that sounds a little bit funny, but I'll describe how that might be feasible in a few minutes. Briefly, one way we do this is we examine existing protocols that aren't blocked in certain countries and we look at their properties and we try to figure out, based on these properties, if the composition of their features provides some form of unblockability, again, as a side effect.

There are a bunch of services that closely fit this model. Skype is a great example, which is perhaps why it was used in Freewave. Frankly Skype almost gets us there. It does a lot of interesting things. In particular, one of the reasons that Skype was so successful in its early days, was its ability to just work, and by just work I mean if you were behind a corporate proxy, or you were NATed at home, you could still receive incoming Skype calls. And that was very different from the SIP softphones and other things that were available at the time, but didn't always quite work. And the way that Skype did that is to basically rely on rendezvous points. So if you are not reachable on the internet, meaning you're behind some proxy, or firewall, or NAT, you find a peer who is reachable and you use that peer as a rendezvous point, in which case both sides of the communication go through that rendezvous point and to the other communicant.

It would be helpful, at least for this talk, if we pretend we don't know any-thing about Prism, or NSA, and we assume that Skype is built like its white papers advertise. So we assume that it has private user-to-location lookup, which means that you can consult a directory service, which is centralised, or at least run by a single administrator, in this case Microsoft, to find out the current loca-tion or locations of the user you're trying to connect to. It provides end-to-end encryption and authentication.

I realise that Skype is a closed protocol. But outside experts have written some not-particularly-detailed explanations as to what's going on. Regardless, you certainly could come up with something "Skype-like" that has end-to-end authentication and encryption. We know how to do that.

And of course, Skype provides a number of communication features: it has VoIP, it has video, it has file transfer that's not particularly good, it has text chat, and then other things I can't probably think of at the moment.

Then we have much more centralised models. We have centralised systems like Google hangouts, which also has a property that it uses a rendezvous point (but really that rendezvous point is Google). So even if you're not reachable, you just always relay your traffic through Google. Again, I'm not making a judgement as to whether or not this is a good or bad thing, but it does work if you're NATed or you're behind a firewall that prevents incoming connections. And it provides VoIP, video, file transfer, and screen sharing, and other things.

And finally, there's the Vuze BitTorrent client. It provides fast file transfers that are scalable: the more users who have the file, the faster you get it. With piecemeal end-to-end integrity checks, and end-to-end integrity checks, it provides file indexing, and the way that it provides file location, or search, is through a distributed hash table. In their case it's based on Kademlia, a fairly popular DHT that's used all over the place. They say it's secured somehow, probably via some sort of simple protection based on IP addresses, which is likely fairly weak. But they're running it, and as far as I know it hasn't been completely taken over yet, and it would seem like an attractive target, so I think there's hope that it hasn't been totally compromised.

We can take some of the aspects of these protocols (Skype, Google Hangouts, and Vuze) to build our "censorship as a side effect" protocol.

To just backup for one second, one point I wanted to make is that Skype achieves almost everything that we want in the sense that Skype is a very difficult protocol in theory to monitor. Now clearly we now know that that's not the case because it leaked information. But in theory, if you take the constituent parts of Skype and do it right, it does provide this nice property that it's used primarily as a communication service. When I use Skype it's not because I'm using Freewave, it's because I want to talk to someone abroad, or call my wife from England. But it's very difficult for a censor to figure out whom I'm talking to, particularly if I'm going through a rendezvous point. The lookup, the user to location service, is through some secure connection with the lookup service. If I go through a rendezvous point and the rendezvous point is located outside of the censor's region, then it's very difficult for the censor to know where I'm going: It's essentially one hop onion routing or using a proxy. So Skype is a service that is difficult to surveil. There's evidence of this. It's why China introduced Tom Skype, and why the US government thought it necessary to build backdoors, or whatever you believe, into these systems.

So Skype I think gets us 99 % of the way there. The problem with it is you have to do something like Freewave because it's not meant as an anti-censorship service: it doesn't natively support things like web browsing. To get web browsing out of Skype, you have to do something weird like Freewave–you're building a modem in software, and encoding web requests as audio signals; that's a very strange thing to do, and the cost of doing something like that is obviously bandwidth.

So I think that we can take and compose some components from existing systems to meet our goal of building something that's useful, that does things like NAT piercing, or gets around firewalls, that offers reliable communication, that has privacy; and, gee golly, just so happens to have censorship resistance as a side-effect.

You could build a username to IP lookup in a decentralised manner using a distributed hash table, an idea that Vuze currently uses. I didn't bother to look up what they actually did, but I would imagine it's something like: you have a user ID, which is say a hash of an email address that you publish in the distributed hash table along with your public key and IP address keyed by your UID, if you're reachable. If you are reachable, if someone wants to look you up, they do a DHT request on your UID and can figure out where you out, and also learn your public key, which, you might want to have this signed by some authority you trust. If you aren't reachable then you might publish your public key in a rendezvous point of your choosing, in which case if Alice needs to communicate with Bob it just looks up Bob's public key, and might have to do iterative lookups to figure out how to connect to the rendezvous point. I should mention that the rendezvous point would be the UID of the rendezvous point, in case that isn't clear. And all this would be done over a TLS. How user authentication would work is relevant to yesterday's talk, but I could imagine bootstrapping something into DNSSEC, or using trust on first use, or using the PGP web of trust model.

But this design is nice in that it provides a bunch of features that are just genuinely useful for application developers. It provides NAT firewall piercing, and scalable lookup. To be useful as an anticensorship service, it turns out that you need more than this: you need support for inband redirection, so when Alice talks to Bob she wants to be able to tell Bob, hey actually I want you to communicate, or relay this communication, to Charlie. This is essentially onion routing. Although it may seem like this is only useful for censorship resistance, there are other reasons why you would want to do this type of redirection: The two that I thought of are, if there are triangle inequality violations on the Internet this is a good way of leveraging that to get higher performance. And the second is that, just in terms of reachability again, if there are failures on the Internet, routing or otherwise, you can route around your failures at the overlay layer, which is a common technique. You may want to bundle additional performance and reliability features, again to sell this type of communication suite as a service or library that developers would want to use.

And finally, you could add some additional features. For example, SPDY for prefetching pages, which is a Google-based protocol, and that's actually a very good idea. There's resilient overlay networks, which is an early version of multi-path routing. And things like IP mobility, or transparent mobility, which would fit naturally here.

So why would this approach be censorship resistant? The destinations would be obscured through the use of rendezvous points and inband redirection. Those two things together should provide you with some type of censorship resistance.

Notably, the service *is* blockable. I talked about its use of a DHT. Clearly, the censor can just block access to the DHT. The idea is that, although it's easy for the censor to block it, hopefully the service will be widely used for a variety of applications, in which case it would be prohibitively expensive from an economic, or financial, or political, point of view, for the country to block access to it. And I think there's evidence that such logic holds in practice. If you look at Skype, for example, this is a good illustration of something that other countries, not the US or England, aren't particularly able to surveil, but still allow. So Skype is allowed in China, for example. I can do the same thing in Iran, although I'm told that whether Skype is allowed kind of changes on a weekly basis.

So is this feasible? Arguably yes, definitely maybe. As I mentioned before, Skype is nearly sufficient, it achieves almost all of our goals in the sense of being a widely deployed, useful, and not a censorship technology that is inherently difficult to surveil and censor. As I mentioned before, most nations state censors don't block all crypto. So it's feasible to run something that they don't necessarily understand the content of, since metadata is more important than content. And components for a "censorship as a side effect" system already exist, which I just talked about before. The tricky part is combining them into a useful library without introducing too much bloat, and not have it be so complicated that no-one wants to use it. And the even trickier bit is getting a lot of developers from diverse projects to actually use this thing.

I think it's plausible to get widespread deployment. Here's a very optimistic scenario. Lets assume that application developers want reliability, performance, privacy, and the features that we're going to basically sell to them for free in this library that we're developing. And they also want to develop quickly, so they don't necessarily want to build these things from scratch all the time, as long as it doesn't hurt their business model. Computer science is all about using abstractions, which is what our system will provide.

So some organisation, for example Microsoft or Google, releases this communications library as Open Source software. And they say, "hey look, this does a lot of awesome things for you as application developers, you should use it"; they don't promote it as an anti-censorship technology. I would imagine that there's some first mover app developer who uses the library, not related to purposes for censorship resistance; perhaps they use it for some photo sharing, social networking app. They then sell their company to Facebook for $36trillion, and additional startups take notice and say, "hey I want to develop something like this, I don't need to build my own directory services, I don't need to build my own overlay, or build my own NAT piercing system, I can just plug in this library and use it". So what you end up with, and what we really need is not just widespread deployment for one type of communication, but a diversity of uses of this particular library. And this is important because it means that the censor can't do easy forms of traffic analysis and say, "hey this likes look a file transfer therefore it must be anti-censorship", because you have file transfers used for things that aren't related to anti-censorship.

In summary, we propose the half whacky idea of achieving censorship resistance, not through protocols that are designed for censorship resistance, but instead through protocols that are generally useful for a lot of different performance and reliability reasons, and that just so happen to have censorship resistant properties, which we're calling a side effect. We think this is a better approach than what's currently done, just because for a large part it really does avoid the arms race of detecting and countering the detection of anticensorship protocols. And in order to get this to work we really need to make the protocol generally useful, and ubiquitous, and again, having some disincentives for the censor to block it.

We've got a few minutes for questions.

Yvo Desmedt: So on the last row you were actually mentioning that Microsoft has changed the path of the Skype system, dramatically, so beware of that. And also if you look at the relationship between Microsoft and China, it is actually very good.

Reply: Yes, I think that's a relevant point. Skype supernodes, eight years ago, were actually peers that were the rendezvous points. Microsoft has done away with that model entirely. Now, Microsoft servers are the supernodes. Again, I'm not suggesting that we actually use Skype, because you know, maybe they're in bed with censors– who knows?. But what I'm proposing is that we build something that has some of the promised properties that Skype has failed to deliver.

Nikita Borisov: But given this move, right that Microsoft made to eliminate supernodes, it seems that it was at least more profitable, and more natural for them to use their own services as these rendezvous points. And so why would any app developers not follow suit. There's been this huge practice towards using centralised services where possible.

Reply: If you're an application developer and have a staff of two people then you can scale up fairly organically by allowing nodes to become super peers, and then I guess if you want to move to the Microsoft model, so be it. I actually don't think that the more centralised rendezvous point model is any less useful here, as long as you have all your centralised services on the other side of where the censor sits. So, for example, if you trust Google you can do what I'm suggesting using Google.com as your rendezvous point as long as Google.com doesn't cooperate with your censor. So people may be moving to that direction, but I think in order to operate 10,000 servers around the globe you have to be a rich company, and startups would be most attracted to the decentralized design I spoke about earlier.

Yvo Desmedt: You mentioned this may have been done before economically, however, if you look at the requirements in the United States for legal wiretapping, you can wonder whether this was done in order to satisfy the goals of the wiretapper.

Reply: Yes, so there's a whole CALEA-II discussion which I probably shouldn't even mention – revising CALEA to put wiretap capabilities inside of peer to peer systems like Skype. But that was being debated before Snowden, and as far as I can tell is totally dead.

Shishir Nagaraja: So my question is really that when you talk about censorship resistant properties I think this idea that there's an adversary who's invested in wholesale elimination of sensitive channels everywhere is something hard to really understand. The reason is because there are easier ways to do that; sort of going after Tor, for instance. What I think you ought to be looking at in terms of essential properties is how help to people who are being placed under surveillance, and you look at their communications and try to distinguish whether or not they're using anonymous communication.

Reply: Yes, so my take on that is, and I was at CCS in Berlin a while ago where Jacob Appelbaum gave this talk, he works with Der Spiegel, analysing some of the Snowden documents, and one of the things that he spoke about which wasn't in the press yet was how the NSA intercepted your recently purchased Mac and added some hardware in there that bypassed air gaps, and spied on everything you did. And in that model where I now need to x-ray my machine every time that I turn it on in order to figure out whether it's been tapped—if you're that targeted, I don't know how to solve that problem. I think that's a very difficult problem and it's not one that I'm specifically trying to address, because I think the answer might be that you're just totally screwed.

I guess I would disagree with your first point though, I mean, I think that we see things like the great firewall of China, which does have specific functionality where it identifies Tor bridges by essentially reaching out and trying to use them as a Tor bridge. It identifies a candidate Tor bridge, and then tries to use it as a Tor bridge, and if that succeeds it blocks it. So they are actually spending human resources developing technological resources to do countrywide censorship, or blockability of anti-censorship systems.

Shishir Nagaraja: When you say that we use the existing user behaviour as cover traffic, is that is something that you're after?

Reply: Well, maybe. If you have protocols that use this library for things like web access, browsing webpages, and VoIP, and video, and a few others, and that it's widely deployed and not used primarily for censorship, then it's very easy to build one that does use it for the purposes of getting around blockability that looks like the other thing in the same class of application.

Shishir Nagaraja: Right, so you will be upper-bounded by the extent to which the user engages in the first time.

Reply: Yes, the user is going to have to have traffic that looks like stuff that's not blocked.

Shishir Nagaraja: So then you will have bandwidth issues won't you, which you wanted to solve in the first place?

Reply: I imagine that if you want to browse the web without censorship for an hour, you just need to browse the web with censorship for another hour later in the day. And I don't know that that's problematic, maybe it is, I'm not informed enough to make a judgement on that.

Max Spencer: So you have this Open Source like software library which you can use to build these applications and some would be censorship resistant and some of them wouldn't, I don't see how this addresses the problem. So there's some great app that can use the censorship resistance, what's to stop the state just going and like pressuring the owners, or the developers of that application to enable them to censor traffic like that's going via that thing.

Reply: Right, so if you have a programme and the censor can actually apply pressure to the service operators, then I think that that is problematic. But I don't know whether in the real world that actually matters so much, because I'm less concerned about someone from the United States. In the United States and here in England there's not a lot of censorship, right, I can go access some webpage, I may get arrested for accessing that page, but you know, my Comcast, or my cable modem connection, is going to be able to get there.

Max Spencer: If I can look at a page, even if I don't know it's specifically censored, I could be questioned by the authorities, then that's a sort of like form of censorship by a chilling effect. The threat of being prosecuted is a form of censorship.

Reply: OK, I agree with that but let me answer this in a different way. The service operators aren't going to be necessarily Chinese companies that can be easily pressured by China. Maybe they're pressured by the NSA, or GCHQ, or whoever, right, but that doesn't mean that they're going to be sharing that information with the censor, which is operating in China. Again, the country that censors doesn't have the ability to put significant pressure on the application developers, so they will have to make a choice of whether to cut off all users.

Yvo Desmedt: I think you should look at basically the Google data that clearly reveals that Google has been asked to remove links to certain webpages, inside the United States, so it's not that easy in the United States to look at all the webpages. Moreover, if you look at the Tor pages it clearly mentions that. You might still be able to get to those pages, I don't know, but Google had to remove links to those.

On the Feasibility of a Technological Response to the Surveillance Morass

Joan Feigenbaum[✉] and Jérémie Koenig

Yale University, New Haven, CT 06520-8285, USA
{joan.feigenbaum,jeremie.koenig}@yale.edu

Abstract. We consider mass surveillance from a computer-science perspective. After presenting some objections to the behavior of the US National Security Agency and its counterparts in allied nations (emphasizing technical problems associated with such behavior, rather than political, legal, and social problems), we propose a grass-roots, technological response: decentralized cloud services, facilitated by open-source, decentralized configuration-management tools.

1 Introduction

Since June 2013, information leaked by Edward Snowden has revealed that the US National Security Agency (NSA) has for years been conducting dragnet surveillance both domestically and internationally, covertly sabotaging security standards and products, and pressuring major US technology companies to cooperate in its activities. Apparently, sister agencies in allied nations (particularly Canada, the UK, Australia, and New Zealand – the four other Anglophone nations of the "five eyes" consortium) have collaborated with NSA in the collection, storage, and mining of unprecedented amounts of sensitive information. In other words, "all our paranoid dreams of the past twenty years have come true."[1]

In this paper, we consider the surveillance morass from a computer-science perspective. In Sect. 2, we present some objections to government surveillance of entire populations, emphasizing the technical problems associated with it rather than the political, legal, and social problems. In the same section, we ask whether the US business community has both the incentive and the power to bring about change in its government's policies on mass surveillance and security sabotage; we conclude that there are some reasons for hope but also some reasons for despair on that front. In Sects. 3 and 4, we outline a possible grass-roots, technological response to our current predicament, to wit: a transition to more decentralized cloud services, facilitated by open-source, decentralized configuration-management tools.

---

[1] Call for Papers, Cambridge Security Protocols Workshop, 2014.

© Springer International Publishing Switzerland 2014
B. Christianson et al. (Eds.): Security Protocols 2014, LNCS 8809, pp. 239–252, 2014.
DOI: 10.1007/978-3-319-12400-1_23

2   The Surveillance Morass

2.1   Problem Description

We use the term "surveillance morass" to refer both to intelligence-agency practices that we find objectionable and to ambient conditions in the Internet that enable these practices and may make it difficult to put a stop to them.

Objectionable practices have been covered steadily by the news media since the Snowden story broke in June 2013. Indeed, as reported in [1], the NSA itself provided the following summary of its "collection posture" in a slide presentation at a multinational meeting of intelligence agencies in 2011:

> Collect it all. Process it all. Exploit it all. Partner it all. Sniff it all. Know it all.

To accomplish its panoptic goal, the agency, often in cooperation with its sister agencies in allied nations, has been collecting massive amounts of communications "metadata" (including but not limited to the phone numbers, date, time, location, and duration of every cell-phone call made in the US), surveilling both corporate databases and user-generated data of major Internet companies (with the companies' cooperation when it can be obtained and by breaking into data centers when it cannot), and engaging in security sabotage (covert and deliberate undermining of cryptographic standards and products and of the standardization process). A comprehensive explanation of these practices is beyond the scope of this paper and has been undertaken by others; see, for example, Greenwald's recent book [1].

An essential enabler of this breathtaking surveillance regime is the ubiquity of computers, smart phones, and communication networks in everyday life. More and more of our daily activities in commerce, education, government, recreation, and even friendship and romance are mediated by electronic devices that create records of these activities, either as their primary products or as by-products. A growing number of ad-supported cloud services require companies to retain, interpret, and mine records of our daily activities so that ads can be targeted well enough to fetch high prices. Arguments against targeted advertising and the data mining that supports it have been advanced for years, but their abolition could spell the end of the Web as we know it [2]. The troves of personal data created by modern communication networks and cloud services are and will always be irresistible, fat targets for intelligence services.

To explain one of our technical objections to intelligence-agency overreach, we first recall a legal objection that many (but not all) participants in the debate have raised, i.e., that dragnet surveillance is a *prima facie* violation of the Fourth Amendment of the US Constitution. Recall that the amendment guarantees that

> The right of the people to be secure in their persons, houses, papers, and effects, against unreasonable searches and seizures, shall not be violated, and no warrants shall issue, but upon probable cause, supported by oath or affirmation, and particularly describing the place to be searched, and the persons or things to be seized.

Unlike the First, Second, and Fifth Amendments, the Fourth has not traditionally played much of a role in American popular culture, but it played a huge role in American history. Rejection of "general warrants," under which agents of the British government subjected entire communities to search and seizure, was one the main reasons that 18th-century American colonists fought the Revolutionary War.

The Fourth Amendment is an early expression of a consistent theme in discussions of law enforcement and intelligence generally and of electronic surveillance in particular: the belief that privacy and security are both important goals but that they are inherently at odds with each other. One straightforward interpretation of the amendment is that, under normal circumstances, citizens are entitled to personal privacy but that, if there is credible and particularized suspicion that a specific citizen has committed a specific crime (thereby violating others' security), government authorities may be granted a warrant to search his home and seize his possessions (thereby violating his privacy). This simple example of the need for law-enforcement agencies to "balance" or "trade off" privacy and security makes sense intuitively, and US citizens have centuries of experience with lawfully obtained search warrants' enabling police officers to catch criminals and collect evidence that can be used to convict them in court.

In the debate about NSA surveillance, however, some people have implicitly made a much stronger and more general assumption that is *not* supported by real-world experience or by scientific research, *i.e.*, that there is a robust, tunable tradeoff between security and privacy in which the security of society at large is always guaranteed to improve if the privacy of individuals within the society is allowed to erode. Even some civil-liberties supporters who argue that limits must be placed on NSA data collection say things like "it's a tradeoff. If we had perfect information, then we'd have perfect security, but we cannot tolerate the level of government intrusion necessary to achieve perfect information." *Nothing in the scientific literature establishes the existence of this type of robust, tunable tradeoff.* The fact that some effective security measures, *e.g.*, lawfully authorized search and seizure, cause some loss of privacy does *not* imply that loss of privacy *per se* causes or is even positively correlated with increased security.

2.2   Threats Posed by Personal-Data Collection on a Massive Scale

It is entirely possible that storage and mining of personal data on the scale implied by the NSA's collection posture is inherently insecure and destined to cause the nation more harm than good.

One threat clearly posed by the mere existence of personal-data hoards of unprecedented size is mission creep. Just as cloud-service providers' treasure troves of personal data proved too tempting for intelligence agencies to resist, intelligence agencies' troves are, in our opinion, likely to be used for purposes other than intelligence. Indeed, there have already been reports of diverse organizations' requesting access to NSA data in order to thwart drug trafficking, cyber attacks, money laundering, counterfeiting, and copyright infringement [3]; as of August 2013, the NSA claimed to have turned down all of those requests, but will it resist forever, no matter what it is offered in return? On a more banal note, there have been reports of NSA employees' abusing their access to surveillance data in order to spy on their romantic partners and ex-partners [4]; the practice is known as LOVEINT, by analogy with SIGINT (signals intelligence) and HUMINT (human intelligence).

A second clear threat is infiltration and corruption of data hoards. Given that the NSA has itself infiltrated data centers of Google and Yahoo! [5], the agency would be foolish to assume that no one could infiltrate its data centers. Infiltrators need not act dramatically and quickly, *e.g.*, by appropriating large amount of money using stolen banking credentials (although that would be destructive enough). They could, for example, alter data in critical but subtle ways that are hard to detect, particularly since most of the data in these hoards will be accessed rarely if ever.

Although dragnet collection of sensitive data poses substantial threats, whether it provides substantial value remains unclear. A presidential review group convened to study the NSA controversy found no evidence that universal collection of cell-phone metadata contributed useful information that could not have been obtained using conventional intelligence-gathering techniques [6]. Even sensible uses of cell-phone calling records by intelligence agencies are apparently carried out in a more privacy-invasive manner than they need be. For example, the NSA's "co-traveler" program [7] finds unknown associates of known (presumably legitimate) surveillance targets by first intersecting cell-tower dumps from times and locations at which a particular known target appeared and then interpreting the intersection as the set of cell-phone numbers of people who may be "traveling with" the known target. By using *privacy-preserving set intersection*, a well studied cryptographic problem for which there are efficient solutions [8–10], the agency could arrive at the same (small) set of co-travelers' phone numbers *without* learning the phone numbers of the (large) set of innocent people who happen to have used one of the same cell towers at a relevant time. No doubt there are other well understood protocols in the vast cryptographic literature that could be used to find truly useful intelligence without revealing massive amounts of private information about ordinary citizens.

The claim that dragnet surveillance is acceptable when "metadata," rather than "data," are all that is gathered is highly dubious. Technically, there is simply no well defined distinction between metadata and data: One program's metadata are another program's data; for example, from an email client's point of view, sender's and receiver's IP addresses may be metadata, but, from a router's point of view, they are data. Socially, the claim that "who, when, where, and for how long" information about a person's cell-phone calls (aka metadata) is less revealing or less deserving of privacy protection than the content of his calls (aka data) does not pass the laugh test. Clearly, there are situations in which all of the metadata are pretty well known to the authorities anyway, and the interesting question is what the people on the phones are saying; there are just as many situations, however, in which the questions of interest are precisely "with whom, when, where, and for how long is this person communicating?"

Government agencies should not obtain answers to any of these questions without particularized suspicion.

The claim that communications have only been "intercepted" or that data have only been "seized" when a human being hears, reads, or otherwise consumes them ignores the reality of the Big-Data era we live in. The shift from human-mediated to computer-mediated surveillance does not make mass surveillance less objectionable. It may even make it more so, because imperfect, probabilistic algorithms now interpret people's words and activities on behalf of government agencies with enormous power (not just on behalf of companies that want to target ads).

2.3   Security Sabotage

Recall that we use the term "security sabotage" to refer to government agencies' covert and deliberate weakening of crypto and security standards and products through interference in the work of standards bodies or companies. Sabotage is one, but by no means the only, approach taken in the NSA's Bullrun program [11], the goal of which is to "defeat the encryption used in specific network communication technologies."

For security sabotage to be effective as a tool of intelligence and law enforcement, the weaknesses inserted into standards and products must be usable by intelligence and law-enforcement agents but not by the very terrorists and criminals that they are intended to defeat. *There is no reason to believe that this is the case.* On the contrary, security sabotage has backfired before, *e.g.*, in the case of the mobile-phone system built by Vodafone Greece [12]. The system was intended for use by members of the Greek government and senior civil servants; it contained "built-in wiretapping facilities" for official use. Hackers subverted these facilities and managed to eavesdrop on the Prime Minister, the Mayor of Athens, and many other high-level officials.

Crypto and security researchers have worked for decades, often at taxpayer expense, to create the mathematical and technological foundation for a secure information environment. Security sabotage is tantamount to betrayal of those researchers and the taxpayers who support them and to vandalism of that foundation. It is not only unethical and heavy-handed but potentially economically destructive; to remain dominant, the US tech industry will require customers' trust, and that trust has been violated.

Finally, we believe that security sabotage invites bad product design and implementation. If inventors and developers believe that standard cryptographic protocols are likely to have hidden features that enable government eavesdropping, they may opt to use nonstandard, inadequately vetted protocols or even attempt to design their own. Cryptography and security are difficult, highly specialized areas in which expert evaluation and standardization processes have developed over decades (and are still developing). This painstaking and expensive development effort will have been wasted if the resulting processes are perceived to have been corrupted by government surveillance agencies.

2.4   The US Business Community

As described by Schneier [13], pervasive use of cloud computing has given rise to a regime of Internet use that is reminiscent of feudalism. By entrusting all of our personal data and the records of all of our online activity to one (or a very small number of) for-profit cloud-service providers (Google, Facebook, Yahoo!, *etc.*), users play the role of feudal peasants; we are dependent on these providers and must be loyal to them or endure significant switching costs. Similarly, the providers play the role of feudal lords in that they command our loyalty and profit from it, but they are to some extent obligated to treat us decently, because we could abandon one of them for another, and the most talented and entrepreneurial of us could even rise up and overtake them. Other technology critics have explored the feudal metaphor, most notably Lanier [14], who calls the providers "Lords of the Cloud" and argues that their business models are destroying the world economy.

Unsurprisingly, the Lords of the Cloud are unhappy about NSA's surveilling their users, breaking into their data centers, implying to journalists that they have willingly cooperated with NSA's data-collection programs, and refusing to allow them to clarify the extent to which they actually have cooperated (in the sense that they have responded to subpoenas and National Security Letters, details of which are usually classified). Their CEOs have met with President Obama to express their unhappiness, and eight major firms have issued a joint objection to the current surveillance regime, together with five principles that could inform a better regime [15].

We applaud the Lords for this action and think that their proposed principles are reasonable. Moreover, we recognize that business lobbies can have enormous influence on US electoral politics and congressional legislation; tech-industry support for anti-surveillance candidates and legislative efforts would be welcome. Unfortunately, we see at least two reasons that such efforts cannot be expected to lead to significant change in the near future. Although the tech industry is rich and powerful, it is not nearly as powerful in Washington DC as the military and intelligence communities. Furthermore, the Lords of the Cloud have limited credibility in opposing surveillance. At the core of their business models is the exploitation of personal information for the purpose of targeting ads, and, as explained in Sect. 2.1, their collection of that personal information is a key component of the surveillance morass.

Of course, tech is not the only business sector in the US, and corporations in general probably do not like the extent to which they and their customers are beholden to the Lords of the Cloud. Perhaps they will lend their support to the vision outlined in Sect. 4 below, just as they lent their support 15 years ago to open-source development of webservers and other Web 1.0 components.

3   The Still Somewhat Decentralized Internet

As explained in Sect. 2.1, one major enabler of mass surveillance is the popularity of ad-supported cloud services. A crucial feature of these services is that they are *centralized.* We use this term to describe a service or system that is controlled by one principal; note that centralized services may be *distributed, i.e.*, they may be executed on multiple machines. By contrast, *decentralized* services or systems are not only executed on multiple machines but controlled by multiple principals that may have little or no trust in each other. In this section, we identify some of the factors underlying this trend toward centralization.

By managing Internet services for a large number of users, the Lords of the Cloud are able to realize huge economies of scale and provide services that are "free" in that end users are not charged directly. Because their revenue model revolves around the exploitation of user data, their incentive is to centralize those data on their servers. The costs associated with this centralization, namely the loss of privacy and the ease of mass surveillance, are borne mainly by society as a whole rather than by individual users of the Lords' services. They are treated by cloud-service providers as externalities.

We argue that the utility provided by the Lords of the Cloud resides primarily in their production of a particular kind of software. We look to the open-source movement for an alternative regime for the production of this software that can better account for the overall public interest.

3.1 The Internet's Decentralized Roots

The core infrastructure of the Internet was built to support a decent amount of decentralization. The Domain Name System (DNS) provides a decentralized global namespace in which administration of subtrees can be delegated. Other services can then take advantage of this infrastructure: Domain names can be embedded in the names of protocol-specific resources and used to resolve the hosts that provide the corresponding services.

For instance, in order to deliver an email message, a Mail Transport Agent (MTA) first extracts the domain part of the recipient's address. The MTA then performs a DNS request and obtains the Mail Exchanger (MX) records associated with the domain. These records specify a set of servers capable of receiving email for the domain, as well as associated priorities. The MTA can then try to contact these servers in order of priority until mail delivery succeeds. Because many other Internet services follow similar patterns, the procedure has been generalized across protocols and unified in the DNS Service (SRV) resource records [16].

Email and web are the most popular Internet applications built in this way, but many others exist. For example, the Andrew File System (AFS) is a distributed file system commonly used in large infrastructures. It relies on the Kerberos authentication protocol, which is often used in conjunction with user-account data published using the Lightweight Directory Access Protocol (LDAP). These protocols include a notion of independent administrative *realms* that are able to interoperate without prior trust. They can all function as global protocols by using DNS to record the servers associated with a realm.

Many of these decentralized technologies have been available since the 1980s, and some of them have been widely adopted in the context of information systems for medium-sized and large businesses. Indeed, LDAP and Kerberos form the basis of Active Directory, the service used on Microsoft Windows for sharing account information and authentication over the network. Nevertheless, despite great potential, none of them has become ubiquitous as an Internet protocol to the same extent that email and web protocols have, and Internet users tend to rely on centralized solutions instead.

3.2   The Lords' Economies of Scale

That a small number of companies dominate mass-market cloud services is unsurprising given the massive economies of scale that centralization enables. From the point of view of an isolated user, the services provided by the Lords of the Cloud are essentially free, because the Lords' marginal costs are essentially nonexistent. Alternatives are cost-prohibitive: Even for open, decentralized services such as email, small-scale providers incur significant costs per user, *e.g.*, for hardware and labor.

Large service providers maintain infrastructures in which every part of the administration process is automated. At very large scale, system administration is essentially software development, where the "machine" that runs the software in question is the whole infrastructure rather than a single computer. As in all software development, there are huge initial costs, and a highly skilled workforce is required; however, the marginal cost per user is essentially zero.

Like traditional proprietary-software companies, the Lords of the Cloud develop infrastructure software that addresses users' needs only as a secondary objective, to the extent that such development efforts enhance the companies' profits. As a consequence, infrastructure-software development is focused on centralized solutions in which users' data are collected by the service provider, rather than remaining under users' control. Although it has been pointed out repeatedly that these solutions come at the expense of users' privacy, they are sustainable: Many of us do not suffer directly from loss of privacy to a faceless corporation or even to the surveillance state; more importantly, one person's choice of provider has very little impact even on his own vulnerability, much less on prevailing forms of cloud-service architecture.

Rather, centralization has problematic consequences primarily in the aggregate, when a large percentage of the world's email transits through a few companies' servers, and most electronic communications on the planet are made available to at least one country's espionage agencies and their associates. These consequences do not factor into the economic calculations of a service provider, its users, or its paying customers (most of whom are advertisers).

3.3   Open-Source Software as a Model

A development regime for infrastructure software that prioritized users' interests would look very different. To an extent, such a regime can be found in the open-source community, where users of the software, among them many corporations, pool their resources and collaborate directly on its development (instead of pooling their resources indirectly by paying the developer of a proprietary product).

Because the developers are a subset of the intended users, open-source software is constructed with a very different agenda.

It is not entirely clear how the open-source regime of collaborative development can be applied to infrastructure software. However, one thing is quite clear: Decentralization becomes a requirement; participants can trust the *code* that they exchange, because of the transparency and traceability of the development process, but that does not mean that they can trust each other to share *administrative privileges* over a common Internet infrastructure. Fortunately, as discussed in Sect. 3.1, there are many protocols for decentralized systems that could be used as components, including some Internet protocols that are already widely deployed.

As costs of both hardware and bandwidth have continued to decline, self hosting has become more and more affordable. In the US and other wealthy countries, always-on Internet connections are very common. One can purchase small plug computers the size of a home router for $50 – $100. Alternatively, one can rent a virtual machine in a data center for a few dollars per month. Still, the skills and time required to operate servers of any kind remain obstacles to widespread use of self hosting. This has prompted several groups to develop home-server operating systems targeting plug computers with enhanced privacy and control as a stated goal.

In 2010, Eben Moglen gave a series of talks in which he invited the open-source community to create the *Freedom Box*: a plug computer packed with ready-to-use privacy-enhancing software [17]. More recently, the arkOS project [18] has focused on self hosting of email and web content. In both of those cases, the model is that of a home-network appliance: a small box with a limited purpose and few parameters that can be tuned using a convenient web interface. Here "infrastructure as software" applies literally: A general-purpose operating system is pre-configured to fulfill a certain specialized role; very little configuration remains to be done by the end-user, and project proponents hope that this will facilitate deployment.

Projects of this kind are interesting, and appliance-style servers may have an important role to play in a shift towards decentralized cloud services. However, the network-appliance paradigm by itself cannot provide service comparable to that provided by the Lords of the Cloud; the Lords' level of availability and reliability can only be achieved through redundancy, and one needs a mechanism by which plug servers can cooperate to provide it. Furthermore, Freedom Box and arkOS target only very small institutions, *e.g.*, households and perhaps small businesses; in order to replace the Feudal Internet with a more open and democratic Renaissance Internet, we will need to enlist the participation of many sorts of institutions, including large ones.

We believe that *decentralized configuration management* can address these limitations by bridging the gap between decentralized, but low-level, Internet protocols and well established, but centralized, system-administration methods that are typically used for large infrastructures.

4   Decentralized Configuration Management

While many Internet protocols are designed to operate in a decentralized manner, the methods and software currently used by the participants to deploy them typically assume centralized control over the infrastructure. By relaxing this assumption, we can build an open-source framework that would allow groups of people to cooperate on the provision of the same kinds of services that are now provided by the Lords of the Cloud in a centralized, albeit distributed, fashion.

4.1   Configuration-Management Systems

The theme of "system administration as software development" is of course not exclusive to the very large-scale infrastructures of cloud-service providers; it can be useful for smaller deployments as well. Systems for centralizing the configuration and administration of medium-sized and large infrastructures are usually known as *configuration-management systems*.

Typically, the configuration for the whole infrastructure is stored *as code* in a central repository. The configuration is usually placed under revision control (as is done for more typical software-development tasks). The configuration-management system provides mechanisms to propagate the configuration from the central repository to each client machine in a reliable and repeatable way.

In principle, because a configuration-management system captures the state of an infrastructure as code, it should be possible to use it for collaborative system administration. Indeed, in a typical enterprise setup, a team of administrators shares access to the configuration repository, perhaps following a process similar to those used by teams of programmers. In a hypothetical collaborative cloud service, participants would pool their resources and set up their machines to use a common configuration repository, collaborating and "contributing" to this shared configuration so as to accommodate their common needs in a mutually agreeable fashion.

Unfortunately, this model cannot scale. In this arrangement, the participants must trust each other. In most cases, granting a set of participants access to the configuration repository is tantamount to giving them full privileges on each others' machines. Although it is sometimes possible to set up fine-grained control of access to the configuration repository, every configuration-management system that we are aware of relies on a centralized database in which the configuration of the whole infrastructure is stored. The integrity of this database has to be trusted by all participants in an all-or-nothing fashion.

4.2   Decentralized Configuration Management

Truly *decentralized configuration management* would allow two or more independent participants to express configuration *policies* in a repository that they alone control. Such policies may specify that some forms of collaboration are desired or permissible. The host-configuration mechanism of a given machine could then

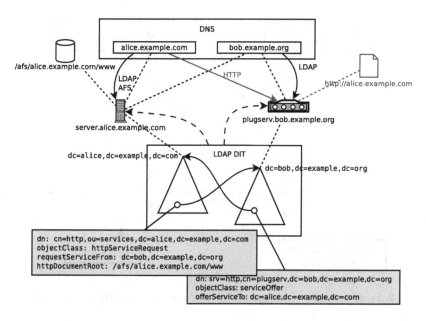

Fig. 1. Example scenario for the envisioned configuration-management framework. Dotted lines denote the associations between servers and the services they provide, solid lines denote references, and dashed lines show the flow of configuration information.

access the repositories of several participants in addition to that of its owner and derive a configuration for that machine that satisfies all of the policies.

As a concrete example of such a system, consider the situation depicted in Fig. 1. Alice and Bob own `alice.example.com` and `bob.example.org`. Because they control the contents of these DNS zones, they can designate LDAP servers for the subtrees rooted at `dc=alice`, `dc=example`, `dc=com` and `dc=bob`, `dc=example`, `dc=org` in the global Directory Information Tree (DIT). Therefore, they also control the contents of these subtrees, which they use to hold their configuration policies.

Alice's machine `server.alice.example.com` hosts her DNS zone and the corresponding DIT, as well as the AFS volume `www`, where the data files for her website reside. Bob's server `plugserv.bob.example.org` likewise hosts his DNS zone and LDAP DIT. Now suppose that Alice and Bob are to cooperate on hosting the website http://alice.example.com; Bob's machine is to serve the static contents of Alice's website, which it can find in `/afs/alice.example.com/www`. For this to happen,

- Alice has to trust Bob to provide the service faithfully;
- Bob must to be willing to host Alice's website on his server.

If these two conditions were met, Alice would modify her DNS zone in such a manner that `alice.example.com` would point to Bob's `plugserv` as the associated HTTP server, and Bob would configure that machine to serve the appropriate content.

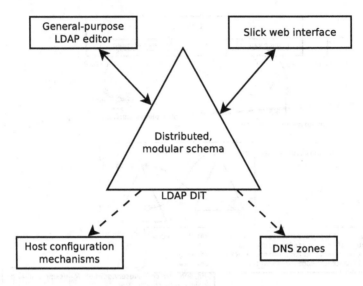

Fig. 2. Several possible components of the framework and their relationships

Our goal is to automate this process so that Alice and Bob can express their preferences in a common configuration repository in the form of *service requests* and *service offers*. These requests and offers could then be matched to one another so as to compute the configuration of each individual host.

4.3   Overall Structure

Figure 2 shows the overall structure of the system we envision. An LDAP directory is the obvious candidate to hold the configuration policy, because it is possible to delegate maintenance and control of subtrees in the directory to different administrative principals. Ultimately, such a system would provide a user interface to assist the administrator in creating this configuration policy. However, in the prototyping phase, a general purpose LDAP editor would be enough. It could also serve as an escape hatch for advanced users who wish to access parameters unavailable through user interfaces or to introduce their own.

Host-configuration software can then compute the configuration of each individual machine using data from different participants. Assuming the LDAP schema has been carefully defined, it would be possible for different implementations of such host-configuration mechanisms to coexist. In Fig. 1, the machines `server.alice.example.com` and `plugserv.bob.example.org` might be running completely different operating systems. The computed configuration can include any DNS zones that have to be published. In the case of Fig. 1, `bob.info` is served by both Alice's `server` and Bob's `plugserv`. In fact, the two servers can independently compute the zone's contents from the data in the repositories, eliminating the need for DNS zone transfer.

Furthermore, these configuration mechanisms could use substantially different approaches. At one end of the spectrum, a human administrator could inspect the contents of the directory manually and carefully configure a given machine to match its role in the infrastructure. While this approach would ultimately defeat the purpose of automating configuration, it could be useful as a stop-gap measure when prototyping new schema components. As an example of the other extreme, the data from the directory could be used to specialize and compile a complete operating system image, possibly of the kind proposed in [19]. Most likely, the usual case would comprise some kind of automatic host-configuration tool operating on a conventional operating system. This could be achieved by a new tool, a preliminary version of which we have prototyped and are experimenting with.[2] Alternatively, one could set out to modify or specialize an existing configuration-management system to integrate similar capabilities.

5   Conclusions and Future Directions

After exploring the surveillance morass from a computer-science perspective, we have concluded that centralized cloud services play a crucial role in perpetuating the current, objectionable state of affairs. We have proposed an alternative approach to the construction of global-scale cloud services, based on open-source, decentralized configuration-management tools.

Research on the question of how simultaneously to provide scalable cloud services, user privacy, and support for *lawful* surveillance is fairly new, and open questions abound. We give just two of them here.

As we have argued in Sect. 2.2, collection and storage of massive numbers of phone-call records and other communications "metadata" are potentially harmful and may not even be necessary for effective pursuit of criminals and terrorists. In at least some realistic use cases, well studied cryptographic techniques, such as privacy-preserving set intersection, can be used to identify and track suspects while *not* identifying or tracking innocent bystanders or any other non-suspects. There may, however, be inherent limitations to this approach. In order to use most of the relevant techniques in the literature, one must start with a well defined function that one wants to compute and then design and implement a protocol that computes it in a privacy-preserving manner. An intelligence agency, however, may not know in advance exactly what it wants to compute. For example, it may uncover information that appears relevant to an investigation and suggests other sources of potentially relevant information but does not by itself suggest a well defined function to compute in a privacy-preserving manner; indeed, it may be precisely by collecting and examining more sensitive information from the suggested sources that the investigators figure out what they need to compute.

Clearly, the technical approach put forth in Sect. 4 must be fully fleshed out before it can seriously challenge the centralized cloud-service regime that prevails today. Because a successful challenge would require the buy-in of large organizations, probably including for-profit corporations, analysis of incentives and other economic aspects of our proposal is necessary along with technical development.

---

[2] https://github.com/jeremie-koenig/ldapmin

References

1. Greenwald, G.: No Place to Hide: Edward Snowden, the NSA, and the U.S. Surveillance State. Metropolitan Books, New York (2014)
2. Goldfarb, A., Tucker, C.E.: Online advertising, behavioral targeting, and privacy. Commun. ACM **54**(5), 25–27 (2011)
3. Lichtblau, E., Schmidt, M.S.: Other Agencies Clamor for Data NSA Compiles. The New York Times, 23 Aug 2013
4. Gorman, S.: NSA Officers Spy on Love Interests. The Wall Street Journal, 23 August 2013
5. Gellman, B., Soltani, A.: NSA Infiltrates Links to Yahoo, Google Data Centers Worldwide, Snowden Documents Say. The Washington Post, 30 Oct 2013
6. Clarke, R.A., Morell, M.J., Stone, G.R., Sunstein, C.R., Swire, P.: Liberty and Security in a Changing World, 12 Dec 2013. http://www.scribd.com/doc/192387819/NSA-review-board-s-report
7. Soltani, A., Gellman, B.: New Documents Show How the NSA Infers Relationships Based on Mobile Location Data. The Washington Post, 10 Dec 2013
8. Freedman, M.J., Nissim, K., Pinkas, B.: Efficient private matching and set intersection. In: Cachin, C., Camenisch, J.L. (eds.) EUROCRYPT 2004. LNCS, vol. 3027, pp. 1–19. Springer, Heidelberg (2004)
9. Kissner, L., Song, D.: Privacy-preserving set operations. In: Shoup, V. (ed.) CRYPTO 2005. LNCS, vol. 3621, pp. 241–257. Springer, Heidelberg (2005)
10. Vaidya, J., Clifton, C.: Secure set intersection cardinality with application to association rule mining. J. Comput. Secur. **13**(4), 593–622 (2005)
11. The Guardian: Project Bullrun - classification guide to the NSA's decryption program, 5 Sept 2013. http://www.theguardian.com/world/interactive/2013/sep/05/nsa-project-bullrun-classification-guide
12. Prevelakis, V., Spinellis, D.: The athens affair. IEEE Spectrum. **44**(7), 26–33 (2007)
13. Schneier, B.: When It Comes to Security, We're Back to Feudalism, 26 Nov 2012. https://www.schneier.com/essay-406.html
14. Lanier, J.: Who Owns the Future?. Simon and Schuster, New York (2013)
15. AOL, Apple, Dropbox, Facebook, Google, LinkedIn, Microsoft, Twitter, Yahoo!: Global Government Surveillance Reform (2013). http://reformgovernmentsurveillance.com
16. Gulbrandsen, A., Vixie, P., Esibov, L.: A DNS RR for specifying the location of services (DNS SRV). RFC 2782 (Proposed Standard), Feb 2000. http://www.ietf.org/rfc/rfc2782.txt. Updated in RFC 6335
17. Vaughan-Nichols, S.J.: Freedom box: Freeing the Internet one Server at a time, 16 Feb 2011. http://www.zdnet.com/blog/networking/freedom-box-freeing-the-internet-one-server-at-a-time/698
18. Henderson, N.: Open Source Project arkOS Brings Simplicity to Self-Hosting, 12 Nov 2013. http://www.thewhir.com/web-hosting-news/open-source-project-arkos-brings-simplicity-to-self-hosting
19. Madhavapeddy, A., Mortier, R., Rotsos, C., Scott, D., Singh, B., Gazagnaire, T., Smith, S., Hand, S., Crowcroft, J.: Unikernels: library operating systems for the cloud. In: 18th International Conference on Architectural Support for Programming Languages and Operating Systems, pp. 461–472. ACM Press, New York (2013)

On the Feasibility of a Technological Response to the Surveillance Morass (Transcript of Discussion)

Joan Feigenbaum$^{(\boxtimes)}$ and Jérémie Koenig

Yale University, New Haven, CT 06520-8285, USA
{joan.feigenbaum,jeremie.koenig}@yale.edu

When I read that the theme of this year's workshop started with "now that all our paranoid dreams of the last 20 years have come true," I assumed that that meant that this workshop was about the surveillance morass. That's because I am obsessed with the surveillance morass. Now that I'm here, I realize that, regardless of the official theme, this workshop is about whatever the participants are obsessed with. So I guess Jérémie's and my paper is in scope.

What do I mean by the phrase "surveillance morass"? Well, the NSA and related government spy agencies all over the world have been conducting dragnet surveillance on all of us – on citizens of advanced democracies who supposedly have legal rights that preclude that type of thing. That's what we learned from the Snowden revelations. We also learned that our governments (led, it seems, by my own government) have deliberately compromised the security of our information and communication environment. To answer the question with which Bruce started the workshop, namely "who's the enemy," I guess we're all the enemy, because I think that the surveillance morass really constitutes an all-around failure. Everybody who had a chance to step up and do the right thing failed, including us.

I won't go through every word on this slide, because I think you can easily get the point. We failed each other, the governments failed us, the tech industry failed us, ..., you know, it's really a very sad situation. Last semester, I taught a course in which I tried to persuade all the students to think about the surveillance morass; the title of the course is "Sensitive information in a wired world." Most of the students were more interested in other things, like digital copyright, censorship, and online privacy in general, but a few of them, including Jérémie Koenig, took me up on my charge to think about the surveillance morass. So he's going to use the second half of this talk to present his technical vision for something we might do about the surveillance morass – how we might deal with the fact that the enemy is all around us and, in fact, *is* us to some extent.

But first I'd just like to spend two slides ranting about some underplayed aspects of this all-around catastrophic failure. This will be a very US-centric rant. When a US court authorizes dragnet collection of telephone metadata, it's issuing what a US-constitutional historian would call a "general warrant." The 4th Amendment of the US constitution was written to preclude general warrants. It says that the government must have particularized suspicion in order to conduct search and seizure – particularized suspicion about who and what is to

© Springer International Publishing Switzerland 2014
B. Christianson et al. (Eds.): Security Protocols 2014, LNCS 8809, pp. 253–262, 2014.
DOI: 10.1007/978-3-319-12400-1_24

be searched and about what may be seized. General warrants are the opposite: Just search everything, seize everything, search everyone. I'm somebody who never conceived herself as a naïve patriot, but I see this as a huge issue. The rejection of general warrants was actually one of the reasons that American colonists of the 18th century fought a revolutionary war! I had some trepidation about mentioning the revolutionary war in this context, but Bruce began the workshop by mentioning George Washington in his introductory lecture. Bruce is also from a former British colony; so I guess I'm off the hook on that.

It's a terrible thing that general warrants are going on all around us and that the US government is telling us that a court authorized them. What do you mean a court authorized them? They're unconstitutional! I recently heard Senator Rand Paul of Kentucky saying the same thing. He went on to say that the 4th Amendment is every bit as important as the 2nd Amendment, which is the right to bear arms. I'm horrified that I'm in the same bed as Rand Paul, who's a right-wing nutcase.

Virgil Gligor: Based on this, maybe he's not entirely nutty.

Reply: Right, there is a right-wing version of the anti-surveillance position.

Virgil Gligor: He's a libertarian.

Reply: So he says. I don't really believe those people when they talk about libertarianism, but, OK, I believe he's anti-surveillance. But I also want to ask him "what do you mean the 4th Amendment is as important as the 2nd Amendment? The 4th Amendment is much *more* important than the 2nd Amendment, you jerk." That's first bullet of my rant.

The second bullet is a *bon mot* not from Rand Paul but from Joan Feigenbaum: "One program's metadata are another program's data." We've heard endless blah, blah, blah, about the collection of telephone metadata, why it might be bad, and why it might not be bad. We've heard from the privacy advocates about why metadata might be as revealing as data. But no one has just come out and said that this distinction between metadata and data is very poorly defined. There is no bit string out there that is inherently "metadata," as opposed to "data."

The intelligence agencies are collecting data. There are programs, such as the cell-phone billing programs, that use them as data. And then there are other programs, such as the actual cell-phone call-delivery programs, that regard them as metadata; such a program may display the metadata on your cell-phone screen while you're listening to and creating the primary data, namely the content of the call. Analogously, to the internet routing programs, our email addresses are data, but, to an email client that displays our email messages, those addresses are metadata. The focus in public discussion on "how dangerous is the collection of metadata" is a red herring; they're collecting data, and who knows what they're going to use it for later? I wish people would start saying "One program's metadata are another program's data." You don't have to credit me, just plagiarize; if you think it sounds good, say it.

Virgil Gligor: If we are not being censored.

Reply: Indeed. The next bullet is about security sabotage – deliberate and covert weakening of cryptographic standards and of other security products and standards. There's been a lot of talk about that but not as much as there should be. I want to point out that it's evil and stupid, as other people have, and I want to give you my take on why. The reason it's evil is that it's a severe betrayal of *us*. Our government, certainly my own government, has been claiming for decades that a secure internet is really important. It's been funding a lot of research on internet security, cryptography, and information security generally. Many of us have taken that money and have done that work in good faith. And our own government has been sabotaging that work. It has been vandalizing the secure information infrastructure that we were trying to build, and I take that very personally. I find it very offensive.

Ross Anderson: But the trouble is it just sees the world differently. The Snowden papers make it clear that the NSA sees security as a complement of privacy.

Reply: Well, nonetheless, I was very upset about security sabotage. I call it "under-emphasized," because there hasn't been much written about the idea that they're purveying; it's the idea of having weaknesses in the security infrastructure that *only they can exploit*. This is not a new idea; it has been tried, and it has failed, for example in the Greek cellphone system, where the government insisted that there be backdoors, which were of course later used to spy on government officials who were using this cellphone system. So whenever somebody tells me "I'm inserting this weakness, and only I can exploit it," my immediate reaction is *bullshit!*

I said "everybody failed," and that includes us. For many years, we the people have not reckoned with this stuff. We have not made the 4th Amendment, or personal privacy, or information privacy in general a voting issue. So our elected officials don't care about it, and that's at least partly our fault; in fact, I would say it's greatly our fault. We haven't demanded that they explain what they mean when they say there's a tradeoff between security and privacy. We hear a lot of allegedly intelligent people say "of course, we do want to respect privacy, but if we had total respect for privacy then we could not have any security." Or they say "if we had all the information that's out there, then we would have perfect security. If we knew every single byte of data that's out there that somebody might want to keep private, then we could prevent terrorism." We haven't asked them "Really? Exactly how would you do that?" We haven't made them admit that they have no evidence for that claim, and so they keep assuming that we believe them and therefore that they can keep pushing the envelope on how much of our private information they take.

We also can't claim that we didn't know about the enabler for all this, namely the surveillance-based ad targeting that supports cloud services. We can't claim that we didn't acquiesce in that, because I remember very well the beginning of the mass-market internet and the mass-market web. While we didn't quite know that cloud services were going to look like what they look like now, we sure as hell knew that free services were not free. We knew that, if we weren't going to pay directly, then we were going to pay indirectly, one way or another. Yet we went ahead with "free services."

The security-research community has not stepped up. There have been very few public statements by pillars of the research community opposing mass surveillance. I know this because I myself put one together; Rebecca was one of the signers of an open letter that I put together with a few colleagues opposing the NSA power grab. Maybe I shouldn't say "NSA power grab," because NSA is not actually a policy-making organization; let's say "opposing mass surveillance." I put together this open letter, and I had a very hard time getting prominent security researchers to sign it. I had a very hard time even eliciting what I thought was a proper degree of emotional attachment to this issue.

Joseph Bonneau: So is the problem that there haven't been enough public statements by the security community or that it hasn't been clear how much weight they have? Because I've seen at least three or four.

Reply: That's about right.

Joseph Bonneau: To me, the issue is that we don't have the kind of professional organization that the public recognizes, like doctors in the US have in their AMA.

Reply: There was an ACM statement; it was sort of wimpy.

Joseph Bonneau: But nobody's heard of the ACM outside of computer science.

Reply: All right, so you're saying maybe it's not just that the security-research community has not stepped up to this issue. Rather, it's that the security-research community doesn't have a vehicle for stepping up to issues at all.

Joseph Bonneau: Yes. We didn't invest in building an effective organization for years and years the way doctors did.

Reply: Yes, that could be, but let me just say that my personal experience of trying to rally the community to do something didn't only run up against the lack of a vehicle. It ran up against the lack of enthusiasm.

Alastair Beresford: Maybe that's because people thought their efforts wouldn't have any effect because of the lack of a vehicle.

Reply: There are actually some people I know pretty well who fleshed out their reasons for not giving a shit, and some of them said they didn't think it would be effective. Some of them said "I don't want to jeopardize my ability to get funding," and some of them said "I don't really think scientists should mix in politics." They didn't say "I don't think we would be effective if we got mixed up in politics" but rather "I don't think it's our place."

Yvo Desmedt: Did you talk to the EFF?

Reply: I've talked to the EFF, but the EFF is not the security-research community.

Yvo Desmedt: I know.

Reply: There *are* people who care passionately about this. I'm saying that we as a community did not step up. One more remark because I want to get to the technical vision.

Yvo Desmedt: There are people in England who wrote a manifesto.

Reply: Bristol crypto group

Yvo Desmedt: There were also people from other places who signed.

Reply: OK, the Bristol crypto group and some of their friends and associates wrote a letter, an open letter that I *loved*, in September 2013, and my first thought was, "Why don't we in the US just simply say that we agree with them?" That would have been good enough for me. But that didn't work, and it took me until January 2014 to get four paragraphs that a bunch of well known US-based security researchers would sign.

Occasional oppositional media coverage is not going to work. I thought that Glenn Greenwald's drip, drip, drip approach was interesting for a while, but it's gotten very tiresome. The Snowden revelations and the surveillance controversy have now become just one more thing that is intermittently on the front page, which is not enough to rally consensus outrage in the Washington establishment. At this point, it competes with, you know, Ted Cruz, Crimea, missing Malaysian planes, and whatever; it's just going to be one more thing that every once in a while you hear some quasi-intelligent blather about, but I don't think that the media coverage will cause it to be more than that, which is a shame. You would like to think that media interest would matter, but nothing seems to be able to rally enough attention to this issue. OK, end of rant.

Ross Anderson: But you have much more coverage in America than we have here.

Reply: Well that's even sadder.

Ross Anderson: And your government, in the form of the review group, came up with a response that they clearly thought would be sufficient to stop Snowden's frightening the horses.

Reply: Well what it really was sufficient to do was to stop people who were passionate about the issue from pushing it further. I won't condemn it entirely, but that response was very weak.

Ross Anderson: But that's part of political management. It's what you or I would have done had we been the tenant of the White House.

Reply: You or I as the tenant of the White House is a sufficiently false hypothesis that we don't have to entertain it.

Transition to a technical vision! So Bruce Schneier, who definitely is passionate about this issue and has been blogging his butt off about it, says what we need to do is to make mass surveillance more expensive. Why is mass surveillance so inexpensive in today's internet? Because we have arrived at what Schneier calls, and maybe other people also call, a "feudal internet." So my slide title

("Time for a Renaissance Internet") means that it is time to get over the feudal internet and to go to something else. I picked "a renaissance internet," but, if you have some other period of history that sounds better than renaissance, by all means use it.

What is the feudal internet? The feudal internet is populated by monopolistic or oligopolistic cloud-service companies, which Jaron Lanier refers to as the "Lords of the Cloud." They are ad-supported, and hence they have an infrastructure for massive, dragnet collection of personal data at the core of their business model. So once all of these data are collected and centralized by a few Lords, it's sort of inevitable that not only government intelligence agencies but all kinds of potential bad actors will get their hands on them. If we're going to avoid this situation, we need to move to a world in which we can have the benefit of cloud services not provided by data-hoarding Lords of the Cloud. Jérémie has a technical vision that can accomplish this, and he's going to present it to you. Not a security guy, a PL guy, who has a technical vision for us.

Jérémie Koenig: All right, so the idea is, we want to move towards a more decentralized internet. But actually, there's nothing new about this. From the beginning of the internet, the whole idea is to decentralize. So the technology is here, it's just that we decentralize between Google, and Hotmail, and Facebook, and maybe five or ten very big actors. Whether it's email, and web, and DNS — so the very core of the internet — this capability is already there. We could, each one of us could receive our email if we had the resources to do that. And in many other areas of the internet we have decentralized protocols that work very well, but that we use in a centralized way. So for instance, Kerberos is this decentralized authentication protocol where identities can be managed by many, many people, and you can actually hook Kerberos into DNS to make it a global authentication system. The same thing with LDAP, which is a distributed directory service, and it's interesting that both Kerberos and LDAP are very popular in companies; for instance, Microsoft Active Directory, which is Microsoft's account sharing system for business networks is basically Kerberos and LDAP, and it's used in many companies with a central server. But both of those can be much more decentralized, and we can hook them into DNS to obtain a global thing. Same thing with AFS, which is this wonderful distributed filesystem. You can run AFS on a machine and have access to a global filesystem shared with the 20 people in the world who use AFS. Yes, there are more than that. But I mean, when you think of Dropbox in this context — we've known how to do this for quite a while, that's why the next slide says, when do we catch up with the 90s, because all of those protocols are nothing new.

Virgil Gligor: You mean the 80s?

Jérémie Koenig: The 80s, yes, I'm not sure like Coda, and LDAP, maybe?

Virgil Gligor: The 80s.

Joan Feigenbaum: So Jérémie was not born in the 80s.

Jérémie Koenig: No I was born in the 80s. So yes, it's kind of paradoxical that Dropbox is this new fancy thing. So now the issue is: can we take all of these wonderful things and actually deploy them in a way that is truly decentralized? One idea that has been floated around in recent years is, now we have very cheap computers; you can buy a so-called plug computer for $50, and it's just a small piece of hardware, you plug it into permanent internet connection which nowadays all of us have, and then it could manage your email, and so on and so forth. And so in 2010, before the Snowden revelations, Eben Moglen who is the chief lawyer for the Free Software Foundation had this tour of Free Software conferences and events where he floated this idea: we're going to build the software for this Freedom box, this small piece of hardware that anybody can just buy and bring home, and it will be wonderful, it will manage their email, and you don't need the cloud anymore where we all give up control of our own data. It's a nice idea but it has been vaporware ever since. More recently, the ArkOS project is kind of a reaction to this where they said, we need to focus on the important things. Eben Moglen's version was, we need everybody to run Tor and these privacy enhancing proxies and so on and so forth. ArkOS is kind of a reaction to this where they say, let's start with email and it will already be a huge step when 90 % of the world's email is not stored permanently on Google servers, right. But in both cases the model is that of the home router. You have a piece of hardware, you put it there, you configure it through a web interface, and you don't worry about it anymore.

Jérémie Koenig: The issue is, it is not enough because you cannot support an internet domain with just one thing that you plug at home. First of all, you need at least two DNS servers to host a DNS zone, right, so from the very beginning you need some way of pooling resources with someone or purchasing additional resources if you want to manage your domain. And then you don't want a situation where, if you trip the wire, then your email starts bouncing, for instance. We also need to go towards an idea of collaborative system administration because it's just not possible for everybody to put in the system administration work to host their own domain. And we know that when you are doing system administration of large infrastructures, you need to do it as a software development process where everything is in a central repository, and then from there your entire installation would be configured magically, right? The problem with this is, it assumes that someone has central control over the configuration of the whole system. So the idea, in order to pool resources over a large number of small servers, would be to say: we're going to take this configuration management idea, but the configuration has to be stored in an LDAP directory. LDAP is distributed, so like in DNS you can delegate parts of your directory, and you can hook it up in DNS to have a global thing.

Jérémie Koenig: You could have this situation where Alice says, I have this website, but maybe my internet connection is not very good, so I prefer Bob to host it. So Alice will have an entry in her part of the directory saying, Bob.info, please can you serve the website that you'll find at this path in the global AFS filesystem, and Bob says, oh actually I can provide service for anything Alice wants. And so by computing this intersection of requests and offers, the software can figure out that Bob's server should be configured to provide the documents from this part of the filesystem. And independently Alice's software can figure out that Bob's server is providing her website, and so can add the appropriate entry in her DNS zone. So that's the basic idea, it's this notion of having a modular LDAP schema that can be used at the same time by host configuration mechanisms to create this configuration automatically. And at the same time it can be the articulation between more systems. So if you are a geek you can use an LDAP editor to modify your configuration manually, but you could also imagine having some kind of web interface to do this configuration. You could imagine things like load balancing systems to manage a large number of servers, and services, and match them in an appropriate way. So that's the idea, if you have a few questions—

Robert Watson: I love all the technology you've described here, DNSSEC, Coda and AFS are all wonderful things, but I wonder if you've actually made the job of the adversary any harder, or if you've just made it easier. One of the big challenges of the structure you described is you need a supply chain, and if I'm the adversary what I will attack is the supply chain, and that sounds pretty easy to do I think, especially if you're telling everyone they should buy the same modular router, use the same software. Do you need diversity to make this work?

Jérémie Koenig: So yes, that's one of the points, right, if you have this standardized way to describe the requirements for your infrastructure, and how you'd like things to articulate around one another, then you can imagine several possible host configuration mechanisms, so one for a Windows server, maybe my Debian Prototype, and likewise you can imagine several ways to edit this configuration. So the idea is also, we have this standard in the middle, and then we can implement it in different ways.

Robert Watson: I think many of these systems are designed to be Byzantine fault tolerant, right, so that means they're going to suffer from weakest link rather than improved security as a result of adding more parts. So even if you have multiple supply chains, problem is they make this weaker as opposed to stronger. So to me that's just the elements you're describing being assembled in this system aren't the right building blocks, you would need new building blocks that really are designed for a more Byzantine fault model.

Jérémie Koenig: Interesting.

Virgil Gligor: Actually I think what he's doing, he is trying to get away from collaborating with the Lords of the Clouds, not against state actors.

Joan Feigenbaum: Yeah I don't think it's a Byzantine threat model, I think it's the—

Robert Watson: Well I think when we challenge the cloud more, that's kind of what we're saying is, the problem with these big clouds is that they're kind of of Byzantine in a sense, we go to every one of the cloud providers and they've all been compromised, they're all willing to sell our data.

Jérémie Koenig: So if we spread out, if we make the number large enough, then it's harder to compromise them all. I think that's the point of going towards something more decentralized.

Joan Feigenbaum: So where's your economic argument that there will be many providers? You have now outlined a technological platform that could enable many providers. Why doesn't the business case still drive towards a few Lords of the Cloud?

Virgil Gligor: Right, and that's the problem.

Ross Anderson: Well one of the interesting things here is that in our industry everybody thinks about network effects. If you go to Washington, or London, or Brussels, and you talk to the policy wonks there, the guys who did their PhDs in international relations or public choice, they've never heard of network effects, they just don't understand this at all. There's an enormous gap in economic thinking between the IT industry on the one hand and the regulators on the other. You can't expect the regulators to catch up. They still think that enabling the EU to compete with the USA in the IT businesses, for example, is a matter of economies of scope, sheer market size, that the single market will be enough to do it. And as for thinking through what's involved in regulation, and of a world in which you get network effects in industry, they've not even started that task yet.

Joan Feigenbaum: OK, but you must have some reason you think this would lead to more diversity of service providers. Is it just build it and they will come?

Robert Watson: I see lots of individuals in this model, but I don't see what the supply chain is. If you have one implementation of AFS why would you find a second implementation of AFS? Why will that exist?

Jérémie Koenig: It does.

Robert Watson: Well it did, and the other project from KTH went away as soon as AFS was open sourced by IBM, because a second implication didn't really make sense. The only reason two implementations existed was that there wasn't an Open Source one, so the Open Source people came along and said, I'm starting to build one, but they never finished because OpenAFS came.

But sometimes by its nature a distributed Open Source project is harder to bring pressure to bear on. This is what Apache found, we were talking about this at lunch. It is wonderful being a foundation, because, you know, foundations aren't worth suing, and they are sufficiently distributed so that it is quite hard to persuade them to put in anything they don't want to put in.

Ross Anderson: But the network effects still work, right, once you've got an Open Source project building, for example, something like Apache, every ambitious developer will contribute his code to that particular project rather than start a new one.

Robert Watson: I'm not sure it is like that, I mean, Open Source projects often do compete in the same spaces, but they do so for technical reasons, not so much for social reasons, I think, right, they come up with alternative implementations, they take different approaches, or embody different design philosophies. Can we cause all those things to come together, these are big distributed systems, they're the hardest systems to build, and design, and test, and specify, we have enough trouble doing it with local operating systems.

Ross Anderson: Well I'm going to be giving a talk next month in Berkeley where I point out that thanks to the likes of the NSA we now have strong network effects in government, and so governments are going to have start thinking about this stuff. So if you go back 30 years to the Cold War, a neutral country like India would happily buy its jet fighters from Russia because the lock-in wasn't all that great, and we decided to change from MiGs to Mirages, they'd have to do some pilot retraining, and buy a few million bucks worth of spares, and it wasn't a big deal. Now, on the other hand, the Indian intelligence agencies of course prefer to swap information with the NSA rather than with the FSB because the NSA has the bigger network. And so we maybe moving towards a world in which for various reasons network effects become evidence in policies, as well as evidence in our industry. Now we have seen some previous examples of this in the cities, and languages, and religions, are also examples of structures that benefit from network economics, but of course the politicians never thought of them in those terms, they thought of these as given platforms on which you erected your power structures. But now that we're building infrastructure ourselves which can lead to substantial shifts in power structures worldwide, then that if nothing else should get the attention of our ruling classes.

Strange Bedfellows: How and When to Work with Your Enemy

Aaron D. Jaggard[1] and Rebecca N. Wright[2]([⊠])

[1] U.S. Naval Research Laboratory, Washington, DC, USA
aaron.jaggard@nrl.navy.mil
[2] DIMACS and Department of Computer Science, Rutgers University, Piscataway, USA
rebecca.wright@rutgers.edu

Abstract. There are many examples of parties that are seemingly in opposition working together. In this position paper, we explore this in the context of security protocols with an emphasis on how these examples might produce long-term benefits for the "good guys" and how a formal model might be used to help prescribe approaches to collaboration with the "bad guys."

Collaboration is usually thought of as a joint effort where the parties involved have the same or similar end goals. However, there are many examples of collaboration between parties that are actually or seemingly in opposition. We sketch some of these below. Parties may choose to participate in these types of collaborations even though they believe that their opponents are rational and thus must see some benefit from the collaboration. We suggest that a reason for this is that the parties may have different time horizons or discount rates. For example, law enforcement may value the capture of a major kingpin highly even though it requires years of work, while their informants may have a much shorter term focus. Beyond seeing this as a possible explanation, we propose that this should inform strategy. A party such as a police force can, and in some cases should, collaborate with parties that have short time horizons in an effort to attack common opponents with longer time horizons.

Collaborating parties have their own incentives and their own reasons for collaboration. They also know that the other parties are often behaving rationally (although the utilities that they are trying to maximize may be quite different and even opposed in some ways). In the language of game theory, the "good guys" collaborating with the "bad guys" can be viewed as the good guys trying to find bad guys who maximize the good guys' utility (perhaps in equilibrium) and then collaborating with those bad guys to defeat other bad guys whose presence hurts both the good guys and the bad guys with whom they collaborate.

Work supported by ONR and DARPA.

Work partially carried out with support from the National Science Foundation under grants CNS-1018557 and CCF-1101690.

© Springer International Publishing Switzerland 2014
B. Christianson et al. (Eds.): Security Protocols 2014, LNCS 8809, pp. 263–267, 2014.
DOI: 10.1007/978-3-319-12400-1_25

There are a number of (not necessarily mutually exclusive) reasons that such collaborations might occur:

1. Parties who normally have opposing goals find that they have common or similar goals in a particular context, even if for different reasons. For example, in a political race with three candidates, the two weakest candidates sometimes work together to attack the strongest candidates, because they both believe they can beat each other once the leading candidate is eliminated. Similarly, in criminal investigations, criminal suspects may be offered the opportunity to act as informants (or coerced into doing so, in some reported cases). The informants then help the police to investigate other suspects in the same case or other cases, in exchange for more lenient treatment in their own cases (such as avoiding arrest or being charged with less serious crimes than they otherwise could have been).
2. Due to incomplete or misleading information, a party may be able to take advantage of an opposing party who does not realize he is not acting in his own best interest. This, for example, is how con men operate.
3. If two parties have different risk tolerance or different time horizons (as in the purchase of insurance), then even if they have conflicting end goals, they might both be acting in accordance with their own preferences. For example, such a collaboration between two parties might allow party A to benefit in the short term and party B in the long term, with each choosing the arrangement because it fits their preferred time horizon. Or, in a situation where the most likely outcome for a given set of collaborative actions is moderately good for party A (but bad for party B) and a less likely outcome is very good for party B (but bad for party A), they may still be willing to work together to carry out the necessary collaborative actions.

As these and other examples illustrate, such collaborations are not without ethical perils, even outside the context of cybersecurity, and also have risks to their potential success. In a high-profile case related to cybersecurity, Albert Gonzalez reportedly became an informant for law enforcement in 2003 after being arrested for charges of ATM and debit card fraud. He is said to have provided information that led to the arrests of 28 people related to an identity-theft ring trafficking in 1.5 million stolen credit card and ATM card numbers. However, Gonzalez was later sentenced for 20 years in prison for continued work as a criminal hacker even while cooperating with law enforcement. He was charged with running an identity theft ring involving more 130 million card numbers and personal information stolen from five large companies via Internet attacks, much larger than the operation he had helped investigate [9].

Starting with technical issues, we consider how such methods might be effective in the setting of cybersecurity. As a oversimplification, consider a world in which there are two classes of parties: the good guys (defenders) and the bad guys (attackers). One strategy the good guys might employ would be to work with some of the bad guys to defeat the other bad guys. For example, the good guys could work with the kingpin bad guys to drive the smaller bad guys out of business, perhaps by driving up the market price for zero-day exploits to the point that only the kingpin bad guys can afford them. This could actually be good for both parties—the kingpin bad guys could increase their market share of the attack market (thereby potentially increasing their profits) while the size of the overall market could be decreased (thereby potentially decreasing the overall impact of attacks). This seems more plausibly workable but less desirable than the related option of working with the smaller bad guys to drive the kingpin bad guys out of business. Even absent such collaboration, the good guys might still assess some adversaries as preferable to lose to over others. In such cases, doing things to foster their rise to the top (relative to adversaries who would be worse) might be worthwhile.

A promising approach to this seems to be modeling the utilities over time of the various participants, including some discounting of future utility over some time horizon. We suggest viewing the good guys as being able to take a longer view (i.e., caring about utility further into the future) than the bad guys. For example, good guys might care both about their utility now and when only one adversary is left or when all have been defeated, far into the future, while the bad guys care only about the present and near future.

At least in a static (but unrealistic) setting where no new adversaries arise, this could lead to exploring an approach to picking off the adversaries one-by-one in decreasing order of their time horizons. In such a setting, we suggest that the good guys should take a long view and then collaborate with adversaries who take a short view to defeat those with a long(er) view.

There are a variety of modeling issues involved with discounting future utility in general [2]. While we believe that capturing this will provide useful insight and even prescriptive guidance, there remain many questions to answer in constructing a useful yet workable formal model. Some natural assumptions and questions include:

- The modeling of time. Discrete time periods seem like a natural starting point.
- Aspects of time discounting that should be explicitly captured. We will want to consider at least preference for current consumption and uncertainty about the future. Are there others that should be considered in an initial model? What are reasonable effects of these?

A natural starting point is to assume the utilities of the good and bad guys are of the form

$$U^t(c_t, \ldots, c_T) = \sum_{k=0}^{T-t} D(k) u(c_{t+k}),$$

where $D(k)$ is an exponential discounting function and $u(c_i)$ describes the "instantaneous utility" derived from consumption c_i, as in Samuelson's discounted-utility model [6]. While this model plays a significant role in the economics literature, there are various issues with it, both theoretical and in comparison with experimental data; these have been surveyed by Frederick et al. [2]. Our perspective requires considering utilities over different time periods for different parties. We might also allow different discount rates for different parties, even if just one rate for the good guys and one rate (or a small number of rates) for the bad guys.

Frederick et al. note that the use of multiple discount rates is a natural extension to the basic discounted-utility model and that the correlation between greater discounting and greater risk or uncertainty (in the life of the discounting party) has been suggested throughout the study of intertemporal choice. While the discount rate may be difficult or impossible to prescribe, the potential difference in it between good guys and bad guys argues for enriching the basic model in this way.

As noted by others, there may also be settings in which the defenders and attackers have different but not necessarily strictly opposite security concerns. For example, after an attacker A steals defender D's data (e.g., customers' credit-card numbers), it is in A's interest that the data not be disseminated further, while it is in D's interest that the data not be disseminated except as D sees fit (for example, by purchase from D). Indeed, criminals are aware of this shared incentive, and can use it to offer D the chance to buy back D's data (but then requiring D to trust that A won't go ahead and sell the data elsewhere anyway).

A well-studied example of working with the bad guys (or trying to turn them into good guys by providing a desired pathway for their endeavors) is for the good guys to offer bounties for detected software vulnerabilities (such as put forth in [7] and later explored by others, e.g., [4,5]). However, the cost to do so can be high, and just as in the previous case of purchasing data, there is no guarantee that the vulnerabilities won't still be sold to other bad guys in addition before they can be remediated. We note that the bad guys themselves suffer from lack of trust; researchers (e.g., [1,3]) have sought to better understand the underground markets used by cyberattackers and to use that understanding to suggest methods to disrupt those markets, including by introducing mistrust into them.

There are difficult questions of trust and incentives in all collaborations, but particularly so in collaborations between typically opposing parties. What is the role of trust? If the end goal of the good guys is to wipe out the bad guys, and the end goal of the bad guys is to disrupt the good guys, and the good and bad guys are all rational, why should either trust the other? What sort of partial trust might be reasonable? [8] Does "trust" imply trust to act irrationally?

The area of intertemporal choice has been of interest has been of interest to economists for well over a century. We have argued that a variety of time horizons should be assumed when studying collaboration between entities with opposing goals and that this might be of use, both descriptively and prescriptively, in studying security. The formal model can be enriched in a number of other ways, drawing on work in economics, to inform a richer analysis of this problem and identify beneficial approaches to collaboration that might be realistic to implement.

As noted above, there are non-trivial ethical issues involved in such collaborations that may be difficult or impossible to capture in a formal model. While models might prescribe approaches to collaboration—and we argue that such approaches should be investigated—careful consideration is needed before the adoption of any methods.

References

1. Franklin, J., Paxson, V., Perrig, A., Savage, S.: An inquiry into the nature and causes of the wealth of Internet miscreants. In: Proceedings of the 14th ACM Conference on Computer and Communications Security (2007)
2. Frederick, S., Loewenstein, G., O'Donoghue, T.: Time discounting and time preference: a critical review. J. Econ. Lit. **40**(2), 351–401 (2002)
3. Holz, T., Engelberth, M., Freiling, F.: Learning more about the underground economy: a case-study of keyloggers and dropzones. In: Backes, M., Ning, P. (eds.) ESORICS 2009. LNCS, vol. 5789, pp. 1–18. Springer, Heidelberg (2009)
4. Kannan, K., Telang, R.: An economic analysis of markets for software vulnerabilities. In: Proceedings of the Third Workshop of Economics and Information Security (2004)
5. Ozment, A.: Bug auctions: vulnerability markets reconsidered. In: Proceedings of the Third Workshop of Economics and Information Security (2004)
6. Samuelson, P.A.: A note on measurement of utility. Rev. Econ. Stud. **4**(2), 155–161 (1937)
7. Schecter, S.: Quantitatively differentiating system security. In: Proceedings of the First Workshop of Economics and Information Security (2002)
8. Syverson, P., Meadows, C., Cervesato, I.: Dolev-Yao is no better than Machiavelli. In: First Workshop on Issues in the Theory of Security WITS'00, pp. 87–92 (2000)
9. Zetter, K.: TJX hacker gets 20 years in prison. Wired Magazine (2010). www.wired.com/threatlevel/2010/03/tjx-sentencing

Strange Bedfellows: How and When to Work with Your Enemy (Transcript of Discussion)

Rebecca N. Wright[✉]

DIMACS and Department of Computer Science,
Rutgers University, Piscataway, USA
rebecca.wright@rutgers.edu

Before we talk about collaborating with the enemy, let's consider why anyone would actually collaborate. In some cases, some parties clearly have a common goal, and working together helps them achieve it. For example, maybe we all want to build a bridge between two places, so we all put in our resources to build a bridge and there's an obvious benefit to this collaboration. But in many cases parties have apparently opposite goals, and are still willing to engage in a transaction, for instance, selling an object. If I want to sell you this pen, you can imagine this pen has some value, and either you're going to pay me more than that value, in which case it's good for me but bad for you, or you're going to pay me less than that value, in which case it's good for you but not so good for me. The reason such transactions can work is that we all have our own valuations and our own incentives for doing things. Maybe you value the pen more highly than I do at this particular time and so you're willing to pay a price that I'm willing to accept.

Similarly, one might think purchasing term life insurance is something where the parties have apparently opposite goals. With term life insurance, if I'm buying insurance from you for a term of, say, 20 years, if I die within that 20 years, then you pay my estate, and if I don't, then you don't pay me anything. So it would seem from a financial perspective that I would like you to pay me during these 20 years, and that you would like not to pay me, but in fact both of us would prefer that I not die in the next 20 years, because then you don't have to pay me and I get to still be alive. These examples demonstrate that even in non-opposing situations, non-enemy situations, there can be complicated incentives and individual valuations.

For the purposes of this talk, I'm going to divide the world into the good guys and the bad guys as a convenient shorthand. In the context of enemies, then, the question that I want to look at is when and how can it make sense for the good guys to collaborate with the bad guys, given that both are presumably acting rationally and in their own interests, and so it would appear to be one of the cases where the goals are particularly divergent, a win for the good guys is a lose for the bad guys, and vice versa.

As noted earlier, there are many reasons why people collaborate. Common interest is perhaps the most straightforward case. This can happen even when

Work partially carried out with support from the National Science Foundation under grants CNS-1018557 and CCF-1101690.

B. Christianson et al. (Eds.): Security Protocols 2014, LNCS 8809, pp. 268–275, 2014.
DOI: 10.1007/978-3-319-12400-1_26

parties who are normally in opposition find that in a particular situation they actually are very much in agreement, and so they work together for that particular situation. For example, in a political race with three candidates, sometimes the two apparently weakest candidates will work together to attack the strongest candidate, because each one of them believes that if they can just get that strong candidate out of the way, surely he or she will be the winner afterwards. If they actually succeed and get the strongest candidate out of the way, they'll go back to their position of being clearly in opposition.

Another reason sometimes people with opposing goals collaborate is because they don't realize that they have opposing goals, due to incomplete or misleading information. In this case, party A might be able to take advantage of party B because B doesn't realize that he's not acting in his own best interests. In fact, A may foster this situation, trying to convince B of certain information or valuations that would cause B to do this. This is, for example, how con men operate. Some salesmen do this as well. In the computer security context, honeypots can be seen as an example of this: they're put there as something to look valuable to the attacker, but that typically don't have that real value, and that are hiding the fact that they're actually a dangerous place for the attacker to go in the sense of being more likely to be caught.

Criminal informants are an example of an apparent good guy/bad guy collaboration. In law enforcement, criminal suspects are sometimes offered—or in some reported cases, coerced into—the opportunity to act as informants, helping the police to investigate other suspects in the same case, or in other cases, often in exchange for more lenient treatment in their own cases. In a high profile case of this, actually related to cyber security, a man named Albert Gonzalez reportedly became an informant for the US Secret Service in 2003 after being arrested for charges of ATM fraud and debit card fraud. As an informant he reportedly provided information that led to the arrest of 28 people related to an identity theft ring trafficking in 1.5 million stolen credit card and ATM card numbers. But it turned out that later he was sentenced to 20 years in federal prison for continued work as a criminal hacker at the very same time that he was working with the government, and he was charged with running an identity theft ring involving more than 130 million card numbers, allegedly using his stature and feeding information to the police to help him carry out the larger fraud. This serves as a good example to illustrate that collaborating with people, or entities, that appear to have opposing goals can be fraught with peril.

Another reason that sometimes people collaborate, which we think may be strategically appropriate and interesting to consider for the security protocol setting, is when there's different risk tolerance or different time horizons. Even if A and B have conflicting end goals, they might still be able to both act in accordance with their own preferences in a collaboration. A collaboration might allow party A to benefit in the short term, and party B in the long term, and each chooses the arrangement because it fits their preferred time horizon. Some criminal informant cases may fit into this model, where in the short term it's the best choice available. Or perhaps in the Gonzalez case, it was his long-term plan all along to use his relationship with the police to enhance his criminal status or to misdirect their attention.

Another example of this would be if you are an experienced adult playing chess with a less experienced child you can often win the game by baiting the child by setting up obvious and attractive single-move options that they'll take for apparent short-term gains, while you're setting yourself up to win later.

Audience member: It's a model for venture capital, too.

Reply: Yes.

We think this seems to be a promising approach, where the good guys may be able to collaborate with the bad guys in this kind of way where the good guys take a longer view, and the bad guys find this advantageous in the short term, but then the hope is that in the long term, it would be good for the good guys. It may also be more ethical than the lying and conning approaches, though they may not be entirely unrelated.

I'll come back to a couple of examples of this in the law-enforcement context, where it seems fairly common that there are these kinds of interactions between the good guys and the bad guys. In law enforcement, the good guys might more highly value capturing the big bad guys—the major kingpin criminal—even though it may require years of work, and so they can work with informants who have shorter-term focus, even if it may result in a short-term gain for the informant or other criminal associates. Also looking at different sizes of bad guys, so the good guys might collaborate for various reasons with a large criminal organization like the Mafia to rid the streets of the small-time criminals, which could be beneficial to the good guys because at least then they're dealing with one big organization once the small ones are gone, there's less street crime, so normal people on the street could be safe and happier.

However, this example seems sort of the opposite of what we might hope, in that it might be good for the good guys in the medium term, but then in the end they're going to have this very strong, large criminal organization that's become even more strong with no competition, so that might not be the best thing to do. Further, it may be a closer collaboration than our society typically desires between the good guys and "big" bad guys. Perhaps more usefully, but arguably less plausibly, the good guys might be able to use the small bad guys to help out by providing some resources to the small-time criminals, whether it's financial resources, or other kinds of resources, to help them weaken the large organizations, with the thought that later then the good guys can go after these now weakened large organizations. However, because of the dynamics of the big and the small guys, it's not clear that the small-time criminals can have an impact, nor that they would want to participate, because they may fear the large organizations more than they fear or care about the good guys.

There are also some examples already out there proposed and even in use, some in the context of cyber security. Bounties for software vulnerabilities have been discussed (including at earlier instances of this workshop) and even used. They can take various forms, but the basic idea is that if people find software vulnerabilities, you pay them for those vulnerabilities. Doing so creates a legitimate market for vulnerabilities and can keep them from being used in the criminal market. In some cases, people have found a software vulnerability and then demanded to be paid for it, threatening to sell it to the highest bidder. Similarly, attackers have demanded ransoms to terminate denial-of-service attacks or to return kidnapping victims in the physical world.

In terms of game-theoretic incentives for a ransom for an individual case, it is often rational to pay the ransom to get back a kidnapping victim, or for your data not go be given away, or to get your service turned back on, etc. However, in the long term this can actually contribute to the creation of these market, leading to increased activity as well as increased prices. There is also an issue of trust in transactions with the bad guys. For example, how do you trust that the parties will do as they say they will, and not, for example sell a vulnerability you have bought to other people before you have a chance to fix it? In the kidnapping context, you don't know for sure that you're going to get your loved ones back unharmed. Or in data theft, you don't know for sure that the attackers are not going to give or sell the data to someone else anyway, or that they just won't come back and do the same attack again.

Bruce Christianson: Those two issues are antithetical to some extent though, because if you don't keep faith with the person you're blackmailing, you're destroying the market.

Reply: Yes, that's true. And the bad guys have incentives, too. They may seek to gain as much as possible in a particular transaction, or they may wish to behave differently in order to create a long-term market. Similarly, bad guys seeking ransoms have some incentive to increase the cost to victims who won't pay the ransom in order to establish the importance to victims to be in the market.

Bruce Christianson: So you are creating a market for lemons.

Reply: Yes, potentially. In some sense it's the pull between what's best in an individual transaction vs. what's best in the long term, and that's true regardless of which side of the market you're on.

Bruce Christianson: Exactly.

Frank Stajano: If someone kidnaps my daughter, and I pay the ransom to get her back, I wouldn't call this "me collaborating with the enemy." I'm only doing it under duress; I mean, I would not collaborate with them, they're just forcing me to do something.

Reply: Clearly this is not a transaction you would willingly enter into. But once the transaction has been initiated, even against your will, there is still a question whether you are going to "work with" the kidnappers by paying the ransom, or instead try to work with the police to restore your daughter. This points out that even the very definition of collaboration can depend not only what the final goal is, but also where in the process you are. This phenomenon is present in both the informant situation and the multi-candidate election case as well.

Frank Stajano: Yes, some of the police and criminal scenarios that you had are similar: do I get thrown into jail or do I get my legs broken by the Mafia? Which is worse? I'm not really collaborating.

Reply: Right, it's not the choice you wanted to be making.

Bruce Christianson: It's Prisoner's Dilemma, but the two sides have different views about how many rounds there are going to be.

Frank Stajano: What I would call "collaborating" is a situation where I find that these are in theory the bad guys, but I can see some advantage in being on their side and doing something a bit naughty.

Reply: That is more like the example of the two lesser candidates, or the case where you have both the very liberal and the very conservatives in favor of the option for home schooling in the US, and they disagree with each other on lots of things, but they agree on this particular issue and they will pool their resources for that purpose.

Audience member: When we accuse someone of collaboration we don't mean they're uncoerced, we just mean that we think that they shouldn't be collaborating—for example, when someone is accused of collaborating with the Nazis. Coercion fits into the model of collaboration, sadly.

Reply: "Collaboration" as a word can convey more positive emotions than some of these cases would have.

Turning to how we model the utilities of the different parties in these kinds of settings, in the particular case of time discounts there is work from 1937 modeling time discounts that is a natural starting point. The basic idea is that if you want to look over a period of time at a bunch of consumptions, or actions, or outcomes, then the utility of the result will be the sum over each time period of the utility of the thing happening at the particular period weighted by a discount factor that depends on the time period. Some much more recent work pointed out some problems with this model, in the sense that if you look experimentally at what people do and how they value things, it seems that more parameters are needed to capture their behavior, and that you may need a discount factor that depends not just on the time, but on the item itself to be consumed and additional context, because there's some potential dependence on how much parties value different outcomes at different times, having a lot to do with what's happened so far as well as with changing uncertainty about the future. Presumably, with understanding these issues a bit better, and maybe adding lots more parameters, one could come up with a reasonable model to understand these kinds of decisions.

I also want to talk about the role of trust, because usually some measure of trust is associated with collaboration. (Maybe this is related to why Frank didn't like the kidnapping example being described as "collaboration.") In particular, and related to Virgil's talk yesterday, if trust means that you're going to allow someone to violate your policies, why would you ever want to trust your enemies? Trust is not as simple as "I trust you" without conditions or parameters. Usually, if I want to be precise about it, I trust you to do certain things, to carry out certain kinds of activities, etc. The kind of trust that is relevant here is when can you trust that you know enough about your enemies' capabilities, or incentives, or knowledge, or other relevant circumstances, that you have enough knowledge about how they'll behave, that overall you feel you'll end up better off from these actions that you're going to take. Just like in any other setting, trust can be viewed as a willingness to take on risk. In working with a bad guy, then, you are not necessarily trusting them to act in your best interest by explicitly considering your interests, or to become a good guy instead of a bad guy, rather, you're trusting that your beliefs or assumptions about how they (and others) will behave in the situations you think are likely to arise are sufficiently accurate to warrant a choice to work with them. There is a risk that you're wrong, and perhaps the bigger and badder the bad guy is, the worse the risk is.

Another option, rather than trying to work directly with the bad guys, would be to set the bad guys against each other and then step back and let it all happen. That can also be framed in the spirit of collaboration, or at least in the spirit of working with the bad guys, for example by anonymously providing resources—financial or otherwise—to the bad guys to work against each other, or by cultivating existing mistrust that the bad guys have for each other. If they don't already have mistrust, it may be possible to inject some mistrust, or to share information or misinformation to foster mistrust.

To summarize, it might be necessary to collaborate with the enemy in order to make some progress in securing systems in today's world where there are so many enemies infiltrating our systems. There are many questions for possible discussion: Is any of this a useful way to think about things at all? If we look specifically at a time discounting formulation, does it apply to any of the security ideas that we've been hearing about today and yesterday, or are there other existing cyber security solutions that fit this model? Can thinking about things in this framework, and thinking about what is and isn't a collaboration, drive innovative solutions that use this kind of collaboration with the bad guys in order to ultimately advance the good guys position? There are some ethical issues here—some kinds of collaboration seem more appropriate, or more legal, than others. Do those ethical perils get too much in the way? What about the difficulty of trust, is it inherently too difficult to trust the bad guys to make this be a workable approach, or is it ultimately workable?

Frank Stajano: It's a pity Virgil isn't here because I think that what you mentioned relates to his idea that the party you must trust can put up some collateral that protects you against the risk of them misbehaving. If they misbehave, you receive the collateral as compensation, and that would certainly help.

Reply: He also had this distinction that there can be the adversaries you understand completely, which you could view as being the ones that you can trust to behave in a certain way because you know enough about them. And then there are the ones that you don't know enough about, for whom having collateral can reduce risk to an acceptable level.

Frank Stajano: If they put up some collateral, then your risk is bounded, because you know that if they misbehave then this compensation comes your way.

Audience member: This often implies a trusted third party is needed to manage the collateral and it's potential collection. Finding a third party that both the good guys and the bad guys trust is often hard.

Bruce Christianson: If often doesn't matter if they don't trust the same third party, you just need enough third parties that everybody's got a correctness proof, so long as they don't have to reveal what their proof is.

Reply: Right, but each has to trust someone.

Michael Roe: Well that's interesting. In economics you quite often see the time discount, but you very rarely see it in this kind of field. The only thing in security field that's kind of similar is when you're talking about cover time and secrecy, the idea that if you've got some secret, then it's probably going to become public eventually, but you've got some notion of how long it is useful for you to keep it secret for, and maybe becoming public after that horizon doesn't matter.

Bruce Christianson: But the number to be less than one. It may be that there's something that increases in value for me over time, whereas for you its value is never going to be bigger than it is now. And the fact that things have different values to different people decides what makes commerce worthwhile in the first place. We don't sufficiently take that into account for security, rather we tend to say everything has a market price and that's the same for everyone, and I think that is a fallacy.

Reply: Yes. Part of it is that many of these things are of unknown value—people don't know their valuations. This is true in the economic world as well, but economists seem willing to overlook it, presumably as a useful or even necessary simplification.

Bruce Christianson: Yes. For example, "I will sell you this sack for $10."

Reply: We don't know how much our data is worth; we don't know how much our systems are worth. Solutions that require you determine valuations in advance require a different way of thinking about things.

Luca Viganò: There are several interesting dimensions for what concerns time. You mentioned the temporal aspect very briefly—long term vs. short-term goals, but that is also from a matter of perspective. Think for instance of three-player chess which is continuing on the example that you mentioned. There, a typical winning strategy would be to ally with one of the two other players, destroy the third one, and then it's between you and the other one. But it could be a losing strategy depending on how you actually play this alliance. A typical example, which you might want to consider, is when the Allied troops invaded Sicily and Italy in the Second World War, they made a pact with the Mafia, because they had local control. The Mafia was then actually quite low in power because the fascist party in Italy had imprisoned most of them, and still many Italian Americans came back from Italy to organize the invasion, and it worked. However, the long-term undesired effect is that the Mafia rose again. So that aspect has to be considered also for the economics, because it will play a major role. It's kind of related to the question that Frank asked me yesterday with the guardian agent, what will happen if you had it inside the system, at some point it might fight back against you, and indeed, that is what can happen.

Reply: Yes. In particular, all of these examples in which the strategy is to pick of multiple adversaries one by one can be at risk of leaving a too-strong adversary standing. There's a risk that you appear to be making all this progress, but then the end state is not necessarily better than where you started. If done well, the weaker adversaries help you neutralize the stronger adversaries, but don't themselves become too strong in the process.

Dieter Gollmann: I think it fits to your example of Albert Gonzalez, collaboration and espionage as a theme. However you view the spy, whether the spy is the bad guy or the good guy (because he spying for you). In the case of a certain level of high-quality spy, the spy would collaborate with you when he's actually being spied on, in order to become an insider and learn more about the situation. So maybe there are ideas from counterespionage that could be useful here.

Reply: Right—infiltration as a long-term strategy that may look less useful in the short term, but sets the infiltrator up for future success.

Joan Feigenbaum: But that's not just a matter of long term vs. short term. If someone is going to be a mole long term, he is going to have to continue to get wins for the enemy, There will be an ongoing, very fine line between being a mole and being a true double agent who really is working for both agencies (presumably at any given time for whichever agency he can get the biggest win for). You probably don't want true double agents.

Audience member: I was wondering whether you could apply this to storage of personal data that you may later regret. Students often do things in their student days that they regret later. Perhaps people could come to say: the value of the service you are giving me now needs to be much higher if you want to store my data for longer. For example, you can store information about my phone calls for 10 years as long as you give me a really good system, and you can only store it for a year if you give me a bad one.

Reply: Right, you want it to be valued for the valuation of your future self as opposed to your current valuation.

On the Key Role Intelligence Agencies Can Play to Restore Our Democratic Institutions

Yvo Desmedt[1,2](✉)

[1] The University of Texas at Dallas, Richardson, USA
[2] University College London, London, UK
Yvo.Desmedt@UTDallas.edu

Abstract. After the Snowden leaks, it has become evident that a discussion is needed on how to reorganize the huge intelligence agencies so that they fit a Western thinking and to avoid that they are evolving into a clone of what the KGB and the Stasi used to be. Well before the Snowden leaks, the author had been thinking along this line.

On the 26th of October 2012, at the closed workshop on "Online Security & Civil Rights: a Fine Ethical Balance," Hertfordshire, UK, the author put forward the idea that modern intelligence agencies should be split. The part which is involved today in mass surveillance, should work for the people and no longer for the government. That means that the intelligence agencies should spy on these working in the government and these working for lobbyists. The recipient of this information should be the public at large. The foundation of this idea comes from the Magna Carta and the US Bill of Rights that regard "We the People" as the trustworthy party and the government as potentially corrupt.

In this paper we present the above ideas put forward by the author at the aforementioned 2012 Hertfordshire workshop. We also reflect on these 2012 ideas in the context of the Snowden leaks.

1   Introduction

Since the summer of 2013 the Snowden leaks have dominated the discussions on privacy. So far, only a small fraction of the data collected by Snowden has been published in newspapers [20].

Although most of the information revealed by the newspapers was well known to technical experts who took a broader interest in the topic, it seems the public at large only became aware of these activities after the Snowden leaks. Prior to these newspaper publications, books such as "The *Codebreakers*" [17] and "*The Puzzle Palace*" [2] revealed NSA capabilities. Moreover, the Patriot Act [22], gave the government the legal means to move to the current situation. Finally, for several years now NSA is interested in the "Black Hat" conference, not hiding the fact that in today's world, intelligence agencies are hiring hackers, buying malware, etc.

When in 2012, the author, who was aware of NSA's capabilities and the legal means the Patriot Act provided, was invited to the closed workshop on "Online

© Springer International Publishing Switzerland 2014
B. Christianson et al. (Eds.): Security Protocols 2014, LNCS 8809, pp. 276–285, 2014.
DOI: 10.1007/978-3-319-12400-1_27

Security & Civil Rights: a Fine Ethical Balance," Hertfordshire, UK, he decided to reflect on the ethical and civil rights aspect of massive eavesdropping. In the light of the Snowden leaks and the debate on privacy, it is time to have this 26th of October 2012 presentation published. Note that this lecture was given prior to the leaks.

In putting these 2012 ideas forward, the author was largely influenced by his statement during the Question/Comment part of the panel at the ACISP 1997, Sydney, Australia. Since the panel had only representatives of the *pro-key-escrow* viewpoint, a careful reaction was needed. The author then stated[1]:

> At the height of the industrial revolution, Marx pointed out that *private ownership* can be abused. The solution he proposed was to have the *government* nationalize all private property. Today, during our information technology revolution, we see governments argue that *private data* can be abused and they have proposed as a solution the reduction of the rights of the private owner. In the light of the analogy to Marx's reasoning, we call this philosophy: cyber-communism.

In this paper we put forward the ideas as they were presented at the aforementioned 2012 workshop. To avoid being influenced by the Snowden leaks, and to reflect the original ideas, we will quote as much as possible from the slides that were used on the 26th of October 2012. To maintain the quality of the publication, comments received during the aforementioned 2012 workshop are discussed in a separate section (see Sect. 7) and in footnotes. When we refer to the 2014 presentation given at the Security Protocols Workshop, we refer to "SPW 2014." Finally, Sect. 8 incorporates what was learned from the Snowden leaks and discusses some of the reactions. We also remind the reader that these proceedings contain a transcript part, which we also recommend to consult.

2 Justifying Governmental Eavesdropping

According to the foundations of "communism, fascism (and Nazism) the government is[2] considered as a *trusted power.*"

"Western society, on the other hand, finds its foundations in such documents as: [the] Magna Carta [and the] US Bill of Rights. Looking at the US Constitution, we see it starts with: 'We the People'. We see that government is considered as a potential threat and that freedom protects us against abuse *by the government.*" This is quite clear from documents such as [30], which explains the reasoning behind the (US) 2nd Amendment.

---

[1] The exact wording not having been recorded, the statement is based on the author's and participants' recollection.

[2] A more appropriate use might have been "should be" considered. However, one of the SPW 2014 participants, originally from China, confirmed after the 2014 lecture that in her classes on Marxism, Marx viewed the government as being the trusted party. Whether the population of communist countries regard their government as trustworthy or not, is beside the point.

As a *logical* consequence of these very different viewpoints on trust in the government, we concluded that: "in communist and fascist countries, governmental eavesdropping (using, e.g., malware) is easy to justify." Moreover, "seeing the foundations of freedom [and] the different role of the government in Western societies, eavesdropping by the government should only be an *exception*, where the exception is truly limited."

We can wonder "what are the exceptions? September 11 has been used as an example," which we discuss in the next section.

3   Impact of September 11

As stated at the 2012 workshop "11 years after the September 11 attack, security seems more important than ever. However, we should wonder [why] governments are taking measures, *year after year* bringing us further away from a free society [that is] based on Civil Rights, Human Rights, etc.

We should be willing to compare this trend to what happened in Germany after the November 7 1938 terrorist attack in Paris that killed Ernst vom Rath, a German diplomat. In contrast to popular believe it did *not* trigger *immediately* the requirements for Jews to wear the Star of David on their right arm. In fact, it took until November 23, 1939 until the Nazi Governor-General of occupied Poland, introduced the requirement" [26].

"In these 11 years after September 11, we have seen:

- in the *UK*: new rules were introduced from [the] 1st of February 2005 requiring marriage visitor visa, *except for Anglicans*." Moreover, "certain [UK] Islamistic organizations" have been declared "terrorist organizations. These acts imply it is *illegal to even mention the names of these organizations*! This implies that one cannot debate whether these organizations were indeed terrorist organizations or whether they were just expressing freedom of speech.
- the dress code rules, [such] as: the anti-scarf law (10th February 2004) in France." It is remarkable that one can "easily find pictures on the internet of famous non-islam people using a scarf." Moreover, more anti-Islam measures such as "no-face covering laws in France (since April 2011) and in Belgium (July 2011)" have been introduced.
- in the USA [we now have] the Patriot Act [and] the DHS fusion centers" [25].

One can wonder whether this trend will continue? "The answer depends from region to region." Indeed, in 2012, the "Tokyo Governor Shintaro Ishihara,... created a new extreme right wing party [and] a new extreme right wing party in Greece received lots of votes. In the US, a US Senate subcommittee... stated" [29]:

> DHS' work with those state and local fusion centers has not produced useful intelligence to support federal counterterrorism efforts... sometimes endangering citizens' civil liberties and Privacy Act protections

Finally "on October 16, 2012, a US appeals court quashed the earlier conviction of Salim Hamdan, Bin Laden's driver." The reason given by the court was that "he had been jailed for 'aiding and abetting terrorism' between '1996 to 2001', but that only became illegal after September 11, 2001" [21].

4   A Critical Look at Our Modern Western Democracy[3]

When we look at "the '*democracy*' we live in, we see that checks and balances of our modern democracies are failing at an alarming rate! We find that except for the judicial system, both the executive [and] the legislative branches of government have been hijacked by lobbyists. Examples are:

- After banks lobbied for deregulation, we have seen that we now have *neo-anarchists*[4] in the government, i.e., Greenspan, who caused the trillion dollar "Great-Recession" [10,13,15].
- According to the "official report of The Fukushima Nuclear Accident Independent Investigation Commission [27][5] lobbyists played a key role in the Fukushima disaster!
- On the 60th birthday of the German invasion of Poland, the EU made the selling of 60 Watt (and over) Edison bulbs illegal and forced it being replaced by the Compact Fluorescent Lightbulbs. These lightbulbs are quite controversial, since: they contain mercury [12] [and are] well known to cause migraines [7]!" By having overruled the rights of the individual, we see that capitalism has been replaced by what [is called Inverted Totalitarianism] in which the rights of corporations outweight these of the individual and that the government is there to facilitate this.
- the exclusion of the EPA [US Environmental Protection Agency] rules to *inside areas* of homes and other buildings." As an example, the American Lung Association [5] warns that
  > Chemicals used in some new carpets, carpet pads and the adhesives used to install them can harm your health. Some of these chemicals and glues are made with volatile organic compounds (VOCs), which emit odors and pollutants.
- deployment of full-body scanners. "Michael Chertoff, Secretary of Homeland Security (2005–2009), [is] now [the] founder of the Chertoff Group [and] represents manufacturers of full-body scanners [11,18]. We have seen the rushed adaptation of this technology *without* the proper medical checks, as became clear when the EU stopped its deployment on November 13, 2011 [16].
- the massive use of antibiotics in soap, sprays at airports, etc.

With a US president who promised not to take lobbyist[s] in his government, but did anyway, we should wonder whether democracy has been replaced by: *Demagogcracy.*

[We can wonder what happened to] your grandfather's *capitalism*? [In classical capitalism,] failed corporations go bankrupt. In Nazism, corporations too

---

[3] The original title of the corresponding slide was "Not your grandfather's capitalism/democracy."

[4] "Proponents of anarchism (known as "anarchists") advocate stateless societies" (from Wikipedia). In this context a *neo-anarchist* could be regarded as a proponent advocating societies without proper regulations.

[5] At the 2012 workshop, this statement was received in a very critically way. The author responded that the cited web page is at a Japanese governmental site.

crucial from a national viewpoint, were nationalized. Today, we see that corporations that view themselves as too important, get bailed out. Examples [include] Citibank and several UK banks, Chrysler and GM. As in Nazism (see, e.g., IBM[6]) we see a collaboration between corporations and government. [Modern] examples [include the] location obtained by mobile phones [and] social networks.

Moreover, we can wonder whether the foundation of capitalism, i.e., *competition*, still exists? Indeed, we have seen [that] prices of products are kind of arbitrary and competition is limited. [An example is the high cost of] Apple's (pre-Samsung) iPhones. [Moreover] outsourcing did *not* reduce the cost of products in Western shops." For example, Western toothbrushes sold in Beijing stores cost a fraction of what they cost in the West. Finally, "shareholders are often the real 'customers' of modern corporations." The classical economic theory of 'supply and demand', assumes an increase in supply, will decrease the costs. However, such theories ignore the fact that today "shareholders are often the real 'customers' of modern corporations."

5   Potential Solutions

"Having neo-anarchist[s] in the government causing the Great-Recession [see Sect. 4], having lobbyist[s] dominate the government [see e.g. [1,6]], we have moved [to] a society in which the biggest threat to our Western society comes from the government and lobbyists, no longer [from] a disorganized individual anarchist, [or from] unions (who lost their power), etc. So, how can we restore our democracy?

Potential solutions [could be to] make government[s] responsible: [such] as in Ukraine"[7]. However, [relying on] the judicial system may lead to unexpected problems, [as shown by] the *New York Times* [23] article titled: 'Italy Orders Jail Terms for 7 Who Didn't Warn of Deadly Earthquake.'

Another potential solution is to "increase salary of governmental employees: e.g., [an approach] used in Singapore. [Indeed] today the salary of the UK prime minister is less than the one of several US Computer Science professors." Alternatively, some Gulf countries, such as Saudi Arabia, have a "negative tax," which means that instead of requiring citizens to pay tax, it is the state who pays its citizens!

The main focus from now on, "will be on using *Intelligence Agencies* to solve the problem.

Current intelligence agencies are active against foreign countries, foreign spies, etc., [and] their own population (e.g., MI5). They provide information about the individual *to* the government.

However, with the US Constitution starting with 'We the People,' the *government is there for the people* and *not* the other way around. With Western

---

[6] The fact that IBM electromechanical sorting machines were used by the Nazis to identify these who were Jewish is well known [3].

[7] In 2011 Prime Minister Yulia Tymoshenko was convicted for 7 years for her deal on Russian gas [28].

governments failing, we *need to split these agencies* into these that spy for the government (minor, except when the target is foreign), [and] these that *spy for the people*. This proposal could be implemented as following: [the] *target* [would be] lobbyists and anyone working for the government." Related to the question/comment, what part of the communications and which ones should be eavesdropped, we are inspired by "the Theresa May proposal" [9].

"We adapt the proposal of the UK Home Secretary's (Theresa May) to keep track of who talks to who via internet, i.e., the People Intelligence Agencies inform the public who inside the government talks to who inside a lobbyist organization." Moreover, we suggest the *"Starting date* [to be] 2014." Indeed, "2014 is the year one can regard the fight against terrorism to be won sufficiently to have NATO pull its troops out of Afghanistan." Moreover, "George Orwell predicted a Big Brother society in his novel: *Nineteen Eighty-Four.* 2014 is 30 years later, a good moment to undo the current Big Brother society that has damaged freedom." Related to the question how long this should go on, we propose a "test period for 10 years. If Theresa May is right that this does not violate human rights, then the Western governments cannot complain. After the 10 years test period, a debate among the population could start to see whether her arguments to introduce this against the UK population as a whole, makes sense or not."

We now analyze potential impacts of this proposal. We consider several scenarios. We first start with looking at the UK "Leveson Inquiry." During a part of this inquiry on the involvement of the "Murdoch family and the UK governments, only 1 (former) prime minister said that he [felt] pressured by Murdoch. With the intelligence information: (former) prime ministers may be more careful, checking their records before replying."

The Fukushima accident might have been prevented if the advice to increase the height of the Fukushima stormwall would had been followed. However, the link between lobbyists and the Japanese government implies relaxed rules. If the Japanese People Intelligence Agencies would have revealed this link and its potential consequences, the accident might have been prevented.

Similarly, if in the US the cozy relation between lobbyists and the government would have been undermined, lobbyists might have failed in rushing full body scanners without a proper medical study.

"So, *People Intelligence Agencies* can help restore the check[s] and balance[s] in our democratic Western institutions." By having intelligence information flow in both directions, we see we move towards a more *balanced way.*"

6 Original Conclusions

The following conclusions were drawn. First, one can state that: "It is ethical for a communist country to have cyber-communism and for a Nazist regime to have cyber-Nazism (in which cooperations and the government collaborate in cyber space and the rights of corporations dominate the one of the individual). However, in a democratic society, believing in human rights, wiretapping should only be [performed] in exceptional circumstances."

The second conclusion was that "Western societies should stop handing over a victory to Al Qaeda. Indeed, September 11 has changed our society to a frightening degree. Due to the reactions to September 11, we are now on a slippery slope! We should stop installing technology and laws which will facilitate the next Holocaust. That means that each camera used by the FBI should be regarded as violating the restriction on 'random search.' [Moreover,] $10,000 cash laws make escaping the next Holocaust impossible as became clear when [former] US Senator Lieberman convinced Mastercard, VISA, etc., to stop accepting donations to WikiLeaks."

The third conclusion was that "Western societies should restore human rights, otherwise they will continue being criticized by China for being hypocrites."

The fourth point made was that: "We need to extend human rights to include cyber-freedom and virtual-freedom." The following examples were mentioned. We need to:

- "introduce privacy at the constitutional level.
- [make] it much harder to violate the constitution."
- We need to take into account that "today we live in a virtual world in which we have many nomads (businesses travelers, crew on a ship, etc.). The current constitution does not extend to nomads."

Finally "we hope the proposal to have People Intelligence Agencies may restore the checks and balances we used to have."

7   Feedback from the 2012 Workshop

Several questions and comments were given after the 2012 lecture. Some of these comments were given during the banquet of the workshop.

It was pointed out that Brin's book "*The Transparent Society*" [4] predates the ideas put forward. However, as pointed out by Schneier [24] Brin's proposal is *symmetric*. Today the role of eavesdropping is *anti-symmetric*. The proposal made here is primarily anti-symmetric, so different from Brin's. Moreover, the proposal is more refined. Indeed, intelligence agencies would still collect military intelligence and continue to spy on foreign countries and this information would *not* be released to the public.

One of prediction Brin made in his book came true. The size of cameras became so small one can hide them everywhere. However, the argument that this authorizes the government to use cameras to massively spy on their citizens is wrong. Indeed, some types of guns fit in a purse, and so can easily be hidden. However, this is not a valid argument to argue that gun regulations, used in many countries, should be abolished. In this regard, the proposal we make is again quite different from Brin's, since we stated that (see Sect. 6) "each camera used by the FBI should be regarded as violating the restriction on 'random search'."

Another question that was raised is why intelligence agencies would change their role? To answer this, we focus primarily on the US, although some of the ideas generalize. First, the former KGB has been replaced by two organizations, showing such organizations are sometimes reorganized. Second, the *US Supreme Court* might reduce the role of intelligence agencies. The recent Supreme Court case involving the search of data on smartphones [19] is a step in the right direction. However, such ruling would not reverse the role of intelligence agencies. A third solution would be when citizens sue the government and sue the phone companies to have the metadata of government employees released under the freedom of information act. Using such an argument to obtain the metadata of communications from lobbyists might be more difficult. Fourth, once in a while idealist follow their viewpoint; an extreme example was former Secretary of State Frank B. Kellogg, who was instrumental to outlaw war in 1928. Such idealist may succeed in convincing the government and/or congress. Fifth, a new cold war may force the West to stop its hypocracy and force it to restore freedom and human rights to what they used to be before the invention of the telephone. The following solution was suggested to the author *without* his endorsement: the suggestion was that citizens could start planting eavesdropping devices inside non-military governmental buildings.

Obviously, our proposal would only work if we can trust this task to agencies. One should not forget that people who join such agencies are very patriotic. Given them a new target, they will likely take their task seriously.

Finally, the following references were suggested to the author [8,14].

8   Putting the Proposal in the Post-Snowden Context

The Snowden leaks confirm the 2012 idea that the focus of agencies has to change.

Snowden only leaked NSA data. What other Western agencies are working against human rights in the West? Do we need leakers in other agencies (CIA, DHS, FBI, MI5, MI6, etc.)?

International agreements should *extend* the rights of foreigners visiting *friendly* countries. In other words, we need agreements on *limiting* spying on foreigners from friendly countries.

Finally, it should be pointed out that although NSA has built a huge eavesdropping capability, it is not a decision making agency. When asked by e.g., CIA, FBI, etc., they will provide information.

Acknowledgment. The slides used at the aforementioned 2012 workshop thanked the organizers and "the anonymous people from intelligence agencies for privately expressing their concerns about the US Patriot Act, and researchers consulting for European Governments stating that what they are doing on the cyber topic violates their constitutions."

The author also thanks Bruce Christianson for encouraging him to submit the position paper to the Security Protocols Workshop, Cambridge, and the many participants of both this workshop and the 2012 "Online Security & Civil Rights: a Fine Ethical Balance" workshop for their feedback.

References

1. Anonymous: Word of Mouth Democracy for the 99%: A Corporate Spiritual Democracy. CreateSpace Independent Publishing Platform, 26 September 2013
2. Bamford, J.: The Puzzle Palace. Penguin Books, New York (1985)
3. Black, E.: IBM and the Holocaust: The Strategic Alliance between Nazi Germany and America's Most Powerful Corporation. Three Rivers Press, New York (2001)
4. Brin, D.: The Transparent Society: Will Technology Force Us To Choose Between Privacy And Freedom?. Perseus Books, Cambridge (1999)
5. Carpets. http://www.lung.org/healthy-air/home/resources/carpets.html
6. Connolly, M.: Granite state could use more 'blue sky'. Concord Monitor, 5 March 2012
7. Cooke, R.: Migraine and me. The Guardian, 9 May 2009. http://www.theguardian.com/lifeandstyle/2009/may/10/migraine
8. National Research Council: Protecting Individual Privacy in the Struggle Against Terrorists: A Framework for Program Assessment. The National Academies Press, Washington, DC (2008)
9. Dunn, T.M.: Track crime on net or we'll see more people die. The Sun, 3 December 2012
10. Evans, K.: Jeffrey Sachs rails against ex-fed chief Greenspan. The Wall Street Journal (2009)
11. Fear pays: Chertoff, ex-security officials slammed for cashing in on government experience. The Huffington Post, 23 November 2010. http://www.huffingtonpost.com/2010/11/23/fear_pays_chertoff_n_787711.html (updated 25 March 2011)
12. Fischetti, M.: The switch is on. Sci. Am. **298**, 98–99 (2008)
13. Goodman, P.S.: Taking hard new look at a Greenspan legacy. New York Times, 8 October 2008. http://www.nytimes.com/2008/10/09/business/economy/09greenspan.html
14. Hosein, G.: Threatening the open society: Comparing anti-terror policies and strategies in the U.S. and Europe. Comparative report. https://www.privacyinternational.org/sites/privacyinternational.org/files/file-downloads/comparativeterrorreportdec2005.pdf. Privacy International, 13 December 2005 DOI:10.1007/978-3-319-12400-1
15. Isely, L.: Alan Greenspan's deregulation and inadequate regulation led to another bubble. The Nation, 7 February 2013. http://nationbuilders.thenation.com/profiles/blogs/alan-greenspan-s-deregulation-and-inadequate-regulation-led-to DOI:10.1007/978-3-319-12400-1 •
16. Jaslow, R.: Europe bans airport scanners over cancer fears: How about U.S.? CBS News, 17 November 2011
17. Kahn, D.: The Codebreakers. MacMillan Publishing Co., New York (1967)
18. Kindy, K.: Ex-homeland security chief head said to abuse public trust by touting body scanners. The Washington Post, 1 January 2010. http://www.washingtonpost.com/wp-dyn/content/article/2009/12/31/AR2009123102821.html
19. Liptak, A.: Major ruling shields privacy of cellphones: Supreme court says phones can't be searched without a warrant. New York Times, 25 June 2014. http://www.nytimes.com/2014/06/26/us/supreme-court-cellphones-search-privacy.html
20. Only 1% of Snowden files published - Guardian editor BBC News UK, 3 December 2013. http://www.bbc.com/news/uk-25205846

21. Osama bin Laden driver's conviction quashed by US appeals court, 16 October 2012. http://www.theguardian.com/world/2012/oct/16/osama-bin-laden-driver-conviction-quashed

22. Patriot Act, bill summary & status 107th congress (2001–2002) h.r.3162. http://thomas.loc.gov/cgi-bin/bdquery/z?d107:H.R.3162:

23. Povoledo, E., Fountain, H.: Italy orders jail terms for 7 who didn't warn of deadly earthquake. The New York Times, 22 October 2012

24. Schneier, B.: The myth of the 'transparent society', 6 March 2008. http://www.wired.com/politics/security/commentary/securitymatters/2008/03/securitymatters_0306

25. State and major urban area fusion centers. http://www.dhs.gov/state-and-major-urban-area-fusion-centers DOI:10.1007/978-3-319-12400-1

26. The ghettos (a teachers guide to the holocaust). http://fcit.usf.edu/holocaust/timeline/ghettos.htm

27. The official report of The Fukushima Nuclear Accident Independent Investigation Commission, executive summary (2012). http://warp.da.ndl.go.jp/info:ndljp/pid/3856371/naiic.go.jp/wp-content/uploads/2012/09/NAIIC_report_lo_res10.pdf

28. Tymoshenko convicted, sentenced to 7 years in prison, ordered to pay state $188 million. Kyiv Post, 11 October 2011. http://www.kyivpost.com/content/ukraine/tymoshenko-convicted-sentenced-to-7-years-in-priso-114528.html

29. U.S. senate report on fusion centers, committee on homeland security and governmental affairs (full text) October 2012. https://archive.org/stream/446657-fusion-centers/446657-fusion-centers_djvu.txt

30. Vandercoy, D.E.: The history of the second amendment. Valparaiso Univ. Law Rev. **28**, 1007–1039 (1994)

On the Key Role Intelligence Agencies Can Play to Restore Our Democratic Institutions (Transcript of Discussion)

Yvo Desmedt[1,2]

[1] The University of Texas at Dallas, Richardson, USA
[2] University College London, London, UK
Yvo.Desmedt@UTDallas.edu

So I'm going to talk about the key role intelligence agencies can play to restore our democratic institutions. So this talk has a very interesting history. I was invited to a conference, a workshop actually organized by philosophers called the Online Security & Civil Rights: a Fine Ethical Balance in 2012, October 26th to the 27th, here in the UK. It was a workshop on invitation only, and so this means the talk was pre Snowden. Unfortunately the philosophers did not like the talk, and so the talk wasn't actually one of the invited ones for publication. And I would like to thank basically Bruce for encouraging me to submit the position paper here.

So what I will do is I will actually first of all talk about the 2012 talk, I actually keep the page numbers and the format exactly the same, so you basically will see a pre Snowden talk, but then being repeated, and Bruce has heard the talk before, so if I don't do as a good job as I did then, then please tell me OK. So then I will actually talk about the feedback, the feedback that I received at the end of the talk, and also the feedback I received during a dinner and at other occasions. And then I will put it in the basically post Snowden context, and then I will entertain questions and discussions.

So here now starts the 2012 talk, and as you see this starts to basically be back at zero. So the same title, except that the date has changed, OK. There are a few other changes if you pay attention. And so what I actually said then is, I thanked the organisers for inviting me, although I have not published a lot on ethics, and I also thanked the anonymous people from intelligence agencies for privately expressing their concerns about the US Patriot Act, and researchers consulting for the European governments stating what they are doing on the cyber topic violates their constitutions.

Frank Stajano: The first day and the last line.

Reply: D, it's D.

Frank Stajano: Is it the researchers or the governments?

Reply: European governments. So what I did decide, basically start with Introduction, then Justifying Government Eavesdropping, the Impact of September

11, we are no longer in your Grandfather's Capitalism or Democracy, what are the Potential Solutions, and the Conclusions.

So the potential issues I was considering to talk about was basically when I was invited, the Western Great Firewall, the defence against malware, an idea I proposed in 1998, ethics of teaching hacking, a big discussion with Gene Spafford, don't forget this was a workshop on ethics, but instead I decided to reflect back on a paper with Rebecca Wright, who is just coming in the room, and also with Mike Burmester and Alec Yasinsac, which was presented in 2004, exactly at this workshop, and which was heavily influenced by September 11. And so it actually also, I wanted to reflect back on my statement that I made during the completely pro-key-escrow panel that took place at ACISP, which is basically Australasian Conference in Information Security Protection in 1997, which took place in Sydney. And so I stated there as basically a comment, at the height of the industrial revolution, Marx pointed out that private ownership can be abused. The solution he proposed was to have government nationalise all private property. Today, during our information technology revolution we see governments argue that private data can be abused and they have proposed as a solution the reduction of the rights of the private owner. In the light of the analogy to Marx's reasoning we call this philosophy cyber communism. So my talk will focus on spying of the governments on the population. That's a comment that I did make, I mean, this is the talk basically spying of the governments on the population in respect to basically democracies.

So first of all can we justify governmental eavesdropping? And it's easy to do if you are a communist country or a fascist country, because what happens is that the government is considered a trusted authority, a trusted power. Western society, on the other hand, finds its foundations in such documents as the Magna Carta, and the US Civil Rights Bill. And if you look at the US Constitution then you see it starts with the words "We the People". So we see that governments are considered as a potential threat and that freedom protects us against abuse by the government. So in communist and fascist countries, governmental eavesdropping, since they are a trusted power, is easy to justify. So now the question is, what about the Western societies. Seeing the foundations of freedom, the different role of the government in Western societies, eavesdropping by the government should only be an exception, where the exception is truly limited. So the question then is, what are the exceptions, and September 11 is usually used as the example, or I would say, as an example.

Now what's the impact of September 11. And in particular that's why in 2012 after the talk there was given here before with Rebecca, Mike Burmester and Alec Yasinsac, it was time to reflect back to that. So 11 years after the September 11 attack, don't forget it's 2012 this talk, security seems more important than ever before. However we should wonder governments are not taking measures year after year bringing us further and further away from a free society based on Civil Rights and Human Rights, etc. So we should be willing to compare this trend to what happened in Germany after November 7 1938 terrorist attack in Paris that killed Ernst vom Rath, a German diplomat. What is important is that in contrast to popular belief it did not trigger immediately the requirements for Jews to wear the Star of David on their right arm. In fact it took until November 23 1939 until the Nazi governor of occupied Poland introduced the requirement. And then afterwards others actually followed in Germany and occupied countries.

So while we see in these 11 years after September 11, we have seen in the UK new rules were introduced from the 1st February 2005 requiring marriage visitor visa except for Anglicans. How can you do that in a Western society? The declaration that certain Islamic organisations are terrorist organisations. Now the way it's done in Britain is that these acts imply it is illegal to even mention the name of these organisations, and this implies that one cannot debate whether these organisations were indeed terrorist organisations, or whether they were just expressing freedom of speech. I lived here in the UK when this thing happened and I can tell you that in the United States there are similar organisations, and they would be regarded as under freedom of speech, I'm not saying all, but some. But I cannot mention these organisations or I would break the UK law, and so I cannot even argue for or against, we cannot debate it, because we cannot mention the case.

The dress code rules, as for example, the anti-scarf law, 10th February 2004, in France. Even though you easily can find pictures on the Internet of very famous non-Islam people using a scarf, and here is for example one webpage, also the Queen of England uses frequently a scarf. So if you go to Australia and you are a kid, and you don't bring a scarf or a hat to school, you are not allowed to play on the playground because they are worried about the destruction of the ozone layer, and the cancer it causes to you, OK. Now with global warming France does not care about that apparently. There are also now face covering laws in France since April 2011, and in Belgium July 2011. In the United States we have the Patriot Act, which we all know about it, heavily debated. We have DHS fusion centers, etc. So the question is, will this trend continue.

So the answer depends from region to region. So for example, yesterday, don't forget it was 2012, the Tokyo Governor, Shintaro Ishihara, has created a new extreme right wing party. A new extreme right wing party in Greece received lots of votes. And in the US a US Senate subcommittee recently in 2012 stated, DHS work with those state and local fusion centres has not produced useful intelligence to support federal counter-terrorism efforts, blah, blah, blah, sometimes endangering citizens civil liberties and Privacy Act protections. On October 16 2012 a US appeals court quashed the earlier conviction of Salin Hamdan, Bin Laden's driver. The argument was that he had been jailed for aiding and abetting terrorism between 1996 to 2001, but that only became illegal after September 11 2001, and so therefore he couldn't actually be convicted on that.

So now the question is when we actually see all these reasons to bring in, or which we could say, are we on a slippery road with bringing in all these measures, how is our society actually working today, how is our capitalism and democracy working. So let's start with democracy first we live in. We see that checks and balances of our modern democracies are failing at an alarming rate.

So we find that except for the judicial system, and even there you can debate it post Snowden, but I'm not going to talk about post Snowden, now both the executive, the legislative branches of the government, have been hijacked by lobbyists. Examples: after the banks lobbied for deregulation we have seen that we now have neo-anarchist in the government, for example, Greenspan, who caused the trillion dollar "Great Recession". Abolishing all this regulation for banks has had a disaster impact. According to the official report of the Fukushima Nuclear Accident Independent Investigation Commission, and this is go.jp, this is not some nut organisation, this is go.jp, which stands for government in Japan, I've actually met some people who were involved in this report. The report says clearly, and I strongly encourage you to search the Internet, and do the search on it, lobbyists played a key role in the Fukushima disaster.

Other examples include, on exactly the 60th birthday of the German invasion of Poland, the EU made the selling of 60 watt Edison bulbs illegal, OK, and forced it being replaced by the Company Fluorescent lightbulbs. These lightbulbs are quite controversial since they contain mercury, see Scientific American, they are well-known to cause migraines, in some cases very severe, people being sick up to one month afterwards. If I remember correctly this was an article in The Guardian. So we see that basically government is overruling the rights of the individual, so we have seen that basically capitalism has been replaced by what one would call reverse fascism, in which the rights of the corporation outweigh these of the individual, and that the government is there to facilitate this.

There are more scary stories, for example, the exclusion of the EPA rules to inside areas of homes and other buildings. If the EPA rules would actually apply to inside buildings, many buildings you wouldn't be allowed to live in. Carpets are an example that basically start distributing chemicals for a long time in your house, the EPA rules don't apply there. For those of you who are not American, this is the Environmental Protection Agency. The EPA is not there for you, it is there for the animals, OK. Another example is Michael Chertoff, the former Secretary of Homeland Security from 2005 to 2009, and now the founder of the Chertoff Group represents manufacturers of full-body scanners. So if you go to Heathrow you will see that almost immediately after the after the actual setup of this organisation, this lobbying organisation, that Heathrow actually bought full-body scanners. They were used, I lived in Britain at the time, they were used, and then the EU ruled that actually they had to be stopped, so the EU stopped its deployment on November 13 2011. They're still being used in the US, but you can basically say that you deny to basically be used against you. So then we have the massive use of antibiotics in soaps, sprays at airports, etc., while it's well-known when you talk to people in medicine that this may endanger your immune system, may actually cause bugs that are resistant against this antibiotics, etc., but we have seen lobbyists at work. So we've also seen that the US President basically promised not to take lobbyists in his government during his campaign, but did anyway. So with all this we should actually wonder whether we are still living in what we call a democracy. And I think we should actually wonder whether it has been replaced by a demogogracy.

What about your grandfather's capitalism? We have seen that in capitalism as failed corporations go bankrupt, that's basically one of the main pillars of capitalism. In Nazism corporations too crucial from a national viewpoint where nationalised to basically make sure that they cannot go bankrupt. Today we see that corporations that view themselves as too important get bailed out, for example, Citibank and several UK banks, Chrysler and GM, and the list goes on. So as in Nazism, see for example the IBM collaboration, with Nazism we see a collaboration between corporations and government, examples are, location of obtained by mobile phones, social networks, those are just two. Moreover we can wonder whether the foundation of capitalism in this competition still exists, indeed we have seen price of products are kind of arbitrary, you can think about your Apple where the price is kind of independent of how much it has cost Apple to make. Another example is outsourcing did not reduce the cost of products in Western shops. When I go to China I buy toothbrushes, they cost one eighth than when you buy them in the UK, they are exactly the same toothbrushes. So we had no inflation we say, yes, we had no inflation, we should actually have prices go down. So you see the people actually have, who are basically outsourcing that are making their products so indeed we wonder whether capitalism still works where competition actually should be used. And in fact the reason why we have that is that shareholders are often the real customers. And so the models, which we use which have competition, they don't take the shareholders into account.

Now a final story, which is a very interesting one, was about air conditioners. In Norway an air condition costs $800, and so some people actually, who moved from China to Norway, realised that in China air conditions are much cheaper. So what they actually did, they had a whole, so they sent a whole load over from China, a whole container, they bought a whole container full of air conditioners, then they shipped them to Norway, then they basically looked into whether they had to pay import tax, because if you carry an air conditioner through customs, you as a person have to pay import tax. However, in Norway if you are a company and you import something which is not made in Norway, as electronics is not made in Norway, you have to pay zero import tax. So they sold their air conditioners for $600. So you see when you basically have this $800 versus $200, I when I basically went the first time, shipped the furniture from the Belgium to US, I know quite well how much it costs to ship a container, it is a very small amount, it's almost negligible.

So what are the potential solutions to the abuse? Having neo-anarchists in the government is causing the Great Recession. Having all these dominate the government, for example, the Fukushima accident, we have moved from a society in which the biggest threat to our Western society comes from the government and lobbyists, no longer a disorganised individual who claims to be an anarchist, who basically has no power, and unions who have lost their power. So how can we restore our democracy? There are many potential solutions. One of the potential solutions is make the government responsible. Don't forget this was 2012 when I gave this talk, as in Ukraine, it came back in the news the former Prime Minister was actually put in jail, and basically was freed a few days ago as you may remember. There are other problems with that. So at the time in 2012, if you look at the New York Times October 22 2012, it made the news that Italy, the justice system there, ordered jail terms for seven scientists who didn't warn of an upcoming deadly earthquake. So you cannot always trust the judicial system, it doesn't always produce what we hope it would produce.

Another one is to increase the salary of the governmental employees, so for example, if you look at what's done in Singapore, so if you compare that to the UK, and you look at the salaries of the UK Prime Minister, it's actually less than the one of several US computer science professors. So if you want to do the Singapore approach then you pay basically salaries similar as CEOs of corporations. So they don't have them no longer have to basically be in bed with the lobbyists. So another approach is the negative tax, for example, is done in Saudi Arabia, where it is the government who pays you tax, it's not you who pay tax to the government, no, the system works the other way around. Now evidently they have oil, so there is something that they can do with their money.

So instead of looking at all the solutions and talking more about how they could work, my main focus will be on using intelligence agencies to solve the problem. Government intelligence agencies are active against foreign countries, foreign spies, etc., and their own population, and that's, some other speakers have spoken about that problem. And they provide information about individuals to the government, this work too is very important. However, if you look at, I will take questions at the end, when you look at the US constitution starting with "We the People", the government is there for the people, and not the other way around. So that means that in Western governments that are actually failing, we need to split these agencies into two, these that spy for the government, which is basically a small part, except when the target is foreign, so here it should be exceptions for national spying should be minor and basically well regulated. And then agencies that spy for the people. So now you could wonder how can you make that work? So how can you implement it? So the target would be lobbyists and anyone working for the government. So what would you now actually spy on, don't forget this is pre Snowden talk.

I would do exactly the same as Theresa May's proposals, and Theresa May's proposal was basically, do the same as the United States is doing, but then for metadata. So we adapt the proposal, the UK Home Secretary, to keep track of who talks to whom via Internet. The people intelligence agencies inform the public who inside the government talks to whom inside the lobbyist organisation. What starting date, 2014, it couldn't be better, we are 2014 now, but it didn't happen, why, because 2014 is the year one can regard the fight against terrorism to be won, indeed, NATO has decided to pull out its troops in Afghanistan, at least in 2012 they decided that, now they are talking about different things, but let's talk about now. And secondly, George Orwell predicted a Big Brother society in his novel, and the date of that novel was basically 1984, so we are 30 years later, a good moment to actually look back at his book and see how much our freedom has been damaged.

And then the question is, how long would we actually, when we look at this we could say we have a test period for 10 years, if Theresa May's idea is right, that it does not violate human rights, then the Western governments cannot complain. So after the 10 years that we actually introduce that, and that the spying takes place to get information about to who they are talking, after the 10 years test period a debate among the population could start to see whether her arguments to introduce this against the UK population as a whole makes sense or not.

What's the potential impact? So for those of you who are not actually living in the UK, the Leveson Inquiry is about basically all this eavesdropping that some newspapers owned by Murdoch were actually doing, and this breaks the law. So during the Murdoch family and the UK governments the only one former Prime Minster said that he felt pressured by Murdoch, very strange, I mean, if you look at basically who are the godfathers of certain children of certain Prime Minister, etc., this number seems way too low. So now if you have basic intelligence information that's given to the public, then former Prime Minister may be more careful when actually checking the records before replying, because information would leak it anyway how often the Prime Minister of Britain has spoken to people in the Murdoch, etc. Another example is Fukushima, and I mentioned the report on go.jp. And also full body scanners, etc. So people, intelligence agencies, can help restore the check and balance in our democratic Western institutions. By having intelligence information flow in both directions we see a move towards a more balanced way. Nowadays it's all only in one direction.

Conclusion. I believe it is ethical for a communist country to have cyber-communism, and for a Nazist regime to have cyber-Nazism, in which corporations and the government collaborate in cyberspace and the rights of corporations dominate the one of the individual. However, in a democratic society, believing in human rights, wiretapping should only be in exceptional circumstances. Western societies should stop handing a victory to Al Qaeda. So Al Qaeda said that they would actually change our society, and they have succeeded with that. September 11 has changed our society to a frightening degree. Due to the reactions of September 11 we are now on a slippery slope, we should stop that, we should stop installing technology and laws which facilitate the next Holocaust. Some examples, I don't think a next Holocaust will take place, I'm just saying that we are doing very dangerous things. That means that each camera used by the FBI should be regarded as violating the restriction on random search. The law on $10,000 cash laws should be basically abolished. The reason is that if you look at what happened to Wikileaks, US Senator Lieberman convinced Master-card, VISA, etc., to stop accepting donations via Mastercard and VISA, very frightening. Western societies should restore human rights, otherwise they will continue being criticised by China for being hypocrites. Not only that, we need to extend human rights, to include cyber freedom and virtual freedom, examples, introduce privacy at a constitutional level, making it much harder to violate the constitution. Today you have to wait years and then the whole thing goes to the Supreme Court before some action of the President of the United States is basically ruled illegal. I'm not saying that this was invented by Obama, I'm not saying this was invented by Bush, this was even done by Roosevelt, so this is a very old trick, and Roosevelt knew very well that it was going to take a long time and helped solve the depression, to basically violate the constitution.

So indeed today we live in a virtual world in which we have many nomads. There's another problem, business travellers, crew on a shop, etc. The current constitution does not extend to nomads. When you travel in the US and you are a US citizen, at the moment you leave your house the constitution stops, OK. If you go by car, they can search your car without having basically a warrant. Then when you stay in a hotel, that is no longer regarded as your, basically your house, and therefore they can search it. This should be expanded. We need to basically make sure that the constitution is adapted to the 21st Century. So we hope that the proposal to have People Intelligence Agencies may restore the checks and balances we used to have. And this is basically the end of the 2012 talk. Are you going to say am I going to talk as long for the 2014, I'm almost at the end.

So the 2012 feedback was, there's a book called The Transparent Society, but Schneier is right, Schneier said, look Brin in his book proposed symmetric, we can spy on the government, the government spy on us. Today the role is anti-symmetric. Also this proposal is anti-symmetric, it is not symmetric, and it also more refined. I do not object that we have intelligence agencies that collect military intelligence and continue to spy on foreign countries, and that this information would not be released to the public. So one prediction that Brin made in his book came true, the size of cameras have become smaller. There was this argument, why they could be used at the very large scale, but nowadays guns are so small they actually fit in purses, does it mean that every person who carries a purse should actually carry a gun, no, guns are heavily regulated in many countries, even in the United States, in certain parts of the United States guns are very heavily regulated, and so cameras could as well.

So a question that was also asked is, why should intelligence agencies change their role? So although we focus on the US some of the ideas are generalised. The KGB has been replaced by two organisations, so organisations can be split up. The US Supreme Court might reduce the role of intelligence agencies. And citizens could sue the government and phone companies to have their metadata be released, the one related to the government under the Freedom of Information Act. For lobbyists I realise it is more difficult. And then there are always idealists, as for example, former Secretary of State Kellogg who basically outlawed war. A new Cold War may force the West to stop its hypocrisy and force us to restore freedom and human rights.

Finally, it was suggested by somebody else, citizens could start planting eavesdropping devices inside non-military governmental buildings, this is not my idea, this was somebody else who said, maybe people need to take basically this in their own hands. So the question then was also asked can we trust this task to agencies, and basically the answer is yes, because many people who join such agencies are very patriotic. Evidently you can always have moles, and this was discussed when Rebecca gave her talk.

So putting it in the post Snowden context. So first of all, only 1 % of Snowden leak got actually released to the public. Those of you who read the Puzzle Palace and similar books know that 1 % is actually not too much new in there. More interesting I think is the leaks that were made by the government afterwards as, for example, if you order a CAT5 and CAT6, they may actually be, bugs may have been put inside. There are many other interesting leaks that the government made afterwards in reaction to the Snowden leak. So the 2012 presentation is now in a new daylight, the Snowden leaks confirmed the 2012 idea that the focus of the agencies has to change, either by changing their role as explained higher on, or by having their budget dramatically cut to a bare minimum. Snowden only leaked NSA data, what about CIA data, DHS, FBI, MI5, MI6. I hope that Britain doesn't have the same law as Japan, because if I would actually say, should we have more leaks, I may be thrown into jail in Japan just for suggesting that.

So international agreements should extend the rights of foreigners. So, if you have a right in your country and you go visit a friendly country, then your constitution should extend to the country that you visit. Today basically these rights are limited, as I said, to your house, the moment you leave your house the US constitution doesn't hold anymore, at least a lot of parts of it. So how has the world changed and its interaction to IT things? There are two examples. China, so what China has done, I heard it two weeks ago, is that now CISCO has a very hard problem to sell CISCO equipment to China. Two, for many years there has been the Great Firewall of China, which has implied, China has it's own search engine called Baidu, it's own social networks, as for example, renren, it's own Twitter, wechat, and actually there are more than just those. And last, Huawei, which is a Chinese telecommunication company has offered £300,000 for a researcher to start a research group. The person who told me declined the offer.

So what have we seen on the other hand in Europe. In Europe we have seen anti eavesdropping action, and here you see basically Germany, Chancellor Merkel, keeping a phone, and she has been successful because Merkel's phone is no longer tapped, at least that's what Obama says. But if you say that only Merkel's phone is no longer tapped, basically what you see is that Merkel speaks very loudly but she carries only a small stick, basically her cellphone, which is a small stick. What we also see is that many countries in Europe are talking about firewalls, great firewalls, Belgium has a great firewall, Britain wants to have a great firewall, etc. But those, and they talk about children, children shouldn't be able to look at this, and children shouldn't be able to look at that, and therefore we need restriction on import of data, but what about export of data. So today we see all these children from different countries exporting all their data to basically the United States, and there's no talk about that. And we know quite well that some of this data can be career ruining. So I think that if you compare Europe with China, China is taking action and doesn't say so much, Europe is talking a lot and taking no action. Thank you.

Partha Das Chowdhury: The point about increasing salaries of politicians, we tried that in India, it was not successful, and with the kind of money they get from bribes, there's recently a case going on between Rolls Royce and the government, where Rolls Royce gave a lot of money. Now so the kind of money the politicians earn from these deals doesn't match however much you increase. And again, there is this cost to companies, the Prime Minister gets a lot of things for free.

Reply: I mentioned this one solution, and I said there are many, many things that are discussed, what I'm focusing on is, can we actually use the intelligence agencies. So I'm not proposing to copy Singapore, OK.

Joan Feigenbaum: So I just wanted to make a comment that your definition of reverse fascism is actually a well-studied concept in political philosophy, the term inverted totalitarianism, coined by the Princeton political philosopher Sheldon Wolin, is exactly the same on here.

Reply: OK, thank you very much.

Joan Feigenbaum: And if you're interested in this I think you should look into what social scientists and philosophers have studied that, because it's not a whacko idea, it's like actually

Reply: No I know it's not a whacko idea.

Joan Feigenbaum: It's actually been studied, and there's a whole theory that goes with it.

Reply: So, for example, when I mentioned Greenspan there were people on PBS who were actually serving on the Federal Reserve who clearly stated two people came forward saying, we told Greenspan what you're doing is the same as what happened in Japan, and you will get the same problem, collapse basically of the economy as has happened to Japan. As you know, Japan has still not recovered from that collapse. And Greenspan just ignored it.

Joan Feigenbaum: There was actually a recently article in Bloomberg News saying that the Federal Reserve seemed to be the only group of people who did not know that the credit bubble was about.

Simon Foley: So at the moment the people who spy on the government for us are the press, but they spy on us as well, which is interesting. But we pay for those in various different ways. If you have an intelligence agency that's spying on the government, who do you think will be deciding its level of funding, and allocating funds to it.

Reply: So that's basically what I said is that, so first of all the press, they only have been allowed to 1%, and if you look at the person who used to work for The Guardian who now has moved to the US, no longer working for

The Guardian, has basically said that a lot of the ideas from the Snowden leak that they wanted to publish, they were told by their lawyers, in particular the lawyer of The Guardian, that they were not allowed to basically publish this. So if you want to see, for example, when Snowden basically tried to get asylum in countries, the power of the US administration, by basically bullying country after country after country, saying, no don't actually allow him to stay, he needs to be extradited, even if there is no extradition agreement with that country. And what he had to do is basically go to the second most powerful country in the world to actually deal with this. So the press is not doing their job, or, I mean, I'm not saying that they're the fault, I'm not saying that the editor, or former editor of The Guardian, that he isn't doing his job, but due to everything that related to law and pressure of the government, it doesn't work.

So now the question, your second part of your question, I know it was not a question that there are the press, but I wanted to make a comment on that, the second part about basically the amount of money, it is very simple. What happens is there are oversight committees, as for example in the United States, there is the Senate I was talking with you about basically the relationship between the Senate and the CIA at the moment, but there are oversight committees, oversight committees could basically look at the NSA and say, how much of your effort is actually going towards foreign, and how much is going about spying on the US. I have been several times at the NSA, I've been there before September 11, and I have been there after September 11. There very interesting things that they didn't have, etc., but since they have ballooned, OK. And so it's easy, you basically say, OK, one argument was made after the end of the Cold War is, what are these agencies used for? And people said, maybe we should let them spy for US companies so we can compete with overseas companies, and people said, no, that's not the goal. So you should go back, the question is, is there going to be a new Cold War with Russia, for example, and in that case, the NSA should go back to basically as it was before September 11. If there's going to be no, then maybe it should be as shrunk as it should have been shrunk at the end of the Cold War. So that's basically the reply, and I don't think it's too difficult to do that. The oversight of the agency should not be abolished, that's the one that should spy for us.

Simon Foley: I think you should become a lobbyist for this idea.

Reply: I'm not a lobbyist, I'm a researcher, OK, I was asked to give a talk at an ethics conference, and so I said, what can I talk about.

Virgil Gligor: There is an insight in your presentation which I don't quite share. You say that in communist countries people trust the government.

Reply: That's what Marx said.

Virgil Gligor: That's not

Reply: No they don't, I know, in reality

Virgil Gligor: Marx was a theorist, and he did not live under communism.

Bruce Christianson: The government has the power to violate your

Reply: I live in the US and I often tell people that Europeans, they basically, they are following socialism, but Europeans don't trust the government. In the United States people trust the government, but the constitution is made for a system in which it shouldn't be trusted.

Virgil Gligor: Right, but I would massage that statement because the way it is presented right now is demonstrably false.

Reply: No, I said the logic, the logic from Marx following, is that in a communism system people should trust, I will add the word "should" trust the government.

Virgil Gligor: OK, well that's missing.

Reply: OK, thanks for pointing that out, I appreciate it.

Virgil Gligor: Oh, one more thing I forgot to mention. What, do you think that Wikileaks approximates that people see intelligence agency, does Wikileaks approximate your notion of people's intelligence agencies?

Reply: Wikileaks is a very strange agency, I mean, it's not an agency, but a very strange entity, because what happened is that Assange said that if they would get their hands on the data from Snowden they would publish it all. Why hasn't he done so? His girlfriend went to talk to Snowden, why hasn't he done so. So I don't think that Wikileaks is that trustworthy.

Virgil Gligor: You don't think that Snowden's data is completely published, fully published?

Reply: No, definitely not, and so that's actually very well mentioned. If you look at the Internet you will actually see this figure, this is not the figure that I have just basically made up. Also there have been basically contradictory reports about whether the US government knows what has actually been taken by Snowden to China or not, which is another issue. I'm not saying that Snowden is a hero, I have never said that OK. But what they do know is what files did Snowden have access to, and there's a concern that some of these files actually contain a lot of military secrets of the United States. So they don't know whether all these files have been taken by Snowden to Hong Kong, and then afterwards to Russia. But if we can take Assange on his word, if indeed the girlfriend of Assange got these files, why hasn't Wikileaks leaked all this. And I'm not saying they should, but they haven't even a fraction.

Virgil Gligor: Well so you're arguing that we don't know what Snowden has.

Reply: No, we don't know what Snowden has.

Virgil Gligor: So consequently we can never tell if they leak them all or not.

Reply: No, it's for sure they didn't leak them all, OK.

Virgil Gligor: We don't know.

Reply: I mean, I think that the figure came from, it might have come from the editor of The Guardian, it might.

Luca Viganò: So I see the political, ethical, moral challenges and so on, but from your point of view what are the research challenges for us, I mean, given that we are not lobbyists who can enforce this vision, how can we make sure that it is realisable in the first place if we wish to.

Reply: So, this was given, as I said, at an ethics conference. Now as basically Joan said, the title of the workshop this time, or subtitle, is about basically working with the enemy. I'm not saying the NSA is the enemy, but there are some serious concerns about the dragnet, as it has been called, and so, you suggested I become a lobbyist, I don't plan becoming a lobbyist, so what I do is just propose ideas, and if others who are more interested in actually looking at their proposing this to the government, or bring it to the press, etc., basically provided that they mention this presentation, I have no problems with that.

Bruce Christianson: The question in essence is how can Theresa May be persuaded to take her own medicines. How can forcing them to use the same infrastructure as the rest of us use?

Reply: So that's why some people said that basically we should start bugging all these governmental buildings. I don't think this is the right solution. Actually in the text that I submitted I said that probably have to be ruled on whether this violates laws or not. It's a very interesting question, yes, indeed, how can we convince the government, in particular Theresa May, that they are basically doing damage. I think that we should speak out, and the question is, what fraction of time do we want to put in this, as I said earlier on, I'm a researcher and basically this is just, when you think about ethics, and you are asked to talk about ethics, or asked to talk about basically how do we deal with the adversary, it's an interesting topic that has to be brought out. You shouldn't also forget every idea from a scientist is not necessarily implemented. If you look at a number, in particular in cryptography, where our work, we have had hundreds of ideas, hundreds, or maybe more, hundreds of ideas, a fraction is implemented. And then from the implemented ones a fraction is deployed. If you're now going to say every talk at a crypto conference, what will you do with this work, you will basically ruin the whole crypto community, no papers will be accepted anymore. So the crypto community is very different from the Oakland community where you have to have made basically a prototype implementation and then show that it works. In crypto we don't have to do that, and so that's why a lot of the crypto research isn't deployed at all. So it's very common in my community that I come from to basically suggest an idea, and then go on and work on something else.

Petr Švenda: I have just one comment with respect to bugging the government, I think this is already happening to some extent because every time there is a demonstration everyone is holding his phone with a camera, and making a movie from the event. It's published later somewhere although it may not be completely legal to post the movie on the public webpage like YouTube.

Reply: But this is very small compared to what I proposed, what you say is epilson.

Joan Feigenbaum: Well there is citizen journalism, you know, movement of sorts, there are more and more people who view it is essential.

Reply: So I've been asked by Jean-Jacques Quisquater who has made the news recently to actually forward this to a professor in Harvard who works on this topic, and so now that I have given this talk I will actually forward it. If I have the time before the banquet I will do that before the banquet. So I will do something, OK, it's not that I basically, and also it's been, the reason why Bruce and myself have had a chat, and I was not very happy about it not being published, so by publishing it at least more people will see it. So I think publishing is an important part, and that's what I was not too happy about, about what happened in 2012 when this wasn't selected. Now I do realise that philosophers don't know about the NSA, and so I can understand that basically it wasn't selected. So yes, there are things that are going to happen, it will be hopefully published, and then I will forward it to people, and I'll put it on my website, etc.

On Node Capturing Attacker Strategies

Filip Jurnečka[✉], Martin Stehlík, and Vashek Matyáš

Faculty of Informatics, Masaryk University, Brno, Czech Republic
{xjurn,xstehl2,matyas}@fi.muni.cz

Abstract. In distributed environments, such as wireless networks, a common adversary is considered to take control over a fraction of the nodes and hence to affect the system behaviour. We have examined several key management schemes for wireless sensor networks where the adversary compromises all the secret keys stored on captured nodes. We propose a number of realistic movement strategies that an actual attacker could pursue to capture nodes and examine the fallout of these attack approaches.

1 Introduction

Wireless sensor networks (WSNs) are multi-hop networks composed of low-end devices called nodes or motes, usually equipped with sensors monitoring some physical phenomena. Sensor nodes are generally very limited devices with restricted computational, energy and storage resources. Reported applications include scenarios such as battlefield management, wildfire, wildlife and medical monitoring or emergency response information.

Physical protection of nodes is difficult to provide, as the nodes are generally not considered to be equipped with tamper-resistant hardware and the network can be deployed in uninhabited or even hostile areas. Yet, the information stored and/or processed within the nodes can be of a significant value. An attacker can easily *capture* some of these nodes and read out all the stored data. For example, a poacher can read out location information about monitored endangered species or an attacker might even to get secret keys used for a critical military monitoring network.

Capturing nodes is usually done either by a malware application or, more realistically, by physical access. In this paper we define various movement patterns of an adversary to attack a wireless sensor network and examine their impact on selected key management schemes (KMSs) securing the network. From this point of view, we are examining the advantage provided to the attacker by the network design and also by the strategy the attacker pursues.

Knowing one's enemy better definitely helps to devise a better defence strategy. Knowing the physical location and deployment of the network, we can make reasonable assumptions about the possible attacker strategy used. Based on this, we can either improve the security of the most critically exposed areas or use a key management system least vulnerable to that sort of attacker strategy.

© Springer International Publishing Switzerland 2014
B. Christianson et al. (Eds.): Security Protocols 2014, LNCS 8809, pp. 300–315, 2014.
DOI: 10.1007/978-3-319-12400-1_29

We make the following contributions:

1. We introduce (the first version of) our WSN key management scheme evaluation framework and provide the first publicly available [9] collection of WSN key management scheme implementations.
2. We define a unified parametrizable node-capturing attacker against wireless sensor networks.
3. We define a set of node capturing strategies and evaluate their effect on sample networks protected by three different key management schemes.

The rest of this paper is organized as follows. We first describe the key management schemes that we evaluate in Sect. 2. Following is Sect. 3, defining the attacker model in use together with various node capturing strategies. In Sect. 4 we describe settings of our experiments. Evaluation of the experiments is provided in Sect. 5. Related work is discussed in Sect. 6. We conclude the paper with Sect. 7.

2   Key Management Schemes under Consideration

All our work ultimately aims at evaluating security of general key establishment and management schemes for WSNs. In this section, we briefly introduce the principles of the three schemes implemented and evaluated in this work. We examine the master-key based BROSK scheme [12], the original Eschenauer-Gligor random pre-distribution [6] and the PIKE scheme [3].

2.1   BROSK

The BROSK scheme is based on a single network-wide master key k_M that is preloaded to all nodes. After deployment, nodes start to broadcast their identifier together with a fresh nonce. Node A with identifier ID_A, nonce n_A then broadcasts message $ID_A|n_A|h_{k_M}(ID_A|n_A)$, where h_{k_M} is a MAC function parametrized by the master key.

After receiving a similar message from node B, node A can compute a new shared key k_{AB} out of the two nonces, e.g., as $k_{AB} = h_{k_M}(n_A|n_B)$.

2.2   Eschenauer-Gligor

The original Eschenauer-Gligor random pre-distribution has been examined and improved many times over. This work does not aim at evaluating the scheme as such, only uses it as a sample key management scheme for the attacker strategy evaluation.

The basic principle of the random pre-distribution is to generate a large pool of P keys, to randomly draw k keys and to load them as the key ring to each node independently. After deployment, nodes broadcast the identifiers of stored keys and establish shared keys as either the single shared key or compute a new shared key out of all shared keys. In our case, we use the SHA-2 hash function of the concatenated shared keys to generate a new one.

2.3 PIKE

The PIKE scheme delegates the responsibility of additional key establishment between nodes A and B to a mutually trusted third node C. All the nodes in the network are pre-loaded with a set of $2(\sqrt{n}-1)$ keys, where n is the number of nodes in the network, each shared with a single other node in the network. The nodes are installed in a grid based on their identifier and each node shares pairwise keys exactly with the nodes in the same row and column. To establish a new key outside of the row and column, assuming the node n is a square power of $x \in \mathbb{N}$, there are always two nodes such that both A and B share a pairwise key with them.

The trade-off between the number of stored keys and communication per node can be adjusted by installing the nodes in m dimensions, i.e., $m \cdot (\sqrt[m]{n}-1)$ keys would have to be installed per node. Additionally, if n is not a power of x, there is always at least 1 node that shares pairwise keys with both A and B.

2.4 Other Remarks

Note, however, that due to the unreliable nature of wireless communication, using these schemes, it is possible for one node to establish a shared key, while the other may not.

Unlike the first two schemes, PIKE is not based on physical proximity and hence the communication between distant nodes can be only partially protected by end-to-end means.

3 Attacker Model

In computer network security protocols, a common attacker model defined by Needham and Schroeder in [13] has frequently been considered. This attacker is considered to be able to interpose a node in all communication paths and thus can alter or copy parts of messages, replay messages, or emit false material. This extreme view was long considered and can still be argued for to be the only safe one when designing security protocols. This attacker is sometimes referred to as *global active*.

In the area of wireless sensor networks, this model is extended by following assumptions and called *node-compromise* attacker model [6]:

1. The key pre-distribution site is trusted.
2. The attacker is able to capture a fraction of deployed nodes.
3. The attacker is able to extract all information from the captured nodes.

Due to the nature of wireless sensor networks, Perrig et al. argued for the inadequacy of a *global passive* adversary and defined the *real world* attacker model in [1]. This attacker model is relaxed in several important assumptions:

1. The attacker has no access to the deployment site during deployment.

2. The attacker can only monitor a small portion of the network communications during the network deployment.
3. The attacker is unable to execute active attacks during the network deployment.

Obviously, this model cannot be assumed in extremely hostile scenarios such as battlefield deployment, but is very relevant for most applications. This attacker can be referred to as *local passive* – and evolves to *global active* once the network deployment phase is over.

In this paper, we are principally focusing on the *node-compromise* attacker. However, we encompass the *real world* attacker model as well, due to the attacker evaluation being performed after every significant phase in the key management schemes life-cycle.

Definition 1. *The unified **node-capturing** attacker operates in stages. Each stage takes place after a significant phase of the key management scheme is completed and before the next one starts. Each attack is independent of the previous ones and every time the attacker is able to compromise δ percent of nodes in the network.*

The significant phases depend strongly on the actual scheme in consideration, but generally include phases such as *deployment, node authentication* or *initialization.* The attacker efficacy is given by the set of percentages of compromised links in each measurement. The relevant value for the scenario has to be selected manually, based on the environment and other assumptions. The percentage of compromised nodes δ is not cumulative throughout the experiment as each round evaluates separately.

Note that we do not consider backwards computability of shared keys based on eavesdropped communication. We are solely interested in the node capture attack.

3.1   Attacker Strategies

The aforementioned ability to capture a fraction of deployed nodes is important from the viewpoint of theoretical analysis. However, it considers only a single attack strategy, namely a random one. In this paper, we add three other strategies of node capturing based on a possible physical movement of a person through the network. Additionally, we open discussion of other possible strategies that we would like to add to our framework.

Random Attacker Strategy. The random attacker strategy is usually the only considered strategy for key management scheme evaluations. It is parametrizable by the percentage of nodes the attacker is able to take control of. However, there is little correlation between the strategy and real world attack vector path. Considering a real person, moving through a network in the random pattern would be inefficient at best. The strategy is depicted in Fig. 1a.

Outermost Attacker Strategy. In a network with better defences at its centre, the outermost attacker strategy provides an easy attack vector. In this strategy the nodes captured are the nodes farthest from the centre of the network up to a threshold. The threshold can be defined similarly as with the random attacker strategy to a percentage of nodes compromised. This attack is easily executable by a real person by walking around the network and picking the outermost nodes.

An interesting result would be whether or not is the attacker able to capture keys enabling them to communicate "securely" with the centre of the network. An advantage of this strategy is the reduction of the chance of being caught inside the network.

Note that the dotted line in Fig. 1b depicting the outermost attacker strategy is only visualized to help the reader to better distinguish the distance from the network centre.

This strategy can be generalized to capturing nodes farthest away from a selected location. In our case, that is the network centre.

Direct Centre Attacker Strategy. A general objective of a wireless sensor network might be to protect sensitive items around which the network is deployed. An attacker might want to reach these items. A physical attack would then commence simply by moving directly to the centre of the network from a random location on the edge of the network. Alongside, the attacker can pick up nodes in close vicinity of his trajectory. The strategy is depicted in Fig. 1c.

The *direct centre* strategy could be generalized from using a random starting point and a fixed target point in the network to using two randomly picked points on the edges of the network and interpreting the movement as "walk through".

Centre Drop Attacker Strategy. Similarly to the previous strategy, an attacker might want to reach the centre of the network. In this strategy, we are considering additional possible ways of movement instead of a simple "walk through", namely a possibility to simply appear at a target location and to collect nearby nodes. A realistic equivalent might be a parachute drop or digging under the network. The strategy is depicted in Fig. 1d.

Again, this strategy can be generalized to drop at a random location within the network.

3.2   Comments

Currently, we define a percentage of nodes to be captured by the attacker in the first two strategies and a *reaching range* of the second two. It could be, however, unified simply by capturing the closest nodes to the trajectory or the location up to the threshold defined by the percentage.

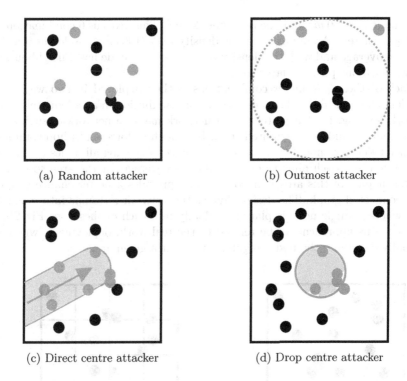

(a) Random attacker

(b) Outmost attacker

(c) Direct centre attacker

(d) Drop centre attacker

Fig. 1. Attacker node capturing strategies.

4   Experiment Setup

In this section we describe the experimental setup that we used to measure the efficacy of the proposed attacker strategies.

For the evaluation, we use the Omnet++ [19] simulator based on the WSN framework MiXiM [10]. We have built a complex key management scheme evaluation framework called KMSforWSN, available online for evaluation of various metrics of key management schemes [9]. The framework is continuously being developed and the results provided in this paper are the output of the 6th SVN revision found online.

We define 216 scenarios with various number of nodes present in the network, various density of nodes in the network, various key management schemes used and various percentage of nodes being compromised by the attacker. Furthermore, each of these scenarios was executed twice with a different seed. For each of these scenarios we measure the percentage of link keys compromised by an each attacker strategy with given input parameters as described in respective subsections of Sect. 3 of this paper.

The network is composed of $n = 16, 100$, and 1024 nodes, respectively. These network sizes are such that $\sqrt{n} = x \in \mathbb{N}$ in order to better fit the second deployment strategy described below. We consider two different densities of the network of one node per $100\,m^2$ and one node per $225\,m^2$. This gives us 6 combinations of input parameters. Assuming the node density $node/100\,m^2$, a node has 9 neighbours on average and with the density $node/225\,m^2$, a node has 4 neighbours on average with our physical layer settings.

Each of these parameter combinations is then deployed in two ways. The first deployment is a simple random uniform distribution in an adequately small network, see Fig. 2a. Adequately small network means a network of such a size where nodes would be distributed sparsely enough to force multi-hop communication yet densely enough to have a high chance of keeping all nodes connected. The second approach aims to ensure a better coverage for the area so that no significant part of this area is uncovered and provides a better chance of keeping a connected graph. The design divides the network rectangle into n smaller cells, where a single node is placed randomly into each of these, see Fig. 2b. In addition, this approach can be related to the real world deployment, where we manually distribute the nodes regularly to cover a given area.

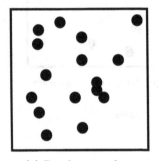
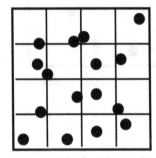

(a) Random topology   (b) 1 node per cell random topology

Fig. 2. Example topologies deployed randomly and randomly within each cell.

Finally, we measure the attacker success against three different key management schemes.

For the signal propagation modelling, we use the log-normal shadowing model [7] with the parameter α set to 2.3, which should correspond to the outdoor environment, based on our earlier work [16]. Additional physical layer settings are based on our results from [16,17].

The experiment itself is executed as follows. The nodes are pre-loaded with necessary information for the key management scheme. To select appropriate key pool size and key ring size for the EG scheme, we limit ourselves in the experiments by the size of RAM memory of a standard TelosB mote. That is $10\,kB$ and thus we assume one fifth to be available for the key storage. Assuming 32-byte long keys, we have space for up to 64 keys. Hence, we choose the ring sizes of $21, 42$, and 64 with key pool sizes $200, 400$, and 800 keys, respectively, based on the network size under consideration. Furthermore, these values have been chosen in such a manner that reflects the size of the network and based on the analysis in [8] provides > 90 % actual local connectivity. Additional details on the schemes and their parameters can be found in Sect. 2 or in the respective papers.

After deployment, each attacker strategy is performed and evaluated independently of each other. Further on, if some initialization phase is required by the key management scheme, it is executed. Then all nodes try once to establish shared keys with their neighbours and finally later on, each node tries once to establish a shared key with each other node in the network, where the node does not share a key with. After each of these steps, the node-capturing attacker executes each strategy.

The attacker strategy is then evaluated as a percentage in terms of number of links compromised to all established links. We evaluate the experiments with 5 %, 10 %, 15 %, and 20 % of nodes being captured by each attack strategy. Note that some links can be only unidirectional due to various connectivity issues and hence we consider each copy of a key for a link as a standalone link. Yet capturing one key of a symmetric key based link compromises both "standalone" links.

The principle is depicted in Fig. 3. Consider three separate scenarios, where in the first case only one direction of a "shared key" between nodes A and B is established. In the second scenario, it is the opposite direction and the third one establishes the secret shared key in both ways. These links add to the number of existing secure links in the network by $1, 1$, and 2, respectively. An attacker capturing only node A then compromises $1, 0$, and 2 links, respectively. Let us denote the number of established links in the network l and the number of compromised links c. The success ratio of the attacker strategy is then computed as $\frac{c}{l}$.

Fig. 3. Compromised links with various key establishment success.

5   Evaluation

In the following text and graphs we present the mean numbers from all relevant runs of each experiment. These include the same experiment settings with various seeds and all assumed topologies. Altogether, each data point in the graphs is generated as the mean value of 4 experiment runs, two topologies with two seeds.

In the first graph Fig. 4 we can see number of links, secured by a shared key, established by each KMS in each relevant phase of our experiment. Several interesting facts can be observed.

First, we can see the master key characteristic of BROSK after deployment, where all nodes share a single key. Thus the number of *secured* links is equal to number of logical links in the network. Despite not being specified in [12], our implementation expects the master key to remain after the initialization phase, but is not used directly any more except for "only" establishing new shared keys. Hence the number of links drops rapidly to 16, 154, and 1575 on average for the respective network sizes. Interestingly, the number increases significantly after the repeated attempt to establish keys with all neighbours after the network is initialized to the average number of links of 65, 549, and 5821. Finally, the number of established links after the *attempt to establish keys with all nodes in the network* phase is on average 83, 705, and 7685 per the network size.

Secondly, we can see that there is no bar in the graph for the EG scheme after initialization. That is due to the fact, that the number of established links is 0. That does not mean that they would not share any keys, but prior to additional communication, the nodes have no way of knowing what keys they share with whom and hence do not consider any keys to be shared. The average numbers of links established after the initialization phase, the *attempt to establish keys with all nodes in the neighbourhood* phase and the *network* phase are 13, 42, 57; 121, 350, 468, and 976, 3321, 4536 respectively, per network size.

Thirdly, PIKE does not require any initialization phase, hence the corresponding bar is left out as being identical with the deployment phase. The preloaded keys also help with a large number of existing logical links being in the network from after the deployment. The average numbers of links established are 96, 176, 240; 1800, 2905, 9900, and 63488, 78811, 1047552 per phase and network size. The main drawback of these experiments are the large computational requirements and communicational overhead that result from the usage of an intermediary node used to establish key with new nodes.

Note that all the reported values and possible issues are the result of various implementation choices and have little to no consequence for the examination of the attacker strategy. For example, the experiment was set up to try to establish a shared key with each node only once and not until it succeeds. Therefore, a blocking communication channel at a small timeframe can completely block a number of key establishment attempts.

The actual number of compromised nodes, regardless of the attacker strategy, is based on the number of nodes in the network and the percentage of nodes to be compromised by the attacker. In our case, for the 16-node network, the 5% of nodes is unfortunately floored to 0 nodes and this case will be excluded in the following discussion. For the 10, 15, and 20 percent the attacker captures 1, 2, and 3 nodes. In the case of 100 nodes in the network, the number of captured nodes is straightforward 5, 10, 15, and 20, respectively. Finally, in the case of 1024 nodes in the network, each attacker strategy captures 51, 102, 153, and 204 nodes, based on the attacker parameter.

In Fig. 5 we can see the results for the BROSK scheme and all corresponding parameters. On the x-axis, there are results grouped by the network size for the aforementioned phases of the network application. On the y-axis, we can see the

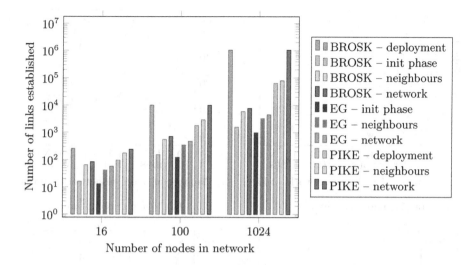

Fig. 4. Number of links established in each phase by each KMS.

resulting percentage of links captured by each attacker strategy in average for given parameters.

From the graphs we can observe the expected behaviour of each attacker strategy based on the characteristic of BROSK. Since BROSK establishes keys locally, mainly with neighbours, the *random* attacker strategy capturing nodes at distant locations has actually the best results in average. On the other end of the spectrum, the *outermost* attacker strategy captures nodes with the least neighbours and thus the least links established.

The EG scheme results are harder to interpret. Due to the randomized nature of the scheme, we can see very similar results for all strategies in Fig. 6. This holds true especially for larger networks, where each strategy has almost the same averaged result across the 4 runs of each experiment. The small network experiments provide some difference, but we believe that across more runs, the results would average out across the strategies. However, this observation highlights the possibly easier to perform attack strategies such as the *outermost* attack strategy.

Additional observation signals the actual security provided by the EG scheme. While for the smaller networks the results seem still quite random, for larger networks, despite larger percentage of nodes captured, the actual percentage of links captured stays very low. However, this is mainly due to the way multiple shared keys between nodes are handled by computing a new shared key as a hash of the pre-distributed shared keys. Due to the way the sizes of ring and pool were selected, arbitrary two nodes have a large chance of sharing multiple keys and hence this process introduces a large number of new keys in the network that are actually not used to create links and thus the node capture of a small fraction of keys contributes little to the overall percentage of captured links.

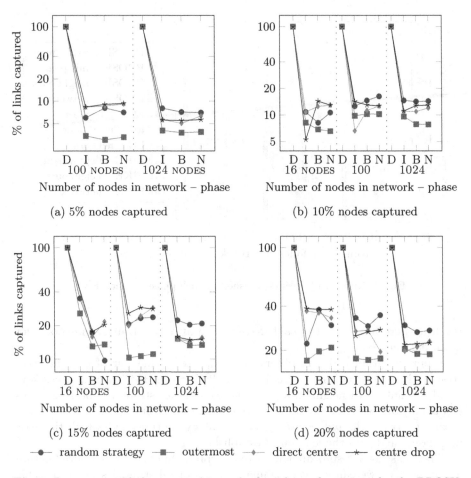

(a) 5% nodes captured

(b) 10% nodes captured

(c) 15% nodes captured

(d) 20% nodes captured

—●— random strategy   —■— outermost   —◆— direct centre   —✶— centre drop

Fig. 5. Percentage of links captured in each phase by each strategy for the BROSK scheme. To save some space, we substitute the deployment, initialization, neighbours and network stages for D, I, B, and N, respectively. Note the logarithmic scale of y-axis.

Finally, in Fig. 7, we can see again the expected behaviour of the PIKE scheme, where a large portion of keys are pre-distributed and hence upon capturing a few nodes, a large fraction of the links is compromised. Further down the network application lifetime, more links are created and the percentage of compromised links drops.

The results for various strategies differ only slightly, with the *outermost* strategy being the least impactful and the *centre drop* strategy being just barely more efficient than the rest of the proposed and tested strategies. Again, this result is expected based on the average number of neighbours and thus links being established by nodes at the edge of the network and in the centre.

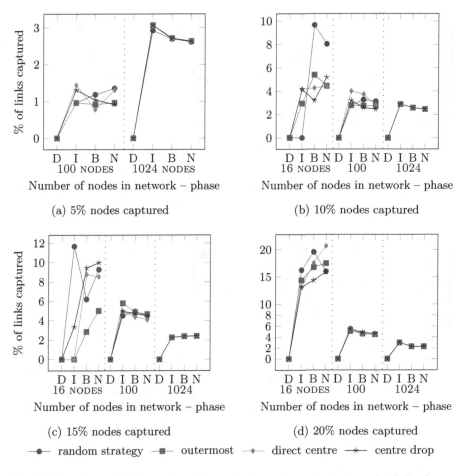

(a) 5% nodes captured

(b) 10% nodes captured

(c) 15% nodes captured

(d) 20% nodes captured

—•— random strategy —■— outermost —♦— direct centre —✳— centre drop

Fig. 6. Percentage of links captured in each phase by each strategy for EG scheme. The notation and concept of graphs is the same as in Fig. 5.

Note that graphs in Fig. 7 are missing the *initialization* phase measurement, as PIKE does not require any initialization phase.

6   Related Work

Attacker strategies have been examined in a several papers. The foundation came with the work of Needham and Schroeder [13] with their definition of the network attacker model, followed by Dolev and Yao [5] with an algebraic model of an omnipotent attacker.

For wireless sensor networks, the node-compromise attacker model by Eschenauer and Gligor [6] is typically considered. An argument was given for the real-life attacker model by Perrig et al. in [1]. These models are examined in Sect. 3.

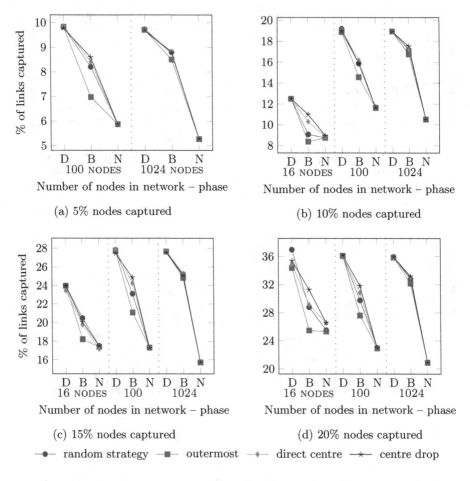

(a) 5% nodes captured

(b) 10% nodes captured

(c) 15% nodes captured

(d) 20% nodes captured

—●— random strategy   —■— outermost   —◆— direct centre   —✱— centre drop

Fig. 7. Percentage of links captured in each phase by each strategy for PIKE scheme. The notation concept of groups is same as in Fig. 5.

A formal model of a node capturing attacker has been formulated in [18] by Tague and Poovendran. They additionally discuss two attack strategies named set coverage and subset coverage due to their relationship to the well known set coverage problem.

Bonaci et al. design a control theoretic framework to model physical node capture in [2]. However, similarly to [1,6], they also assume only the random capturing strategy.

An automated design of attack strategies using evolutionary algorithms has been proposed by Kůr et al. in [11]. These strategies are understood in a broader sense than in our paper and include other attacker actions such as manipulating messages. The design rests on an educated guess of elementary rules and on definition of the fitness function. Four attacker strategies have been examined for the Eschenauer-Gligor scheme. However, these strategies do not take the physical attacker into account. Instead, they focus on optimal strategies to capture the maximum number of keys, the most frequently used keys, etc.

Evaluations of key management schemes have been previously done mainly analytically, by hand; a necessary step but prone to mistakes and failures. In [15], Roman et al. are assigning pre-defined values to various WSN key management schemes' properties based on the common understanding of these schemes' behaviours. However, if the property is reported incorrectly, the resulting value is wrong as well.

Automated evaluation of key management schemes with respect to various properties has been proposed and implemented in [20] by Vu et al. and in [14] by Özdemir and Khalil.

Vu et al. implemented a WSN simulator with support for key management scheme evaluation, most interestingly the node capture model. However, they only focus on the Eschenauer-Gligor scheme and its extension *q-composite* [4] and provide only the random attacker strategy.

The work of Özdemir and Khalil is built on top of the Omnet++ simulator and focuses mainly on performance characteristics of the Eschenauer-Gligor scheme, the q-composite scheme, master key pre-distribution and pairwise key pre-distribution. Too little attention has been paid to the reported node capture resiliency of these schemes, and the results are merely reporting number of keys captured by capturing a single node.

7 Conclusions

In this work, we have introduced our automated key management scheme evaluation framework built on top of MiXiM. In comparison to previous works, our framework is highly adjustable, very detailed in terms of simulation level and more comprehensive in terms of various WSN key management schemes being implemented.

We have defined four different attacker strategies for node capturing and observed the effect against three different KMSs. While the results of our experiments were to be expected in most cases, a few interesting results arose.

The localized characteristic of the BROSK scheme makes the random attacker strategy the most efficient in terms of percentage of links compromised, while the outermost strategy is the least efficient. On the other hand, with the EG scheme, all the evaluated strategies performed equally and hence the easiest strategy to perform, for a particular attacker and environment can be seen as advantageous.

The surprisingly small effect of any attack strategy against the EG scheme in large networks (even with a large fraction of nodes being captured) suggests possible future work on examining the EG scheme more exhaustively with various key pool size and key ring size parameters.

Acknowledgement. This work was supported by the GAP202/11/0422 project of the Czech Science Foundation. We are also grateful for helpful discussions and notes provided by our colleagues Petr Švenda, Dušan Klinec, Jiří Kůr, and by participants of the Security Protocols Workshop 2014, particularly Daniel Thomas and Virgil Gligor.

References

1. Anderson, R., Chan, H., Perrig, A.: Key infection: smart trust for smart dust. In: Proceedings of the 12th IEEE International Conference on Network Protocols, pp. 206–215. IEEE Computer Society, Washington, DC (2004)
2. Bonaci, T., Bushnell, L., Poovendran, R.: Node capture attacks in wireless sensor networks: a system theoretic approach. In: 2010 49th IEEE Conference on Decision and Control (CDC), pp. 6765–6772 (2010)
3. Chan, H., Perrig, A.: Pike: peer intermediaries for key establishment in sensor networks. In: INFOCOM 2005: Proceedings of 24th Annual Joint Conference of the IEEE Computer and Communications Societies, vol. 1, pp. 524–535, March 2005
4. Chan, H., Perrig, A., Song, D.: Random key predistribution schemes for sensor networks. In: 2003 Symposium on Security and Privacy, pp. 197–213, May 2003
5. Dolev, D., Yao, A.C.: On the security of public key protocols. IEEE Trans. Inf. Theory $29(2)$, 198–208 (1983)
6. Eschenauer, L., Gligor, V.D.: A key-management scheme for distributed sensor networks. In: Proceedings of the 9th ACM Conference on Computer and Communications Security, CCS '02, pp. 41–47. ACM, New York (2002)
7. Hekmat, R., Van Mieghem, P.: Connectivity in wireless ad-hoc networks with a log-normal radio model. Mob. Netw. Appl. $11(3)$, 351–360 (2006)
8. Hwang, J., Kim, Y.: Revisiting random key pre-distribution schemes for wireless sensor networks. In: Proceedings of the 2nd ACM Workshop on Security of Ad Hoc and Sensor Networks, SASN '04, pp. 43–52. ACM, New York (2004)
9. Jurnečka, F., Stehlík, M., Matyáš, V.: Key management schemes for wireless sensor networks (2013). https://sourceforge.net/projects/kmsfwsn/. Accessed 22 May 2014
10. Köpke, A., Swigulski, M., Wessel, K., Willkomm, D., Haneveld, P.T.K., Parker, T.E.V., Visser, O.W., Lichte, H.S., Valentin, S.: Simulating wireless and mobile networks in OMNeT++ the MiXiM vision. In: Conference on Simulation Tools and Techniques for Communications, Networks and Systems & Workshops, Simutools '08, ICST, pp. 71:1–71:8. ICST, Brussels (2008)
11. Kůr, J., Matyáš, V., Švenda, P.: Evolutionary design of attack strategies. In: Christianson, B., Malcolm, J.A., Matyáš, V., Roe, M. (eds.) Security Protocols 2009. LNCS, vol. 7028, pp. 3–17. Springer, Heidelberg (2013)
12. Lai, B., Kim, S., Verbauwhede, I.: Scalable session key construction protocol for wireless sensor networks. In: IEEE Workshop on Large Scale RealTime and Embedded Systems (LARTES), p. 7 (2002)
13. Needham, R.M., Schroeder, M.D.: Using encryption for authentication in large networks of computers. Commun. ACM 21, 993–999 (1978)
14. Özdemir, S., Khalil, O.: Performance evaluation of key management schemes in wireless sensor networks. Gazi Univ. J. Sci. $25(2)$, 465–476 (2012)
15. Roman, R., Lopez, J., Alcaraz, C., Chen, H.H.: Sensekey - simplifying the selection of key management schemes for sensor networks. In: Proceedings of the 2011 IEEE Workshops of International Conference on Advanced Information Networking and Applications, WAINA '11, pp. 789–794. IEEE Computer Society, Washington, DC (2011)

16. Stetsko, A., Stehlik, M., Matyas, V.: Calibrating and comparing simulators for wireless sensor networks. In: 2011 IEEE 8th International Conference on Mobile Adhoc and Sensor Systems (MASS), pp. 733–738 (2011)
17. Stetsko, A., Smolka, T., Jurnečka, F., Matyas, V.: On the credibility of wireless sensor network simulations: evaluation of intrusion detection system. In: Proceedings of the 5th International ICST Conference on Simulation Tools and Techniques, SIMUTOOLS '12, ICST (Institute for Computer Sciences, Social-Informatics and Telecommunications Engineering), pp. 75–84. ICST, Brussels (2012)
18. Tague, P., Poovendran, R.: Modeling adaptive node capture attacks in multi-hop wireless networks. Ad Hoc Netw. **5**(6), 801–814 (2007)
19. Varga, A.: Using the OMNeT++ discrete event simulation system in education. IEEE Trans. Educ. **42**, 372 (1999)
20. Vu, T.M., Williamson, C., Safavi-Naini, R.: Simulation modeling of secure wireless sensor networks. In: Proceedings of the Fourth International ICST Conference on Performance Evaluation Methodologies and Tools, VALUETOOLS '09, ICST (Institute for Computer Sciences, Social-Informatics and Telecommunications Engineering), pp. 30:1–30:10. ICST, Brussels (2009)

On Node Capturing Attacker Strategies
(Transcript of Discussion)

Filip Jurnečka[(✉)]

Masaryk University, Brno, Czech Republic
172641@mail.muni.cz

Hello everyone, and thank you all for coming, even though the dinner is already passed. Today I'm going to be talking about a little bit narrower a topic than the previous talks were. As my latest work focuses on automated evaluation of key management schemes for wireless sensor networks, and this is just a part of that. We have built a framework on top of an existing simulator, and one of the main metrics, or parts, that you want to characterise, to evaluate in a key management scheme is the network resiliency of such a scheme. And usually it's always considered one kind of attacker, the random attacker strategy of capturing nodes. We thought that, well if I were the attacker I would want to go the most efficient way, and is there some way like that. First, I will give a brief introduction to several things, and then we'll see the results of the evaluations.

Wireless sensor networks, as I've said, is a narrower topic. It's a distributed ad-hoc network where the nodes are very limited in computation, power, in memory, and one of the most important characteristics for today is that they are not tamper resistant, and they are usually deployed in unattended, or even hostile, environments. Favourite applications for this, I always love to mention the battlefield management, and there are various applications for climate monitoring. We have a network of thousands of nodes, very limited and unprotected, and if we want to protect them somehow we usually reach for cryptography, and that means giving some key management. In this work, I will be presenting the evaluation of three different key management schemes.

The first one is BROSK by Lai and Kim, and it's a very simple master key based scheme where initially all nodes are preloaded with a single network-wide master key that every node shares. And after deployment each nodes constructs a message like this, composed mainly of the identifier and some fresh nonce. And then they broadcast this message, and upon reception of a similar message from neighbouring nodes they can construct a shared key, for example, in that manner.

The other one, the EG scheme, Eschenauer and Gligor, are randomised pre-distribution, we generate a large pool of keys, and we preload each node with a random subset of keys, known as the key ring. And then after deployment nodes broadcast the identifiers of the keys, and in case of matching keys they use those keys for secret communication. However, if an attacker captures a node he does not compromise only the nodes on that, the keys on that node, but also the keys, the same keys that may be employed somewhere else in the network.

© Springer International Publishing Switzerland 2014
B. Christianson et al. (Eds.): Security Protocols 2014, LNCS 8809, pp. 316–320, 2014.
DOI: 10.1007/978-3-319-12400-1_30

The third one is PIKE by Perrig, and this one preloads in such a manner that the nodes are installed, for example, by their ID in some grid, and each node is preloaded with two times the $2(\sqrt{n}-1)$, verifies keys that it shares with nodes in the same row and column. And if we want to establish a shared key with some other node in the network we have two neighbours to choose from that will intermediate the process. So if we want node 11 to establish a shared key with node 93, we can either ask node 13 or node 91 to intermediate that.

We are interested in the node-capturing attacker. Usually there are in the analysis of key management schemes resistance authors assume some things, some assumptions, about the attacker, and they usually are restricted, like the presence prior to the end of the initialisation phase has to be restricted, maybe eavesdropping something, but there is very often some sort of limitation. And then they are evaluated just at one point, and that's very sound, that's very good, but we are interested also in the lifetime of the key management scheme and whether it changes its nature throughout. So we've devised the following experiment, and it goes as follows, where the nodes are obviously deployed with already some preloaded information, then the key management scheme performs the initialisation phase if it needs one. Then we've devised two custom phases, the first one where nodes try to establish keys with their neighbours that they do not share a key with yet, and finally nodes try to establish keys with all the nodes in the network they don't have a shared key with yet. They try only once so there may be

Frank Stajano: Is it not the case that sometimes the first two steps are reversed, that you perform the initialisation phase before the planned nodes?

Reply: Can you give an example?

Frank Stajano: It's in the EG, don't you have to first preload the random subset in the nodes before deploying them in the field.

Reply: Yes, well I call this predeployment phase maybe. You always have to load some data to the node, and only after they're usually deployed in the field, so I was, I know what you mean, but in this case I would call it the initialisation phase, rather the phase where the nodes broadcast their identifiers, and they

Frank Stajano: Figure out who's in the..

Reply: Figure out, exactly, the matching keys. And then after each of these phases we evaluate the attacker strategies that we are interested in to see whether it changes somehow significantly throughout the lifetime of a key management scheme.

Just to briefly touch on how do we actually evaluate the attacker strategy, basically it's just the ratio of compromised links in the network to the number of links overall, secured links obviously. However, due to the wireless nature and problems with communication in these networks, there may arise some cases where one node thinks it shares a key while the other one does not. There are just three subcases, where in each of them the attacker actually captures only node A while it does contribute to the number of compromised links, in the first case 1, in the second 0, and in third case 2 links. That's how we evaluate the attacker, and now the attacker strategies that we've proposed and are taking a look into. Obviously the random attacker is a must, but then usually with wireless sensor networks they are surrounding something we want to protect or monitor. So if we want to avoid detection maybe the best approach would be to just sort of pick the nodes on the outskirts of the network, we call this the outermost attacker strategy. Then what we are trying to protect normally is usually in the centre of the network, so if I were a smart attacker I would just dash towards the centre, maybe pick the nodes closest to me. Hence, the direct centre attacker strategy, where we pick a random point on the edge of the network, and we pick up to a percentage of nodes, a given percentage of nodes closest to the path we're taking to the centre. And finally the drop centre where we can imagine some hidden attacker being already in the centre, or parachuting there, or whatever, that does capture again up to the parameter nodes from the centre of the network.

Furthermore, we have devised a lot of settings, mixed it up a little bit. On the following graphs, each of the data points is actually an outcome of 8 independent simulations, just to briefly touch on the experiments of things. So each experiment has two repetitions different, with different seed. Then we are taking a look at how it behaves on various sized networks. Usually wireless sensor networks are considered in 100 s, or 1000 s of nodes, while actually deployed ones usually have a smaller amount of nodes. That's why we are taking a look at 16, 100 and 1024 nodes. Then in the terms of actually spacing, or the area size, we are taking a look at two different node densities, and we're examining for different parameters, for different percentages of the nodes to be captured. And finally two deployment strategies where obviously the uniform random distribution, it can again form unconnected graphs, and uncovered areas. That's why we proposed this second strategy where we divide the deployment area into cells, and we randomly deploy a node, with one node within one cell, which just gives us a better chance of keeping the graphs connected, and covering the area.

So just for some overview, the number of links established overall in the, just in the dense networks, since I've forgotten to run the other part of the experiments prior to making this graph, is what we can see here, yes.

Daniel Thomas: So you did two experiments for each?

Reply: Yes, but then again I will get to it in the next slides, where if I can, where I can show that each of these data points then are, is an average value of not only the two directly but of 8 different experiments, because we are actually considering the deployment strategy as well in there, so we average all these values, OK?

What we can see here is obviously the BROSK right after deployment shares one master key that keeps, or that makes the logical full graph, and then it drops. Similarly, there is no value for the EG scheme after deployment, because they just don't really share any links prior to matching the keys that are preloaded. And finally there is no value for the PIKE after the initialisation phase because it really doesn't need one.

If we take a look now at the outcomes. For the BROSK scheme we can see a few interesting characteristics, and that would be namely that the random strategy actually gives overall a very good, to the best results, and I would say that's mainly due to the fact that BROSK is a very localised scheme working with neighbours. If we cover various points in the network we get better, yeah?

Daniel Thomas: What does the DIBN stand for?

Reply: Oh right, that's not on this one, it's the deployment phase, initialisation phase, neighbour phase and network phase. And then we can also see that the outermost attacker picking the nodes from the outskirts of the network actually has the least effect, least success ratio. That would be mainly due to the fact that the nodes on the outskirts have the smallest connection degree, while they do have least number of links that they are contributing in the network. With the EG scheme we can see some very random values for the smaller networks, presumably also due to the smaller number of experiments. However, the interesting values come in the larger networks where we can see a strong convergence of the strategies.

The other interesting thing here is a very small success ratio of arbitrary strategy, even with a large number of nodes captured, and I would actually like your opinion on that because I'm mainly thinking it's due to the sizes of key pool, key ring, and also the way of making a shared key with nodes we actually find, which (a) we do not share keys with, and (b) do share more than one key. There has to be some way, and in our implementation actually we do just concatenate all the shared keys, and hash them to create a new shared key, so that might be why. And finally PIKE, by the way there is an error in the pre-proceedings where the first value is double what it should be, so if you divide it you would get here. And again, what we can see is, in the larger networks the strategies are converging, maybe with the exception of the outermost again for the same reason that it actually contributes the least.

These are the things that I've come up with after evaluating three simple schemes, and that's namely that the random attacker strategy is actually very effective on localised schemes such as BROSK. Then the outermost strategy, since it contributes the least, it is also the least effective. However on the EG scheme on larger networks it seemed to have very comparable results, and if it, or actually any attacker strategy that is easiest to perform on the EG scheme would yield the same results, we could just go the easiest way, and that's pretty much it from me. I have one more idea, and that's slightly cheating, but if I want to be the smartest attacker I would just capture the nodes that are contributing the most in the network. Is that something I should also do, what do you think?

Daniel Thomas: Absolutely.

Reply: So if there are any questions now is the time.

Simon Foley: So if you could go back to slide 10. So when you considered the two deployment strategies, did you notice any significant differences in the results?

Reply: Well they were not really that significant overall, so yes we did get some unconnected graphs, but we actually prepared some fixed topologies after we were satisfied with some generated results, and those fixed topologies are being used for all the experiments.

Simon Foley: Because I think when you think of building a management, energy management scheme, and the way that they would deploy sensors, wireless sensors. So that they wouldn't really use either of those schemes because what they're more interested in is putting in the smallest number of sensors possible while getting maximum coverage.

Reply: Absolutely.

Simon Foley: So, they may perhaps be closest to the second scenario where you've got a one node per cell. Even then though you would have situations where you have two sensors physically next to each other. So do you think carrying out the experiments on a topology where there's a more even distribution of the nodes across the topology would make a difference.

Reply: I don't, well yes it would, but then again I think it would be, the trends I think would be still the same, so we've included two, just in case it would really make some significant, more significant impact, but I think the overall trends would be the same.

On the Reliability of Network Measurement Techniques Used for Malware Traffic Analysis

Joseph Gardiner and Shishir Nagaraja[✉]

University of Birmingham, Birmingham B15 2TT, UK
{j.gardiner,s.nagaraja}@cs.bham.ac.uk

Abstract. Malware attacks are increasingly popular attack vectors in online crime. As trends and anecdotal evidence show, preventing these attacks, regardless of their opportunistic or targeted nature, has proven difficult: intrusions happen and devices get compromised, even at security-conscious organisations. As a consequence, an alternative line of work has focused on detecting and disrupting the individual steps that follow an initial compromise and that are essential for the successful progression of the attack. In particular, a number of approaches and techniques have been proposed to identify the Command & Control (C2) channel that a compromised system establishes to communicate with its controller. The success of C2 detection approaches depends on collecting relevant network traffic. As traffic volumes increase this is proving increasingly difficult. In this paper, we analyse current approaches of ISP-scale network measurement from the perspective of C2 detection. We discuss a number of weaknesses that affect current techniques and provide suggestions for their improvement.

1 Introduction

Malware detection and mitigation is a significant security challenge. In the last several years, the number of attacks, their sophistication, and potential impact have grown substantially. On one hand, opportunistic attacks have continued to flourish: these attacks are financially motivated, are responsible for the compromise of large numbers of machines, and result in the stealing of financial data, such as credit card numbers and online banking account credentials [9].

At the same time, targeted attacks have emerged as a new threat. These attacks target specific organisations or individuals with the intent of obtaining confidential data, such as contracts, business plans, and manufacturing designs [13].

Statistics and anecdotal evidence indicate that *preventing* attacks, either opportunistic or targeted, is difficult. For example, news reports have indicated that even security-conscious, well-funded organisations have fallen victims to attacks [12,15,16].

Considering the difficulties in effectively preventing attacks, defenders have looked at ways of *detecting* and *disrupting* the individual steps that follow an initial compromise and that are essential for the successful progression of an attack.

© Springer International Publishing Switzerland 2014
B. Christianson et al. (Eds.): Security Protocols 2014, LNCS 8809, pp. 321–333, 2014.
DOI: 10.1007/978-3-319-12400-1_31

This is the so-called kill chain approach to defence [11]. In particular, considerable effort has been spent in identifying the establishment of Command & Control (C2) channels, i.e. the communication channel through which attackers control compromised devices and receive any data stolen from them.

Focusing on the C2 step has several advantages. It is a general, widely applicable measure, since both opportunistic and targeted attacks rely on the establishment of C2 channels. In addition, if defenders can detect the attack before sensitive data is ever ex-filtrated, the damages suffered by the attack's target are limited considerably. Even in the event of successful data theft, an understanding of the C2 structure could prove essential to determine what has been stolen and where it ended up. Furthermore, the analysis of the C2 channel may provide indications useful to attribute the attack to specific groups of people, which may facilitate legal actions against them.

However, C2 channel detection techniques make a critical assumption. They assume the existence of a measurement system that collects traffic containing C2 and non-C2 traffic. As traffic volumes increase, the measurement goal of storing all traffic becomes increasingly difficult. Core routers operate in the order of 100 Gbps and are expected to increase to 1 Tbps in a few years time. Enterprise routers are expected to scale up similarly, from 10 Gbps to 100 Gbps. At these throughput rates on a per-router basis, storing all traffic for a few days is a task that is practically impossible.

The scope of this paper: is to conduct the first security analysis of traffic measurement mechanisms, specifically those which C2 detection techniques depend upon. The research question we examine is: how hard is it for malware to evade current measurement mechanisms?

The main insight of our work is that all major sampling-based measurement mechanisms have security vulnerabilities. Thus we can expect that in the near future, malware designers will exploit these vulnerabilities to evade measurement and collection. Thus malware detection based on statistical pattern analysis of command and control traffic could be rendered useless.

2   The Command and Control Problem

Command and Control identifies the step of an attack where the compromised system makes contact back to the attackers to obtain additional attack instructions and to send them any relevant information that has been collected up to that point. It is one of the phases of malware intrusion. There are several others which we document briefly, as follows.

In the *reconnaissance phase* the attacker learns more about its target and identifies the weaknesses that will be exploited during the actual attack.

In the *initial compromise phase* the attacker attempts to compromise the network via various methods: spear phishing [20], social malware [14], or a "watering hole" attack – a opportunistic drive-by-download attack [18], in which victims are attracted, by different means, to a malicious web page. If successful, the

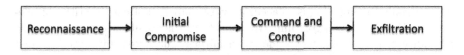

Fig. 1. The attack life cycle

exploit downloads malware on the victim's machine, which as a consequence, becomes fully under the control of the attacker [17] (Fig. 1).

In the *Command & Control phase*, the adversaries leverage the compromise of a system. More precisely, compromised systems are forced to establish a communication channel back to the adversary through which they can be directly controlled. The C2 channel enables an attacker to establish a "hands-on-keyboard" presence on the infected system (via so-called remote access tools), to install additional specialised malware modules, and to perform additional malicious actions (e.g. spread to other machines or start a denial of service attack).

In the *exfiltration phase*, the attackers extract, collect, and encrypt information stolen from the victim's environment. The information is then sent to the attackers, commonly through the same C2 channel that was established earlier.

In the following sections, we analyse existing measurement techniques that can be applied to detection and disruption of targeted attacks, with a view to understanding unsolved challenges and open problems.

3   New Attacks on Network Monitoring

Recording complete traces will prove increasingly difficult. Enterprise networks carrying a few tens of terabytes a day could result in hundreds of gigabytes of traces. It's currently possible to store traffic header traces for a few days at a time. However, the growth in network speeds will change this for the worse in the future. In the case of ISPs, the volume of traffic flow records is immense. A tier-1 ISP carries close to a hundred petabytes of user traffic per day [1], resulting in hundreds of terabytes of traffic header traces. Even with low storage and transmission costs, storing entire traffic traces beyond a short period of time is not feasible for ISP traffic while storing the entire traffic including packet data is outright impossible.

Currently, traffic monitoring is performed by routers, commonly using the Netflow [4] or sFlow feature. Alternatively, standalone measurement devices [6] observing traffic via network mirroring devices or splitters (optical or electrical) are more flexible than in-router methods. In both cases, traffic traces are exported to collectors which store the traces.

Network monitoring needs to guarantee that C2 traffic will be recorded. This can be hard to achieve as the malware can transform behaviour to evade measurement, as a consequence detection fails. Therefore apart from scalability, network measurement systems must address evasion resilience for which network-wide control is necessary.

The goal of monitoring is to accurately estimate statistical quantities of relevance to the detection algorithms. We show that it is possible to compromise the reliability of monitoring techniques with fairness guarantees by targeting their *estimation accuracy*. The relevant metric for analysing measurement evasion, is the upper bound on the variance of estimation accuracy. We will consider two sampling methods (**uniform sampling** and **weighted sampling**) and two notions of fairness (**Max-min fairness** and **Proportional fairness**).

3.1   Attacks on Uniform Sampling

Uniform sampling involves sampling each event with equal probability. A monitoring system based on this approach is Sample and Hold [8]. Uniform sampling is also used in Netflow and sFlow measurement methods which are in current deployment in most routers.

Feature distribution attack (passive): C2 traffic can easily evade uniform sampling by modifying distributions of relevant traffic features. Uniform sampling is particularly ill-suited for estimating power-law distributions. A power-law distribution is of the type $f(x)\ x^{-\gamma}$. Thus sampling with uniform probability p will mostly obtain samples representing the majority while C2 traffic escapes in the tail-end.

Spurious flow attack (active): As a variant of this attack, an active attack can be carried out by inducing a few large legitimate flows which increases the probability that a majority of the recorded packets belong to the induced flows. Note this does not require a DoS attack against any router.

To estimate the value of a traffic feature x, applying elementary sampling theory [10], an unbiased estimate for feature x is $o_x n/k$, where n/k is the uniform sampling rate and o_x is the number of observations of x within the sample set. The accuracy of the estimate is given by its variance $o_x n/k(n/k - 1)$. Increasing n by a factor of n' (active attack) decreases accuracy by a factor of n'^2. Thus most of the packet sampling budget is spent on large flows, allowing low-volume C2 flows to go systematically undetected.

3.2   Weighted Sampling

Weighted sampling [7] addresses the underlying bias of uniform sampling to accurately record traffic features used by detection algorithms such as byte count of a traffic flow. It does so by preferentially sampling from relevant traffic sub-populations. For instance, preferential selection of long-lived flows enables accurate byte count. Without fairness guarantees, weighted sampling is also damaged by the same attacks as uniform sampling, although to a lesser extent.

Given a set of n flow records with byte count $\{x_1, x_2, \ldots, x_n\}$, sampled independently, the goal is find the best sampling function $p = \{p_1, p_2, \ldots p_n\}$. Applying Horvitz-Thompson [10], an unbiased estimation of each x_i is given by (1).

$$x_i' = \begin{cases} \frac{x_i}{p_i}, & \text{if at least one sample of } x_i \text{ is observed} \\ 0, & \text{otherwise} \end{cases} \tag{1}$$

This formula is used by all sampling methods and is a root cause of monitoring problems, as we shall see.

The variance in estimation accuracy is given by: $Var(x_i') = x_i^2 \left(\frac{1}{p_i} - 1\right)$. Finally, sampling theory introduces a cost function. By optimising different cost functions, we can generate different sampling methods.

Proportional fairness: counters the weaknesses of uniform sampling that allows flooding attacks, by sampling packets with an Inclusion Probability Proportional to Size (IPPS). Thus $p_i = c_i / \sum_i c_i$. The resulting inclusion probability (into the sample set) is $\pi_i = 1 - (1 - p_i)^k$. Proportional fairness allocates sampling budget in proportion to the data rates of different traffic sub-populations.

Max-min fairness: A sampling budget allocation is fair if there is no way to increase the budget of any traffic sub-population without decreasing the allocation another sub-population. Max-min fairness is trivial to evade once the allocation is known, by applying the intelligence variance attacks. Uniform allocation is equivalent to uniform sampling and its attacks.

Minimal cost sampling method [7]: Minimises cost function $\sum_i (x_i^2/p_i + z^2 p_i)$ subject to $p_i > 0$, where z is the sampling threshold. Small flows $x_i < z$ are IPPS. Large flows $x_i \geq z$ are included with probability 1 (up to maximum sampling budget).

Proportional sampling method: Combines proportional fairness maximising a cost function of the sum of the logarithms of the allocated sampling budgets.

Other methods: There are three other methods which improve upon the ones above. VarOpt sampling [5] uses both IPPS and max-min notions of fairness. It has a fixed sampling budget (selects exactly k items on average $\sum_i p_i = k$). It minimises the cost function minimising variance across traffic sub-populations.

Attacking proportional fairness: Having discussed weighted sampling, we now propose an generic attack on all sampling techniques based on proportional sampling: proportional fairness, IPPS, and VarOpt sampling. Given the observed samples S, the information theoretic uncertainty (entropy) of the distribution over flows is the sum of two parts: $H = -\sum_{i \in S} p_i \log p_i - \sum_{i \notin S} p_i \log p_i$. One part is the contribution of observed samples and the other is the contribution of unobserved packets. Thus an error due to the **contribution of unobserved sub-populations** adds up to $-\sum_{i \notin S} p_i \log p_i$.

This could be far from negligible and its size depends on the p_i for $k \notin S$. This error arises due to weight-based inclusion where rare packet constructions have extremely low sampling probabilities. To exploit this vulnerability, we can apply the signature evasion attacks where C2 traffic continually changes form in a random manner, thus entering the noise floor as far as sampling is concerned, contributing to a negative entropy balance.

3.3   Network-Wide Orchestration

Secure measurement techniques require more than just data collection. Since sampling budgets are fixed, attackers can exploit this by flooding the sampling buffers with random data. For instance, gradually increasing the bitrate of random transmission in advance of actual C2 transmission impacts both machine learning and measurement: a high-entropy traffic feature would program ensemble based approaches such as RandomForests to look elsewhere as well as overwhelming local sampling resources.

To address these requirements, we need network-wide orchestration of measurement resources combined with flexible sampling budgets at each router. Network-wide coordination between routers can leverage unused sampling budgets at one router to cover the overflowing sampling budgets at an upstream router. Similarly, in response to localised flooding, the router might wish to initiate a change in routing topology to improve measurement. There have been a few attempts at designing such systems but these are very early days. Optimal Network-wide Sampling [3] tries to maximise the probability that every flow is sampled at least at one of the routers; cSamp [19] coordinates sampling over multiple locations to avoid duplicate measurement.

The paradigm of software-defined networks (SDN) is ideally suited for implementing such systems. SDN de-constructs a hardware router into a software controller based on a general purpose computer and specialised packet-forwarding hardware. This separation allows rapid response to dynamic changes in network state, such as efficiently dealing with localised flooding attacks intended to overwhelm the measurement system. As an early example, OpenSketch [21] proposes an extensive framework for scalable and adaptive measurement based on the Software-Defined Network paradigm. OpenSketch seeks to achieve a optimal coordinated measurement in response to network events. It uses fast hardware primitives to drive coordinated measurement of statistically significant traffic across wide-scale networks, but does not support the monitoring of low-volume traffic sub-populations such as C2 channel traffic.

4   Evaluation

To evaluate the different sampling methods, we apply each method to the CAIDA UCSD Internet Traces 2012 dataset [2]. This dataset contains anonymised internet traces captured passively on high-speed internet backbone links. We then sample the data according to flow size, use the output of each sampling method to estimate the ground truth, and measure the amount of lost information (in terms of estimation error). A positive error means an overestimation from sampling, and a negative error shows underestimation. Negative error can be seen as worse, as it indicates that significant information has been lost. The ground truth of flow sizes in the dataset can be found in Fig. 2. The majority of flow sizes are in the range of 50 to 100, with a maximum of 298500 (resulting in a mean of 441).

We evaluate four sampling strategies on the dataset: uniform, proportional fairness and inverse proportional (computed as $1 - p$, where p is the probability density function used be proportional fairness). The fourth sampling strategy is one of our own design called threshold inverse sampling, which we describe

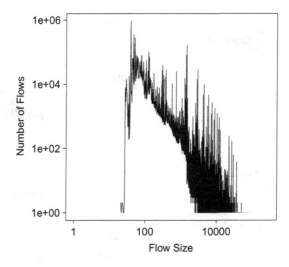

Fig. 2. Distribution of flow sizes in dataset

below, and is used to test if sampling can be improved by using a combination of the previous strategies.

Threshold Inverse Sampling. We propose a simple sampling strategy that could be used to evaluate the possibility of improving the accuracy of the sampled output. For this, we suggest threshold inverse sampling. In this approach, traffic is sampled using the inverse proportional fairness method, i.e. the sampling probability is inversely proportional to the event probability. This ensures that rare events are almost always captured. To avoid the possibility of an adversary "hiding" within frequent events, where the probability of being sampled is low, we also apply uniform sampling. By doing this, the probabilities for common flow sizes are raised to a threshold, meaning that all traffic has a minimum probability of being sampled. This level can be set appropriately. In part this will define the overall amount of data to be sampled as this will represent the most common events which will make up the largest proportion of sampled data. While this is not proposed as a full solution, we use it to measure if improvements can be made by combining sampling approaches into a single approach. As with the previous approaches, this is a static sampling strategy.

4.1 Results

Figure 3 shows the amount of error observed by the estimation of the ground truth from the various sampled outputs. The error is computed as the estimation minus the ground truth, which results in the estimation error. Figure 3(a) shows that uniform sampling results in error across all flow sizes. While the error is relatively minor for frequent sizes, for rarer sizes (small and large flow sizes) the error is significant. As the error values are largely negative, this indicates

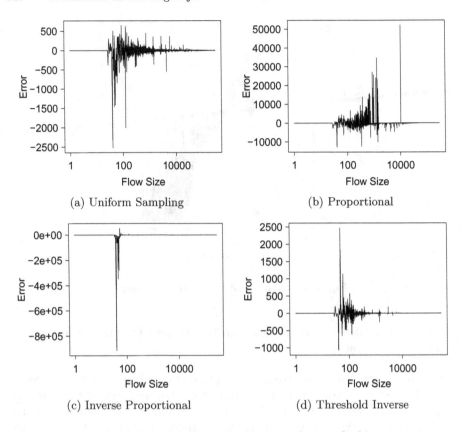

(a) Uniform Sampling   (b) Proportional

(c) Inverse Proportional   (d) Threshold Inverse

Fig. 3. Error of estimation from sampling methods

significant information is being lost. This is down to rare flow sizes being sampled with the same probability. In this case the probability is set to 0.2, so those flow sizes that feature less than 5 times are unlikely to be captured.

Proportional fairness, as shown in Fig. 3(b), achieves a slightly higher error rate for common flow sizes, but performs comparatively worst for rare sizes. Again, this is down to rare events being assigned a much lower probability than frequent events, meaning they are very unlikely to be captured. Common events are over-sampled resulting in positive error amounts, while rare events are under sampled, or in most cases not at all, resulting in negative error.

Inverse proportional sampling solves this problem by assigning the highest probabilities to rare events, meaning that they are almost always captured. The main downside is then the reverse or proportional sampling – frequent events are assigned a low probability and are therefore not sampled as accurately, as illustrated in Fig. 3(c). In this case, the frequent flow sizes result in an under-estimation error of up to 80000 for the common sizes, indicating severe under sampling of flows. There is also error on the middle-ground flow sizes of up to a few hundred under estimation.

Finally, the threshold inverse method (Fig. 3(d)) that we have put forward features the best accuracy across the entire distribution of flow sizes. In this experiment, the threshold was set to 0.2, applied to the inverse proportional density function. The method samples common events with a high accuracy (less than 2500 errors), and accurately samples the rare events (events that occur a limited number of times feature, on average, an error of <0.0001). The error is relatively evenly distributed between positive and negative values. The error for common events is on the same scale as uniform sampling, which is to be expected.

4.2 Discussion

Our experiments demonstrate that the major sampling methods (Uniform, Proportional, and Inverse Proportional) exhibit vulnerabilities in the form of sampling bias. These biases enable adversaries to shape traffic behaviour to evade sampling. Even the threshold approach (proposed by this paper) that attempts to prevent this by ensuring all behaviour has a minimum likelihood of being sampled still loses information. Flows of common sizes only have a one in five chance of being sampled. Both uniform and proportional sampling poorly represent less common behaviour. In any sampling strategy that is used for detection these rarer events are useful so should always be sampled. The common behaviour cannot be ignored as it also provides valuable information and could contain malicious behaviour. All of these static approaches have to trade off collection on one type of traffic over another in order to maintain the effect of sampling, so each provides means for an adversary to hide.

The threshold sampling method will work well in cases where common events are large in number, thus need to be sampled to limit the amount of data, whilst maintaining accuracy, in particular for rare events. This is down to the fact that rare events will almost always be sampled, while the common events can be sampled to the desired rate by setting the threshold to an appropriate value. The distribution of events, such as flow sizes, should have tall, narrow peaks (power law and log normal distributions can provide this). Where it will not work so well, however is if the distribution features wide peaks with gradual slopes (such as a normal distribution).

A common limitation that all of these strategies, including threshold inverse, fall victim to is that they are all static in nature. They all assume constant behaviour and do not take into account that an adversary can change their behaviour. They are also static in terms of the probabilities assigned for sampling, no matter how much traffic there is to be measured.

It is clear from this that dynamic strategies need to be developed in order to maximise the effectiveness of sampling given the current state of the network. A simple solution could be implemented by changing sampling strategies regularly in an unpredictable manner, with regards to the adversary. So, for one time period use proportional sampling, then for the next use inverse proportional. This would make it difficult for the adversary to shape traffic in order to evade sampling.

A point to consider is that the amount of traffic flowing through a network will not be static throughout the day. For example, a corporate network will have far less traffic outside of business hours than during. It does not make sense to keep the same sampling strategy in place during this time, when a greater percentage of the traffic can be collected and processed. So a sampling strategy should be in part influenced by traffic characteristics (such as cumulative traffic) other than that which is the key measure for sampling (such as the flow size), and be adjusted regularly.

With increases in computational power it may also become possible to apply in-line analysis to exclude certain flows from being sampled. Allowing resources to be used on more interesting flows. Of course this would have to be an extremely lightweight system that could, for example, recognise known legitimate web requests (for example, those to bbc.co.uk which are highly unlikely to be malicious). This solution will need to be carefully designed however; to avoid opportunities for an attacker to hide themselves. Rather than simply exclude flows from being sampled, flows to known safe locations (such as bbc.co.uk) could be sampled at a lower rate than to those domains that are untrusted or provide greater opportunity for abuse (such as twitter.com).

In larger networks that feature many different entry points to the network, as well as various levels of sub-nets within, sampling can be carried out at multiple points over the same traffic, using the same sampling strategy. This will provide more opportunities to capture malicious traffic while not increasing the strain on resources on any one point.

5   Conclusion

Behavioural analysis techniques depend on traffic collection mechanisms to detect malice or anomalies in network traffic. However to deal with high traffic volumes whilst ensuring low processing latency, network operators rely on measurement techniques that record a subset of the traffic, as opposed to recording full traffic traces. In this work, we have analysed the resilience of current network measurement techniques against intelligent adversaries that shape network traffic with the intent of evading collection.

One insight of our work is that current network measurement techniques are easy to evade. They exhibit biases that are readily exploitable. The second insight is that it is possible to do better; we have proposed a new measurement technique that has better evasion resistance properties. However, it is far from perfection and further investigation into evasion resistant sampling techniques is necessary.

Both academia and industry have been fighting malware C2 communication channels for close to a decade now. The focus of most of the current work is in the direction of detection mechanisms. However little attention has been paid to measurement techniques – the assumption that all traffic can be recorded is increasingly under stress as traffic volumes increase. In this context, reliable measurement techniques are an important requirement. If C2 traffic cannot be recorded, then detection algorithms cannot work, no matter how good they are.

From time to time, experts have proclaimed that the problem has been solved, only to find their confidence has been misplaced due to subsequent attacks. In this paper we argue that a focus on global-scale measurement architectures for C2 traffic is missing and needs attention. Current ISP-scale measurement techniques do not offer the properties necessary for C2 detection, thus creating a gap where surveillance apparatus can work without encumbrances.

Thus an important challenge is the scalable collection of traffic traces. With increasing traffic rates it will soon become hard to store all traffic even in enterprise networks thus forcing defenders to rely on estimation via sampling techniques. This is already required at ISPs and datacentre networks.

In the light of these challenges, the problem of characterising C2 traffic behaviour from sampled traffic requires a shift of perspective. Researchers need to take a step back to focus on the big picture. First, the challenges of building secure measurement techniques has not received the necessary attention in the security community — the 'needle-in-the-haystack' problem is challenging and some approaches have been outlined from sampling theory but these do not work in an adversarial setting. Apart from sampling techniques, the measurement architecture has to be open and extensible, allowing network wide coordination to focus measurement resources on attack traffic rather than trying to work out broad trends as it has historically done.

There is a pressing need for the research and development of better publicly available C2 defence techniques, especially built into routers, which are essential to routing information, and where data naturally aggregates. The need for open and flexible frameworks might benefit from Software-Defined Networking. These open-source platforms are of great value. SDN deconstructs current hardware routers into controllers (running on general purpose computers) and programmable hardware running on specialised hardware. This allows incorporating innovations in sampling and detection directly into the router. SDN massively slashes the costs of evaluating and deploying techniques. Expensive hardware routers costing hundreds of thousands of dollars, are replaced by general-purpose computers and a one-off investment in routing hardware. Thus enabling rapid deployment of new techniques that keep up with attacker advances.

The increasingly targeted nature of todays attacks are indicative combined with high levels of attacker motivation presents a challenging problem. Judging from innovations in targeted malware, we see the need to develop traffic measurement mechanisms which can accurately instrument traffic characteristics of malware with high-stealth properties. Since C2 is a critical part of malware design, we expect malware capabilities to shape and morph traffic in order to achieve full measurement evasion. We hope that this paper will help with the development of novel measurement techniques which can keep up with malware agents that incorporate dynamic traffic morphing behaviour.

References

1. AT&T global networking facts. http://www.corp.att.com/gov/about_ags/fact_sheet
2. The CAIDA UCSD Anonymized Internet Traces 2012. http://www.caida.org/data/passive/passive_2012_dataset.xml. Accessed 20 March 2013
3. Cantieni, G.R., Iannaccone, G., Barakat, C., Diot, C., Thiran, P.: Reformulating the monitor placement problem: Optimal network-wide sampling. In: Proceedings of the 2006 ACM CoNEXT Conference, CoNEXT '06, pp. 5:1–5:12. ACM, New York (2006)
4. Cisco Systems Inc., Cisco IOS Netflow. http://www.cisco.com/web/go/netflow
5. Cohen, E., Duffield, N.G., Kaplan, H., Lund, C., Thorup, M.: Stream sampling for variance-optimal estimation of subset sums. In: Mathieu, C. (ed.) Proceedings of ACM-SIAM Symposium on Discrete Algorithms, pp. 1255–1264. SIAM (2009)
6. Cranor, C., Johnson, T., Spataschek, O., Shkapenyuk, V.: Gigascope: a stream database for network applications. In: Proceedings of the 2003 ACM SIGMOD International Conference on Management of Data, SIGMOD '03, pp. 647–651. ACM, New York (2003)
7. Duffield, N., Lund, C., Thorup, M.: Learn more, sample less: control of volume and variance in network measurement. IEEE Trans. Inf. Theory **51**(5), 1756–1775 (2005)
8. Estan, C., Varghese, G.: New directions in traffic measurement and accounting: Focusing on the elephants, ignoring the mice. ACM Trans. Comput. Syst. **21**(3), 270–313 (2003)
9. Franklin, J., Paxson, V., Perrig, A., Savage, S.: An inquiry into the nature and causes of the wealth of internet miscreants. In: Proceedings of the 14th ACM Conference on Computer and Communications Security, CCS '07, pp. 375–388. ACM, New York (2007)
10. Horvitz, D.G., Thompson, D.J.: A generalization of sampling without replacement from a finite universe. J. Am. Stat. Assoc. **47**(260), 663–685 (1952)
11. Hutchins, E.M., Clopperty, M.J., Amin, R.M.: Intelligence-Driven Computer Network Defense Informed by Analysis of Adversary Campaigns and Intrusion Kill Chains. Technical report, Lockheed Martin Corporation, 2010. http://www.lockheedmartin.com/content/dam/lockheed/data/corporate/documents/LM-White-Paper-Intel-Driven-Defense.pdf
12. Krebs, B.: Security Firm Bit9 Hacked, Used to Spread Malware. Krebs on Security, 13 Feb 2013. http://krebsonsecurity.com/2013/02/security-firm-bit9-hacked-used-to-spread-malware/
13. Mandiant. APT1: Exposing One of Chinas Cyber Espionage Units. Technical report, 2013. http://intelreport.mandiant.com/Mandiant_APT1_Report.pdf
14. Nagaraja, S., Anderson, R.: The snooping dragon: social-malware surveillance of the tibetan movement. Technical Report UCAM-CL-TR-746, University of Cambridge, (2009)
15. Nakashima, E.: Confidential report lists U.S. weapons system designs compromised by Chinese cyberspies. The Washington Post, 27 May 2013. http://articles.washingtonpost.com/2013-05-27/world/39554997_1_u-s-missile-defenses-weapons-combat-aircraft
16. Perlroth, N.: Hackers in China Attacked The Times for Last 4 Months. The New York Times, 30 January 2013. http://www.nytimes.com/2013/01/31/technology/chinese-hackers-infiltrate-new-york-times-computers.html

17. Polychronakis, M., Mavrommatis, P., Provos, N.:. Ghost turns zombie: Exploring the life cycle of web-based malware. In: Proceedings of the 1st Usenix Workshop on Large-Scale Exploits and Emergent Threats, LEET'08, pp. 11:1–11:8. USENIX Association, Berkeley (2008)
18. Provos, N., Rajab, M.A., Mavrommatis, P.: Cybercrime 2.0: When the cloud turns dark. Commun. ACM **52**(4), 42–47 (2009)
19. Sekar, V., Reiter, M.K., Willinger, W., Zhang, H., Kompella, R.R., Andersen, D.G.: Csamp: a system for network-wide flow monitoring. In: Proceedings of the 5th USENIX Symposium on Networked Systems Design and Implementation, NSDI'08, pp. 233–246. USENIX Association, Berkeley (2008)
20. TrendLabs APT Research Team. Spear-Phishing Email: Most Favored APT Attack Bait. Technical report, Trend Micro Incorporated, 2012. http://www. trendmicro.com/cloud-content/us/pdfs/security-intelligence/white-papers/ wp-spear-phishing-email-most-favored-apt-attack-bait.pdf
21. Yu, M., Jose, L., Miao, R.: Software defined traffic measurement with opensketch. In: Proceedings of the 10th USENIX Conference on Networked Systems Design and Implementation, NSDI'13, pp. 29–42. USENIX Association, Berkeley (2013)

On the Reliability of Network Measurement Techniques Used for Malware Traffic Analysis (Transcript of Discussion)

Shishir Nagaraja[✉]

University of Birmingham, Birmingham, UK
s.nagaraja@cs.bham.ac.uk

Morning everybody. I'm going to talk about work along with my PhD student, Joe Gardiner, who's sitting here. A while back we surveyed the literature on targeted attacks and defenses, for the CPNI[1], and we found a number of unsolved challenges in the area. One of them is the challenges of measurement in large scale networks, which this talk is about.

This is a slide showing the importance of targeted attacks. Initially we have had reputation based viruses, and then we had DDoS attacks (still have them), cyber crime, botnets, and so on, and now we have got a fair amount of targeted attacks. And the main difference is, of course, that in a targeted attack the adversary decides on a particular victim that they want to compromise; they're not opportunistic, so they're adaptive and persistent. A key step in this, this is sort of connecting to the kill chain that the other speakers mentioned on day 1, is you make an intrusion into the user's network, you set up a C&C channel, and then you get involved in some kind of data exfiltration or sabotage.

So the point we are trying to make is that existing defences are only partially effective. When Ross (Anderson) and I worked on this in 2009 we discovered the first publicly documented intrusion, which could be considered a targeted attack, into the office of the Dalai Lama, in the foothills of the Himalayas. And this was in 2009, in 2011 Google and the government of India were compromised with a very similar attack, and there have been loads of them since. If you look at the current story, targeted attacks according to Symantec constitutes 24 % in the manufacturing sector, sort of 20 % in other areas as well, about 10 % to 15 % in finance and aerospace according to the Mandiant Report.

Frank Stajano: 24 % of what? Of the attacks on Symantec?

Reply: No, it's 24 % of targeted attacks, it's the percentage of where the targeted attacks take place.

Frank Stajano: So can we compare them across the reports made by different people?

Reply: Yes, but all the numbers are for targeted attacks.

---

[1] Centre for the Protection of National Infrastructure, http://www.cpni.gov.uk/advice/cyber/idata/.

© Springer International Publishing Switzerland 2014
B. Christianson et al. (Eds.): Security Protocols 2014, LNCS 8809, pp. 334–339, 2014.
DOI: 10.1007/978-3-319-12400-1_32

Frank Stajano: So in the second column we have 17 % of the targeted attacks found by Mandiant are in aerospace.

Reply: Yes, correct.

Frank Stajano: And the other column 24 % of the attacks found by Symantec?

Reply: Yes, correct, so these are two different sources. We also see a fair amount of attacks in large as well as small organisations, so the organisation size is not really an indicator of where targeted attacks take place. They take place along a fair number of sectors. If you look at the total number of attacks then according to Symantec it's about 25 % of the total number of attacks they see are targeted attacks at the moment. So attacks span multiple sectors, and organisation sizes is not a predictor for attack likelihood.

On the defence side, what we see is a combination of measurement and detection, so you've got S-Flow and NetFlow, which are traffic collection techniques. And then we've got a whole slew of detection algorithms in the literature, many of which claim fairly high accuracy rates, detection rates, and low false positive rates, and underlying these are various machine learning approaches. Whether these are or are not capable of defending against targeted attacks is a different talk. In this talk I'm going to look at the measurement approaches, and see to what extent they can actually support the detection literature. Detection algorithms assume that the traffic can actually be captured, whereas I think in the first place that is a questionable assumption.

So this is a cartoon[2] showing the defence industry/anti-virus industry in 1998, and the bad guys are running, and we're kind of winning, and here are the tides turning, and the bad guys are winning quite a bit. So the question is, why is this actually happening? If you look at the targeted attacks, I think the threat model has fundamentally changed. We started to see machine learning approaches being proposed around early 2000s, some even late 1990s, and started off in the intrusion detection community first. And the assumption was, I think, that the attackers were opportunistic, they were trying to get into your network, but if they couldn't they would get into somebody else's network. And that's no longer true with targeted attacks, because the adversaries goal is to compromise your network; they don't care about somebody else's, they're after you. So this means that the measurement technique that you have should give reliable guarantees that the attack traffic will be recorded in the first place. Whatever policy you operate on the routers needs to give you that assurance. Similarly detection should be invasion resistant as well.

So let's look at the first part, invasion resistant measurement. What we want is, we want an ISP or an enterprise operator to be able to execute a drill down query on a suspicious bit of traffic. You've got incoming traffic, your intrusion detection flags this bit of traffic as suspicious, well you need to be able to then go on and get everything about that type of traffic in your network, and be able to dig in and do some sort of deep inspection and so on. So the naïve approach to

---

[2] http://blogs.msdn.com/b/tzink/archive/2012/06/08/evolution-of-the-antivirus-industry.aspx

that is, hey let's store all the traffic, and then we can go back in time, if you had infinite storage capabilities, but that of course can be impractical, or it can be inefficient at the very minimum. A tier-1 ISP, which is carrying a large amount of traffic, can find it difficult, but in theory at least it's possible. Certainly it is inefficient in all the cases. If you have limited sampling budget you can't store everything, what policy would you operate on your routers to get a complete view of what's going on?.

So let's look at current measurement techniques. The basic one that's operated by NetFlow, as well S-Flow, is one or the other version of uniform sampling. What uniform sampling says is that each traffic population is sampled with the same probability, whether it's low volume or high volume flow, all types of packet constructions will be sampled with the same probability. This has the nice property that the attacker can't really change the probability with which events are recorded, at least on the face of it. So the probability for low volume as well as high volume of DoS flows, is going to be the same. The assumption is of course that the traffic features vary according to our normal distribution, and if you have a normal distribution, a uniform sampling strategy can give you a reasonable view of what's going on.

One possible attack against this is you exploit the Gaussian assumption, right. Why should the traffic flow, a variable in the hands of the attacker, follow a particular feature distribution? Assuming that it's distributed like that, as an attacker controlled variable, and they can distribute that way, as a parallel, for example. So this is saying that, this can be interpreted in two ways: (1) that the packet flow, packet sizes, or any other traffic feature, instead of following a single static value could vary. Alternately, if this is the distribution, a feature distribution of all flows that the router is seeing, well you locate yourself in the part where you're least likely to be sampled, because sampling budget is fixed, if you've got uniform sampling, well that's going to take a major chunk of the sample budget, so you just locate yourself at a place where you're least likely to be sampled. That's a passive attack. An active approach would be that if there aren't enough places to hide, well you can induce spurious flows, large flows, that consume the sampling budget quickly, so that wherever you're located in the statistical frame, you're not going to get caught or the probability is kind of lower.

So if ox is like the observation (number of observations), and n is the sampling (total number of samples), then the sampling budget, you're looking at n/k samples; out of every k you record n, so the unbiased estimate is the number of observations divided by the sampling probability. The accuracy is the variance over the estimate, which is actually a function of the square of your n. So if you change n to n' then the effect on the accuracy of the estimation is actually square of what the attacker is able to change.

So what we did was we looked at the CAIDA[3] dataset from 2012, and looked at just the flow sizes, and that's the distribution on a law log scale, basically the number of flows on the y axis and the flow sizes. We've got a fair number of small

---

[3] http://www.caida.org/home/

flows and quite a few large flows. So if you do uniform sampling then basically you get something like that kind of distribution. And as you can observe the difference is in that part, and also in that part. So it's fine to get a picture of the global trends, but if you're trying to understand the rare events in your network then uniform sampling isn't going to work very well. So that's the estimation error from the ground truth, which is the estimated minus the ground truth, and that gives you the actual number of errors. So for small volume traffic you're looking at a fair amount of error there.

In response to that in the literature we've got weighted sampling, which says, let's not look at every event with the same probability, we'll have different probabilities associated with different events. And so if you have got a low probability or a rare event, we'll sample that with a higher probability, and therefore we can make up for these errors. So the basic idea is fine, you have two variants, you've got inclusion probability proportional to the number of events, and inclusion probability inversely proportional to the size of the traffic, so the population you're interested in. This can also be attacked, and well the basic observation is that it's better than low volume, in dealing with low volume proofs than uniform, but the problem is that rare events still have an extremely low probability mass associated with them, and so they don't actually get included. When you look at the evaluation this is proportional to the size, so it's a really bad outcome, it's sort of the lower bound, the upper bound on the error in a way. But if you inversely associate it, slightly better, but you still see a gap in the small volume communications that turns up. This side is much, much better than uniform sampling, so certainly an improvement.

So we compare the error rates in uniform, then in proportional, inversely proportional, and thresholded inverse, so these are the various existing schemes in there, so the point I'm trying to make is, they can all be attacked by the attacker either carrying out passive statistical transformations, or active attacks, which changes the statistics of the recorded traffic. So the fact we need a better algorithmic approach is basically one of the conclusions of our study. And one approach which is rather pretty naive and basic, I think, is, well I think it is a good idea for sampling probability to be inversely proportional to the traffic, so population and size, but you also need to raise the probability of frequent events high enough so that you don't lose out in that sense. So you increase any sampling probability below the threshold, normalise the whole thing to add up to 1, and that's a slightly better approach we felt.

So when you run that up, so that's the ground truth, and that's the estimate, it seems much, much closer than any of the others, but I think fundamentally the problem is kind of different. Algorithmically it looks better, but I'm still not too pleased with it, and the reason is basically I think the issue is that if you operate any static policy on your routers you're going to lose no matter what that policy is. You can have slightly better static policies than others, and we've proposed one, I'm sure others could propose much better ones. But what you need is you need a dynamic policy where, on the router, so that the amount of sampling resources which you have can be dynamically allocated and altered depending on what you want to measure in the network. So if you've got a link with four routers, for example, and the first one isn't able to look at completely at whatever you wish to look at, then the second, third and fourth one need to sort of chip in with their unused sampling budgets in order to ensure that you have a fair picture of what's going on.

Again, when you talk about drill down queries, and your detection mechanism tells you that a certain statistical profile is important, and that's the one that we need to be focusing on rather than setting up NetFlow to say that, OK, this is what we do we record source, IP and port numbers, and packet sizes of everything, and that's the static policy we operate. But it's not exactly, you know, a silver bullet, but if you have a dynamic policy, dynamic policies can also attract possibly more interesting attacks than static policies, because they can be altered. They are traffic dependent, and so one criticism against dynamic policies could be that they're actually more vulnerable because attackers can control them much more easily. But on the face of it clearly static policies are, I think, non-serviceable, not up to the job, and so we need better stuff.

So in this context SDN could be a promising tool. You have the controller, which is talking to various switches, and can ensure network-wide coordination, and orchestration of resources to be placed at different parts of the network depending on what is it that you need to be focusing on. Instead of each router trying to do the whole job, you sort of divide it up in a proper organised manner, coordinated manner, and the controller can achieve that necessary organisation.

Robert Watson: Are you imagining that the SDN would be used in response to actual network traffic, or it would be used in response to your change in understanding of the things that you want to monitor, and it's known that an issue of SDN is scalability, a router, it ties the routers to controllers, and if we're really talking about high levels of traffic, that's not really plausible, to hold up every flow as it comes in to decide what to do with it.

Reply: I guess the scalability issues are with respect to, for instance, verification of the changes to the forwarding plane, but if you're just focusing, for instance, you could still have that static if you have scalability problems, but just ensure that the monitoring techniques that you apply across a set of routers has a feedback loop from the detection algorithms where you apply a scalable version first, and then you decide that, this is what I want to look at further, so well let's get the monitoring to generate the kind of amount of traffic so the appropriate detection algorithm can go into it.

Robert Watson: I guess the real trick there is just to make sure that you deal with the limitations on SDN scalability in a way that you're not vulnerable to exploitations.

Reply: Yes.

Robert Watson: If your SDN switch isn't somehow limited to monitoring 10,000 flows, or 20,000 flows, and you take a 20 to 40 millisecond round trip every time you have these flows.

Reply: Well SDN switches are now around 128,000 flows, and it's been increasing as more and more of the vendors are convinced that is a possible.

Robert Watson: Yes, the roundtrip time there is a big issue, it's not that they can actually fill 128,000 rules if you frequent changes in flows.

Reply: Yes, there's also the amount of TK memories on most of the switches is a bit of a problem. But I think those are primarily engineering challenges, which are waiting for the appropriate amount of capital to be injected.

Robert Watson: Speed of light is a tricky engineering challenge.

Michael Roe: How do you know whether an event is a rare event or not, so uniform sampling is easy, this packet comes in, you generate a random number and sample it, whereas presumably you just do estimate from some features of the packet where you think it's a rare event.

Reply: You make the judgement based on the historical frequency of event occurrence.

Beyond Trust

Partha Das Chowdhury[✉] and Bruce Christianson

University of Hertfordshire, Hertfordshire, UK
partha.dc@gmail.com, b.christianson@herts.ac.uk

Abstract. Risk as studied conventionally and risk as manifested in actuality differ widely both in semantics and content. In this paper we explore the possibility of managing risk without resorting to transitive and compulsive relationships termed as "trust". We draw an exploitable analogy with the assumptions under which cooperation is observed in repeated strategic games and posit that voluntary cooperation between players with mutually incompatible commitments is indeed possible provided that such cooperation can be promiscuous.

1 Introduction

Christianson [1] draws a distinction between latent trust and actuated trust where trust can be interpreted as a measure of risk [4]. We start with the converse of this and draw the same parallel between latent risk (risk as defined and studied) and actuated risk (risks as manifested and accepted). In the conventional literature on computer systems and security we find extensive coverage of the former, while the latter seems to have blown off all the behavioural and threat assumptions of this analysis.

Conventionally the basic modeling unit in systems and their interactions is the individual agent. This modelling includes the agents' beliefs, preferences, and possible actions. Security literature, traditionally, has the good principals Alice, Bob and Carol, with Carol as the system/service owner. There is also Eve who wants to listen and Moriarty who tends to be more aggressive than Eve in his adventures to harm Alice, Bob and Carol. Carol, Alice and Bob are all aware of Eve and Moriarty, and thus define – and share – a risk model.

The realized actuality (actuated risk) seems to be wide apart in both semantics and content from these conventional definitions (latent risk). For example, although Carol, Alice and Bob are cooperating, they may have different goals and agendas, and consequently can well be adversaries and so be a threat to each other along with Eve and Moriarty. Eve and Moriarty may be providing part or all of the system infrastructure. There is no clear distinction between participant and attacker. Even if Carol is not the attacker then a subcontractor Snowy for Carol can be a whistleblower without any incentive to protect either Alice or Bob or Carol. However the risks for Alice and Bob differ from those of Carol. This tryst between latent risk and actuated risk presents a deeper challenge than the study of latent trust and actuated trust, as the latter in many ways is dependent on the

© Springer International Publishing Switzerland 2014
B. Christianson et al. (Eds.): Security Protocols 2014, LNCS 8809, pp. 340–344, 2014.
DOI: 10.1007/978-3-319-12400-1_33

former [4]. Nonetheless it is impossible for either Alice, Bob or Carol to achieve anything meaningful without the cooperation/participation of one another in the system.

In this position paper we explore the assumptions and possible security innovations that can allow Alice, Bob and Carol to cooperate in a manner that takes into account the shifting assumptions of the risk model.

2   Case for Departure

In [1] Christianson argues that in the distributed world trust relations are not really promiscuous: all trust relationships that the system can warrant must turn upon meaning in the sense of intension, and consequently system design is more like diplomacy than engineering. Different principals can have different, undeclared, reasons for trusting a system. Threat perceptions differ, expectations differ but the same set of countermeasures can satisfy divergent expectations.

Given the overwhelming realities that attackers are omnipresent, relationships are intensional, and cooperation is a requirement, we posit that promiscuous cooperation between various stakeholders of a system can facilitate risk management. Promiscuous cooperation, we believe, is an obvious fallout of intensional relations. In the example cited in [1], Alice trusts Carol since Bob does so, but Carol's broadcast about Bob's state information has different meanings for Alice than for Bob. So the cooperation between Carol and Alice, though not harmful to Alice, is certainly promiscuous in nature. We elaborate the duality of cooperation and promiscuous behaviour in Sect. 4.

3   Assumptions

Alice and Bob (who are otherwise political opponents) are under enemy occupation and Carol controls the system infrastructure Alice and Bob use to communicate between them as well as with principals of friendly nations. Alice and Bob must pretend loyalty to Carol and not burn each other in the process. However Alice's own safety is paramount to her and the same applies to Bob. So in spite of their common cause of defeating Carol they ought not reveal information to each other which can be used by the other in the event of any coercion by Carol. The relation between Alice and Bob like many relations in the real world is not contractual in a formal legal sense, but is a human contract and ongoing. However there are no side channels, arbitrators or side payments involved to sustain this cooperation.

In our quest for an understanding of whether cooperation between Alice and Bob is feasible in this case we draw from the fundamentals of non-cooperative game theory [3,5,8]. In repeated yet finite (where the participants know the exact number of iterations) iterations of the Prisoner's Dilemma, we observe a tendency among the participants to defect, as that is the dominant strategy. Since the participants are going to defect anyway at the last period so their cooperation unravels even on the previous stages. For example among final year students in relationships in colleges, if there are pairs which would be taking up jobs far away from each other, one or both participants in such pairs might show signs of warming up to other potential partners in the final year.

However, in case of strategic games (like Prisoner's Dilemma) if we tweak the rules of iteration and toss a coin twice after every period with the rule that only two heads will stop the game, participants (in absence of the knowledge of the exact number of periods) start to cooperate. Principals tend to cooperate initially to set a reputation, but then back out the following times only in absence of reciprocation. For our purposes let us assume that the enemy occupation will end but neither Alice nor Bob knows when it will end. So the phenomenon of cooperation (in absence of any specific knowledge about the duration of the relationship) can be represented as

Play C ; { if (NONE Plays D) then (Play C) else (Play D) }*

This concept is being formalized in the literature on non-cooperative games as the Grim Trigger Strategy. In order for this to be an equilibrium it must satisfy the following condition:

Temptation (defect) $\leq$ d $\cdot$ [Temptation (reward) $-$ Temptation (punishment)]

where $d = P(\text{Tomorrow}) < 1$ since tomorrow might not happen, i.e. the enemy occupation might end. In case of Prisoner's Dilemma it can be shown that cooperation can be induced using Grim Trigger (as a sub game perfect equilibrium) if $d \geq 1/3$, i.e. Alice and Bob cooperate if the possibility of interaction tomorrow is greater than 1/3. For a detailed proof the reader can refer to [3,5,8].

It can also be shown that even when the interactions are limited (say the enemy occupation ends soon and the time frame is known to Alice and Bob) if there are several Nash Equilibriums in the stage games then we can use the prospect of playing different equilibria tomorrow to provide different incentives (rewards and punishments) to induce cooperation today.

In business or personal relationships, promises and threats of good and bad behavior tomorrow may provide good incentives for good behavior today, but, to work, these promises and threats must be credible. In particular, they must come from equilibrium behavior tomorrow, and hence form part of a sub game perfect equilibrium today. We find that the grim trigger strategy forms such equilibria provided that we are patient and the game has a probability $\geq 1/3$ of continuing.

4   Promiscuous Cooperation

Further to the discussions in Sect. 3 we learn that the cooperation between Alice and Bob would only sustain under the conditions of a credible threat (enemy occupation) when the probability of the credible threat to continue at each stage is greater than 1/3. There are no side payments, nor an arbitrator, nor a side channel. However game theorists tend to assume that there is consensus about the object of the game, and that the players will act rationally: thus discounting the reality that Alice and Bob can have mutually incompatible commitments and objectives, which can be perfectly rational (though mutually opaque). So Alice and Bob would need the (technical) ability to protect themselves from each other's mutually incompatible commitments, for this cooperation to sustain[1]. Herein lies the need for cooperation and promiscuous behavior to coexist.

Thus, we propose to include the service of Plausible Deniability [7] in the mechanisms that Alice and Bob use to communicate. Roe considers the problem of ensuring that an instance of semantic communication between computer systems leaves behind no unequivocal evidence of its having taken place. Features of communications protocols that were seen as defects from the standpoint of nonrepudiation can be seen as benefits from the standpoint of this converse security requirement, which is termed "plausible deniability".

In a scenario where Bob defects to Carol or is coerced Alice needs to repudiate all communications Bob claims to be from Alice. Oneway this can be achieved is by using symmetric keys as explained in [1]. There are other mechanisms for large groups to sustain such deniable cooperation under threat. Ring signature [2,6] is one of them within a reasonably large group. We are not particularly tied to a particular mechanism but more to the possibility and semantics of such cooperation. We focus on the possibility where protocols leave an independent observer unable to resolve disputes of the form "Alice says Bob created the message but Bob says Alice created the message". Various mechanisms to support Plausible Deniability are discussed in detail in [7].

It is worth pointing out here that even if the number of interactions is limited i.e. Alice and Bob are aware of the tenure of the relationship, still they will not defect, in contrast with the results we have in Prisoner's Dilemma. The ability to deny (effectively, to defect with retrospective effect) provides the incentive to cooperate given the common threat of enemy occupation. So even if Bob defects tomorrow Alice can always deny all past communications and defect in future. Thus they will not unravel the dominant strategy of the last period as seen in case of Prisoner's Dilemma. The service of plausible deniability, we believe is a significant improvement in limited interactions as well because (technically) it provides different incentives (rewards and punishments) to facilitate cooperation today.

5 Conclusions

The narratives of conflict in computer systems have undergone a sea change in the last twenty years. The distinctions between insiders and outsiders are blurred more than ever. Traditional assumptions about the honesty and competence of insiders do not hold anymore. If we aim to sustain cooperation between individuals with disparate interests and preferences, it is important for a credible

---

[1] To reflect the Grim Trigger Strategy which allows reciprocation following defection by the other participant. See Sect. 3.

threat to exist with real rewards and punishments along with a service of plausible deniability. Promiscuous cooperation then becomes an attractive option in systems design.

However the cooperation we propose in this paper is not a strong cooperation as in the classical byzantine problem. All we get to know is that someone in a group cheated. Although we learn from game theory, we do not necessarily include their assumptions that principals behave in a transparently rational way, and that payoffs are public knowledge. Mutually incompatible commitments are an integral part of our model and thus define different rational behaviours for the different agents.

In the case of distributed systems the advantage we have is the presence of so many players that apparently irrational individual behaviour can potentially cancel out. For example players with mutually incompatible commitments who are in a collaboration can lose out on a particular occasion in order to gain later (on average) in their long term pursuit. Such decisions when applied by multi-players can cancel each other out without having any impact on collective cooperation.

What is significant to us is the availability of a strategy that enables us to defect in response to a defection without caring much about the rationale for such behaviour on the part of the partner/adversary. The ability to defect/retaliate retrospectively in case someone cheats, thus acting as a deterrent, we believe to be a significant improvement. Since we do not commit at every stage of the game there is no longer the same risk involved in trusting a potential enemy. So far as using our model for negotiations (legal or financial) is concerned, we believe that there is significant amount of research that will be required; however it seems useful to have the ability to repudiate retrospectively any transaction while there is still a possibility that the deal may go wrong.

References

1. Christianson, B.: Living in an impossible world. Philos. Technol. **26**(4), 411–429 (2013)
2. Das Chowdhury, P., Christianson, B., Malcolm, J.A.: Anonymous context based role activation mechanism. In: Christianson, B., Crispo, B., Malcolm, J.A., Roe, M. (eds.) Security Protocols 2005. LNCS, vol. 4631, pp. 315–321. Springer, Heidelberg (2007)
3. Dixit, A., Nalebuff, B.: Thinking Strategically. Norton, New York (1991)
4. Harbison, W.: Trusting in computer systems. Technical report 437, University of Cambridge (1997)
5. Dutta, P.K.: Strategies and Games: Theory and Practice. MIT, Cambridge (1999)
6. Rivest, R.L., Shamir, A., Tauman, Y.: How to leak a secret. In: Boyd, C. (ed.) ASIACRYPT 2001. LNCS, vol. 2248, pp. 552–565. Springer, Heidelberg (2001)
7. Roe, M.: Cryptography and Evidence. Ph.D. thesis, University of Cambridge (1997)
8. Watson, J.: Strategy: An Introduction to Game Theory. Norton, New York (2002)

Beyond Trust (Transcript of Discussion)

Partha Das Chowdhury[✉]

University of Hertfordshire, Hertfordshire, UK
partha.dc@gmail.com

The motion before us in this workshop is that attackers now control so much of the infrastructure that it's impossible to do anything without their active cooperation. In one of Bruce's recent papers[1] he speaks about latent trust and actuated trust. I find some reflections of that in the theme of this workshop, where we can distinguish latent risk, like risk as we study it, and actuated risk, risk as we find it manifested. So in this paper we are trying to analyse if it's possible to have a collaboration, a cooperation between people who are otherwise opponents or have some mutually incompatible commitments, and if cooperation is possible then what direction we can take so that we can implement that kind of cooperation.

In conventional computer science security we have Alice, Bob and Carol, who are supposedly the good guys, and there is Eve, who wants to listen, and there is Moriarty, who is a bit more aggressive. Now in this conventional model, Eve and Moriarty are more or less outsiders. Even in such a threat model you always have an element of the unknown, where every participant will at some point assert something about their state of the system, which somebody else will believe to be true, and act upon that.

Bruce Christianson: Alice can never sure of what the state of the system is remotely, because she can't see it. So in some sense, when you design the protocol, you have to get someone else to tell Alice what that part of the remote state is, and then she has to act as if she believes what they tell her.

Reply: Now this kind of arrangement leaves us in a scenario where there is an element of unknown about what's happening at the other end, and that gives rise to the dreaded T word, the trust word. So these kind of relationships we usually term as trust relationships. Now the word trust becomes a cover for everything we don't know, everything that is unknown, so we tend to perceive them as somewhat compulsive, and undesirable[2].

Now we learn from a thesis which was presented by Bill Harbison, that trust is a measure of risk: if I trust my doctor to keep my information safe, that means the doctor has the potential ability to harm me. Now in that recent work by Bruce he says that one reason we don't have transitive trust relationships, is because participants can be reticent about what they trust, whom they trust, and why they trust, and that reticence can block transitivity. So basically my trust *assumptions* are not dependent on what others assert about a system.

---

[1] Living in an Impossible World.
[2] Even though we can't do without them.

© Springer International Publishing Switzerland 2014
B. Christianson et al. (Eds.): Security Protocols 2014, LNCS 8809, pp. 345–349, 2014.
DOI: 10.1007/978-3-319-12400-1_34

The idea is, the less the need to trust, the better it is for participants, so this lack of shared knowledge about the trust assumptions of other participants, or maybe even of its principles, actually can aid in system design, and this explains why in practice your system design becomes more a matter of diplomacy than engineering. Now participants can agree on security properties without having to reveal the reasons why *they* believe such security properties hold.

Such an approach we believe can cater to the scenario we have already described, where there are defined outsiders and insiders, where the threat model is pretty much conventional, what we are used to. Now the real challenge becomes, when you collaborate with an enemy, or with somebody you don't know who can have different commitments on a system. Then is it possible to agree on countermeasures without actually agreeing on the threats? Risk evolves over time, as we read in the theme of this workshop, that all our bad dreams of the last 20 years have come true. So can there be a scenario where you actually agree on countermeasures with your enemies?

So let's think of a new scenario, more in line with the theme of the workshop. Alice and Bob can be opponents who are under some kind of enemy occupation by Carol. Alice and Bob see each other as threats, and Carol can cause either of them to doubt the other. Now there are no side channels, arbitrators, or side payments, or Mafia, to enforce the collaboration between Alice and Bob. The collaborative relationship between Alice and Bob will end but no-one knows when, Carol's occupation over Alice and Bob will also end, but no-one knows when. Now if it is possible to have collaboration in such a scenario between Alice and Bob, the example we think of is Prisoners Dilemma. We know that if we keep on playing the game forever then we get out of the dilemma. In that case we can have cooperation without side payments, Mafia, or other enforcements. The problem is, in the case of Prisoners Dilemma, if we know exactly how long the game is going to continue, then the dominant strategy starts unraveling from the back, so participants tend to defect, because that's a dominant strategy. Now we change the rules of iteration a bit, say we toss a coin twice after every round and if it's two heads then the game stops. Above some threshold probability of the game continuing we see that the participants continue to cooperate. The strategy becomes: Play C unless somebody plays D. So I'll cooperate unless somebody defects.

Now this strategy has a name, it is called a Grim Trigger Strategy. What we find in Grim Trigger is, whether this is an equilibrium or not, that we have the temptation to defect is less than or equal to the temptation for reward minus the temptation for punishment tomorrow. Now we don't know if tomorrow exists, so if we denote tomorrow existing as p, then it's strictly less than 1. So if there is a sufficient probability of the relationship continuing, without the participants knowing when this relationship will end, then we can have collaboration. And what is significant for us that this, for this collaboration to work, there should be credible threats that if the opponent defects then I can subsequently defect, so there should be credible threats, and incentives, for this cooperation to work. Now this is somewhat relevant to us because somewhere it eliminates this unknown, or compulsive trust relationship, which we have always previously used to enforce collaboration or cooperation between parties.

Now we term this new kind of cooperation as promiscuous cooperation. Promiscuous cooperation gives us the ability to reciprocate in case of defection. But how is it relevant to us in the computer security community? Now for the next step, I read a thesis by Michael Roe, which speaks about plausible deniability as a security service, which is when I can always retrospectively deny a particular instance of communication taking place. I'm not saying this gives an instant solution but this is a direction I would like to explore more: that plausible deniability can give us the ability to defect *in retaliation*. It reflects the strategy that if somebody defects then I can also defect as well. So for example, if Alice and Bob are communicating using symmetric keys, now if Bob pops up and shows Carol a message claiming to be from Alice, Alice can always deny that. Now for Bob and Alice, unforgeable authentication is a threat, because that would require Alice to trust Bob, and Bob to trust Alice. So plausible deniability somewhat gives both of them the incentive to cooperate, without invoking an unknown domain where they are required to trust each other, by giving them the ability to defect retrospectively in retaliation.

Now what can be interesting about this is that it is unlike Prisoners Dilemma in the case of a known number of iterations, where we know the participants will defect, that the dominant strategy will unravel from the back. Actually plausible deniability can get over this problem, where knowing that I have the ability to defect in case somebody defects, means that people can still collaborate, even in the case of relationships which are tenured, which have a limit, and that limit is known to the participants. And the good thing about this is, that you can enforce collaboration without side channels, Mafia, or payments, or other kinds of things, even for Prisoners Dilemma.

So we intend to provide a direction where we would like to reduce, or even eliminate, the reliance on trust, this unknown specification of the state of the system in other domains.

Ross Anderson: Well it's not a very strong form of cooperation is it, because then you've got all the usual Byzantine problems, all you know if something went wrong is that one of this following group of people cheated.

Bruce Christianson: Yes, but you're already thinking ahead to the multi-party case. I think even in the two party case it's harder than we want to admit to apply game theory to system design, because game theorists make all these questionable assumptions, for example: everybody knows the payoff matrix, and it's the same for everyone, it's agreed what the objective function is, and eveyone can measure what's happening at the outcome, and everybody behaves rationally, and so on.

So game theorists can build these nice logics based around common belief, you know, Alice knows that Bob knows that Alice knows that Carol knows, that you know. Whereas in the world where you're collaborating with an enemy, just as you don't want to reveal your trust assumptions, you don't want to reveal the value to you of particular things happening, you and the enemy have a very different objective functions, and you both want to conceal what they are.

One of the best ways of concealing what you're trying to achieve is to behave slightly irrationally, not enough to compromise your payoff by very much, but it's often worth losing 5 % in order to conceal from the counterparty that you're collaborating with what it is that you're actually trying to get out of the collaboration. And so my conclusion from looking at the logics that guys like Robert Stalnaker have developed for reasoning about game theory and strands[3], is that those logics still have far too strong an epistemology, and we need a way of reasoning about threats using a much weaker epistemology.

Reply: Another interesting observation from the economics of security is, why would I even enter into an interaction with somebody I don't trust?

Virgil Gligor: But I think Bruce's point is that if you know the utility function of the guy, and you know the payoff function, then you can solve the game.

Bruce Christianson: Yes.

Virgil Gligor: There are examples where you don't necessarily have to know the utility function of your adversary, but you do have to know the discount rates they assume in interacting with you. And even that's hard, how do you measure the discount rate, you can't have that, and that's why co-operation is hard when you don't know much about the adversary.

Bruce Christianson: Maybe you just want to say, well I've got a proof that we've got a viable strategy provided the discount rate is somewhere between 0.3 and 0.7, that's the best we can do.

Virgil Gligor: With grim strategies in general there is an assumption that sometimes isn't stated, that the grim strategy deters defection. And one would have to argue that that's the case, in other words, if I refuse to play the game anymore because he did something wrong, if I refuse to continue the game he loses also, right, and if that doesn't deter him then there is no hope. So grim model already assumes that there is a degree of deterrence.

Frank Stajano: There is also in some cases an element of greed and trying to cheat the other guy, in a situation where if both knew each other's utility function they could find something that is in some sense fair to both. But if you don't know that, I really think that you've got an antique saw, which is worth a lot of money, to you it's just a decoration, I can get it from you for the price of a decoration, which is maybe £50, and I know that it's actually worth £500,000, but I don't want to go halfway and pay you £200,000, I'd just rather have it for £50 then keep all the profit myself. So it's in my interest not to reveal my strategy, because I know I want to screw you, and if we both knew each other's utility function we would turn to something that is advantageous to both of us, but that would not be nearly as advantageous to me as the case when you don't know anything and I can screw you.

Virgil Gligor: So if there is asymmetry in this utility function, then you can screw each other?

---

[3] See for example Robert Stalnaker, "Knowledge, Belief and Counterfactual Reasoning in Games", Economics and Philosophy, 12(1996), 133–162.

Frank Stajano: Insofar as I am collaborating with the enemy, I don't want something fair with the enemy, I want something where it's the most I can extract out of the situation from the enemy. And of course then I want that to have an asymmetry.

Bruce Christianson: Yes. But alternatively you might be negotiating with me, but my objective might simply be to screw you, out of malice. I might be a troll and my motivation is, I'm not concerned with how much money I get out of it, I just want to cost you as much as I can. A lot of tedious legal negotiations ends up being my preferred outcome[4].

Frank Stajano: Financial vandalism.

Bruce Christianson: Yes, financial vandalism, I'm *that* kind of enemy.

Michael Roe: You said what was interesting about this was having a connection between game theory and protocols with a role of commitments. Usually in iterated Prisoners Dilemma you've got somebody that will move, and the game re-starts at each step, you can't go back and defect, that is kind of like doing a non-repudiation because then you've committed to the transaction log what your move was. Whereas with a non-repudiable protocol where you've actually got a move at the end where you can deny it, that's changed the game.

Bruce Christianson: Yes, you can say, well if you're going to be like that, then I'm going to take my last move back.

Michael Roe: So it looks to me like you really could formalise that right out of the game theory as different protocols, with the non-repudiation with symmetric cryptography corresponding to different games, and look at the game theory for them.

Bruce Christianson: Well you could look at the game theory, but the game theory approach already assumes access to too much information. Really you're playing with much more partial information, for example we might both agree that the system is secure, but neither of us is willing to reveal the real reasons why we think that.

You think it's secure because you think this protocol is unbreakable, I think it's secure because I know the protocol is broken and so I know that I control the server, but I'm not going to tell you that. But the hope is that we can come to an agreement about useful public fictions that justify the countermeasures that need to be there, without revealing why we really think we actually need those countermeasures.

Hannan Xiao: Can you use information theory, because you do know strategy and occupational end-points, so you can get some information.

Bruce Christianson: Daniel Polani at the University of Hertfordshire is looking at stuff a bit like that, where you try to get such things coming up as emergent properties[5].

---

[4] cf Andrew Loeb in Cryptonomicon.

[5] For background see Touchette and Lloyd, "Information-theoretic Approach to the Study of Control Systems", arXiv:physics/0104007v2 [physics.data-an].

Fawkescoin

A Cryptocurrency Without Public-Key Cryptography

Joseph Bonneau[1]([⊠]) and Andrew Miller[2]

[1] Princeton University, Princeton, USA
jbonneau@gmail.com
[2] University of Maryland, College Park, USA

Abstract. We present, Fawkescoin, a simple cryptocurrency using no public-key cryptography. Our proposal utilizes the distributed consensus mechanism of Bitcoin but for transactions replaces Bitcoin's ECDSA signatures with hash-based Guy Fawkes signatures. While this introduces a number of complexities, it demonstrates that a distributed cryptocurrency is in fact possible with only symmetric cryptographic operations with no dramatic loss of efficiency overall and several efficiency gains.

1 Introduction

Bitcoin [9] is a distributed, peer-to-peer digital currency system, which uses a public append-only ledger to maintain consensus about the ownership history of all coins in the system. The ledger is maintained by a community of mutually distrusting miners using economic incentives to maintain consensus. Bitcoin has demonstrated the possibility that an append-only ledger can be maintained in a decentralized manner. The consensus mechanism requires no public key cryptography, utilizing only hash computations.

However, coins in Bitcoin are controlled by public-key signatures. Technically, all bitcoins are controlled by a transaction script which indicates the conditions under which they may be transferred to another script. Most often, this script requires a signature from one or more designated public keys, so ownership of the key entails ownership of the bitcoins assigned to the transaction script. The only signature algorithm currently supported is Elliptic Curve DSA over the NIST P-256 curve.

We propose a new cryptocurrency scheme called Fawkescoin which shows that, surprisingly, it is possible to build a system with similar properties to Bitcoin using no asymmetric cryptography at all. The only cryptographic primitive required is a one-way, preimage-resistant[1] hash function with no length extension attacks. SHA-3 (Keccak) [2] is a candidate, or any Merkle-Damgård function with the length unambiguously prepended to the input [3]. Fawkescoin is extremely simple for clients, with coin ownership controlled by knowledge of a hash preimage instead of knowledge of a private key.

---

[1] Collision resistance is a more challenging property, but this is not necessary here.

© Springer International Publishing Switzerland 2014
B. Christianson et al. (Eds.): Security Protocols 2014, LNCS 8809, pp. 350–358, 2014.
DOI: 10.1007/978-3-319-12400-1_35

We could build a cryptocurrency without public-key operations in a very straightforward manner by adapting a variant of Lamport's one-time signature scheme [5], as Bitcoin keys need only be used to sign one message. However, even with compression techniques [8] these schemes result in signatures which, at thousands of bits, are considered unwieldy by the Bitcoin community.

Instead our construction builds on the Guy Fawkes signature protocol [1], demonstrated by Anderson et al. in 1998 to enable secure signatures using only a hash function and a secure timeline service. Observing that Bitcoin's block chain must serve as a secure timeline service for the currency to work, we can replace Bitcoin's ECDSA signatures with Guy Fawkes-style signatures and achieve an efficient digital currency with only symmetric cryptography.

2 Simplified Fawkescoin Protocol

We assume the existence of a mechanism for maintaining global consensus on an append-only log, which is usually called the *block chain* in Bitcoin. The block chain imposes a partial ordering over transactions, which need not be a total ordering. Transactions may be published in batches, usually called *blocks*.

In Bitcoin, this is achieved (with some issues [4,10] and objections [6]) by a community of miners a solving a proof-of-work puzzle in exchange for newly minted coins and a longest-chain rule in effect to establish consensus, but other mechanisms would be suitable for our purposes. We assume, like in Bitcoin, that the log may occasionally fork but consensus will eventually be re-established. Temporary forks introduce a number of subtle issues to deal with, but we must tolerate forks to be able to build on top of Bitcoin's consensus model instead of an ideal append-only log with no forks.

2.1 Minting

To mint coins, one inserts a special transaction into the ledger:

$$\text{Mint} : v; \mathbf{H}(X)$$

A value of v now belongs to the address $\mathbf{H}(X)$, where X is a random, secret value known only to the owner of the new address $\mathbf{H}(X)$ for a preimage-resistant hash function $\mathbf{H}$. The community must agree to rules about who has the right to mint coins and with what values; this is outside the scope of our technical definition. In Bitcoin, for example, miners may currently mint 25 new coins when they find a new block, with this value scheduled to decline gradually over time. A number of alternative cryptocurrencies have adopted different rules.

2.2 Transfer

To transfer coins from address $\mathbf{H}(X)$ to address $\mathbf{H}(Y)$, the owner publishes an initial transfer message:

$$\text{Transfer} : \mathbf{H}\{X; \mathbf{H}(Y)\}$$

If this appears in the block chain in block i, this will serve as proof that whoever crafted this message knew the value X at block i, which is crucial for establishing that the coin was transferred by its proper owner. The owner of X must wait until a sufficient number of subsequent blocks are published to ensure that this message is permanently in the block chain before actually revealing X, so that this proof of knowledge of X at time i is not overwritten by a block chain fork.

Once this is achieved, the owner of X publishes a second message to finalize the transaction:

$$\text{Finalize} : X; \mathbf{H}(Y)$$

This message allows anybody to verify the initial Transfer message in block i committed to a transfer from $\mathbf{H}(X)$ to $\mathbf{H}(Y)$ and knew the value of X at the time. Security rests on that fact that the Transfer message was published before X was public knowledge, so only the legitimate owner of the address $\mathbf{H}(X)$ could have inserted the Transfer message. Note that, because X is public once the Finalize message is sent, $\mathbf{H}(X)$ can never again be used as an address.

As with Bitcoin, the owner of $\mathbf{H}(Y)$ must wait an additional confirmation period before accepting that they control the coins to guard against double-spending, since the owner of $\mathbf{H}(X)$ may have published a different Transfer message that could be opened in the case of a fork. After a suitable confirmation period, the address $\mathbf{H}(Y)$ owns the value v, which can be transferred to a subsequent address $\mathbf{H}(Z)$ using the exact same protocol.

3   Complete Fawkescoin Protocol

The simplified protocol is limited to transferring indivisible coins that forever retain their initial value from the time of minting. We can easily modify the messages to enable arbitrary splitting and merging of values. We also want to include block index numbers in messages to avoid searching the entire block chain during transaction verification. The Mint transaction needs no changes.

The Transfer messages now contains a list of input and output addresses:

$$\text{Transfer} : \mathbf{H}\{[(X_0, i_0), (X_1, i_1)...], [(\mathbf{H}(Y_0), v_0), (\mathbf{H}(Y_1), v_1), ...]\}$$

The input addresses X_j must all be known to craft this transaction. The indices i_j indicate in which block each X_j's receipt of funds was finalized. Each output address $\mathbf{H}(Y_k)$ receives some value v_k, with the obvious constraint that the total of the inputs is greater than or equal to the total of the outputs.

The Finalize message is now simply:

$$\text{Finalize} : i; [(X_0, i_0), (X_1, i_1)...], [(\mathbf{H}(Y_0), v_0), (\mathbf{H}(Y_1), v_1), ...]$$

with all of the information from the Transfer message repeated and, for efficiency, the block i in which the Transfer message appeared.

As with Bitcoin, it is now possible to implement a transaction that transfers some holdings to a new address $\mathbf{H}(Y)$ and keep the "change" at a new address. Bitcoin clients already create fresh addresses for change to increase anonymity, though with Fawkescoin the change address *must* be new to ensure security.

4   Preventing Race-Condition Theft and DoS by Miners

Without further mechanisms, the owner of a coin is vulnerable to a race-condition after broadcasting their Finalize message. Anybody receiving this message (including the miners, who must see it in the pending transaction pool) could observe the value X and attempt to block the publication of the Finalize message by quickly crafting and publishing their own Transfer and Finalize messages sending the value held by X to their own address Z.

4.1   Earliest Transfer Wins

One mitigation is an "earliest Transfer wins" rule, which specifies that if two Finalize messages are published for the same X, then whichever one corresponds to an earlier Transfer message wins. This ensures the legitimate owner can always control transfer of the coin, since they can always publish a valid Transfer message before anybody else.

However, this introduces a double-spending attack. The recipient of a coin can never trust that their ownership is beyond dispute, because the legitimate owner may have published an earlier Transfer message that remains latent in the block chain. To prevent this we must establish a maximum time-limit Δ beyond which a Transfer message is considered invalid if not matched by a Finalize transaction. A recipient can then be confident in their ownership of a coin if no other party tries to claim it after Δ have been passed since the Transfer message transferring the coin to them.

4.2   Optimization via Transaction Tagging

The Δ block waiting period for transaction confirmation can be removed by tagging each Transfer message in a way that unambiguously ties the message to X, so one can safely determine that there are no earlier valid Transfer messages in the block chain that might correspond to X. To do so requires appending to each Transfer message a tag $\mathbf{H}'(X)$ computed using a tweaked hash function. This portion of the Transfer message will be identical for any valid Transfer message involving X but reveals no information about X.

4.3   Preventing DoS with Guy Fawkes Multi-use Signatures

The anti-theft mechanisms in turn introduces a potential denial-of-service attack: if a coin owner relays a valid Finalize transaction but miners can prevent it from appearing in the block chain within Δ blocks, then they can use the revealed secret value X to publish their own Transfer and Finalize messages to claim the coin which can't be overridden by the earlier Transfer. We would like a rule then that if a Transfer message isn't matched within Δ blocks, the corresponding value X can no longer be used to redeem the coin. Now miners can't steal a coin by delaying the Finalize message past the cutoff of Δ blocks, but they can cause the coin to be unspendable.

This can be prevented by using a modified Guy Fawkes algorithm which enables multiple signatures per public address, giving the legitimate coin owner multiple chances to overcome a denial-of-service attack. There are two potential ways to implement this. One is by publishing an iterated hash $\mathbf{H}^n(X)$ as the public address, with each preimage $\mathbf{H}^i(X)$ for $1 \leq i < n$ serving as a secret which can be revealed. The second is by using the root of a Merkle tree $\mathbf{H}^{\text{Merkle}}(X)$ with n leaves, each of which is a preimage that can be revealed. Either allows n signatures from a single public address. The first scheme has signatures of size $\Theta(1)$ that require $\Theta(n)$ hash computations to verify; the second scheme produces signatures of size $\Theta(\lg n)$ which require $\Theta(\lg n)$ hash computations to verify. We expect in practice the first scheme will be preferable.

With either construction, we can provide reasonable guarantees against extended denial of service as in the worst case that the legitimate owner can't publish anything for Δ blocks they will have n additional attempts to spend their coin. We also must extend the tag to include the index of the preimage to be revealed, so the transaction tag would be $\mathbf{H}'(X||i)$ if the ith preimage must be revealed.

4.4   Choosing an Expiry Delay

With a first-Transfer wins rule and tagging, we might recommend a Transfer expiry delay of 12 blocks. This lets a client publish a Finalize message 6 blocks after the Transfer message is published, allowing the standard confirmation period of 6 blocks to be confident the Transfer message is permanently in the block chain, and still leaving 6 blocks to get a Finalize message placed in the block chain in case of malicious miners. In the common case this will add no apparent latency to the recipient(s) in the transaction as they will wait an additional 6 blocks' confirmation period to accept the transaction anyways, at which point they can accept that they have received funds.

This could be established as a global constant, or better yet embedded into X itself. For example, we might reserve by convention the high-order 16 bits of a 256-bit X value to represent Δ. This value will then be publicly known as soon as X is published.

5   Comparison to Bitcoin

We claim that Fawkescoin replicates the core functionality of Bitcoin as it is used today, with no public-key cryptography. Some observations:

5.1   Cryptographic Security

Bitcoin's security inherently depends on the security of the hash function used in its signature scheme. Therefore Fawkescoin is strictly more secure from a cryptographic standpoint as it has no reliance on the security of elliptic curve cryptography. This eliminates the risk of a catastrophic algorithmic break of discrete log on the curve P-256 or rapid advances in quantum computing. It also reduces the risk of implementation flaws, as it is considered far easier to securely implement a hash function than asymmetric cryptographic primitives.

Fawkescoin also significantly reduces the risk of subtle entropy failures. Stealing funds from Fawkescoin requires finding a second preimage for a hash output of a random input X, the difficulty of which degrades gracefully as the strength of the random number generator X degrades. With elliptic curves, there are a number of subtle flaws arising from biased random numbers, particularly if a key is used repeatedly with non-random nonces. In practice, the risk is much lower in Bitcoin however if each signing key is only used once which is common practice.

5.2   Forking Security

Fawkescoin has much worse behavior than Bitcoin in the case of a long fork of the block chain. In Bitcoin, an attacker capable of producing of a long fork (i.e., an attacker who temporarily wields a large amount of hash power) may perform effective double-spending attacks; however, the attacker can only double-spend their own coins which they actively relay transactions for in the blocks which are overwritten by the fork. In Fawkescoin, however, after a fork the attacker may steal the value of any transaction whose Transfer and Finalize message both appear in the overwritten fork.

5.3   One-Time Addresses

In Bitcoin it is often recommended (and implemented in most clients) that fresh addresses be used in every transaction for security and anonymity reasons. In Fawkescoin, this is mandatory as addresses can only be used securely once. This can be relaxed by using multi-use Guy Fawkes signatures, as proposed in Sect. 4.3. Other workarounds exist: for example, a business can publish a large number of addresses offline, or can transfer a new address to clients on demand. It would be possible to modify Fawkescoin to allow multiple transfers to an address $\mathbf{H}(X)$, but these would all need to be spent at once at which point $\mathbf{H}(X)$ would need to be retired.

Ostensibly, storing one private key may be more compact than a large number of secret values in Fawkescoin. However, Fawkescoin clients can avoid this by storing a single master-secret and deriving one-time addresses from it deterministically using a PRNG.

5.4   Efficiency

Fawkescoin has a number of small efficiency advantages, for example, relieving clients of the need to perform public-key operations. This might be of benefit on highly constrained devices, though it's unclear if this confers any practical advantage, as in either scheme a device must be able to contact the network and verify the integrity of the block chain. The block chain would also be more compact in Fawkescoin due to the smaller sizes involved and lack of signatures, though by less than a factor of two; we can implement Fawkescoin using a secure hash function with 128 bits of output (since collision attacks are not a concern). A major advantage is complete verification of the block chain; while this process requires millions of signature verifications in Bitcoin, they are replaced by millions of hash computations in Fawkescoin.

A major disadvantage for Fawkescoin is the need for 2 confirmation periods during any transfer compared to 1 for Bitcoin, effectively doubling the latency of the system.

5.5   Transaction Fees, Priority, and Anti-DoS Countermeasures

Transaction fees can be realized in Fawkescoin exactly as they are in Bitcoin by having the total output value of a transaction be less than the total input value and allowing miners to claim the difference. However, this presents some difficulty since two messages are necessary. It would be possible for the transaction to include fees for both miners (the one who mines the block containing the Transfer message and the one who mines the block containing the Finalize message). However, until the Finalize message is published, there is no way to tell a valid Transfer message from an invalid one. At the moment, Bitcoin prevents spam transactions in two ways. The first is by transaction fees, and the second is by transaction priority based on age. Although fees are optional, the standard miner policy is to require fees for transactions without sufficient age/priority. This means the Transfer message carries no priority or fee, so it would not be relayed due to existing anti-DoS measures. There are several potential approaches:

Out-of-band Payments. In order to post a transaction, a user must make some arrangement out of band with a miner, who includes the Transfer message based on some form of trust that the Transfer message contains a commitment to an actual fee.

Split Transaction Fees. Transaction fees might be split evenly between the miner including the Transfer message in a block and the miner including the Finalize message in a block. This incentivizes miners to include Transfer messages on the hope that they will eventually lead to fees if a Finalize message is published. The transaction owner still needs to convince a miner to include the transaction even though it is not evident that the transaction will be finalized. One approach is a proof in zero knowledge that the transfer message has a preimage paying the miner a useful amount. This negates some of the performance benefits of Fawkescoin, but would leave block chain validation very efficient.

Merkle Tree of Transfer Messages. Finally, miners might place all Transfer messages in a Merkle tree and only include the root in their block. The Finalize message would need to include a proof-of-inclusion for the Transfer message. This reduces the need to limit spam, since spam Transfer messages won't increase the size of each block. However, Finalize messages will grow as the proof-of-inclusion will be logarithmic in the number of Transfer messages included in a block. This approach also removes the possibility of the tagging optimization.

5.6 Multi-sig Transactions

Transactions with multiple possible input addresses controlled by untrusting parties are possible (though not widely used) in Bitcoin. For example, the Coin-Join protocol [7] uses them to mix funds for anonymity purposes. There doesn't appear to be a simple way to achieve this in Fawkescoin, as any party finalizing a transaction risks leaking their private key if their counter-party doesn't publish a Finalize message.

5.7 Scripting Functionality

The scripting functionality in Bitcoin is not included in this simple presentation of Fawkescoin. In principal, arbitrary scripts could be included in Fawkescoin transfers just as in Bitcoin. The main difficulty is that Fawkescoin transactions are inherently a one-shot proposition. If a script fails for whatever reason during verification, it effectively destroys the value associated with any input addresses as they will have their secret revealed.

6   Conclusion

Bitcoin itself is something of a curiosity from an academic standpoint in that it was discovered decades after the requisite cryptographic primitives were available. Our work shows that it was in fact possible even before the discovery of public-key cryptography. The subtleties with double-spending and spam transactions support that a public-key based approach is preferable given the efficiency of elliptic-curve operations on modern hardware and their strong security track record. However, Guy Fawkes signatures could be implemented as an alternative option within a cryptocurrency such as Bitcoin. This is not a simple addition which can be trivially bolted on to Bitcoin's existing scripting language given the required validation rules introduced in this paper to prevent double-spending and spam. However, it might be worthwhile as an alternative allowing very simple clients to participate or as a hedge against a catastrophic break of the discrete log problem in elliptic-curve groups.

References

1. Anderson, R., Bergadano, F., Crispo, B., Lee, J.H., Manifavas, C., Needham, R.: A new family of authentication protocols. ACM SIGOPS Oper. Syst. Rev. **32**(4), 9–20 (1998)
2. Bertoni, G., Daemen, J., Peeters, M., Van Assche, G.: Keccak sponge function family main document. Submission to NIST (Round 2) 3 (2009)

3. Coron, J.-S., Dodis, Y., Malinaud, C., Puniya, P.: Merkle-Damgård revisited: how to construct a hash function. In: Shoup, V. (ed.) CRYPTO 2005. LNCS, vol. 3621, pp. 430–448. Springer, Heidelberg (2005)
4. Eyal, I., Sirer, E.G.: Majority is not enough: Bitcoin mining is vulnerable. In: Financial Cryptography (2014)
5. Lamport, L.: Constructing digital signatures from a one-way function. Technical report CSL-98, SRI International Palo Alto (1979)
6. Laurie, B.: Decentralised currencies are probably impossible but let's at least make them efficient (2011)
7. Maxwell, G.: CoinJoin: Bitcoin privacy for the real world, August 2013. https://bitcointalk.org/index.php?topic=279249.0
8. Merkle, R.C.: A certified digital signature. In: Brassard, G. (ed.) CRYPTO 1989. LNCS, vol. 435, pp. 218–238. Springer, Heidelberg (1990)
9. Nakamoto, S.: Bitcoin: a peer-to-peer electionic cash system (2008)
10. Sompolinsky, Y., Zohar, A.: Accelerating Bitcoin's transaction processing. Fast Money Grows on Trees, Not Chains. Cryptology ePrint Archive, Report 2013/881 (2013). http://eprint.iacr.org/

FawkesCoin: A Cryptocurrency
Without Public-Key Cryptography
(Transcript of Discussion)

Joseph Bonneau$^{(\boxtimes)}$

Princeton University, Princeton, USA
jbonneau@gmail.com

This is joint work with Andrew Miller from Maryland. This started as kind of a thought experiment: could we do Bitcoin, or a Bitcoin-like crypto currency, without using any public key crypto?

I gave a talk in the Lab on Tuesday that went over Bitcoin in a lot of detail. This is Bitcoin in one slide, the essential stuff to understand what we want to replace in terms of where you have to actually use public key crypto. Bitcoin has a consensus mechanism. It involves miners, it involves a block chain, probably stuff that you've heard about, or maybe you're quite familiar with. The critical thing is that the consensus mechanism actually already doesn't use any public key crypto, so that's great. The miners are computing a hash-based proof of work puzzle. They don't have to sign anything, there's no long term identity for the miners, so that's already essentially only using hash functions. The consensus mechanism of Bitcoin could have been designed a long time ago. It doesn't require any fancy crypto at all.

So the miners are mining, they mint coins, but when you want to actually transfer coins you need a signature from the key that represents the owner of the coin. This transaction in the first block there said that 25 coins have been minted, they're now owned by K_A and to transfer those coins to somewhere else A has to sign the transaction and then that get's logged.

Obviously the reason we want a signature here is that then only the person who validly owns the coins is able to transfer them. And it's pretty straightforward, the transactions just refer to previous transfers so you can transfer coins around forever. You just designate a new owner by a key, and then when that key signs a transfer message it designates the next key, there's a new owner for the coin. All of these signatures in Bitcoin are ECDSA. It's the P256 curve that everybody knows and some people love and that's the only signature mechanism that you're allowed to do in Bitcoin. It's hard coded into the Bitcoin scripts, there's just one operation each to make and check signatures. People don't have to think about it, they just all "sign" and what they get is ECDSA.

OK, so why would we want to get rid of this ECDSA? It mostly works. A couple of things though: some people are suspicious about ECDSA, or suspicious that P256 as a good curve. There's fear that there might be shortcuts that certain intelligence agencies know and the public doesn't know about yet. The performance is pretty good. If you're just doing a signature to transfer your Bitcoins, it's not anything people really worry about. But if you have to download the

© Springer International Publishing Switzerland 2014
B. Christianson et al. (Eds.): Security Protocols 2014, LNCS 8809, pp. 359–370, 2014.
DOI: 10.1007/978-3-319-12400-1_36

whole Bitcoin log back to the 2009 genesis and re-verify the whole thing, you're eating a cost of millions of ECDSA verifications. So it's not trivial to actually download all of Bitcoin and do a deep verification of the whole history, it's a lot of signature verifications.

We already know a couple of tricks for doing hash-based signatures. We could just use a hash function to create signatures that are one-time and the nice thing is that we only need one-time signatures in Bitcoin because you can use a new public key every time you transfer coins. It doesn't have to have any long term identity associated with it. In fact if you download the standard Bitcoin wallet and use it, every time you transfer coins around it generates a new key for you. It transparently handles it, so you'll have a new key for every transaction. The only reason every signature key in Bitcoin isn't one-time is because some businesses like to publish a long-term address where people can send them coins, and then they can redeem multiple signatures to the same key. But that's kind of an artifact, there's no fundamental reason in Bitcoin why you ever need to sign anything with the same key more than once.

There are Lamport signatures and then there are a bunch of improvements. The main downside to Lamport signatures are that, at least in the original proposal, they take up a lot of space. There's actually been a pretty interesting stream of crypto work on compressing these, usually at a cost of making them a little bit more expensive to verify, requiring more hash computations, but you can get them down to 1 K or 2 K, which isn't that well known. I think a lot of people dismiss the idea of using hash-based signatures out of hand because they say the key size and the signature size is really big. You can actually compress it down so it's not a totally insane size, although the Bitcoin community is pretty serious about keeping the block chain as small as possible. It certainly sank Zerocoin, which proposed putting 25 K zero-knowledge proofs into the block chain every time you wanted to transfer a coin. Could they put 1 K? That would blow things up by a factor of 3 or 4. Maybe it would be OK, but they're still pretty resistant to it.

Bruce Christianson: Are those bits or bytes? Because a public key signature isn't going to be a lot shorter than that.

Reply: Those are bytes. It's less than an order of magnitude at worst, but it's still a very hard sell with Bitcoin if you propose anything that makes the block chain get bigger.

We want to do better and we want to use just one hash computation to do a signature. The trick, the Guy Fawkes signature protocol from Ross and others, is quite old now. Though it's not necessarily that well known. It works like this and lets you do signatures with just a single hash, assuming that you have either a secure timestamping service, or you have a log that's append only. You need this extra time-dimension to make the Guy Fawkes signature protocol work.

The idea is that you publish your public key, which is just a hash value. The private key is going to be the pre-image X there. And then sometime, which is provably later (everybody must be able to tell that you published this second bit later) you publish the hash of your private key and the message that you want to sign. And then at a third time, which is again provably later, either by secure timestamping or because of this append-only log, you just reveal your private key and the message that you were signing. Now everybody knows your private key after it's revealed. So why can't anybody else do a signature? Well, they could try to, but they wouldn't be able to have the signature commitment happen before yours, because you published this before anybody knew what X was.

Bruce Christianson: You are assuming that this hash function has certain properties...

Reply: Yes, I'm assuming it's a cryptographic hash, it's pre-image resistant.

Bruce Christianson: Yes, and you can't just take the hash of X and...

Reply: Yes, the detail is that you're assuming that there is no length extension.

Bruce Christianson: Yes.

Reply: Yes, that's important.

Virgil Gligor: Also pre-image resistant doesn't imply that all the bits of X are unknown, but a sufficient number of them are.

Bruce Christianson: That's right.

Reply: So you mean, it's also strongly one-way? Correct.

Virgil Gligor: Well yes, so when you define pre-image resistant on one image, you have to be careful just how you define that.

Ross Anderson: We did a paper years ago about how there were all sorts of subtleties and whether hash functions are, you can construct pathological hash functions that are collision resistant, but which leak a lot of the input, for example.

Reply: Right. Most standard cryptographic hashes will be OK, though you do have to worry about length extension. Technically speaking, collision resistance isn't a problem for Guy Fawkes, but you need it to be fully one-way and pre-image resistant. So that's the basic idea. This is of course one-time signature only, but there is a pretty simple trick that extends it, which is that when you're signing you commit to a new public key which you then reveal. And then you can repeat this protocol and you can have arbitrary number of signatures, and in the future they form a chain and it will all date back to that one public key that was originally published. So as long as you're able to publish that one message way on the left and have people think it really comes from you, you can keep signing messages with just two hash computations per message. There are two things that you have to publish per signature and they have to have a provable time ordering, but those are the only requirements here. This is nice for Bitcoin because Bitcoin basically gives you an append-only log for free. The block chain fits that bill pretty well subject to the risk that the thing can fork.

The basic FawkesCoin design is now pretty simple. You have a mint transaction, just like in regular Bitcoin, you just say that some new value is going to some public key.

Bruce Christianson: Is forking a problem for you?

Reply: Yes, it will be, I'll get to that later, but it's definitely a problem.

Robert Watson: You have to be careful to distinguish fork and Fawkes?

Reply: Yes, exactly. OK, so you have a mint transaction, and if you want to transfer that you can refer to an arbitrary number of inputs and you can have an arbitrary number of outputs. For each output you assign some of the value coming from the inputs. The rule of course is that the value that you're sending out has to be less than the value that was coming from all those inputs, when you sum it up. You can't create new money, but you're allowed to destroy it if you want. So you just publish this, which is a commitment to all the input transactions that you're consuming all the outputs that you're sending out. And then just like with the Guy Fawkes signature, at some provably-later time you just reveal everything and people can verify that you must have had control of all these input addresses so these are all the new output addresses. There are a lot of numbers and subscripts here, but you're basically just doing a Guy Fawkes signature to do a regular Bitcoin-style transfer of coins to some new addresses. That's the basic proposal on one slide.

If you just do that there's going to be a couple of problems. The first one is a race condition. Remember that in Bitcoin, not everybody has the ability guaranteed to write whatever they want to a block. The miners control this process, they collect transactions and put them into blocks, and miners can misbehave. They can refuse to publish your transaction. Another thing they can do, which is a problem here, is that they can modify what you're trying to say. So let's say that you had a coin, it's owned by Alice and you want to send it to Bob, as simple a transaction as possible. So you have your transfer message, you get it in the block chain, it's buried for a sufficient time period, and now you reveal this Finalize message which is going to finalise the transfer to Bob here. After you announce it publicly on the Bitcoin peer-to-peer network, it goes into the transaction pool and the miners are made aware this is something that you want to be in the block chain. But a malicious miner can take it. They know A now because you've revealed it, they can put another transfer message in the block chain, with a Finalize which sends the coin to themselves. So they can attempt to steal your coin here if when they see that you announce this they swoop in, change it, and publish their own commitment and their own reveal. Hopefully you can come along at some later time and find a miner who is friendlier to you, who's trying to behave honestly, who will publish the legitimate Finalize that you were going for.

Now you have kind of a problem. You might think that this is simple to deal with, we'll just say whatever the earliest transfer message, that has to be the legitimate one, so Bob should be considered the owner here and not you, which is basically how you do things in Guy Fawkes. The trouble is, that's going to lead to a double spending attack. The way this works is that Alice publishes her Transfer and her Finalize, she tries to send the coin to Bob, and then later on she reveals, ah, Alice is evil now, and she actually had previously stashed away an earlier Transfer message that she can reveal later and she can say, well the first Transfer wins so the coin now belongs to me at a new address, but there was a period there where Bob thought that he owned the coin. So you get into a state where you can never really be sure when the first Transfer message was. There could be an early Transfer message buried in the block chain that people aren't able to recognise. So you can never really be sure that anyone sent you a coin. That's obviously not going to work.

Frank Stajano: And is it not possible for Bob to check for the presence of that before accepting?

Reply: In the simple formulation, no, because these are just different hash outputs, but that's exactly what the fix is going to be. We add a little bit of metadata, which is a tag. We use some alternate hash function, $H'(A)$, and that acts as a tag. Now if the miner, or Alice, tries to attack, if they try to publish a different Transfer message referring to the same coin, now anybody can detect there was already a Transfer message referring to this coin that got published and we won't accept the second one. Now Alice can Finalize it and everything looks OK.

So this is pretty simple. It gets rid of the double spending, but it introduces a second problem: denial-of-service. In the same situation, when Alice publishes this legitimate message that she wants to put into the block chain to the transaction pool, the miner can come along and publish another Transfer message which has the right tag, but has some garbage commitment that can never be opened. Now if we only allow one message to ever be published with a certain tag, Alice's coin is never going to be able to be redeemed, because that miner has succeeded in getting this message in there. That's not good as the miner can prevent this coin from ever being spent.

The final patch is that we have to do tagging with a timeout. If this bad Transfer message gets in, the miner can succeed at locking Alice's coin out for a certain period of time, she won't be able to spend it but eventually that will lapse and then Alice can try again to put the right Transfer message in there. As long as she eventually finds a miner who's willing to publish the genuine thing she can get her transaction to go through. But the miners are still able to do some denial-of-service and impose this lockout. You can fiddle with what you want the timeout to be. Maybe something in the 6 to 10 block range. Hopefully if miners realise that they can't do the delay forever it will be less appealing for them to do this.

So what have we achieved with this construction overall? We've reduced the number of cryptographic assumptions; we don't have to assume anything about ECDSA here; verification speed is going to go up; the keys are a lot smaller. So in some ways it's a nice improvement over Bitcoin. A couple of disadvantages remain with no really good way to get rid of. There's a spam problem. Because we want the property that Alice can try to publish multiple things with the same tag, she can also publish as much spam as she wants, because there's no way to tell if a Transfer message is actually genuine or not. The miners have no way to tell what should be allowed in the block chain. This is a requirement of the Guy Fawkes system, that the Transfer messages don't reveal anything. Therefore there's not a good way to tell if they're real or if they're spam.

James Malcolm: So what would be the motivation for doing that, is it really denial-of-service again?

Reply: Yes, to make Bitcoin less usable, to slow it down, try to destroy the system. I mean, a lot of people don't like Bitcoin. There are denial-of-service problems today with Bitcoin. Who knows what the motivation is, perhaps they shorted Bitcoin? If you can introduce a lot of spam to make it less useful maybe the exchange rate goes down and you can profit from it.

Bruce Christianson: So how is spam avoided at the moment, the protocol is that the miners won't put anything in it that doesn't verify?

Reply: Yes, exactly. And since the public key signature check is self-contained, you can check if it verifies before you put it in, whereas here you need to publish this extra stuff that you can't verify until the second thing comes.

OK, and forking, this is what Bruce asked about earlier. If we've had a legitimate transaction from Alice to Bob sending a coin and then some miner is able to come along and fork the whole block chain, which can happen in Bitcoin, they can basically rewind history to before Alice's Transfer message went in. Pretty straightforward attack here, they'll know the secret at that point so they can just do some other Transfer message and get the coin for themselves.

Frank Stajano: So you said there was no solution yet for this spam.

Reply: No, if you have one, lay it on us.

Frank Stajano: Why not? I thought you mentioned you had something with a timeout. Then why can't you time-out and erase from the log anything that hasn't been proved to verify? Wouldn't that solve the spam problem?

Reply: It's an append only log, there's no erase.

Frank Stajano: Well, there could be an erase: it's an append-only log, except that things decay if they haven't been verified within a certain number of months. That would fix the spam.

Reply: You need them to verify the hash that people are working on. If you erase then the hash that people spent all this effort to find is no longer going to have the right property.

Max Spencer: So I guess if you are confident that your initial commitment is buried enough by the time you do the Finalize, then it would be unreasonable for a fork that long, and that's the only level of assurance you could get.

Reply: Yes, exactly. So the assurance against forking is, you'd better be pretty confident that you've waited a sufficient period of time before you publish these two messages, because if there's a fork your coins are going to be gone. So how does this compare to Bitcoin? In Bitcoin forking is a problem too, it lets you double-spend. It's actually worse here. In Bitcoin you have to not only fork, but you have to have actively put in a transaction that you knew the public key that you were going to double spend. Here you can passively fork and then steal money from all of the people who tried to spend during that period even if they weren't you. So forking is a much bigger problem here. Although you can only steal coins from people who publish their Transfer and their Finalize, so if people are waiting a sufficient period of time your fork has to come that far back.

Bruce Christianson: But this recommends putting a long gap between Transfer and Finalize, which is what you were trying to avoid in the slide before last.

Reply: Right, I mean, you obviously want the gap to be shorter because then your transactions are confirmed faster and the system is more usable, but the longer it is the more secure you are against forking.

Another way to look at the difference is that forking here hurts all the people who are trying send coins, whereas in regular Bitcoin forking is only a problem for people who are receiving coins, because their coins might then go to somebody else in the other fork.

Chris Hall: So I was just going to say, a Bitcoin-like transaction, is not considered like confirmed until there are like six blocks on the fork. I presume the recipient doesn't trust that transaction until it is confirmed, so then he could just, in this case like say a similar thing like, you don't finalise until the sixth block and then it still has roughly the same property.

Reply: It has roughly the same property. You can make forking arbitrarily hard here by just waiting longer, but it is worse if there's a fork.

Robert Watson: But just some scheme where you come back later and use one signature to cover many different transactions, so you do occasional signatures, but you do it amortise the cost over many transactions, and what you want to do is name the right fork basically, the fork that I meant for this to happen in is the one that I signed later. So the point of your idea, but I guess I'm saying that maybe the occasional signature helps you out.

Reply: Right, the occasional public-key signature.

Robert Watson: Yes.

Reply: Yes, that could happen. I mean, it would be nice if you could commit to the fork that you're on in the Transfer message that would be great, but of course, if you fork then that gets wiped away so you can't really do it.

Robert Watson: And you can't really name the fork in a cryptographic sense well after the Finalize has actually happened.

Reply: Yes.

Robert Watson: If every now and then you add a new signature then you could actually have greater confidence in the earlier events.

Bruce Christianson: Well you could sort of imagine a two-phase version where you say, we'll publish a journal that contains everything, and then after a certain length of time there's kind of a ledger version which deletes any spam, any entries that haven't closed.

Reply: There's kind of a comparable thing in Bitcoin. They have minimal versions of the block chain history that just have unspent transactions, and they remove everything else.

Bruce Christianson: And everybody has to sort of agree that this is a faithful digest of what's happened?

Reply: One other thing I can show you I believe, well two things actually. One is a kind of downside, although I think it might be doable. In Bitcoin you can do co-signatures, so you can designate that a coin is sent to two people and they both have to sign in order to redeem it or to send it to somebody else. And it seems like that's hard to do with Guy Fawkes, because it's hard for two people to sign something such that it's only valid if they both sign it. With public-key signatures this is easy, you just both sign it, and there's some logic in Bitcoin that says if both parties don't sign then neither signature means anything. But with Guy Fawkes signatures that's kind of a problem because if one party signs but the other party refuses to reveal what their secret was, you can say the signature is meaningless, but that person has revealed their key so they've already lost out.

Ross Anderson: So you create a conditional, a payment transaction that says, I pay this to Virgil if he accepts it, otherwise I pay it back to myself.

Reply: The issue is if you want to pay Virgil and Frank and they have to both sign the transaction to send it somewhere new.

Ross Anderson: OK, so I create a transaction for that, and Frank then offers a signature saying, I've paid Virgil, if he co-signs within 20 steps of the block chain, otherwise I retain it for myself.

Reply: And you designate a new key if it's retained to yourself?

Ross Anderson: Yes.

Reply: Yes, so that could work.

Virgil Gligor: Sort of, instead of having no signature you have a delegation through Frank.

Ross Anderson: Are they both actually indirection?

Bruce Christianson: How is this problem avoided in conventional Bitcoin at the moment though, if I send something to two people and one of them won't collaborate with the other.

Reply: Well it's just frozen until they both collaborate.

Bruce Christianson: Yes, so you're actually no worse off.

Reply: Well the reason you're worse off is that if one person tries to sign and the other person doesn't sign then they've burned that key, so you need to have some more complicated logic where in case one person signs and the other person never signs, then...

Bruce Christianson: What happens then, Ross' proposal.

Ross Anderson: So yes, in fact you delegate a new one-off signed key.

Reply: Although then that also may seem kind of odd, because what if Frank then signs a transaction saying the coin goes to Frank, and then Virgil says, I don't want to send it to Frank, so he never signs, and then the fallback is that it goes to Frank anyway since Virgil never signed.

Daniel Thomas: You need to have to it such that it goes back to the two co-signers, there would be one new one and one old one.

Reply: Right, so then you need to designate.

Bruce Christianson: Yes.

Reply: The proposal I have that might make this better is that you could have a Guy Fawkes signature that lets you sign multiple times without issuing a new public key. I don't know if this has appeared in the literature anywhere, but it's actually pretty straightforward to do. You just make a hash tree, then you publish the root of it as a new public key, and then in this case you'd have 2^n signatures that you could use to do a Guy Fawkes style signature. So if one of them gets burned you have three other chances and you could make as many of these as you want. Obviously this is a little bit more costly but it lets you do multiple signatures and the verification time is $\lg(n)$. There's even another way you could do this, if you want to have different parameters, which is just to have a linear chain designating the different keys. And then instead of $\lg(n)$ you have constant-size signatures, but the verification cost is linear.

Ross Anderson: We did have a paper on this but we marketed it as a market payment scheme. So the idea here was that if you wanted, for example, to be able to pay 10p per page to read the Scientific Journal, then instead of doing a whole lot of 10p credit card transactions, you would in effect use a EMV transaction to sign a whole stick of clients by signing the end hash of a random pre-image, and then you peel off the pre-images one at a time to do the payments. And this means that you could leverage a large number of small payments off one more heavyweight credit card transaction. That was at the 1996 Protocols Workshop and the curious thing was that three other research groups logically, independently, discovered this at the same time.

Reply: Yes, I think these are pretty general ideas and I think that they'd work nicely here. The solution to the co-signing thing would be you send it to Frank and Virgil with some logic that says if they don't both co-sign within some certain period of time then one signature doesn't matter, and then using one of these multi signature keys, if they don't sign they move on to the next one and have another chance to agree.

That's the last crypto slide I think. So, philosophically it's interesting that you can do this. It's interesting that you could do cryptocurrency that reasonably works without any public key crypto at all. Obviously a few things have gotten worse and there's some reasons why this doesn't integrate directly to Bitcoin unfortunately. The initial goal when I was thinking this up was that I would implement this as Bitcoin script and that you could do Guy Fawkes signatures in Bitcoin as an alternative signature scheme.

There is a technical reason you can't do it in Bitcoin. The transactions in Bitcoin have to refer to exactly one input transaction and for these Guy Fawkes signatures you need to refer to two things. You need to refer to the previous transfer plus the time when the coin was transferred to that key. This seems like kind of a minor issue that you need to point at two prior things instead of one, but that's enough to make it impossible to drop on top of Bitcoin. But it's interesting to have this out here. I've seen some thought that something like this could be adapted into the ZeroCash design space where everything is zero knowledge proofs. It's much more expensive to do zero knowledge proofs of public-key signatures, so you can do some nice things here with that. But mostly this was meant as a thought exercise of what we could do in constrained crypto world.

Ross Anderson: There's one other thing that might be of some relevance. I think it was 1998, Vaschek and I produced a paper on the Eternal Resource Locator, which was about how you would use hash trees to protect online books in a world in which you still had to pay royalties to use RSA. And one of the things that we remarked is that you can mix hash trees and signatures more or less promiscuously, so if you had some static content that you were happy to authenticate with a hash tree, such as a book, with each leaf being a page, then you might have a book with an active table in it, which you would want to sign. You would then simply embed the public key into the hash tree, which saves you the trouble of paying your fee to Verisign for the certification authority and so on. So there's all sorts of combinations can be pooled here.

Bruce Christianson: he other interesting case is where NSA have a credible threat for a quantum compute.

Reply: Yes definitely.

Ross Anderson: One of the corridor discussions at the Bitcoin thingy a few weeks ago was that people could use the block chain as a non-censorable means of publication, since enough hundreds of millions are invested in not paying attention to, say, the Prime Minister of Turkey, if he decides that the block chain is unpublishable. Similarly if you have got a really, really strong public timestamping service, which is what this is, there are various things that you can do to supplant some parts of the CA infrastructure, you could publish public keys, for example, in the block chain, in the knowledge that it would be extraordinarily hard to suppress them, and then use them for other purposes.

Robert Watson: Is this not similar to certificate transparency, which is very similar to the block chain but to keep certificates?

Bruce Christianson: It links also to Micah's talk, the idea is to have your hash of a hash, embedded in a financial transaction that so many people use, that it's not feasible to suppress those blocks.

Reply: I think to Robert's point, maybe one of the more interesting things about, Bitcoin, CT, and a couple of other things now, the core thing that let Bitcoin go forward is that we have the memory, the disk space now to have these logs that grow forever and we can commit to storing them. There's some concern about spamming them, but you can keep one log forever and ever and not delete anything out of it and do that cryptographically. It's pretty useful that Bitcoin maintains one for financial reasons and we can build other stuff on top of having a one-way append only log. There have already been a couple of proposals to do secure commitments and to extract randomness and other things where Bitcoin ends up being a nice primitive.

Robert Watson: What if there was a large quantity of undesirable material turning up in some of these long public logs, particularly with people who placed child pornography in the Bitcoin?

Reply: I've heard of people paying for child pornography with Bitcoin and that's kind of a scare tactic about how Bitcoin is evil. I haven't heard about anybody putting it into the block chain.

Robert Watson: You might find yourself in an awkward situation if someone were to do this, I guess, with the observation that it hasn't yet been done.

Reply: That's pretty interesting.

Reply: You could do that with the certificate transparency log much more easily because certificates have a whole bunch of bits you can fiddle with. With Bitcoin you can put whatever you want in the block chain by, instead of sending coins to a public key, just sending them to whatever string you want. You'll never be able to get them back, so you have to send the minimum value that the miners will deal with. It's pretty small though, for pennies you can basically write, you know, Robert Watson is cool, into Bitcoin if you want.

Robert Watson: Eternally preserved in the Bitcoin log, the problem is the hundred people who say he's not.

Reply: Well you can just fork.

Bruce Christianson: Your private key can be enough bits so that it can be the hash of whatever you like.

Reply: Yes, well you don't even have to have a private key, you can just publish some public key that you don't know private key for which is then truly whatever you want.

Bruce Christianson: Oh yes, but it's much funnier if you do it with the private key.

Robert Watson: Presumably you could publish a number of certs to the CT log containing the contents of Snowden's revelations.

Reply: That's an interesting idea. It would be good to calculate what the costs per byte to get stuff into Bitcoin is.

Frank Stajano: And who pays it?

Reply: You would pay it, and if you want to publish megabytes of Snowden PDFs it's going to get non trivial.

Frank Stajano: Well the point is that the cost of eternally publishing all these PDFs is not borne by, entirely by the person publishing.

Robert Watson: It doesn't work. Another discussion a few days ago about placing actual value on energy in relation to Bitcoin transactions, maybe this places an actual cost on free speech, once you put the stuff in the Bitcoin transaction log and everyone is financially committed that it will remain here for the rest of eternity whatever the cost was to place it there is the cost of that is distributing information.

Reply: Right. I wouldn't actually try to do this, I think you would get a very negative reaction from the Bitcoin people.

Bruce Christianson: I'm not sure that they'd be seeking their informed consent.

Reply: Yes.

Ross Anderson: It could be used as a process, given that the Prime Minister of Turkey has just banned Twitter because it said something rude about his family being corrupt, that the market could sort out.

Reply: I think he said it, they just published the audio.

Ross Anderson: There might be a certain temptation to spend a hundredth of a Bitcoin just to do a denial-of-service attack on the Turks using Bitcoin as a process.

Robert Watson: Well the real question is to release a piece of software which extracts these messages reliably from Bitcoin.

The Final Word

Secrecy is for losers. For people who don't realize how important information really is.

Senator Daniel Patrick Moynihan, 1927–2003;
Secrecy: The American Experience,
Yale University Press, 1998.

Author Index

Printed in the United States
By Bookmasters